MONEY
IN POLITICS

By HERBERT E. ALEXANDER

Foreword by Tom Wicker

Public Affairs Press, Washington, D. C.

To ALEXANDER HEARD

FRIEND AND TEACHER

FOREWORD

On few subjects is there so much cant and confusion as upon that of campaign finance; it might be said that everybody talks about political money but few know anything about it. Until the recent round of Congressional debate and action on the subject, it could even be said that practically no one knew anything about it except Herbert Alexander.

As director of the Citizens' Research Foundation, former executive director of President Kennedy's Commission on Campaign Costs, and consultant on the subject to President Kennedy, a Congressional committee and other government agencies, Mr. Alexander has long been *the* authoritative source for reporters, politicians, historians. Now he has crammed his knowledge into this comprehensive book, and reading it is going to surprise a lot of people.

It is well-known, for instance, that in American politics, money not only talks, it dominates. But Mr. Alexander shows that there is little justification for the idea that money guarantees victory. Throughout this century, the Republicans consistently had more money to spend than the Democrats; yet, from the Thirties through the Sixties, the Democrats have been the majority party and were in national office all but the Eisenhower years. In 1936, Mr. Alexander will remind you, the Republicans and the Liberty League blew in $9.4 million to the Democrats' $5.9 million and with that three to two advantage lost all but two states.

More recently, in the 1969 New York Republican mayoral primary, John Lindsay spent $340,000 to lose while the winner needed only $120,000; on the Democratic side, the fifth man in a field of five spent five times what the winner did and wound up paying $14.23 per vote won. Money, in other words, isn't really everything, even in politics.

Or take the prevalent notion that big money often buys political office. Mr. Alexander points out that the real problem is not "that too many jobs are given to political contributors, [but] that too few competent administrators among them are willing to take appointment to responsible posts" at drastically reduced government salaries and other financial sacrifices. (It hurts to think what it cost Robert McNamara in Ford stock to become one of the political victims of the Vietnam war, and it was recently reported that it cost David Packard about $19.1 million in stock earnings to serve three years as Deputy Secretary of Defense.)

In fact, of the first 27 non-career chiefs of foreign missions appointed by President Kennedy, only seven had made contributions to his campaign of $500 or more; of 35 such appointments by Lyndon Johnson in 1964 and 1965, only ten went to large contributors, and of 34 by Richard Nixon, only 15 had been big givers. The same low rates of appointment of big-bankroll types were also generally true of these three Presidents' other major appointees, Mr. Alexander demonstrates.

Even so, it is certainly true—isn't it?—that government policy is heavily influenced by massive contributions from the military-industrial complex. Well, the five largest Pentagon contractors— General Dynamics, Lockheed, General Electric, United Aircraft, and McDonnell Douglas—had officers and directors who contributed $122,677 in 1968. That's a lot of money, but enough to influence government policy substantially? Hardly, particularly since $119,677 of the total went to the Republicans, who were then out of office. This disparity leads Mr. Alexander to conclude that "if the complex has political ties, they are mainly Republican . . . not much money was contributed by corporation executives; that most of the contributors with business ties were directors, not company officers; and that not much of the money on the record (sums of $500 or more) went to Democrats despite their control of the White House and the Congress in 1968." What's more, Mr. Alexander sifts a mass of evidence to conclude that "while undue influence may be wielded by large contributors . . . the financial elite of the country, themselves often sharply divided in political sentiments, are not investing in politics and politicians to the extent one would consider necessary for serious influence."

But anyway, most of us seem to feel, there's something wrong about all that money being spent on political campaigns, and particularly if it's spent by wealthy candidates. Again, Mr. Alexander demonstrates that it's not necessarily so. He argues, for instance, that it was largely personal wealth and his willingness to spend it that enabled John Kennedy to "equalize" his religious handicap in 1960—and to dispose once and for all of the Catholic issue in national politics.

At a lesser level, Mr. Alexander points, for instance, to David B. Kinney, who was reported in 1968 to have spent $77,000 of his own funds to lose a Congressional race to Joel Broyhill in Virginia. "Without Kinney," he argues, "the Democrats might not have been able to field a strong, liberal candidate, and many people might have been without a spokesman in that election." Nationally, by the same reasoning, "Without the ability to raise and spend as much as they did [in the years of Democratic dominance], the Republicans could have been . . . reduced to a status of continuing opposition to the incumbent Democrats, with no prospect of gaining power . . . ." This would have threatened the viability of the two-party system.

With one popular belief, however, Mr. Alexander is in absolute agreement—the cost of politics is going up. "Spending," he reports, "in campaigns for all offices at stake in 1968, from the White House to the courthouse, came to at least $300 million, a 50 per cent increase over the $200 million spent in 1964, itself a record. In 1970, a Congressional election year, as much was spent as in 1964, a Presidential election year."

This overall picture is reflected in some interesting local cases. One study shows that in Wisconsin, for instance, costs of state-wide and county-level politics rose from about $1 million in 1950 to $3.5 million in 1966. It cost Nelson Rockefeller $1.8 million to be elected governor of New York in 1958; $2.2 million in 1962; $4.9 million in 1966; and $6.8 million in 1970. That's a grand total of $15.7 million for four terms, and he is said to be thinking about a fifth at 1974 prices.

Mr. Alexander's book will tell you more than any in print about where that kind of money comes from, and where it goes. He has, for instance, a breakdown of Robert Kennedy's $2.4 million expenditures to win the California primary of 1968 that shows among other things the prosaic items of $10,307 for buttons, $12,209 for bumper strips and $34,772 for candidate travel around the state. Incidentally, the California figures point to one of the factors in Eugene McCarthy's ultimate defeat; in that crucial state, Kennedy poured $1.1 million into all media expenses including television, while McCarthy was spending only $523,200 for the same purposes. The reason, Mr. Alexander relates, was not a lack of McCarthy money; that came pouring in after his upset victory in Oregon a week earlier. But by then, Kennedy had booked so much television time on California channels that little was left for McCarthy's final drive.

On the whole, however, McCarthy was not financially over-whelmed by the Kennedy "juggernaut." The McCarthy campaign spent at least $11 million, which Mr. Alexander thinks notable for proving that not all big political money goes to fat-cat or conservative causes. The Kennedy campaign spent about $9 million. McCarthy actually outspent him in the Nebraska and Oregon primaries, but the crucial difference was that Kennedy concentrated his spending in 11 whirlwind weeks, while McCarthy's was spread over nine months. Note well that this means a total of $20 million was spent on behalf of these two men alone, neither of whom ultimately was nominated (although Kennedy might have been had he lived). All told, it cost the Democrats $25 million to get through the primaries and the convention in 1968, and then they emerged with Hubert Humphrey at the head of the ticket.

But if campaign costs are going up, Mr. Alexander is not as certain as some people that is a bad thing. The major reasons for the rise—which has been the sharpest since 1952, when all politics at all levels cost only about $140 million—are the increased use and cost of television, jet travel, sophisticated polling, reapportionment, and more intensive competition in more states and districts. There is nothing wrong about spending for these things *per se*—quite the opposite. Moreover, while political costs were rising, so were the gross national product and disposable income; what we spend on politics remains a small percentage of both.

In fact, Mr. Alexander thinks that politics in America is not overpriced but underfinanced. The $300 million spent in 1968 was not much more, he points out, than the $270 million Proctor and Gamble spent on advertising in the same year. Considering that every poll shows how little Americans really know about great issues and how few know anything about even the leading politicians—considering also the dismaying record of lost bond issues and defeated propositions, the immense social investments many believe needed, the remaining numbers of uncontested Congressional districts and one-party states, and the shamefully low percentage of Americans who bother to vote even in Presidential races, it can well be argued that we need to spend more, not less, on politics and the political education it entails.

The problem therefore is not so much to limit total spending; in any case, such limits historically have been unenforceable and thus an invitation to violation. A more important question is how the money is to be raised—whether the politician and the political process will become evermore dependent on the big contributor and the wealthy candidate, or whether ways and means can be found to make both the mass of the citizenry and the government itself effective contributors.

Tax incentives for the small contributor and some form of government subsidy that does not shut off private giving—which, most often, is a valuable form of political participation — are the obvious answers; happily, the former will be available, for the first time, in 1972. An additional and equal need is for stringent and enforceable disclosure laws to drive the dubious contributor into the light of day, where he can do little harm.

This is not just a matter of avoiding scandal and influence. Such a spreading of the burden and such assurance that the burden will be carried is vitally necessary if any qualified man, rich or poor, is to have his opportunity for political service, and if the public interest is to be as well represented in politics and government as the special interest. Mr. Alexander discusses, for instance, what is probably all too true, that "The dissension, alienation, and violence characteristic of the United States in the 1960's and early 1970's can be related partially to the creaky workings of the political system and to a failure to enlist wide enough participation and competence for reforming and sustaining democratic processes."

"An incumbent has a forum in the White House, in the State House, in the legislature . . . . Established or wealthy interests have resources to propagandize or lobby. To the alienated or dissenters, with access neither to a governmental forum nor to funds, there seems little choice but to take to the streets for an audience, if not on TV or in the papers, at least in the courts."

But this book is not a propaganda tract for reform; neither is it a dull compilation of statistics. In learning so much about campaign finance, Herbert Alexander necessarily has learned a lot about American politics. This is what *Money in Politics* is about, first and last; it is about how men win power in America, and how much it costs to do so, where the money comes from, where it goes, and what the consequences are. Its theme is that "American society has no excuse to tolerate a debt-ridden, obligation-bound political system."

Mr. Alexander proves that point beyond reasonable doubt, a public service of the first order. It is the reader's good fortune that he also has written a fascinating book.

TOM WICKER

Washington, D. C.

ACKNOWLEDGEMENTS

The preparation of this book was made possible by a grant from the Carnegie Corporation to the Citizens' Research Foundation, and the author is grateful for the generous assistance extended in this connection.

Special recognition is due many individuals for providing information in personal interviews and through correspondence. Since most prefer to remain anonymous, it would be unfair to name some and not others.

I am happy to acknowledge by name, and with many thanks, the assistance of the staff of the Citizens' Research Foundation. First and foremost was the work of Genie Grohman Gans, who helped organize, draft and edit the entire manuscript. Others who contributed substantially to the final product were Caroline D. Jones, Jean Soete, Elizabeth Burns, Katharine Fischer, Linda Sheldon, Alice Bevan, and Marcia Baumel.

The forebearance of my wife, Nancy, and the good cheers of my children, Michael, Andrew, and Kenneth, are also gratefully acknowledged.

As always, I appreciate the encouragement received from officers and members of the Board of Trustees of the Citizens' Research Foundation, but the presentation is mine and does not, of course, reflect their views.

HERBERT E. ALEXANDER

Princeton, New Jersey

CONTENTS

INTRODUCTION

Who gives how much to whom for what?

Applied to the electoral process, this is the shorthand way of asking how America finances its politics. The answer is: In many ways, through many means, some good, some bad. If the question were: How well does America finance its politics? then the answer must be: Not very well.

A wealth of evidence has been gathered to demonstrate that political spending is usually extravagant, often corrupting, ordinarily wasteful, and yet, strange as it may seem, frequently insufficient and absolutely necessary. It has become clear also that some ways of spending are better than others.

Year after year candidates have set new records of expenditures and every additional dollar adds to the chorus of voices that call for better regulation of political finances. Dutifully, legislators regularly draft a seasonal round of bills to govern political spending. Quite as predictably, the legislatures ultimately approve few if any effective measures of control.

As the decade of the 1970s opened, the clamor for reform mounted to a subdued shriek, with a corresponding sense of frustration. Success in enacting effective electoral reforms depends on many factors. All that is certain is that no single measure, indeed no grand scheme yet devised, will provide a wholly satisfying means of managing the money for politics. As the public has shown increased awareness of the need and of the failure to resolve the issues, political finance has become a leading concern in the 1970s.

Spending in campaigns for all offices at stake in 1968, from the White House to the courthouse, came to at least $300 million, a 50 percent increase over the $200 million spent in 1964, itself a record. In 1970, a Congressional election year, as much was spent as in 1964, a Presidential election year.

Political spending cannot, of course, be predicted with accuracy.

It could diminish if legislative controls are enacted or if there is adverse public reaction to the unparalleled spending of 1968 and 1970. On the other hand, costs will continue to rise if there are no restraints or if even more spending becomes considered necessary to achieve a stable and responsive political system.

To ask whether politicians spend enough is to assume the money is spent well. Seen from one vantage, campaigns are underfinanced. The $300 million spent in 1968 is about a tenth of one percent of the amounts spent by governments at all levels, $282.6 billion in fiscal 1968. Procter and Gamble allotted $270 million for its advertising in 1968. In comparison, $300 million is a small price to pay for attempting to gain control of offices that decide how public funds should be spent.

Still, the amounts considered necessary for any single campaign often are unattainable. Political money is relatively scarce, and there is competition among many candidates and committees for financial assistance from the few willing to give. Usually fund raising has not kept pace with the rising costs of running an effective campaign. There should be less concern with the actual costs of campaigning than with the need to raise and use the money in a manner conforming to democratic ideals. Americans like to believe that politics should not be dominated by persons of wealth and vested interests, and that there should be ample opportunity for the person of little or no wealth to enter public life.

The ways we raise, apportion, and apply political money lead to a bizarre combination of virtue and vice. On the one hand, there are exemplary displays of public-spirited contributions with no strings. At the same time, the spirit of *quid pro quo* flourishes in transactions between greedy contributors and needy politicians. Candidates and parties emphasize the virtues of building big totals from small sums collected from the many, yet rely out of habit and necessity on large contributors with special interests.

American history is replete with unsavory tales of political money. The seamy side of campaign financing brings occasional headlines, and enough raw deals to create the impression that political money is more often tainted than not. The stories may exaggerate, distort, or unjustly accuse, but the impression remains because of recent conspicuous examples:

• While serving as an employee of the United States Senate, Robert G. Baker, among his financial acrobatics, collected campaign funds. According to a courtroom statement by a federal prosecutor, he received $99,600 in cash contributions from executives of the savings and loan industry, purportedly for distribution to Senators up for re-election. Allegedly he kept about $80,000 for his personal use.

• Senator Thomas J. Dodd was accused of devoting to personal uses money raised at testimonial dinners for the purported purpose of paying campaign expenses. He was censured by the United States Senate.

• A group using the title of the President of the United States, the President's Club, became a vehicle for obtaining funds for the Democrats from government contractors. One contractor was a known member of the John Birch Society whose political sympathy was hardly congenial to the Democratic administration's Great Society program.

• A major party running on a platform of "law and order" ignored a statute requiring campaign committees to file financial reports prior to election day. Only 1 of 20 committees supporting Richard Nixon in the 1968 campaign filed its reports within the time period prescribed by law. No Senator raised the subject during hearings on the nominations of Nixon's campaign manager, John Mitchell, for Attorney General, and Nixon's finance manager, Maurice Stans, for Secretary of Commerce.

• A few months after his inauguration as President, Richard Nixon accepted a leather-bound, one-of-a-kind book listing the purchasers of $1,000 tickets for a "Republican Victory Dinner." The affair's committee was set up in the District of Columbia where no disclosure was required; the names on the guest list were withheld from the public.

• Jack A. Gleason, an assistant to Maurice Stans in 1968 and later a White House aide, ran a covert fund-raising operation in Washington, D.C., for Republican candidates throughout the country during the 1970 elections. He boasted of raising $12 million, yet he filed no reports. Information leaked out only when candidates credited him as a source of funds in reports they filed under state laws. While perhaps not officially sanctioned, the Gleason enterprise could not have operated successfully without the knowledge and consent of the White House and/or the national Republican Party.

When such incidents come to light, they command the headlines briefly. They do not seem even cumulatively to arouse public insistence for reform.

Artificial limitations on amounts that can be spent in campaigns virtually force violations by all participants, winners and losers alike. Furthermore, those who are detected in violations are punished, if at all, for tax fraud, larceny, or bribery, but not for stretching an already flexible code of campaign finance. Those obligated to instill discipline shirk their duty because they are beneficiaries of the system.

The present system blatantly invites offenses while doing little to discourage them. Even where there is no clear-cut official malfeasance—usually there is not—it may be customary for the beneficiary of governmental favor or preferment to show his gratitude with a political contribution. An official choosing between two men for an appointment or a contract is naturally more inclined toward the contributor than a stranger. When does this procedure become undesirable is the important question.

The price of public prominence has been rising steadily. An increasingly professional approach to campaigning and a complex and sophisticated political technology combine to drive up political costs. The contemporary campaigner must find means of financing professional management, consultants, advertising agency assistance, media specialists, surveys, and polls. A candidate needs expert help to prepare material for the media, negotiate for broadcast time, program strategy by computer, or test public opinion tendencies.

The task of raising funds for such purposes is compounded by the American system of holding many elections simultaneously. As this system accentuates competition for money, services, and the attention of the voters, so costs increase enormously. Candidates of the same party compete aggressively for nomination before facing the other party's nominees. In the primary campaigns, candidates and committees of the same party, at different levels, contend against one another and also are in competition with commercial advertisers.

In this competitive market exploding with commercial bids for the consumer's attention, the attention span of the electorate is constantly and readily distracted. The voter requires fresh stimulation almost daily. Because political activity must be intense enough to attract the voter and propel him to the polls during the brief political season, costs are high. These costs exact a price from those who can afford them; they freeze out those who cannot.

President John F. Kennedy described the dilemma of candidates confronting such costs as "the pressure of opportunity." Politicians who find money knocking at their door may choose not to ask about the source, but they soon find themselves in "moral hock"—the condition of one who for need of money tacitly obligates himself to large contributors or special interests.

Conventional methods of financing campaigns are in themselves obstacles to reform. The present system completely satisfies some interests and many politicians. Heavy contributors representing commerce, industry, labor unions, trade associations, and other groups rely considerably for their influence in government upon their control of political funds in amounts tantalizing to politicians. If politicians could otherwise obtain the sums required, these groups would have to find other ways of influencing legislation. The difficult quest for political funds leads to two unfortunate results: impecunious candidates may accept funds from dubious or even shady sources, innocently or unwillingly, and candidates with strong financial resources of their own gain such an advantage that their relative qualifications for office become secondary considerations.

From the standpoint of both the public interest and the ambitions of most politicians, the murky atmosphere enveloping political finance is exceedingly unfortunate. Neither scholarly research nor practical experience provides significant evidence that most politicians really prefer the questionable sources of funds to financing organized openly and equitably.

*　　　*　　　*

Although the panoramic view of the political scene appears discouraging, close inspection finds encouraging signs. The number of small contributors is increasing. So are persistent experiments to broaden the financial base of political activity. The idea that people should contribute to the party or candidate of their choice as an act of civic responsibility is slowly gaining acceptance among citizens who were not formerly asked to give and may, indeed, not yet know how. Corporations and labor unions step up drives to get people to register, to vote, and to contribute, sometimes on a nonpartisan basis. Occasionally, broadcasting networks and individual stations provide free time or cash discounts for candidates. Prospects for improved legislation were heightened by the initiative of President Kennedy in establishing a bipartisan Commission on Campaign Costs and by the advocacy of reform, however belated, by Presidents Johnson and Nixon. The Congress enacted new laws effective in 1972, which could be instrumental in inaugurating a new atmosphere of improvement.

Experience suggests that the element of free will in campaign giving is related so closely to the proper working of the political process as to be indispensable. Reason and experience indicate that public subsidy, direct or indirect, is both practicable and acceptable for some aspects of campaigning and need not supplant voluntary giving. The two ways of providing money for politics, by voluntary gifts or subsidy, are not incompatible. To make voluntary giving a more productive source, it is necessary to awaken greater numbers to the idea that supporting the political process in its campaign stages is a civic duty: to justify subsidies, it must be accepted that campaign costs are quite as much a governmental obligation as paying the salary in office of the winner.

There is a wry American saying that it is much easier to be honest when solvent. No one, surely, would argue that a political system is working at its best when chronically short of money it needs. Considering the national wealth, American political spending may in fact be too low. The end product of politics, after all, is meant to be an effective political system. Too few inquire today whether the political parties are adequate, whether they might perform more effectively than they do, and what improvement might cost. As it is, the creaky machine seems almost calculated to produce the scandals which headlined the names of Baker, Dodd, and others. At least some of the dissension, alienation, and violence characteristic of the United States in the 1960's appears related to the failings of the political system.

Reaction to criticism of our political finance system invariably has yielded piecemeal legislation which imposed negative controls, restricting spending even as needs and costs rose. To prevent candidates from becoming obligated to special interests, limits were set on the amount of contributions. Contributions from suspect sources were prohibited. To dilute the "spoils system," career civil servants were protected from politicial demands for cash. If there was danger that partisans would dominate the airwaves, all sides were guaranteed equal opportunity for free time— although opportunities to buy time were equal only for those who could pay for it. One after another, traditional sources of political funds were cut down without provision for new sources of supply.

Neither the Populists, the Muckrakers, nor the Progressives directed their wrath against the power and influence of money in politics, except in incidental ways. Most reformers stressed other changes in the electoral process, such as primary elections, more democratic party structure or procedure, a broader franchise, revised administration of electoral machinery, recall, initiative, and referendum. Some such reforms led to higher costs, but still no alternative means of financing were enacted.

No major reform movement has concentrated on money-raising for politics. The demands for prohibitions against corporate giving were peripheral to other concerns about corporate power, such as demands for antitrust legislation. The movement for giving publicity to contributors was only part of the movement against political corruption. In shielding the civil service from politics, the central issue was patronage as it affected hiring and firing practices and the quality of government performance. In short, instead of trying to put political spending on a rational and equitable footing, to break the shackles which discourage the average citizen from exercising political responsibility, Americans have, it seems, done almost everything to institutionalize undemocratic methods, to encourage undesirable contributors, and to protect devious customs by disguise, subterfuge, evasion, and lack of candor. Indeed, the main body of campaign law, that having to do with public disclosure of political funds, is archaic and inadequate. The federal law of disclosure of funds dates from

1910. This law was revised in 1925 but not until 1972 were new limits placed on campaign expenditures. Over all these decades, no legislative action to rationalize political finance was effective. Violations have been commonplace and enforcement at best sporadic, at worst nonexistent.

Although political financing in the United States has been undemocratic, with a strong tendency toward corruption, the system has survived because it has managed to provide sufficient funds. Also, several interests have liked it. Nevertheless, the system is increasingly under attack, not only because of past inadequacies, but also because it is failing to provide funds sufficient to the needs. The increased usage of deficit financing is striking evidence of this failure. If the growing weaknesses of the system encourage politicians to seek changes, reform may be possible.

A large number of reforms, some innovative, have been suggested in studies and proposed legislation. Political reform by legislation has been frustrated for so long, however, that Common Cause, a nonpartisan "citizen lobby," in early 1971 undertook another approach—a suit to have the courts enjoin certain practices, such as the making of multiple contributions to multiple committees in order to avoid the $5,000 limitation on giving. In view of the 1972 action of Congress, the case may be moot.

Efforts to broaden the base of political funds find there are too many candidates and too many committees to be supported by too few volunteers. Also there are few inexpensive ways of soliciting those who might give. These realities discourage widespread independent solicitation for most candidates for public office. If only Presidential, gubernatorial, mayoral, Senatorial, and House candidates were each to try to organize widespread solicitation of small contributors, the duplication of effort would overwhelm the donors. Dozens of appeals would be directed at the same people, the activists on mailing lists, or people on a block previously solicited.

The task of garnering votes and dollars is to match up the candidate with the interested citizen. The citizen has learned to register his interest by going to booths where the votes are collected. There are no comparable institutionalized or government-sponsored places for collecting donations from citizens who wish to register financial interest in politics. Instead, each candidate, each committee, seeks out the individual giver. The expense of advertising for funds, of mailing appeals, is multiplied by competing drives. The job can be done rationally with fewer dollars and less effort, but a rational scheme has not yet been tried on a wide scale.

The aim of this book is to help Americans understand how better to provide the financial resources for politics. The argument is not that political activity is too expensive, but that the country is not properly tapping or using its resources. A democratic system can find fair ways of gathering, awarding, and using political money. The search does not lie in the direction of unenforceable restrictions or in small expenditures but in a fresh look at the whole political system, in a willingness to try such devices as subsidies, tax incentives, matching incentives, and rational methods of mass solicitation and collection. There can be no question that the country can afford the amounts required. American society has no excuse to tolerate a debt-ridden, obligation-bound political system.

Only if the political bill is properly shared will some of the agonies of paying debts subside. Only then will some of the regulatory anxieties disappear. Only in this fashion can the rules of American politics assure that the game is fair to everyone.

MONEY THE ESSENTIAL

Money, Emerson said, represents the prose rather than the poetry of life. In politics, money represents the prosaic rather than the poetic. Money is the fuel that keeps politics alive. It is the basic—some might say baser—element.

Money in politics, of course, is not everything. Issues, organization, leadership, skill, control of information, the prestige of the office, and the advantages of incumbency count heavily. In the end, people, not dollars, cast the vote.

Still, money is essential. It takes money to buy the space and time for advertising, research, writing, and travel—in short, for the broadcasts, billboards, buttons, banners, brochures, even the barbecues which influence votes. Money helps the candidate to publicize his name, his record, and his pledges. Money buys what is not volunteered.

Money also substitutes for energy. Giving money permits citizens with little political talent and less available time to contribute a share of the energy needed in a campaign and to participate in politics. Many affluent Americans find it easier to show their support for a candidate or a party by writing a check than by otherwise participating. Public opinion polls record about twice as many contributors as political workers. If money is a substitute for service, giving it does not require as firm a commitment; some people donate money to both parties but few would give time to both. Money has an advantage over service for the recipient; it does not come loaded with the idiosyncracies of the volunteer.

American attitudes toward political finance, rooted deeply in our folkways, are ambiguous and ambivalent. Money is a highly generalized medium of exchange: it buys the campaign necessities and is assumed to influence votes, appointments, and public policies. At some point, especially in relation to contracts, appointments and legislation, the influence of political money is considered "dirty."

Still, a good connotation is placed on political activity as a civic responsibility. One votes because it is a duty; one is civic-minded if one takes part in community decisions; one is public-spirited if one works hard for a favored party or candidate. Service in these senses is accorded higher social value than money and is considered indispensable to the functioning of democracy, but money is not valued the less since, without it, political services are feeble.

If money is unique because it can be converted into other resources, then other resources can in turn be converted into political money. The politican can use the privileges of public office to award contracts, fill jobs, and make decisions that attract dollars. Skillful use of ideology, issues, and the perquisites and promises of office attract financial support to political actors, in legitimate forms as contributions or dues or in illegitimate ways, as past scandals have demonstrated.

Political money, however, is only symbolic of true political goals. The real competition is for power, prestige, or other satisfactions. Instrumental in this struggle, money's importance lies in the ways in which it is used by people to gain influence, or is converted into other resources, or is used in combination with other resources to achieve political ends. Because of its universality, money is a tracer element in the political process, marking the tracks both of the individual or group seeking influence and of the candidate and party seeking election to office. Revelation of their transactions and associated behavior deepens understanding of the flows of influence and power.

The role of money in the political process is a legitimate issue for public debate. The ties between political leaders and vested interests are always worthy of examination. Politicians, many assume, act at the behest of special interests. If that is true, the sources of financial support for both major parties certainly should be questioned. Many assume that money for politics is supplied primarily by government contractors, by large contributors, by labor unions, and the like. Because the wealthy minority are the source of much contributed money, they could be expected to seek to perpetuate the system which made them and keeps them wealthy. Yet many rich donors contribute to those sympathetic with helping the "poor", and in a sense their contributions often serve as surrogate appeals for the deprived who cannot themselves command influence.

Those with money generally need to enlist the support of other constituencies. The demands of wealth must be tempered to be politically acceptable. In a democratic system the minority representing wealth must win a majority to its side; otherwise the minority can lose to the majority, as it often does despite the financial advantages it can give to candidates or parties.

Democratic theory is based upon the doctrine of political equality, which abides no qualification of property, class, or other factor in regard to the right to vote and register one's opinion, but many political philosophers from Aristotle on have regarded property or economic power as the fundamental element in political power. They have maintained that the form of government is determined by the nature and distribution of property. The basic conflict in politics, then, has been between those who would use political power to protect or augment their economic power and those who would offset economic power with political power or votes.

The American system of government is rooted in the principle of "one man, one vote," but, like other democracies, it is hobbled by an unequal distribution of economic resources. The attempt to reconcile the inequalities is the main source of contention over money in politics. In a sense, broadly based political power, as effected through universal suffrage, was conceived and has been used to help equalize inequalities in economic power, despite frustrations brought on by the system of financing politics.

The mediation of this conflict is hardly eased by the structure of the constitutional and political systems. The Constitution required the election of officers for two of the three branches of government but made no provisions for political parties, which formed spontaneously to bridge the gap between citizen and ·public officials. The party system does not have the benefit of Constitutional status. The Founding Fathers did not, of course, foresee the rise of a highly competitive party system, nor the huge number of popularly elected officials, the direct election of United States Senators, the increased importance of nomination campaigns, the democratization of the Presidency, the advent of universal suffrage, the development of television, or the reapportionment battles—all of which have added to the need for large political expenditures.

Coincident with the extension of the franchise and the democratization of government's institutional framework, the control of money has been increasingly concentrated. Huge industrial, financial, labor, and other combinations not only vie to dominate the economic life of the country but also seek to control the political environment. They do this directly through lobbies and the contribution of services, goods, or money, and indirectly through attempting to influence the public in elections and in other activities.

Superficially, American politics seems to be so simple that it should operate at little cost with what is basically a two-party system, fixed elections, and single-member districts. There is no swarm of major parties, no complex vote counting, no "taking it to the country" on short notice as in England. Yet behind the seeming simplicity is a complex pattern, with primaries, run-offs, conventions, and 500,000 electoral public offices sought by perhaps a million candidates.

The American party system contains a series of subsystems, separated less by regional or geographic differences than by variations in the incidence and intensity of competition. Two-party competition occurs in certain districts only and in certain kinds of elections. In other districts and campaigns, one party may be dominant or there may be a modified one-party system in which a rising second party seriously contests only selected offices, concentrating on these while ignoring others. In a few places minor parties contest elections regularly, although they usually field their candidates only for selected offices, and some, such as the Liberal and Conservative parties in New York State, often endorse major party candidates. In many districts, there are nonpartisan local elections.

Whether the election is nonpartisan or fusion, one party, one-party-dominated, or two-party-competitive, in most places the party plays a minimal or no role in the nominating period except where the incumbent seeking nomination is not challenged. So the candidate for nomination is usually without party financing. He must build his own following and organization and raise his own money. Once nominated, he rarely can rely solely on party funds. In any case, he will probably wish to appeal to voters of all kinds and will establish his own committees for this purpose independent of his party. An incumbent seeking re-election undoubtedly has attracted followers and done favors for people outside his party, so he, too, will seek to appeal widely with his own committees and campaign. If his party is divided by factional disputes, as the Republicans were nationally in 1964 and the Democrats in 1968, he may prefer to campaign with little regard for the top of the ticket.

The political maneuvering within this multi-layered collection of subsystems has much in common with show business. The advertising budget must be large. The politician and the star both treat popularity as a depreciable asset requiring funds for maintenance and growth. In two-party districts, the candidate is thrust center stage, on his own, in the prenomination period, while in one-party districts, where party organization may be passive or non-existent, he is on his own in both the primary and the general election, dependent upon a personal following. Once elected, the politician finds the party he represents in public office rarely pays any of his personal political expenses.

The competition in gathering political money is not simply between Republicans and Democrats. A decentralized party system with open nominations, depending on non-party groups and self-financing candidates, all reliant upon a limited number of established techniques for attracting dollars from financial constituencies too small to serve the diverse needs, sees more competition for funds within the party, by candidates and committees at the various levels, than between the parties. No rational model exists by which party members at the local level pay dues, which the local then shares with state and national groups. No rational model distinguishes financial support of party organization year round from financial support of campaigns emphasizing not party but candidate. Lacking a coherent system, party fund raising to erase deficits after a campaign interferes with fund raising to sustain the organization between campaigns. Both collide with fund raising for prenomination campaigns or efforts to fill the coffers in advance. There are exceptions where the party is a stable, effective, continuing organization. For example, the statewide Republican organization in Ohio is a major money raiser and is normally able to allocate substantial funds to party candidates. The Indiana Democratic State Committee in 1964 was able to give major funds to the Senatorial candidate and $5,000 to each Congressional candidate,[1] and has continued the practice. Such organizations are unusual. In many states the party helps little, if at all.

Some southern states are noted for weak party organizations and high candidate costs. In these states, the party may be organized primarily to secure representation on the National Committee. The party neither campaigns significantly in the general election nor takes sides in the primary. In these states, particularly on the Democratic side, the primary election serves as the main focus of political competition. Recent Republican challengers have generally stressed party unity and have built effective party organizations in certain southern districts.

The primary election illustrates the relation between the type of party organization, the intensity of primary competition, and the nature and amount of campaign expenditures. Since the 1950's there have been indications that primary campaign costs in one-party or modified one-party states were as high or higher than those in general election campaigns in two-party states. In the 1968 Texas Democratic primary, eight major candidates for gubernatorial nomination reported spending at least $2.8 million; the average cost per vote was $1.82 compared with 74 cents for the two-party general election.[2] In a study of expenditures in Congressional campaigns from 1962 to 1966, seven of the ten most expensive were exclusively primary contests; costs were reported to range from $100,000 to $287,000.[3]

Though one would expect political costs to be higher in large urban states with two-party competition and higher levels of voter participation, costs per voter actually may be less in competitive situations than in one-party-dominated areas because voter turnout in one-party-dominated states tends to be less than in two-party-competitive states. In two party situations, where voter turnout in a primary is usually low, the cost per voter in the primary may be higher than it is in the general election when the turnout is larger.

The same phenomena can be documented in other parts of the country, for example in Massachusetts, where primary and general election spending is reported by candidates and committees as required by state law. Cost per vote in the general elections shows remarkable stability from 1962 to 1966, but spending in the primaries increased each year until in 1966 more was spent than in the general election—more, in fact, than in any previous general election. Because there were major Democratic primaries for nomination for governor or Senator in these years, Democratic expenditures comparing primary and general election periods were checked against numbers of voters in Democratic gubernatorial primaries. The results of this analysis show the same upward trend. The cost per Democratic voter was not only consistently higher in the primary than in the general elections, but grew increasingly so; [4] this in a two-party state where inter-party spending in 1970 was $2.5 million, compared with $2 million intra-party spending in the primary.

In Connecticut, where there is a challenge primary, total spending in U.S. Senatorial campaigns in preconvention and primary spending in 1970 was $2.5 million, compared with $2 million reported by three candidates (Senator Dodd ran as an Independent) in the general election. In Florida, which has a good reporting law, spending in the pre-qualifying and primary campaigns for the U.S. Senate in 1970 was reported to be $1.7 million compared with $553,083 reported in the general election, when spending was held down by Lawton Chiles' low-budget campaign. He reported spending only $219,098 to win.

The cost per voter is affected also by the difference in voter turnout in Presidential as contrasted to Congressional election years. Even if the amount spent in a given campaign remains the same, the cost per voter will probably be less in a Presidential election year than in other years simply because of the high voter turnout.

Still another indication of the complex relation between the state party organization and primary expeditures comes from the political broadcast surveys of the Federal Communications Commission, the only major systematic evidence available. These figures show that during the 1960's in the nation as a whole, the Democrats at least matched the Republicans in political broadcast spending. Although the Republicans spent more for broadcasting in general election campaigns, the Democrats significantly outspent the Republicans in primary campaigns. In the 1966 primaries the Democrats spent $10 million to the Republicans' $1.8 million. (In the general election that year, the spending was $10.4 million for the Republicans to the Democrats' $8.5 million.) Eight southern and border states accounted for more than one-half of the 1966 Democratic primary broadcast spending—$5.6 million—demonstrating the premium placed on success in primaries in those states.[5]

In 1968 the pattern was similar: in the primary election, the Democrats spent $12.4 million, the Republicans $5.4 million; in the general election, the Democratic spending was $15.4 million, the Republican $22.5 million.[6] Much of the spending by Democratic candidates was in Presidential primaries, further evidence of competitive demands for funds within a party.

The frequent failure of parties to fund campaigns for candidates, combined with the open nomination system, tends to emphasize candidates rather than party in American politics. Party manifestoes are subordinated to candidate utterances. Face-to-face campaigning, whether by handshakes or television, stresses personality rather than party.

This focus is reinforced by the candidate's almost limitless array of non-party supporters—candidate committees, committees of labor, of doctors, of bankers, of reformers. These committees are organized to raise money; some do nothing else.

Some committees raising funds directly for candidates seek political leverage or, at the least, to influence the complexion of public officialdom. For such reasons labor unions, trade associations, and management groups enter campaigns, both directly and indirectly. Sometimes they campaign independently on behalf of candidates or raise funds which they contribute to the candidate; sometimes corporations operate nonpartisan drives among employees for funds. The success of these groups in raising money indicates a void in solicitation not filled either by candidates or parties at present—perhaps one they cannot fill. Corporations, business, trade or professional associations, and labor organizations all have an advantage in politics: members of these organizations share common political goals, and the organizations command ready-made channels of communication capable of reaching large aggregates of potential contributors.

Folklore has it that candidates are more likely to receive emotional money, funds without strings, and that parties are more likely to receive money tinged with special interest. Surely some of the electoral interest groups, such as labor union committees or the American Medical Political Action Committee, do raise emotional money for candidates from a unique constituency that no other group could tap as well. Certainly some candidates find it easier to raise funds than do party organizations; when a party has an attractive candidate, party fund raising improves. Nevertheless, the generality is tenuous.

Opinions on fund-raising techniques vary, but many finance managers still believe the income is greater from multiple solicitation than from a single appeal. This is true to the extent that each appeal reaches its special audience effectively and to the extent that each fund raiser taps new, perhaps personal, sources not otherwise touched. Thus the ripples of solicitation widen, but the circle still remains too small. The effect of multiple solicitation is vitiated by the exasperation of those who become the target of multiple dunning and by the bewilderment of the uninitiated who do not know where to give or where money is most needed or will be used most effectively.

If competition produces extra money, it also means extra trouble. This is the reason why various charities have organized community chest or united fund drives. In political as in philanthoropic fund raising, unlimited competition is undesirable at best; at worst it proves counter-productive. Unrestrained competition is mitigated only by the differing interests of contributors and by the inability of every appeal to reach a given person.

A coherent fund-raising campaign by the party tends to be lost in an anarchic scramble which can be reduced but never eliminated because the existence of *ad hoc* committees is protected by the First Amendment. The proliferation of political committees happens not without reason—specialized groups need to be appealed to; special cause groups form on their own; and campaign managers often create their own competition on purpose. All this is almost inevitable since interests need representation and citizens are entitled to participate in the electoral process. Electoral interest groups are important to their constituents and can be effective agencies for collecting support. Whether citizen participation can be enlarged and channeled in effective ways is one of the questions to which this book is addressed.

Certain circumstances tend to ease the confusion and competition in the raising and spending of political funds. Not all elections are held simultaneously. Many candidates and committees work closely with the party and with each other. Multiple names of candidates for various offices appear on the same billboard; the local candidate tags onto the end of the broadcast of the Presidential candidate. Still, there is too little of that coordination (in some areas it is unheard of), and the resulting competition for advertising space and time swells political costs as vendors enjoy a seller's market. As political credit is less than certain, the vendor also charges for the risk, no small economic factor in the cost of politics.

3

COSTS AND EXPENSES

The cost of American politics must be measured not only in terms of dollars, but in terms of their impact on democratic values. Relatively, the dollar price is not especially high. But a high price is paid because of the irrational, irresponsible ways in which we raise and spend the dollars.

Size, of course, is relative, and the crucial questions are: too high for whom, too high for what? A wealthy society can naturally expect to spend considerable money on its politics. The stakes are high, but there are no logical threshholds above which costs become too high, which is one reason why statutory limits on expenditures have failed. Amounts necessary for serious campaigning may well seem large to the individual seeking office or to the party backing him. Costs are too high if, because sufficient money is not available, a candidate becomes beholden to those who will provide funds but with strings attached, or a campaigner is not able to achieve equitable access to the electorate, or a potential candidate is discouraged from running. Costs are too high if they place a premium on wealthy candidates and put barriers before the aspirations of poorer ones. On the other hand, costs are not too high for those who can afford them, such as a Rockefeller or a Kennedy who is willing to use his personal fortune, or for a Goldwater or even a Wallace who attracts money charismatically. Nor are they too high for the ambitious young man who takes the gamble and finds himself a Governor or U.S. Senator. Total political spending in this country is certainly small relative to the gross national product, the costs of government, commercial advertising, the take of gambling syndicates, or the value of a successful system of choosing public officials.

Costs of campaigning in the United States are not significantly higher than corresponding costs in some other nations and even less than in others. An index of political expenditures per voter constructed for various countries shows a range of .27 for Australia to $21.20 for Israel. The United States, at $1.12, was clustered near India and Japan in the lower range of the index.[1]

Various factors affect this index. These include depth of political loyalty and partisanship, roles of trade unions and other groups, and traditions. Moreover, costs are affected by the size of the electorate, the means of reaching it, the population literacy and geographical dispersion, and the level of voluntary activity. Another factor is the degree to which public funds are provided and legal controls are effective in minimizing political expenditures. For example, registration of voters is a governmental function in many other countries: in the United States, it is to a major extent a political cost somewhat reduced by volunteer services. Many "volunteers" are compensated with political appointments which do not appear as election expenditures.

Estimates of political spending sometimes exaggerate. People talk loosely and round off figures on the high side. Some candidates, in order to scare off potential opponents, emphasize how dearly it costs to campaign.

The proclivity of politicians to overstate their opponent's spending is typical. The news media often cooperate by publicizing inflated figures. In 1966 New York Democrats charged that Nelson Rockefeller's campaign for Governor was costing $20 million, an amount difficult to spend even for Rockefeller. His campaign was officially reported at $5 million, probably an understatement but not by a factor of four, even considering the number of people on his payrolls. Too many estimates of political spending suffer from what Justice Oliver Wendell Holmes called "all the earmarks of artifice."

Duplicity comes almost naturally to political finance managers. A major Democratic state committee for years publicly complained that it was carrying a $500,000 deficit; no sooner was it reduced than it was added to in a new campaign. Privately, however, large contributors were told the truth; the debt was only half the reported amount. The "poor-mouth" tactic is usually used to rouse the sympathetic and keep the regulars on their toes. If everyone knew the party is receiving more than it is spending who would contribute? The press would rather publish a stated deficit as gospel or enlarge it; rarely are investigative reporters assigned to probe deeply to ferret out the exact facts.

No doubt political spending has been stimulated by the tendency of the American parties to nominate wealthy candidates who become causes as well as effects of high campaign costs. A single candidate able and willing to spend will raise the ante to a level his opponent feels he must meet or risk defeat. Occasionally, however, spending records have been set by other than wealthy men: the Pat Brown-Richard Nixon gubernatorial campaign in California in 1962 cost $3 million, at that time a record.

One reason candidates seem to spend so lavishly is that they know too little about the increment of marginal votes per dollar or about the effectiveness of discrete techniques. Ordinarily they spend traditionally, as their supporters expect them to or as their opponent spends—and then some. New techniques win acceptance and to some extent displace older ones, but few candidates are willing to pioneer with unconventional methods alone. Neither social science nor market research has been able to tell them what kinds of spending achieve the most effect per dollar. What proves most effective for Candidate A may be worthless for Candidate B.

Voters conditioned to expect traditional activities interpret their omission in negative ways. Research does not show that the medium is the message, as Marshall McLuhan says, but the effect of the use of certain media, or lack thereof, is easily demonstrated. In certain states, for example, candidates are not considered as serious contenders unless they plaster their names on a convincing number of billboards: in California, 500 are a bare minimum. Moreover it is necessary to use specific billboards and the key space must be used early to keep out the opposition.

Though ostensibly directed at the public, considerable spending has largely psychological motives: the candidate spends to quiet his anxieties, which, in most campaigns are plentiful, or to stimulate party workers, to show the party that the candidate attracts money and intends to win. Much spending is cathartic. Politicians feel they must do something, anything, to keep the ship afloat. The costliest election is a lost election. Sometimes a campaign manager spends on frills to help support his candidate's morale and his own. Few candidates fail to enjoy seeing their picture lavishly displayed, even where election is assured.

The campaign bill for a single Presidential election could be paid easily, but there are 500,000 other elective offices in the United States to be won at some price. In a single election day in Pennsylvania, voters nominated 13,000 candidates.

In the four-year electoral cycle the Presidential election year is by far the most expensive. The 1968 Presidential hopefuls, including those who campaigned for nomination, spent about $100 million or one-third of the total 1968 political expenditures. This sum included: $37 million for national-level costs for Democrats and Republicans in the general election; $25 million in the Democratic pre-nomination period; more than $20 million in the Republican pre-nomination period; $9 million for George Wallace's American Independent Party, beginning in 1967.[2]

The known costs totaled $91 million. State and local spending on behalf of Presidential candidates in both the pre- and post-nomination periods constituted a large part of the remaining $9 million. In addition, there were party and delegate expenses related to the nominating conventions, and spending for parties, travelling, and telephoning by activists who paid out of their own pockets.

In the year which follows a Presidential election, debts are paid while parties and candidates prepare for the next Congressional elections. The celebration of an inauguration by a party that will be in power for at least four years helps to attract financial support at the start of the administration. Good feelings pervade the atmosphere until the administration's winter of discontent sets in to dampen fund-raising prospects.

The year of least political activity is immediately before the Presidential year. The cycle turns upward again with the invigoration of a new Presidential contest. When it is uncertain who will be the party's Presidential candidate, activity begins early.

Next highest to those of the peak Presidential year are the expenditures in the Congressional or mid-term election year, when Presidential candidates do not preempt billboard and newspaper space and broadcast time. Outlays in Congressional and state contests in these years are often higher than in a Presidential year. The amount of spending is necessarily affected by the number of Senatorial and gubernatorial contests.

Key elections naturally encourage spending, as in the Nelson Rockefeller, Ronald Reagan, Milton Shapp, Richard Ottinger, and Lloyd Bentsen campaigns in 1970.

Although there are few hard statistics for the Congressional years, estimates for political spending at all levels were $150 million in 1966 and $200 million in 1970. Total spending by candidates and their committees, reported to the Clerk of the House of Representatives and the Secretary of the Senate, doubled from $6.6 million in 1962 to $13.1 million in 1970, but these figures account only for candidates' personal reports and the intra-state candidate committees which happen to file reports. Most citizen or volunteer committees within a single state, which handle most of the money for Congressional candidates, have not reported to Washington. Until the 1970 election there was never a comprehensive compilation of spending to elect a Congress, only a sampling.

In 1970 the Citizens' Research Foundation (CRF) undertook a broad survey of U. S. Senate and House campaign costs, drawing information from a wide variety of sources, including filings in Washington and certain state capitols, official receipt and expenditure data available in Oregon and Kentucky, analytical figures from states such as California and Connecticut, newspaper reports and surveys, interviews, cost estimates, and other reliable sources. The 1970 costs, categorized into primary and general elections and party campaigns came to $71,619,301, divided into Senate and House as follows:

UNITED STATES SENATE

	Primary	General	Categorized Total	Grand Total
Rep.	$ 6,636,237	$16,053,124	$22,689,361	$23,393,292
Dem.	10,241,399	13,737,599	23,978,998	25,782,109
Other	27,736	2,583,506	2,611,242	2,611,242
Total	$16,905,372	$32,374,229	$49,279,401	$51,786,643

UNITED STATES HOUSE OF REPRESENTATIVES

	Primary	General	Categorized Total	Grand Total
Rep.	$ 1,952,135	$ 7,200,024	$ 9,152,159	$ 9,378,508
Dem.	2,553,982	7,444,254	9,998,236	10,229,109
Other	6,979	218,062	225,041	225,041
Total	$ 4,513,096	$14,862,340	$19,375,436	$19,832,658

The figures listed as categorized are those which could be divided definitely into primary or general election periods. The grand totals are verified expenditures which did not differentiate primary from general election costs. The total reflects Senate campaigns in 35 states, of which CRF had information for primaries in 33 states and general elections in all 35, and House campaigns in 50 states for which general information was available for most candidates and some primary information was available for each state. Information for House campaigns is much more spotty than for Senate campaigns.

Under federal law in 1970 only general election expenditures were reported in Washington. Two analyses were made to compare federally-reported and state-reported expenditures; both show a great disparity in general election reporting. For Senatorial contests, only $6,332,288, or 20 percent of CRF's general election total, was reported to the Secretary of the Senate; for campaigns for election as Representative, $6,674,217, or 45 percent of the CRF general election total, was reported to the Clerk of the House.

To bring this disparity into sharp focus, state-reported expenditures of Connecticut, Florida, Kentucky, and Oregon (the four states with the most extensive expenditure information available) were compared with their federally reported spending. For the general election period only, the Senate contests in Connecticut reported no money totals to Washington, compared with the $1,153,961 the candidates reported in Hartford. For Florida candidates, the ratio was about 1:1.6, with $350,952 reported to Washington and $553,084 reported to Tallahassee. (There were no Senate campaigns in the other two states.) For the four sets of House campaigns, the disparity ranged from about 1:1.5 in Florida to 1:8.7 in Kentucky. The Washington-reported and state-reported figures for the four states are:

		Washington-Reported	State-Reported
Connecticut	(Senate)	None	$1,153,961
	(House)	$374,056	974,534
Florida	(Senate)	350,952	553,084
	(House)	217,710	327,045
Kentucky	(House)	23,662	205,528
Oregon	(House)	115.822	182.150

The CRF survey, of course, used the state-reported rather than the Washington-reported figures where available. Information on primaries was generally available only in the states or in the press. Considering underreporting and gaps in available state information, the survey must have missed at least 25 percent of the total outlay. That amount, added to the $71.6 million verified figure, would bring spending to elect the 92nd Congress to about $90 million.

The 1970 verified totals for the Senate and House campaigns bear out the point that Democrats tend to spend more in primary battles than do Republicans. In Senate primaries the totals were $10,241,399 for the Democrats and $6,636,237 for the GOP; in the House contests: $2,553,982 and $1,952,135, respectively. In the general election period Democratic Senate candidates spent $13,737,599 as opposed to the Republican expenditures of $16,053,124, and Democratic House candidates spent slightly more than the Republicans even in the general election period: $7,444,254 (Democratic) vs. $7,200,024 (Republican). These figures do not take into account three million dollars which CRF could not divide accurately into specific campaigns. Numerous reporting gaps frustrated efforts to obtain a complete account.

Heavy spending marked the 11 elections in 1970 that installed freshmen in the U. S. Senate. There were 23 candidates for 11 seats and they spent a total of $23.9 million in primary and general election campaigns.[3] In March, 1971, a total of $2.1 million in debts remained, not counting an additional $3.1 million borrowed by Richard Ottinger from his family to finance his primary and general election campaigns.[4] These figures omit the spending by the primary contestants who did not survive as candidates in the general election.

The Ottinger campaign points up the high costs of running for Senator in a state the size of New York or California.[4] Both states had Senatorial campaigns in 1970 which included major primary campaigns. The total outlay in each was a minimum of $7 million. In the three-way general election campaign in New York, Ottinger and Buckley reported spending roughly $2 million each, and Senator Goodell reported close to $1 million. In the Democratic primary, Ottinger spent another $2 million, while miscellaneous other candidates spent at least the $353,200 they reported.

In California, it was reported that winner John Tunney spent $1.3 million in the general election after spending $568,180 in the primary, whereas incumbent Senator George Murphy spent $1.9 million in the general election and $637,761 in the primary. Norton Simon, who contested Murphy in the Republican primary, spent at least $2 million. With other primary and general election candidates for the California vacancy in the Senate, the reported totals for the year came to $7.3 million: $3.6 million in the general election and $3.7 million in the primaries.

The Ottinger and Simon primary campaigns each accounted for $2 million of the $7 million spent in their respective states. Their financing came substantially from the candidate himself and his immediate family. Candidates Buckley and Tunney also come from wealthy families, but the extent of their personal or family financial support is uncertain. Clearly the interactions of wealthy candidate upon wealthy candidate drove up the spending precipitously.

Elections for Governor in New York and California in 1970 were also expensive. In New York, Nelson Rockefeller reported spending $6.8 million in the primary and general election periods combined, although no Republican primary was held. Arthur Goldberg reported spending at least $1.3 million in the general election after a primary campaign in which he reported spending $432,000 while his wealthy opponent, Howard Samuels, spent about $750,000. The total of $9.2 million for the campaign for the Governor's office is probably the single highest outlay for one office other than the Presidency. Of course, the main element was the Rockefeller drive to hold his office in Albany, the most expensive non-Presidential campaign by any candidate in American history.

In comparison, in the California campaign for Governor, officially-filed reports show Governor Ronald Reagan's 1970 campaign consumed approximately $3.5 million, while his Democratic opponent, Jess Unruh, spent $1.2 million; their total was roughly half that for the New York contests for Governor. Unruh had no money for a television campaign.

For 1970, CRF surveyed the campaigns for Governor and

other statewide offices. Information was compiled for all 35
gubernatorial, primary and general campaigns. For the other
statewide campaigns, information was found for only 13 general
and 7 primary campaigns. For the most part, the information for
statewide offices was scanty. As in the Congressional survey, the
categorized totals are for expenditures which could be divided
definitely into election periods. The grand totals include all expenses, as follows:

GOVERNOR AND LIEUTENANT GOVERNOR

	Primary	General	Categorized Total	Grand Total
Rep.	$ 7,715,185	$18,027,375	$25,742,560	$28,491,888
Dem.	17,233,871	14,081,485	31,315,356	31,992,573
Other	8,535	386,773	395,308	395,308
Total	$24,957,591	$32,495,633	$57,453,224	$60,879,769

OTHER STATEWIDE OFFICES

	Primary	General	Categorized Total	Grand Total
Rep.	$ 365,876	$ 612,289	$ 978,165	$ 2,873,085
Dem.	1,288,309	1,839,235	3,127,544	3,693,699
Other	88,522	10,837	99,359	99,359
Total	$24,957,591	$32,495,633	$57,453,224	$60,879,769

The pattern of greater Democratic spending in the primaries
holds true in all types of campaigns shown in the tables—Senatorial, House, gubernatorial and statewide offices. The Democratic spending in the primaries is, in fact, so great that when
the primary and general election figures are added together for
each party, the Democrats outspend the Republicans over the
entire campaign year. This bears out the point made earlier of
how expensive pre-nomination infighting is for the Democrats.

Comprehensive election spending data in any state are seldom
compiled. Although 41 states have public disclosure laws, only
3, (Massachusetts, Oregon, and Kentucky) tabulate the results.

Massachusetts publishes only the totals of all the political
spending reported. In 1966 that total was $7.3 million plus an
additional $805,000 in outstanding debts.[5] In 1968 reported ex-
penditures in Massachusetts were down to $4.8 million ($323,000

in liabilities) but there were no U.S. Senatorial or gubernatorial elections or primaries as in 1966. Although there are possibly understatements in the filings and failures to report, the totals cover most elective offices in the state, excluding local offices. The data give at least a good indication of the magnitude of that state's political spending.

Oregon's compilation itemizes expenditures candidate by candidate, committee by committee. In 1968 reported expenditures totaled $4.8 million, with about one-quarter of that for the Presidential primaries.[6]

The Oregon data show substantial differences in competition and expenditures for the same offices in different years or in different districts in the same year. In 1966, when the general election spending level for the Senatorial seat was $800,000, the gubernatorial contest cost only $215,000. In 1970, when there was no U.S. Senate race, gubernatorial expenditures shot up to $415,518, and 76 percent of that total ($316,777) was spent in the general election period. Individual candidates for U.S. Representative in 1970 reported expenditures that ranged from zero in one district to $12,514 in another for the primary and from $1,320 to $79,120 in the general election. In Oregon the Superintendent of Public Instruction is an elective, non-partisan position; in 1966 one candidate spent $3,246, whereas in 1968 the two candidates in the general election spent $58,911 and $104,098 respectively. In 1970 the spending for this office plummeted to $1,072 in the primary and $150 in the general election; a dramatic display of the way levels of spending can fluctuate, depending on the political climate and the issues in a given year.

There can be no typical campaign cost. Rather there is a wide range of costs. A candidate who spends $500,000 may be opposed by one who spends only half as much. No two constituencies are composed of the same mix of factors, though many have elements in common, especially money. Party structure and political practices differ from district to district and between the parties, even within a state. The prevalence and uses of the communications media vary. The availability of funds, as between opposing candidates or parties, or over a period of time, also fluctuates.

No uniformity in patterns of spending is apparent. Rather,

there is a range of expenditures with different emphases and stresses based on real or imagined needs.

Since 1967 Kentucky's Registry of Election Finance has published detailed information on certain political contributions and expenditures. In 1967 total expenditures were reported to be $2,959,144, including gubernatorial and state legislative campaigns.[7] In 1968, with elections for the U.S. Senate, the seven Congressional seats, and several county offices, total expenditures were $1.3 million. Unlike Oregon, but typical of many other states, the gubernatorial race in Kentucky incites significantly greater expenditures than the Senatorial races, reflecting the patronage and other powers of the Governor's position. The 1967 gubernatorial race cost more than $2 million, close to four times as much as the reported costs of the 1968 Senatorial race of about $520,000.

Political expenditures in other states are difficult to dig out and analyze, but information is available for states and races which attract national attention. The totals appearing on the California political register are especially high. Both a northern and a southern campaign—usually separate—are necessary; a candidate well-known in the one region may need special promotion in the other. In 1970 a private compilation of all primary and general election reports filed in California with the Secretary of State showed $26.5 million spent for gubernatorial and other statewide offices, U.S. Senatorial and House seats, state Senate and Assembly seats, and four positions on the regional Board of Equalization.[8]

California's state legislative contests may run high. During a 1967 election in San Francisco for a state Senate seat, a Republican victory would have created a partisan tie, giving the Republican Lieutenant Governor the decisive vote. Both parties charged excessive spending; official reports showed $360,032 spent by two major candidates in a regular and runoff election. Reports filed for the 1970 state legislature in the primary and general election give a total of $5.7 million spent for 20 Senate seats and 80 Assembly seats. About 25 percent of the campaigns for the state Senate reported expenditures above $100,000, and another 25 percent were in the $50,000/$100,000 category. Individual candidates for the state Senate reported spending

$140,000, $135,000, and $110,000; one Assembly candidate spent
$120,000, and seven others each spent a total of $100,000 or
more.[9] California election spending is high in part because some
legislative districts are almost as large as Congressional districts.
This atypicality points up the urgent need for rational political
financing in appropriate circumstances.

In addition to the $5.7 million spent in state legislative con-
tests in California, $9.4 million was reported for primary and
general election campaigns for statewide offices: a reported total
of $15.1 million. Comparable figures for the legislature in New
York are not available, but the gubernatorial total of $9.3 mil-
lion was augmented by at least $464,458 for primaries and gen-
eral election expenses for Lieutenant Governor, Secretary of State,
Attorney General, and Controller, for a non-legislative total of at
least $9.7 million.

The campaign of John Lindsay for Mayor of New York City
in 1965 cost $2.4 million. An additional million was spent by the
New York Republican Party for all candidates on the Lindsay
ticket. Neighborhood storefronts in New York were rented and
manned at a cost of $900,000. The effort was to retail politics,
to take politics out of the clubhouse and onto the streets. Storefronts substitute for precinct organization, which Republicans
often lack in the big cities. Lindsay's opponent, Abe Beame,
spent $2.3 million in his primary and general election campaigns.
Estimates are that Lindsay's 1969 re-election campaign cost $3
million. If these costs seem high, it is well to remember that John
Purroy Mitchel's mayoralty campaign in 1917 cost $2 million,
equal in purchasing power to $6 million today.[10] Most New York
mayoralty campaigns cost less than Mitchel's or Lindsay's, evidence that spending does not follow a constant trend but is a
result of the availability of money, the stakes, the competition,
the political climate, the issues, and other factors.

A study of major statewide political expenses in Virginia covered the 1965, 1966, and 1967 primary and general elections.
For the 1965 contests for Governor, Lieutenant Governor, Attorney General, and the State House and Senate (the Senate
races, but for a court decision on reapportionment, would not
have come up until 1967), total declared expenditures were
$1,294,000. For the 1966 Congressional and Senatorial races, de-

clared expenditures were $1,348,000. For 1967 elections covering only the State legislature, declared expenditures were $963,000. While the three-year total of $3,605,000 is not high in comparison to many other states, it is a sharp increase over amounts spent in Virginia in previous years. One reason the study cited for the increases has significance for other southern states: it said these increases "reflect the change from a well-controlled one-party political situation to a more competitive two-party system. Voting turnout has gone up at a startling rate." [11] The increased voter turnout also reflects the black voter's increased participation, which has financial as well as political implications.

A recent example of the first point can be seen in the 1969 New York mayoralty primary election. On the Republican side, the winner spent about $120,000, while Mayor Lindsay spent about $340,000 in losing. (He won, unopposed, the Liberal Party's nomination.) On the Democratic side, the candidate spending the most, about $550,000, came in fifth in a field of five, while the winner was spending $100,000. On a per-vote-won basis, the Democratic winner spent 38¢; his runner-up spent $1.82; the third-place candidate, 93¢; the fourth-place candidate, 98¢; and the last-place finisher, a whopping $14.23 per-vote-won. In the Republican primary, the cost-per-vote showed the same ratio as the total costs: the winner spending $1.07 to $3.22 for the loser. [12]

Political costs can be tallied also by functions, that is, according to how the money is spent. In the 1968 elections, the largest single expenditure was for broadcasting: $58.9 million. [13] Production and advertisement of the broadcasts would add another 25 to 33 percent, bringing broadcasting and allied costs to at least $75 million. The largest single expense at the local level is election day expenses: in 1968 such costs—for workers, poll watchers, and even babysitters—ran to at least $25 million. A special 1968 analysis of newspaper advertising on a partial basis made possible a projection of at least $20 million spent for political advertising in newspapers. [14] According to industry estimates, $50 million was paid for novelties such as pins, stickers, and posters. Public opinion polling cost at least $6 million. On the basis of $300 million spent at all levels, a rule of thumb would indicate it cost a minimum of 10 percent to raise the money to pay the other bills; so at least $30 million, and probably a good deal more, went for mail drives, promoting and staging fund-raising events, food, drink, and so on. In total, these outlays account for $206 million, about two-thirds of the estimated 1968 political bill. There are no nationwide accounts for the other forms of political spending, such as salaries, travel, printing, postage, or overhead for headquarters.

Beyond the direct expenses, there are the non-cash contributions: for an incumbent, the legions of political appointees manning departments and agencies of government, at taxpayers' expense, providing information used in campaigning; the corporate or union executive who remains on salary while working full-time in politics; the young students, for example, in the 1968 McCarthy campaign, volunteering services and paying their own way.

How rapidly is campaign spending increasing? From 1940 to the mid-1950's the rise in campaign outlays was not much more than the rise in the price level or the national income. Since, then, however, expenses have risen disproportionately, mostly in response to specific needs and techniques: television broadcasts, intense party competition, jet travel, opinion polling, and reapportionment.

In the wide range of cost increases, advertising studies indicate that rates for television and outdoor advertising led all others. During the 1960's, radio and television advertising for the whole market—not only politics—increased substantially. Between 1961 and 1966 rates for spot television, the most common form used in campaigning, increased 38 percent. Basic rates for outdoor advertising increased 47 percent during the same period while those for newspaper advertising rose by only 11 percent.[15] From 1964 to 1968, television spot announcement prices increased about 35 percent, prime-time television program time rates about 25 percent, newspaper advertising space rates 10 percent, magazine space rates also 25 percent, and rates for network radio time 10 percent.[16] Price rises for printing and buttons and such probably have exceeded the general price rise.

The cost of broadcasting has significantly boosted political expenditures. By 1952 broadcasting had begun to displace other media in the publicity budget of national campaigns. Broadcasting costs now surpass other publicity costs. For the major parties, both the percentage and the actual dollars spent for broadcasting went up during the 1950's and 1960's while the percentage and the dollars spent for other forms of publicity declined.

Of the $14.4 million spent in the 1964 Republican Presidential general election campaign, 39 percent was for broadcasting. Other publicity costs amounted to 11 percent.[17] In 1968, with total expenditures of $24.5 million, all Republican advertising expenses were 49 percent, but the non-broadcasting publicity costs were probably only about 7 percent.[18] These allotments compare roughly to 1952 and 1956, but hardly to the years 1912-14, when about 40 percent of total expenditures went for advertising, mostly printed matter.[19] The 1968 Democratic Presidential general election campaign—operating on a $10.6 million budget, less than one-half the total Republican spending—spent 50 percent on broadcasting alone, and under 5 percent additional for other advertising.[20] Broadcasting expenses, the most important advertising expenditures in a major campaign, are least likely to be cut when the budget is tight.

While not all increases can be calculated precisely, it is clear that since the 1950's political expenses have risen at accelerating rates. In 1952 about $140 million was spent on elective and party politics for all purposes at all levels.[21] In 1956 the figure was $155 million; in 1960, $175 million; in 1964, $200 million; and in 1968, $300 million. These rises progressed at a relatively steady rate through 1964: 11 percent from 1952 to 1956, 13 percent from 1956 to 1960, and 14 percent from 1960 to 1964. From 1964 to 1968, however, the rise was 50 percent, a greater rise over four years than the 43 percent increase in the twelve-year span 1952-1964.

For other than the Presidential years, available data confirm the upward movement. For expenditures in the second year of the four-year political cycle (the year after the Presidential election), the only hard information comes from committees filing reports under federal law. Between 1965 and 1969, the sums reported rose from $10.9 million to $14.6 million, an increase of 34 percent. In the quiet fourth year in the cycle, political expenditures in 1963 were $7.5 million compared to $10.5 million in 1967, which was more than twice the amount for 1959. The

1963 figure may have been diminished a bit by the political moratorium following President Kennedy's death in November.

Most states yield little information on political expenditures for an extended time, but a few examples offer at least an indication of the rate of increase in spending. In Massachusetts, the expenditures of $7.5 million in 1964 were 25 percent above the $6 million spent in 1962. The 1970 California state legislative election cost $5.7 million, 43 percent more than the $4 million spent in 1968. In New York, Governor Rockefeller's first campaign in 1958 cost $1.8 million; in 1962 his re-election campaign cost rose 22 percent to $2.2 million. In 1966, Rockfeller's re-election campaign cost a reported $4.9 million (nearly ten times the amount spent by his Democratic opponent), a rise of 123 percent from four years earlier and of 172 percent from eight years before. In 1970, his campaign reported $6.2 million in the general election and an additional $584,800 in the pre-nomination period, even though there was no Republican primary.

The Democratic-Farmer-Labor Party of Minnesota is a rarity on the American political scene, not only because of its name and origins but because it has maintained and made available detailed records of income and expenditures. From 1948-50 to 1964-66, gross receipts rose from $203,000 to more than $437,000. In the same period, expenditures rose from $203,000 to 359,000.[22] These rises of 175-200 percent in income and expenditures over the 18-year period are probably typical.

A good example of rising costs for state election comes from a study of costs of Wisconsin statewide and county elections, covering expenditures by both parties for a 14-year period. The sums were: [23]

1950	$ 990,000	to	$1,073,000
1954	1,205,000	to	1,308,000
1956	1,488,000	to	1,617,000
1958	1,577,400	to	1,707,000
1962	2,830,400	to	3,073,000
1964	3,772,000	to	4,101,000
1966	3,245,200	to	3,526,600

The highest figure in 1964 was four times the lower figure in 1950, a gain attributable in part to the rise of two-party competitiveness.

The steep increase in campaign expenditures in recent years is only in part a reflection of price and income trend. In the table below, the campaign costs are those of national-level spending in the Presidential election years. These figures include national party, labor, and miscellaneous committee expenditures for the year in addition to Presidential general election campaign expenditures.[24]

	Campaign Cost Increases		Consumer Price	Nat'l. Income
Time Period	(Millions)	(Percent)	Index Increase	Increase
1952-1956	$ 1.3	11%	2.4%	17.8%
1956-1960	7.0	54	8.9	20.6
1960-1964	4.9	25	4.8	25.0
1964-1968	19.4	78	12.1	36.0

When state and local expenditures are included in the data, the rise, expressed as a percentage, is much smaller. From 1952 to 1968, the total of all political spending rose only 114 percent ($140 million to $300 million) while national-level committee expenditures noted in the table above rose 281 percent. (Over the same 16-year period the gross national product rose 150 percent.) Campaign expenditures by national-level committees have shown a steep rise also in relation to the number of votes cast. Between 1912 and 1952, starting from an index of 100, both votes and expenses rose to about 400. (During the same 40-year period, the consumer price index rose from an index of 100 to about 275.) In the middle 1950's, however, political expenditures took off: by 1968 the number of votes cast was at an index figure barely under 500, but expenditures were above the 1500 mark (Appendix A).[25]

As gross national product and disposable income also were rising through the years, political expenses remain only a tiny fraction of either. Nevertheless, the increased costs of political campaigns put new pressures upon the candidates, the parties, and the system of government.

4

POCKETBOOK DIFFERENCES

The conventional wisdom is that pocketbook advantage spells the difference between success and failure at the polls, but the outcome of elections usually depends upon much more than money. Although the odds may favor the side that spends more, voters frequently refuse to respond to frills, blitz campaigns, or wealthy candidates, as noted in the preceding chapter. Other factors compensate for a shortage of cash. For example, the low-budget candidate may be campaigning in an area predominantly favorable to his party or he may be a well-entrenched incumbent. He may be swept into office by a national trend, like the new Democratic Senators of 1958 or the new Republican Congressmen of 1966, or he may benefit from a Presidential landslide which extends national victory to other offices, as in 1964. Any of these circumstances can bring victory if the candidate has sufficient resources to enable him to present his report, his qualifications, his positions, his promises, or merely his name and face to the voters.

Many frugal campaigns triumph over lavish competition. Senator Clifford Case of New Jersey campaigned successfully on not more than $135,000 in 1966. Not enough is known, however, about the bedrock minimum needed to reach the electorate. Few losers are satisfied they had ample resources. There is little agreement on how to eliminate the frills without damaging the fabric.

Although many a candidate tries to outspend his competitor on the assumption that the amount of spending will favorably affect the outcome, in political life there are dangers in abundance and affluence. The most immediate danger is that to the extent money is available, costs escalate, and rising costs tempt candidates in a weak competitive position to accept money from sources they might otherwise reject. Campaign spending varies according to the availability of money, the willingness to go into debt, the nature of the contest, and the constituency to be reached. A candidate may win because he is able to spend money, or he may attract money because he is likely to win. The amount spent bears no statistical relationship to the caliber of the campaign or to the discussion of crucial issues or to winning.

In broad terms, money can be considered as a countervailing force to a natural majority. The minority party feels compelled to spend more money than the party that otherwise commands the most votes. A minority may use wealth to compensate for its handicap in small numbers; in effect, it converts cash into political influence at the polls.

High levels of Republican spending unquestionably helped to overcome distinct Democratic majorities in recent years in both registration and votes. Without the ability to raise and spend as much as they did, the Republicans could have been so weakened politically that they might have been reduced to a status of continuing opposition to the incumbent Democrats, with no prospect of gaining power and responsibility for governing according to their professed views.

During the twentieth century, at the national level, Republicans consistently have had more money at their disposal than the Democrats even when independent labor funds are added to Democratic spending. Republican advantages have been large in many states, yet from the 1930's through the 1960's the Democrats usually have commanded a majority of voters. In 1964, while the Republicans outspent the Democrats, Johnson won a landslide vote. It seems unlikely that more Republican spending would have changed the outcome. In 1936 the Republican Party, in conjunction with the wealthy Liberty League, spent $9,411,095 compared to the $5,964,917 spent by the Democratic National Committee and allied non-party organizations. Despite this three-to-two Republican financial advantage, the Democrats won the electoral votes in all but two states.

A Wisconsin study shows a consistent Republican financial advantage in a ratio of about 60 to 40 from 1950 through 1966,[1] while the Democrats were capturing major offices in the state for the first time in years. If labor and non-party funds are added to the Democratic totals, the ratio shifts only by three percentage points. Similar disparities occurred in Connecticut, Maryland, Massachusetts, Pennsylvania, and Michigan.[2]

The predisposition of the voters, the constellation of issues, group support, the advantages of being in office, the handicaps of being out of office, voters' perception of the issues and of the inability to pick a winner are always related to the electoral count and at times are more crucial than cash. Certain variables, such as the predisposition of voters and the images of candidates, are what they are because the parties spend to create and exploit them. One can argue that contributing voluntary manpower, as labor unions do so well, may be more valuable than money. Spending is only one aspect of the broader issue of access to the electorate through the communications media. Sympathy on the part of those controlling the mass media, or those possessing the skills for teaching the electorate, often can mean as much as money or manpower.

No amount of spending may ordinarily overcome prejudice against a candidate's religion, divorce, or color. A politician without substantial personal resources is ill-advised to fight for a Presidential nomination, as Nelson Rockefeller did in 1964, following an unpopular divorce and re-marriage. His political spending in any event helped him to hold the governor's seat. Money also helped John F. Kennedy compensate for anti-Catholic sentiment in 1960. With an evenly divided electorate, had Kennedy failed to spend liberally, the religious factor might have beat him.

If not decisive, money is capable at least of reducing severe handicaps for all candidates. Certainly, no candidate can make much of an impression without it, especially a maverick who fights the regulars or one who challenges an incumbent. For this reason, there should be opportunity for all qualified candidates to obtain support enough for at least a minimal campaign.

Wealthy Candidates

Some believe that the time is near when only the rich can run for high political office despite recent Presidential history. Although Franklin D. Roosevelt, Dwight D. Eisenhower, John F. Kennedy, and Lyndon B. Johnson had wealth, this was a factor only in the nomination of Kennedy. Though Adlai E. Stevenson and Barry Goldwater were considered wealthy, their fortunes bore no relation to their nominations or subsequent defeats. Their wealth may have helped them at most to enter politics. Hubert Humphrey, Harry Truman, Thomas Dewey, and Richard Nixon (in 1960) were not even moderately wealthy when they became Presidential candidates: all edged out wealthier rivals.

Because of the high and rising costs of campaigning, however, the candidate with wealth may be more readily nominated. Ironically, as the wealthy candidate is expected to spend liberally, his competitors are automatically handicapped. Before he spends a single penny, the rich candidate has incalculable advantages. His name alone makes news. Items about members of his family draw attention. Members of well-known families are able to enter office near the top of the ticket; if they exploit their advantages, they soon may contend for high elective positions in record time, as witness the Kennedy brothers. Except for certain other prominent individuals such as athletes, actors, or astronauts, men less endowed with wealth begin at low elective levels and earn their way upward slowly. Politicians complain that it takes money to publicize an unknown. Even a defeated candidate has the advantage in later elections that his name is known. Of course, if the defeated candidate is wealthy, so much the better for his chances next time.

Superficially at least a rich candidate does not need a political job and hence seems less likely to seek personal gain from public office. He may give the impression of being a dedicated man of principle who can be trusted. (In fact, a wealthy candidate may incur fewer personal obligations and preserve more freedom of action than other candidates.)

Other advantages for a wealthy candidate derive from his access to wealthy friends. Business associations are useful to him both in respect to the availability of corporate facilities as a campaign base and as a means of access to wealthy businessmen, suppliers, and creditors. A well-connected person obtains credit with ease and can guarantee that bills will be paid. His ability to pick up the tab at lunches and dinners, to phone long-distance without calculating the cost, is helpful, too.

Personal wealth confers still another advantage, illustrated by John F. Kennedy from 1956 to 1960 and Nelson Rockefeller from 1960 to 1964. Money permits a potential candidate to maintain a large staff between campaigns, which generates publicity to make his name and actions known. He can put task forces and experts to work on policy development and fact finding. A less affluent potential candidate cannot as easily buy a build-up between campaigns; for example, Estes Kefauver was unable to remain in the public eye between the primaries of 1952 and 1956.

For these reasons, political realities favor the wealthy candidate, whether or not the public believes, rightly or wrongly, that his money makes him immune to the pressures of special interest. This is not to say that wealthy candidates may not be good ones but, merely that their presence gives them an edge over others hoping to enter political life at high levels. Wealth propels, quickens, and catalyzes.

The major drawback for the rich is the notion that they can finance their own campaigns without money from other sources. Even the Kennedys and Rockefellers do not care to pay for their campaigns unaided. Nelson Rockefeller has complained often of the difficulty in raising money.

It is folklore that the average American admires the impecunious candidate who wins elections on a shoestring, beating a well-financed opponent. The voter often casts his ballot willingly for the man who is well-to-do with an expensive organization and a substantial war chest. American voters have been strongly drawn to Roosevelts, Tafts, Kennedys, and Rockefellers.

Two concerns usually are raised in discussions of wealthy candidates. One is that their personal resources give them too great an advantage, in strictly monetary terms, over other candidates. The other is that the rich constituency installs in office more spokesmen than middle-class or poor constituencies.

The first concern is really a "how much is too much" kind of question. Most candidates spend some of their own money and most probably receive some financial help from their families. Few voters would bar all such campaign contributions: they only wonder whether candidates should be limited in spending their own money and at what level of spending a candidate gains an unfair advantage from personal wealth.

In 1968 two candidates for the Board of Education in West Virginia, Mrs. Noel R. Snuffer and Joseph E. Bufferine, each spent $95 of their own money; Richard Keff, a candidate for state auditor in New Mexico, spent $185; North Dakota Governor William Guy reported making a donation of $200 to one of his campaign organizations; Texas Congressman Charles Teague received $7.50 from his father: surely no one would say these sums gave the candidates an unfair advantage. Donald Robertson, a candidate for the West Virginia governorship, spent $250 of his own money, while one of his opponents, Edwin C. Cales, spent $600. Many people could personally spend the lesser amount if running for office, and there is rarely any negative reaction to reports of spending at this level.

In 1968 San Francisco mayoral candidate Harold Dobbs spent $2,170 of his own money; Steve McNichols, a candidate for the Democratic nomination for the Senate in Colorado, contributed $2,500; Congressman Andrew Jacobs and Congressional aspirant Shirley Temple Black each reported contributing $3,000 of their own money. These are amounts which most people probably would not personally have available but yet are not generally perceived as too much.

Further up the scale:

• In Maryland an independent Senatorial candidate, George Mahoney, spent at least $10,000 of his own and lost the election.

• Missouri Senator Thomas F. Eagleton spent $21,254 of his own in his first and successful try for the seat.

• A Virginia Democratic Congressional candidate, David B. Kinney, was reported to have spent at least $77,000 of his own in an unsuccessful attempt to unseat the incumbent Joel Broyhill.

• In Texas one candidate for the Democratic gubernatorial nomination, Edward Whittenburg, spent $200,000 of his own while one of his opponents, Dolph Briscoe, spent $460,000. Neither won.

These levels of spending would likely be viewed as too much. Yet a quick response to "too much" tends to overlook an interesting and important fact which relates to the common assumption that wealthy candidates are conservatives who represent wealthy interests. Actually, many wealthy candidates have been spokesmen for poor and lower middle class constituencies and have been the more liberal candidate in many contests.

Wealthy candidates often are not the representatives of their economic class but spokesmen for those who might not otherwise be represented. Winthrop Rockefeller's role in Arkansas is exemplary. Robert Kennedy's quest for the Presidential nomination in 1968 gave representation to the black and the poor as few other candidates have done. As for David Kinney, few Democrats were eager or even willing to oppose Congressman Joel Broyhill, who is himself wealthy, ultra-conservative, and considered almost unbeatable. Without Kinney, the Democrats might not have been able to field a strong, liberal candidate, and many people might have been without a spokesman in that election. In many cases, the Democratic campaign would have been a poor one (literally) were it not that a wealthy candidate was nominated. To the extent that wealthy candidates shore up the two-party system or give voice to controversial issues or minority interests, they contribute to the political dialogue.

The main disadvantages of wealth in elections may not be in the outcome of financially-imbalanced contests but rather (1) in depriving the voters of potential leaders who haven't the money even to consider candidacy, and (2) in escalating election costs that affect all candidates, rich or poor.

A Case Study: Shapp

Milton Shapp, a wealthy Pennsylvanian, ran for Governor in 1966 and 1970. His 1966 primary bid for nomination and his general election campaign have been recorded in great detail by his manager, Joseph Napolitan, an experienced professional.[3] The account is informative and, for a partisan, well-balanced. It is relied upon here to illustrate several points about financing campaigns: uses of personal wealth, its influence on nomination, the tendency to spend beyond need, the expenditures committed by those unauthorized to do so, and the counterproductive or uncontrolled spending.

It was widely reported in the national press and in feature articles that Milton Shapp officially reported spending $1.4 million in his primary and $2.4 million in the general election in 1966. This was heralded as an example of a man of personal wealth willing to commit large amounts of his money to politics. Shapp made no bones about not wanting to be obligated to large contributors. When he was charged with trying to buy the election, he responded that he was merely selling himself with his own money. He preferred to spend his own money and raised little outside.

Shapp won an uphill battle in the Democratic primary. To do so he launched an extensive media campaign. Early polls showed him far behind his opponent, Robert Casey, the Democratic organization's choice, but Shapp's media campaign had its effect. Casey, lulled by the polls and secure in the feeling that primary voting turnout would be the small band of party regulars, realized only too late what modern techniques and money were accomplishing for Shapp.

Napolitan reports that a prime-time 20-second television spot announcement on a major Philadelphia station (one showing on one station) cost about $2,500. In the general election campaign, approximately $175,000 was spent for 23,000 radio spots on 170 stations. About eight million brochures and handouts were printed. One 16-page brochure, numbering 3,200,000 copies, was mailed to every household in Pennsylvania: printing cost, $120,000; postage, about $100,000; processing, about $32,000.

Despite these costs, Napolitan claims that actually less money was directly spent on the campaigns than the officially-reported figures reveal. His viewpoint illustrates a major difficulty in defining relevant costs. Shapp foresaw that charges would be made against him for spending so much, so he decided to reveal all relevant accounts. He leaned backwards not to understate and in fact, according to Napolitan, overstated his disbursements.

For example, his filings included expenses of two "Shapp Reports," prepared in the winter of 1965-66. One was on the condition of the Pennsylvania economy; one on what Shapp considered an impending crisis in the steel industry in Pennsylvania. About 40 pages each, they were mailed to 50,000 persons at a cost of about $100,000. Since neither mentioned Shapp's candidacy, they need not have been reported as campaign expenses. Napolitan says Shapp's biggest fault was his honesty in full reporting.

Also listed as a campaign expense, were certain amounts Shapp had spent personally in opposing the proposed merger of the Pennsylvania and New York railroads. Costs included legal fees, newspaper ads, and other merger-related expenditures. Shapp had been fighting the proposed merger for years and continued to do so after his defeat in 1966. Napolitan offers this as ample proof that the merger fight was not politically motivated, yet Shapp again insisted upon itemizing certain amounts. Perhaps most candidates would not have—the tendency is to understate expenses. No doubt most law-abiding candidates and treasurers ponder whether or not to report certain expenditures; laws in some jurisdictions exempt the reporting of certain personal items. A broad interpretation of spending by a candidate or incumbent over a period of a year surely involves listing many debatable activities which might be considered private or unrelated. The Nixon Fund of 1952, to be discussed later, raises many such questions. Where do private expenditures of a political person end and where do political expenditures begin? If more candidates came to fear the consequences of failing to report fully all relevant spending, as most Americans fear failure to report personal income, the reporting of political expenditures would measurably improve. The media were quick to pick up Shapp totals but are slow to investigate and report understatement by others.

The 1966 Shapp campaign generated unsual suits and countersuits. As a rule, candidates do not like to bring suits that will make them look like "sore losers" or put their party or party faithfuls (attorneys general, district attorneys, judges) in embarrassing positions. Accordingly, it was surprising that the Republicans brought a taxpayers' suit against Shapp, though this was balanced by Shapp forces, who brought a countersuit. Republicans challenged the official financial report on the last hour of the last day, demanding an audit. Shapp himself took the stand, also unusual.

Not unusual is the fact that both suits were dismissed. Judicial challenges serve to point up amounts spent, command the headlines, divert the opposition, and in the process insure legal fees. The Republican suit succeeded in all points. When Shapp's lawyers pointed to some discrepancies in the reports of Raymond Shafer, his opponent, the judge ruled that the purpose of the hearing was to investigate reported expenditures, to make certain they were legal, but not to investigate expenditures which were not reported.

The audit proceedings proved an embarrassment to Shapp and put a strain on his credibility. They attracted attention to payments to Negro athletes for endorsements, to Negro ministers, and to one Harvey Johnston. Johnston was hired by Shapp for $15,000 after he withdrew from the Democratic primary. It later turned out that Johnston was president of the National Association for the Advancement of White People. Shapp claimed to have known nothing of this affiliation, but in any case Johnston's hiring looked like an effort to buy off an opponent. Shapp claimed the payments to the Negro athletes were committed by a campaign operative not authorized to do so, but which Shapp nevertheless honored. One Negro newspaper was reported to have asked $40,000 for "advertising" with the understanding it would influence their campaign coverage. The offer was turned down.

Shapp admitted shifting $30,000 to a bank for use by a group of labor leaders who formed an Allegheny County Labor Committee for Shapp. This reverses the traditional role of labor supporting a candidate but points up the universal uses to which money can be put by an affluent contender.

Although Shapp campaign expenses got the publicity, Shafer expenditures were hardly inconsiderable, and a Shapp compilation of Republican Party and Shafer committees filing official reports showed, to Shapp's satisfaction at least, that Shafer spent more. In any case, Shafer won and Shapp lost in 1966.

In 1970 Shapp again challenged Casey in the primary and again won, spending a reported $1.1 million. In the general election, Shapp spent at least $1.6 million, and was elected governor. In perspective, the expenses of the two primaries and the two general elections should be added to derive the total cost ($6.5 million) of Milton Shapp's drive for high office. Less money was spent in 1970 than in 1966 because by then Shapp was better known, but again, much of the money spent was Shapp's own, though he publicly stated that politics—along with his personal charities, continuing fees in the Penn Central case, and market conditions—had brought his personal fortune down from about $8 million to about half that amount. A less wealthy individual, or one not so willing to spend his money, might have been discouraged. For Shapp, money made persistence both realistic and feasible.

Wealthy Families

In any appraisal of political contributions by members of wealthy families, the Rockefellers are in a class by themselves. Spending reported in four successful Nelson Rockefeller campaigns for Governor of New York reached a total of at least $15.7 million (Chapter 3), a substantial portion of which came from the family. Add to this an unknown amount in Nelson's campaign for Republican nomination for President in 1960, before his withdrawal; the $3 to $5 million, almost all from the family, in the same cause in 1964; probably $6 million in family funds for the 1968 Presidential nomination campaign; and the personal costs for staff and offices not paid for by New York State.

It is probably not an exaggerated estimate that family funds for Nelson's Presidential campaigns in 1964 and 1968 combined to total $10 million or that $10 or $12 million in family funds supported the 1958-62-66-70 gubernatorial campaigns. To these family efforts, add the three campaigns of Winthrop Rockefeller for Governor of Arkansas, plus his generosity in helping finance the building of the Republican Party of Arkansas, put at $3 million in one early account.[4] He gave a substantial part of the $1.3 million spent in his 1970 Arkansas gubernatorial campaign. A minimum of $5 million over the years would be a fair estimate of the Arkansas fund. Moreover, there are contributions by members of the Rockefeller family recorded in official campaign fund filings totalling at least $147,000 in 1952, $150,000 in 1956, $116,000 in 1960, $65,500 in 1964, and $231,750 in 1968. A conservative estimate of total Rockefeller spending in politics from 1952 to 1970 is about $25 million. Probably it is considerably more.

How generous this giving can be for individual members of the family is illustrated by one set of gifts in Nelson's 1968 campaign. Public records show that Mrs. Martha Baird Rockefeller, Nelson's stepmother, contributed a total of $1,482,625 to one Rockefeller-for-President committee in eight separate lots ranging from $425,000 on June 6 to $10,000 on September 18.

Public records also showed that Nelson gave $350,000 to the same committee. How much was given to other committees which did not report publicly is unknown.

The tax regulations do nothing to make political activity easier for wealthy individuals. A federal gift tax applies to political contributions of more than $3,000 to a single candidate or committee. The rates are progressive and the counting of gifts is cumulative, whether made to others within a family or to an outsider or any organization that is not tax-exempt. Press inquiries revealed that Mrs. Rockefeller paid $854,483.44 in gift taxes, which would bring her total cost of helping Nelson's campaign with a gift of $1,482,625 up to about $2,337,108. She may well have given sums in excess of $3,000 to non-reporting committees as well.

Tax lawyers claim that the $350,000 listed from Nelson probably is not subject to the gift tax because it is an out-of-pocket expenditure by the candidate for his own campaign and does not constitute a gift. It would be considered a gift if Nelson's wife gave the money. The conclusion is that it costs less if the candidate himself foots the bill than if the other members of the family do, but presumably families like to share.

It is also relevant that if contributions are financed by loans, interest must be paid. Also, if stock or other assets are sold to repay loans or raise cash contributions, then capital gains tax may be paid in addition to the gift tax. This illustrates other hidden or unreported costs that political contributions can incur for the wealthy.

There are few reported figures on Kennedy family contributions for politics. They do not show up on public records as Rockefeller funds do. Nevertheless, they helped to support the long career in politics of Joseph Kennedy; three campaigns of John F. Kennedy for the U.S. House, two for the U.S. Senate, one for the Democratic nomination for Vice President in 1956, and one for the Democratic nomination and election for President in 1960; the three Senatorial campaigns of Edward M. Kennedy; and one Senatorial campaign and the 1968 Presidential nomination campaign for Robert F. Kennedy.

A paradox in American attitudes is that, on one hand, voters tend to respect both economic wealth and political democracy when independent of each other, but to suspect alliances between wealth and politics. Americans distrust the use of economic power as a weapon in political campaigns and tend to have a perhaps healthy skepticism as to the motives of individuals who contribute large sums. Yet when voters see wealthy candidates on the hustings, as normal political men, many are attracted.

In contrast, the ordinary candidate faces many hurdles. His campaign will be restricted by the amount of money he can raise or is willing to owe. He must spend valuable time that might otherwise be spent on the campaign trail at fund-raising affairs. He may be tempted to accept money with obligations attached and be less free to operate according to principle, once elected, if he depends on selfish interests for support.

Occasionally, a candidate can turn his financial handicap to political advantage, by making poverty a virtue. He might succeed in pleading for money on grounds of his inability to compete with his opponent's fortune, as Senator Hubert Humphrey tried in 1960. Yet people tire of hearing the cry for money. After a while, they avoid meeting the candidate who always needs funds.

Candidates must be strongly motivated to run for political office, to accept the political wear and tear. Accepting the penalty of public life, Truman said, "If you can't stand the heat, stay out of the kitchen." One can argue that wealthy candidates must have deep psychlological needs or else would not expose themselves and their families to the abuse and costs of politics. Abuse is comonplace in politics, and the wealthy are especially vulnerable to charges of buying elections and seeking personal benefit. Yet, having economic and social power, the wealthy candidate may still desire prestige and political power. He may have felt frustrated in appointive office, as Nelson Rockefeller was reported to have felt. He may need to prove to himself that he can do more than make or spend money. He may feel a genuine social obligation. Any one or any combination of these motives could apply. For many, whether precinct workers or candidates, politics is an addiction, even a religious calling. We do not know the root motives of the wealthy any more than of others willing to take a flier, to indebt themselves and their families, perhaps for years to come, in political life. If we knew more about the conditions and motives that lead men to seek nomination and election to political office, we might improve the political system.

We also know too little about recruitment of candidates, too little about what campaigns, at what levels and under what conditions, seek wealthy entries. We know that wealth is significant in nominations for higher offices. We know that Senatorial campaigns in particular have attracted wealthy candidates. According to one unverified source, in 1970 twenty known millionaires ran for Senatorial nomination or election, and among them were eleven of the fifteen major candidates in the seven largest states. Several sets of millionaires opposed each other, and considering the numbers contesting, a goodly number lost. Several who readily won the primary lost the general election.

Assuredly, the wealthy should be able to seek personal political advancement as well as representation of their stakes in society. The argument has been against the unfair advantages of wealth, not against wealth itself. Correctives, as we shall see, are possible in reducing undue advantages.

THE COST OF PRESIDENTIAL NOMINATION

Costly and complex, a modern Presidential election campaign would appall John Quincy Adams, who said that "the President of the United States was an office neither to be sought or declined. To pay money for securing it directly or indirectly, was in my opinion incorrect in principle." [1] There has not been a time since George Washington when Adams' view, noble as it may have been, was practical. Whether the campaign was by torchlight or klieglight, dispensing cider or cocktails, somebody had to pay for it.

There is no way to measure the precise costs of a Presidential campaign. Money is spent on the national, state, and local levels by a multitude of committees and individuals, with no central accounting system. Campaign managers may complain of a shortage of money and suggest that the opposition has a massive slush fund supplied by a wealthy candidate or sinister interests, but it is beyond doubt that somebody is trying to win the election and somebody, indeed, is paying the bills.

Money wields its greatest influence on the Presidential campaign during the preconvention period, which has been called "that shadow land of our politics where it is decided who will be a candidate for a party nomination and who will not." [2] This is when a candidate's name and image must be given national publicity, when a complex of national and state-level organizations must be created to advance his cause, and when the tactics must be devised to win the delegates, whether or not he has entered the Presidential primaries.

A candidate who is not in office must find money outside the party treasuries. If he is an incumbent, or a Dwight Eisenhower coming to the political wars as a national hero, or a Richard Nixon running in 1960 as the heir apparent, a man without wealth may have a reasonable chance of winning a nomination, but if he is a man with strong ideological or personal constituencies but weak financial backing, his bid for the Presidency is crippled from the start.

Presidential primaries were introduced early in the present century as a plan to break the influence over candidate selection of a few political bosses and financial manipulators gathered in "smoke-filled rooms." Ironically, primaries have increased the costs of Presidential nominations and made candidates more dependent than ever on large contributors. Once common, Presidential preference or delegate primaries were by 1968 held in fewer than one-third of the states, and candidates rarely entered them all. The events of 1968 led to demands for reform in nominating procedures. Since then, three states (Rhode Island, Florida, and New Mexico) have enacted new primary laws. By 1972 there may be as many as 27 Presidential primaries, and there will be pressure on candidates to enter more of them.

Anyone seeking a Presidential nomination must forge a national organization. The expenses are formidable. At the least, the aspirant needs money for media, national and local headquarters, and travel expenses for himself and staff. "Grass roots" precinct-type organizations may be built. If the media are used heavily instead, alliances still must be cemented with state factions and local tickets. In states like West Virginia, the candidate may find himself obliged to shoulder a portion of the costs of local party slates in return for their support on primary day.

Even in states without primaries, the would-be nominee must court the party organization and convention delegates, perhaps by helping to finance their local and statewide contests. The support of political leaders in pivotal states that have no primaries is critical, since they often control an entire delegation.

Translating all this activity into dollar totals is hard enough; to obtain accurate data on costs is almost impossible because there was no federal requirement for disclosure of primary campaign expenditures until 1972. In some states with Presidential primaries, laws require disclosure of receipts and expenditures, but the statutes are not uniform and underreporting is common. Among the traditional primary states, California does not require reporting. A recent change in New Hampshire law has effectively eliminated reporting in that state; only Wisconsin, Florida, and Oregon have satisfactory reporting laws. Other expenses for national headquarters, costs of winning delegates, and a candidate's outlays at the national nominating conventions have been provided only voluntarily if at all.

Even well after nomination, the chances were small of getting authentic information, audits, or contributor lists. No single person is able or willing to give out comprehensive data; people will talk about some of the money that was spent but not, usually, about where it came from. What happened had to be reconstructed from bits and pieces of random information that usually lacked uniformity and was often unverifiable.

It is the more remarkable that there are fairly extensive and unusually reliable details on most of the nomination battles of the 1960's. The 1968 nomination campaigns were the most expensive by far and the least typical in recent years.

The campaigns of the early twentieth century, as Congressional inquiries revealed, could run into hundreds of thousands of dollars for an aspiring Presidential candidate. In 1920 $1,773,303 was spent on the campaign of Leonard Wood for the Republican nomination.[3] In 1952 an estimated $2.5 million was spent for General Dwight Eisenhower; probably as much went toward the unsuccessful candidacy of his opponent, Senator Robert A. Taft.[4] And yet, in a revealing memorandum published seven years later, Taft ascribed Eisenhower's victory to the power of the New York financial community and a publicity blitz by a large portion of the American press. He probably would have done better at the convention, Taft said, "if we had put on a real primary campaign in [certain additional] states. The difficulty was the tremendous expense involved in any such program and the lack of time to make an adequate campaign against the newspaper influences." [5]

John F. Kennedy's prenomination campaign of 1960 admitted to spending $912,500, of which slightly more than one-half ($470,000) was spent in the primaries. Additional spending for Kennedy came from state and local groups, with totals unknown. Kennedy, moreover, was able to minimize costs through skilled relations with the press. His wealth, youth, family, and Catholicism made him automatically newsworthy and permitted him to use his resources to full advantage. In addition to outspending Humphrey wherever they competed, Kennedy had the ability to threaten to spend enough more to discourage competition, as in California and Ohio. By political expertise, Kennedy was able to avoid costly battles in states where he won the support of the Governors and all or part of the state delegations. A California primary would have cost Kennedy, according to 1960 estimates, at least $750,000.

At the convention, with the contest narrowed to Kennedy, Lyndon Johnson, Stuart Symington, and Adlai Stevenson, the Republicans cheerfully talked about the "battle of the millionaires." Johnson's expenses were said to be $250,000, spent largely at the convention itself, and Symington spent $350,000. Against these rivals, Kennedy's wealth gave him no special edge; his advantage, apart from his personal qualities, was a smoothly functioning organization seasoned by months of campaigning.

Kennedy and his family admitted contributing $150,000 (of the $912,500 total) to his bid for nomination—$90,000 from the Senator's parents, siblings and their spouses, and $60,000 from the candidate. Members of the family also formed the Ken-Air Corporation to buy a $385,000 airplane which was leased to the Senator at the rate of $1.75 a mile. Additional family contributions that cannot be measured in dollars included the services of family members, working without salary and paying their own expenses. The Kennedy campaign similarly benefitted from the help of wealthy volunteers.

The Kennedy prenomination campaign left an avowed deficit of $217,000, a debt assumed by the post-convention campaign, although Johnson's prenomination deficit of about $100,000 was not.

It is interesting to speculate about the effects of debt upon campaign strategy. A candidate bases his strategy on realistic estimates of available money. If money is tight, he is forced to skimp. If, with a large debt to pay, he loses the nomination, his credit is so much worse. Senator McCarthy in 1968 was obliged to reduce his summer campaign because of debt. Two months after John Kennedy was nominated, Humphrey, though mounting his own Senate campaign, still owed $15,000. A wealthy candidate, on the other hand, has less reason to fear debt. The Kennedy campaigns were marked by notable risk-taking which a lack of credit might have discouraged.

Before the Republican convention of 1960, the camp of Richard

Nixon spent about $500,000 even without major opposition. Nixon was entered in certain primaries for the purpose of scoring in polls, to build support, and to give practice to his campaign organization. One reason for entering the primaries—and spending so much—was to compete for headlines with the Democrats. Candidates without opposition must spend heavily because otherwise they don't make news; and if the press ignores them, the public forgets them.

In the 1964 Republican competition, candidates willing to commit large resources ran up heavy campaign costs even when they were fairly certain of defeat. Nelson Rockefeller's personal wealth combined with Barry Goldwater's broad financial base accounted for most of the more than $10 million spent for the Republican nomination, more than doubling the record $5 million spent in the Taft-Eisenhower contest. The candidates and their organizations admitted spending the following amounts:

Goldwater	$5,500,000
Rockefeller	3,000,000
Scranton	827,000
Lodge	100,000
Nixon	72,000
Stassen	70,000
Total	$9,569,000[6]

Rockefeller's money came almost exclusively from his family, but the Goldwater fund-raising operation drew at least $5.5 million from hundreds of thousands of contributors who shared his militantly conservative philosophy. This was a phenomenal success story in modern political finance, the largest fund ever raised publicly for a Presidential nomination campaign to that time, without counting the amounts raised by state and local groups. In all, more than 300,000 people gave money to the prenomination Goldwater campaign. Goldwater's main effort was concentrated on seizing state delegations, not winning primaries, and his high expenditures suggested that delegate-hunting can be as expensive as the primaries as a method of seeking a Presidential nomination.

Goldwater mounted his prenomination drive without the traditional largesse from the East, which eventually veered to the

Democrats. When it became clear that massive expenditures by Rockefeller and Goldwater had raised the ante too high, many Eastern and national corporate interests cooled toward the Republican Party. It has been theorized that there was so much Rockefeller, local, and "new" Western money in the Republican Party that many wealthy Easterners supported President Johnson with funds because it was cheaper to buy political attention in the Democratic Party. Also, the Democrats were considered almost sure to win.

Scranton did not become an official candidate until June 12, a month before the Republican Convention opened in San Francisco. A whirlwind $827,000 campaign, including some pre-announcement maneuvering, used $245,000 on radio and television and $200,000 at the San Francisco convention. In addition, Rockefeller spent $70,000 at the convention on Scranton's behalf.

The Scranton campaign benefitted from the "splendid inheritance" of the Rockefeller organization, available after the California primary. Rockefeller's data on delegates were especially helpful. Scranton utilized seasoned Rockefeller personnel whose salaries, under contract, continued to be paid by Rockefeller, though Scranton assumed their expenses.

The combined totals of about $250,000 for the Lodge, Nixon, and Stassen movements indicate that even absentee or futile commitment is expensive. Lodge never announced. He remained in Vietnam while others campaigned in his behalf. Nixon never announced either, but others pushed his candidacy in Oregon and Nebraska. Stassen announced and campaigned for himself, and much of the money he used was his own.

A unique approach to campaign finance was adopted by Senator Margaret Chase Smith of Maine when she, too, sought the Republican nomination. Mrs. Smith's announcement brought unsolicited contributions ranging from 50 cents to hundreds of dollars, many from sympathetic women, but she returned them all. Senator Smith's poor showing in the New Hampshire primary may be attributed to her refusal to spend money, except for travel, or to the fact that she was a woman seeking what many consider a man's job. It is probable, however, that even without her handicaps, she could not have overcome Lodge's appeal. His supporters spent a mere $25,000 on an amazingly successful write-in campaign.

Any true accounting of Presidential nominations would include the cost of forays by candidates in the pre-announcement period or by "non-candidates" on behalf of local interests, as when a Governor arranges at public expense a tour of other states, ostensibly to recruit new industry but actually to seek a wider constituency in key states. Another way a candidate gains exposure is to address fund-raising affairs, with maximum opportunity to meet potentially new constituents in new territory, impress the impressionable, and at the same time earn points with party managers who may, in turn, influence their delegation to the nominating convention. Senator Goldwater was a diligent and outstandingly successful speaker at fund-raising events when he was chairman of the Republican Senatorial Campaign Committee. With his help, these affairs grossed an estimated $7 million for local party committees. During 1967, George Romney followed this route, as did Richard Nixon.

An incumbent President seeking re-election normally has a free ride during the prenomination period, but in 1964 primary bids by Alabama's Governor George C. Wallace posed a minor threat to President Johnson in three states (Wisconsin, Indiana, and Maryland). The President did not put his prestige on the line by campaigning personally, but prominent state Democrats represented him in each state, with a reported total expenditure of at least $190,000.

Wallace, it was reported, received $321,344 in contributions to finance his three primary runs and the costs of the unpledged electoral slate in Alabama. He claimed that his funds came from thousands of voluntary contributions, but newspaper accounts indicate that mail solicitations were sent to voters in some primary states by various right-wing organizations, including the Coordinating Committee for Fundamental American Freedoms, a group that was said to have received $10,000 in Alabama state funds through the instrumentality of the Alabama State Sovereignty Commission. It was alleged also that Wallace travelled in airplanes owned by the Alabama Highway Department, and, according to one source, he "sent an army of state employees to work in . . . primaries, riding in cars rented on credit cards issued by the Alabama State Highway Department." [7] Officials in the Wallace campaign denied the stories, but the accusations continued and were repeated in 1968, along with charges of kickbacks from contractors.

The Wallace ploy of 1964 illustrates how splinter candidates with no serious chance of winning can enter contests to prove the popularity of their cause, to exercise influence on future policies, or to hurt other candidates. The result, in any case, is to drive up political costs.

Campaign spending in 1960 and 1964, impressive as it was, seems a world apart from spending in 1968. Not since 1920 had there been such a combination of hot competition in both parties and so many candidates, wealthy or not, in contention. Whether 1968 was a freak or the taste of politics to come remains to be seen. Certainly, the 1968 experience provided fresh impetus for efforts to bring campaign finance under control.

Although there had been a trend toward earlier opening of the real (as opposed to announced) campaigns—the Goldwater effort, though often conducted under the guise of party fund-raising activities, had begun in the early 1960's—year-long or longer prenomination drives in 1968 were almost the rule. Still another trend accentuated in 1968 was exploitation of unpredictable, crash campaigns based on a swift unfolding of news events.[8]

The Romney, Nixon, and McCarthy drives dated back into 1967. The Romney campaign aborted abruptly in February, 1968. When the unannounced campaign for President Lyndon Johnson ended in March, Robert F. Kennedy, initially hesitant, plunged in suddenly and intensely, as if he knew time was not on his side. Hubert H. Humphrey delayed his entry to avoid contesting primaries. The on-again, off-again campaign of Nelson Rockefeller also avoided the primaries. Ephemeral campaigns by Reagan, Maddox, McGovern, and Stassen served mainly to feed the fever of the main contenders.

About $45 million was spent before Nixon and Humphrey carried off the nominations. More money, by several millions of dollars, was spent by the Democrats than by the Republicans. Democratic competition in the period of the primaries, particularly when Robert Kennedy was contesting, was heavy while Nixon, after Romney withdraw, was without serious competition until Reagan was entered, and then Rockefeller entered the lists.

For the other candidates, the appearance of both a Rockefeller and a Kennedy in one year and the emotional nature of the issues brought out larger contributions on the record than at any time since the 1920's. (Chapter 4) It was rumored that Nixon, McCarthy and Kennedy each received $500,000 from individual sympathizers. Another donor gave $300,000 to Rockefeller and McCarthy. Two and perhaps three each donated $300,000 to Romney's campaign. One person probably gave $300,000 to McCarthy's campaign, which also drew perhaps five other contributors of $100,000 to $300,000. The Kennedy and Rockefeller campaigns all had $100,000 contributors outside the immediate families. Several dozen persons are known to have given between $50,000 and $100,000 to the various campaigns. These contributions were for the most part not publicly reported, though there was more candor and publicity concerning campaign gifts than perhaps ever before.

The combination of Kennedy, McCarthy, Humphrey, Romney, and Rockefeller, moreover, brought out more money from politically liberal sources than in any previous American campaign. Although it is conventionally assumed that liberal candidates are financially disadvantaged, while centrists and conservatives supposedly find ample funds, the notion that political money comes mainly from wealthy conservatives is simplistic. The first modern evidence that the theory is false, ironically, came from the Goldwater campaign of 1964 which, though conservative it was, relied not so much on a few large donations as on many small ones. That campaign attracted some right-wingers previously outside the two-party system, but it also showed that hundreds of thousands of small contributors could be attracted to a conservative candidate. It was yet to be learned whether a liberal could rally such support.

No liberal Democrat had ever raised so much from so many, not John F. Kennedy nor Adlai E. Stevenson. However, 1968 demonstrated that with the proper mix or issues, events, and men, liberals could find money plentiful too, with support from the monied no less than from the many. Perhaps 150,000 contributed to the McCarthy campaign, many of them in politics for the first time. The McCarthy mix may have been in many ways unique, but it helped dispel the notion that only Republicans, conservatives, or sure winners attract substantial financing.

The Republicans in 1968 spent about $20 million, slightly less than the Democrats, in the prenomination period, with Nixon's campaign accounting for more than one-half. Rockefeller, even without entering the primaries, spent $8 million; Romney spent $1.5 million; Reagan, $700,000; Stassen, $90,000.

Nixon's central national organization spent $8.5 million, including $300,000 in New Hampshire and $500,000 in Wisconsin (in both states Stassen was the only competition). The total does not include substantial amounts spent independently in three major primary states—Indiana ($200,000), Nebraska ($100,000), and Oregon ($500,000). When all the numerous state and local organizations are included, Nixon's spending was at least $10 million and probably approached $12 million if 1967 costs are added.

The broad categories of Nixon national expenditures were as follows:

Advertising (some in primaries, some nationally)	$2,500,000
Direct national support of primaries	1,500,000
Convention	500,000
Organizing and funding citizens' organizations	400,000
Financial operation (not counting mailing costs)	150,000
Campaign management, including candidate travel,[9] staff, regional organizational network, research, advance, women's activities, New York and Washington operations	3,500,000

The high expenditures for Richard Nixon, in view of his previous defeats, grew from his need to build confidence in his ability as a vote-getter, a situation that made his success in fund raising even more notable. His was the most expensive prenomination campaign in history, and Nixon was not a rich man spending his own money. The money was raised from a relatively broad base, and the campaign was financed, at times albeit with difficulty, without deficits. Not a single fund-raising dinner was held throughout the prenomination period.

Nixon's base for the national campaign had about half as many contributors as Goldwater, but he raised almost twice as much money. About $2.2 million came from more than

150,000 contributors responding to a direct-mail solicitation of 5,000,000 pieces. Contributions averaged $14. The main source of funds, however, was from contributors of $1,000 minimum who, for the price, became members of the Richard Nixon Associates (RNA). RNA had 1,200 contributors and provided more than half the $8.5 million total; it was a vehicle for recognizing large contributors at receptions, through special privileges at the convention, with gold lapel pins, and with a promised post-election advisory role. It was not as widely publicized (or criticized) as the Democratic President's Club on whose operation it seemed modelled.[10]

Nelson Rockefeller's third try for the nomination was chiefly a media drive aimed at influencing the public opinion polls. The main purpose was to get delegates to remain uncommitted. No efforts were spared for want of money, but Rockefeller in 1968 was even more reluctant than in 1964 to reveal how the money was spent, even though all the other contenders had disclosed significant financial facts. The only reason given was that the figures would not be believed, but it appears that members of the Rockefeller family were sensitive about divulging their share of the campaign. It could be a disarming tactic for Rockefeller, a major public figure for more than a decade, much maligned because of his wealth, to make a frank disclosure of his political political spending. Invidious speculation might be stilled if the truth were told. There may be strategic reasons during a campaign to divulge no financial information, but what purpose is served by secrecy after the ballots are counted?

Available evidence and intelligent surmise indicate that $8 million was spent in Rockefeller's central 1968 campaign, even without primaries. The money was spent roughly as follows:

Advertising	$ 4,500,000
Organization	1,500,000
Travel	1,000,000
Polls and surveys	250,000
Convention	750,000

The central campaign raised about $1.5 million outside the family. Of that, about half was given by perhaps a dozen persons and about $500,000 more by another dozen. Not more than five to ten thousand dollars were raised from newspaper ads or unsolicited sources. A remainder of about $5.5 million came from the Rockefeller family.

One bit of hard data, obtained from an official filing in Albany, was as unusual as it was revealing. In most Presidential prenomination campaigns before 1972, committees handling money were organized in states such as Delaware, where laws did not require public reports of political spending. Although it was rumored that 34 Rockefeller committees were established in Delaware to conceal finances, one major Rockefeller committee, called Rockefeller for President (New York), reported in Albany for a period from June 6 to September 18 receipts and expenditures both totalling $1,840,627, as noted before, with funds mainly from Mrs. Martha Baird Rockefeller, Nelson's stepmother. The committee reported 21 payments totalling $1,460,498.29 to Jack Tinker & Partners, Inc., an advertising agency.

One early effort to persuade Rockefeller to run cost his supporter $100,000. In March, Stewart R. Mott, Jr., (later one of Senator McCarthy's largest contributors) bought newspaper ads, mainly in *The New York Times* and in eight Michigan (Mott's home state) papers. He offered to contribute $50,000 if Rockefeller announced by March 15 on the condition that readers pledge $100,000 and that Rockefeller adopt an acceptable policy for withdrawal from Vietnam. The ads, 21 full pages, brought 7,000 replies, $40,000 in cash, and additional pledges. Mott then set up the Coalition for a Republican Alternative, with the $40,000 plus $100,000 from Mott personally. Rockefeller was not ready to announce then and, when he did, made no effort to embrace Mott's coalition.

For Governor Ronald Reagan of California, no formal campaign was waged. He repeatedly denied being a candidate, and yet more than $750,000 was spent for his nomination. An Oregon primary effort was undertaken and a national Reagan Information Center was established in Topeka, Kansas, both without his active help. Reagan announced formally only at the Miami Beach convention, but his supporters had worked hard throughout 1968.

Some of their most costly efforts were directed at keeping the large California delegation committed to Reagan as a favorite son. Nixon agreed not to challenge Reagan in the California primary, yet $100,000 was spent to circulate petitions to put Reagan on the ballot, to make a good showing in a primary where there was no opposition, and also to investigate and counter a recall effort in California which might have embarrassed Reagan. From February until the convention, Reagan supporters hired F. Clifton White to advise on national prospects and strategy. White's fee and expenses were more than $110,000. Convention costs for communications, receptions and hospitality center were about $150,000.

During 1967 and 1968 Governor Reagan undertook extensive travel to speak at Republican functions. A total of $3.8 million was said to have been raised in a ten-month period. These trips served to gain Reagan national attention, to introduce him to potential supporters throughout the country, and to demonstrate his loyalty and value to the party. The Reagan travels were financed by a trust fund set up under the direction of the Republican State Central Committee of California, and the fund was financed by charging either a portion of the gross amount received at affairs where Reagan spoke or a fixed fee arrived at by negotiation. In all, about $100,000 was collected and spent by this trust to cover out-of-state travel costs for the Governor and his entourage and per diem expenses of political employees who helped with advance work, research, or other needs.[11]

The campaign of Governor George Romney of Michigan was budgeted at $4.2 million from September 1, 1967, to July 31, 1968, but this was a rare case where a candidate spent less, not more. Romney announced early, stalled, and withdrew 13 days before the New Hampshire primary, after 101 days of campaigning. Since its start early in 1967, long before the official announcement, the campaign actually cost $1.5 million.

The Romney campaign in New Hampshire received national attention in early 1968 because a special profile of the state's voters (including 150,000 Republicans) was prepared at computer headquarters in Hanover. This project lent itself to both strategic and operational needs. It facilitated mailings to any or all elements on the list; individuals could be invited to Romney appearances in their areas or to visit the home headquarters planned in every city and village in the state. Prepared by

Campaign Consultants, Inc., the voter profile was documented in a 121-page report with statistical tables two inches thick. The computer program and analysis cost about $50,000. The same firm used the profile to direct the Romney media campaign.

The Romney budget for public opinion studies allowed for national as well as state polls. The polls were estimated to cost, plus or minus ten percent, $50,000 for the national poll and, on average, $8,000 for each of eight states. Special studies for delegate persuasion were put at $40,000. In all about $100,000 was spent.

The main financing for the campaign came from a few sources. One insider estimated that 85 percent of the money came from three individuals, in sums of at least $300,000 each—from George Romney himself, Nelson Rockefeller, and J. Willard Marriott. Others like J. Clifford Folger and Harold McClure, Jr., were probably within the $50-100,000 range. Max Fisher was another large giver, but it is not clear how much these three gave and how much they raised from others.

The fund-raising chores were apportioned in an interesting manner. Fisher, finance chairman, is Jewish and presumably raised money among Jews as well as other contacts. Marriott is a Mormon with access to other Mormons, and Folger has much experience in white Anglo-Saxon, Protestant, Republican circles. There was a division of labor, though jurisdiction overlapped, and Fisher was the key man.

Special efforts to reach two immensely wealthy persons for contributions failed for lack of proper follow-through by the candidate or his finance chairman. Appeals through a Mormon closely associated with Howard Hughes were attempted in vain. (McCarthy fund raisers also tried to reach the elusive Hughes, in the belief that his views on Vietnam were congenial, but apparently with no better luck). A Romney campaigner who performed professional services for J. Paul Getty evidently found Getty cool to the candidacy.

On the Democratic side, more than $25 million was spent in 1968 in the nomination campaigns, much of it on credit. At least on paper, the McCarthy campaign cost about $11 million and the Kennedy campaign about $9 million, although Kennedy committed his total in 11 weeks and McCarthy spent his in 39 weeks. In view, however, of a $3.5 million Kennedy deficit and its settlement at about 33 cents on the dollar, his actual campaign costs were probably nearer to $7 million. The campaigns of Johnson, Humphrey, and their Indiana and California standins (Indiana's Governor Branigan and California's Attorney General Thomas Lynch) spent about $5 million. Humphrey's expenditures accounted for about 80 percent of that total. Senator McGovern's brief candidacy and Governor Maddox's even briefer one involved expenditures of $74,000 and $50,000.

The campaign for the re-election of President Lyndon B. Johnson ended on the launching pad. In January, 1968, his friends opened an office in Washington and proceeded to encourage loyalty among influential party leaders. Before Johnson withdrew on March 31, they had been active in New Hampshire, Wisconsin, and Indiana and had done preparatory work in Nebraska, Oregon, and California. The Johnson effort cost less than $500,000, of which the Washington organization probably spent $100,000, apart from the primaries.

In New Hampshire, organization Democrats ran a write-in campaign on behalf of the President. The state party organization assisted the effort indirectly; although officially the two were separate, most of the key people involved were the same. Probably they spent as much as $100,000 in New Hampshire, not counting polls and other services by the Washington committee. For Wisconsin, filed reports show only $75,000 spent, but Johnson campaigners admit spending close to $200,000, almost one-half of McCarthy's expenditure.

Most of the money for Johnson's Wisconsin campaign came from out of state, and the sources reveal some of the financial leverage of a President in office. Johnson supporters were able to command money from state-affiliated Johnson-Humphrey clubs, which were continuations of the 1964 campaign, and from the state President's Clubs which emerged, as in 1964, as a personal Presidential instrument, described in detail later. Special contributions totalling $50,000 in ten checks of $5,000 were made by the Seafarers International Union in early April, 1968, to ten Johnson committees, as subsequently reported in official filings of the Union with the Clerk of the House of Representatives. Later, the Seafarers also sent a series of ten $5,000 checks to as many committees supporting Vice President Humphrey's Presidential campaign. These contributions were said to be linked to a Johnson Administration ruling on an extradition case,[12] although this allegation was denied.

After Johnson withdrew, some contributors asked for the return of their President's Club gifts, presumably to give the money to Humphrey's campaign. Official fund raising by the Democratic National Committee (DNC) and the President's Club ceased, and most national Club monies were turned over to the DNC. Disposition of certain other state President Club funds is unknown; some may have found their way to Humphrey.

The prenomination campaign of Hubert H. Humphrey had much the same supporters as Johnson—party loyalists, labor leadership, and some minority and liberal group leadership and membership, plus his personal following attracted to his long record of liberalism. While he sought to establish a new identity in foreign policy, Humphrey tried to keep loyalist support and at the same time to attract Democratic dissenters, especially after Robert Kennedy's assassination.

With few exceptions, the leadership of the President's Club engaged in raising funds for Humphrey. These leaders included Richard Maguire, the former treasurer of the DNC under whose guidance the financial policies of the Democratic Party changed, as will be seen, profoundly. Maguire resigned as DNC treasurer in 1965, in no small part because of criticism of his policies, to reappear on the Humphrey team. This was perhaps symptomatic of the Humphrey campaign's dependence on the old guard even as it desired the backing of the new.

Humphrey prenomination expense was more than $4 million, and more than one quarter of it was still unpaid in 1969. Income flowed unevenly, particularly after the death of Robert Kennedy, and staff size was reduced from its high point of $40,000 per week. There were large salaries as well as heavy per diem and travel expenses in a campaign aimed at delegates, particularly those from the large, non-primary states. Delegates were sometimes brought to Washington and entertained. The delegation from Delaware, for instance, was flown to Washington, D.C., in a chartered aircraft and wined and dined there at a cost of

$5,000. Even without primary campaigns, the Humphrey organization spent about $1 million for television advertising in the month before the convention. Earlier, in California, more than $100,000 was spent on television and radio on behalf of the so-called Lynch Delegation, a Humphrey bloc. Though the Lynch slate finished third, behind Kennedy and McCarthy tickets, money was spent by individuals to influence the delegation at the convention.

The Humphrey campaign tried to continue the 1964 Democratic alliance with business, encouraged by the dislike some businessmen felt for Robert Kennedy. Several lunches were held in New York City for major figures of the financial and corporate communities. One luncheon at Le Pavillon was reported as having raised $1 million in collections and pledges, but this was disputed. According to several informants, when pledges were called for, two persons promised $250,000 each. Another promised $100,000, and so on. Each thought of giving some money himself and raising the balance from friends and associates, but as the pledgers each had the same circle of givers in mind, they could not raise as much as expected. Also, at least three pledges were for 40 percent before nomination, 60 percent after. The lunch did eventually produce about $1 million, but not all was collected as contributions. Loans and direct payments for newspaper ads were generated as well.

Another lunch was held at "21," and the Humphrey campaign also ran unpublicized gatherings. Two in California produced about $500,000. Among other fund-raising dinners, one in Washington grossed $1 million and one in New York about $500,000. Frank Sinatra entertained at a series of five galas held around the country netting perhaps $500,000.

Labor's role within the Democratic Party was probably more important than ever before in an open Presidential nomination contest. Labor leadership worked openly to support President Johnson, Governor Branigan in Indiana, and Humphrey, and was in sharp opposition to Senator Kennedy (though there was considerable rank-and-file support for Kennedy and also George Wallace). Officials of labor's national Committee on Political Education (COPE) worked extensively in the major primary states. Where possible, party leaders were often moved by labor to support Humphrey or at least not to support Kennedy, and in some states organized labor influenced the choice of Democratic delegates. Only a few labor leaders, mainly in the United Automobile Workers, openly supported Senator Kennedy. Even fewer supported McCarthy, although an anti-Vietnam policy labor committee endorsed him.

On the ground that Kennedy campaigning never really ceases, some would add Robert Kennedy's build-up prior to 1968 to the millions spent in 11 weeks. Kennedy campaigns, typically, are combinations of strong media use and organization, with the emphasis on the "nuts and bolts" of politics—registration and get-out-the-vote drives conducted by telephone, on foot, and by direct mailings to registered voters. Almost one-half of the Kennedy campaign costs were in the seven primaries in which he was entered, including New York, where about $100,000 had been spent before his death. In the five primary states in which Kennedy and McCarthy met head-on, their total costs differed significantly only in California and South Dakota (where McCarthy hardly bothered to contest.)

	Indiana	Nebraska	Oregon	California	S. D.
Kennedy	$750,000	$150,000	$277,000	$2,400,000	$100,000
McCarthy	$700,000	$160,000	$336,000	$1,000,000	$ 30,022

The details of the California media expenses (excluding production and agency costs) are available for both McCarthy and Kennedy. In both campaigns about 50 percent of the total primary costs went to the media, with about one-half of that for television.

	McCarthy	Kennedy
Total California Expenses	$1,000,000	$2,400,000
Total Media Expenses	523,200	1,100,000
Television	116,600	450,000
Radio	93,100	230,000
Newspapers	288,500	290,000
Other, unspecified	25,000	130,000

Luckily, data found in a form rarely available give the Kennedy media and production expenses in the primary states for comparison with total primary costs. (The figures are rounded.)

MEDIA EXPENSES AND TOTAL PRIMARY OUTLAYS
FOR ROBERT KENNEDY'S CAMPAIGN IN SEVEN
STATES AND THE DISTRICT OF COLUMBIA, 1968

State	Total Primary		Media
Indiana	$ 750,000		$ 288,000
		TV	185,000
		Radio	75,000
		Newspapers	28,000
Nebraska	150,000		$ 68,000
		TV	40,000
		Radio	15,000
		Newspapers	13,000
Washington, D. C.	40,000		$ 20,000
		TV	10,000
		Radio	10,000
South Dakota	100,000		$ 35,000
		TV	20,000
		Radio	10,000
		Newspapers	5,000
Oregon	277,000		$ 103,000
		TV	51,000
		Radio	23,000
		Newspapers	29,000
California	2,400,000		$ 1,100,000*
		TV	450,000
		Radio	230,000
		Newspapers	290,000
New York	100,000		
			$1,614,000
Media Production			759,185
Total Primaries	$3,817,000	Total Media	$2,373,185

*$130,000 discrepancy between the total and the TV, Radio
and Newspaper figures is unexplained.

The Kennedy media production costs were exceptionally high—
47 percent of the total cost of time and space purchased. The
preparation of film biographies cost $300,000; production of spot
announcements and printed materials account for the rest. Costs

were especially high because of the urgency to assemble campaign materials speedily. Also, because the products were used for so short a time, production costs did not average down as in a long campaign. The campaign in Indiana went on the air April 17, a month after Kennedy declared his candidacy. As many as 51 advertising agency employees were working on the campaign at one time. In California, there was a sizeable agency-in-exile away from the New York office. The costs of transporting and lodging the staff were high.

Media expenses in California were $1.1 million. A Kennedy-for-President Committee in California spent, as of June 15, 1968 (after the primary), a total of $684,238. Categories include: operations, $221,192; special groups, $95,893; registration drive, $27,698; candidate travel, $34,772; get-out-the-vote drive, $175,-822; polls and surveys, $10,289; sub-category items including bumper strips, $12,209; buttons, $10,307; brochures, $35,325. Four days later, on June 19, total expenditures were listed in a similar statement at $776,633, mainly as a result of additional payments in the operations category. The deficit of the campaign in California was $650,000. This deficit, Committee charges, and media costs add up to approximately $2.5 million, but even this does not necessarily include all the money spent on Kennedy's California campaign.

Of the $650,000, one telephone bill alone was $100,000. (The total national telephone bill including California came to $500,-000.) The other $550,000 was not fully settled until June 11, 1969. All bills for less than $100 were paid in full value. Most others were settled on the average at about one-third on the dollar. Thus, deficits of $550,000 were settled for about $180,-000. One bill gained national attention: a bill for $85,000 owed to the Ambassador Hotel, where Robert Kennedy was shot. Settlement was apparently negotiated at $28,000 but the Ambassador refused to go along. Finally, the Ambassador agreed to settle for $33,500, which wiped out all Kennedy debts in California.

The deficit of the Kennedy campaign, including that in California, amounted to $3.5 million, of which the DNC assumed $1 million. Some creditors were friends of the Kennedy family or felt sympathetic in the circumstances and voluntarily pared their bills. Other debts were negotiated. Among the deficits were $100,000 from the Indiana campaign, $400,000 owed to the advertising agency, and $200,000 to one of the television production firms. Thus, real expenses were reduced, though the committee costs show what a crash campaign for one Presidential nomination can run to.

A fund-raising campaign began after the November elections to pay off the Kennedy deficit. Five dinners grossed between $1.4 and $1.5 million. Approximate proceeds were: New York, Washington, and Boston, $375,000 each; Los Angeles, $225,000; and San Francisco, $115,000. Proceeds for the California dinners were disappointing, possibly because the Los Angeles chairman took ill and was unable to give the affair full attention.

The Kennedy media campaign was notable for monitoring the television expenditures of the opposition. Documents were prepared summarizing the relative spot television weights, market by market. Such market research, unusual in politics, may forecast tactics in future campaigns. Few candidates may have the resources for this, but it offers invaluable guidance for tactical decisions on response and counteraction.

The Kennedy campaign conducted two other surveys unusual in politics. One, in Nebraska, was a public opinion poll questioning respondents about whether and where they saw or heard advertising for Senator Kennedy, and what their reactions were as to topic and credibility. Another compared reactions to Kennedy and McCarthy.

A survey in California explored voter responses to a range of Kennedy television messages. Eight studies analysed responses of groups of 9 or 10 people in sessions conducted in Los Angeles and San Francisco, four in each metropolitan area. The subjects were undecided Democrats representing a typical range of incomes, occupations, and ages. Each session was guided by skilled moderators. An opening general discussion preceded exposure to one-minute TV spots and five-minute TV programs. Discussion following the films tried to bring out either rational or emotional reactions. In some sessions, the group saw a 30-minute film reviewing the Nebraska campaign. The findings were used to change or modify future advertising and to stress items or issues favorably received.

Techniques such as these may be refined and future politicians may profit from them, if they decide it pays to use them. It remains to be seen whether these techniques will lead to efficient as well as effective campaigns, and if so, whether they will contribute to a rational control of political spending.

The candidacy of Senator Eugene McCarthy, from the financial point of view, was unusual in several ways. At the start, the peace movement backing McCarthy boasted of resources up to $1 million for the drive, but after McCarthy consented to run he found that talk was not dollars. Many committees in the form of coalitions and conferences of concerned and dissident Democrats, however, became McCarthy committees, and his early campaign benefitted from their ability to move behind McCarthy at once.

Most campaigns (those of Kennedy and Rockefeller were exceptions) are relatively decentralized in fund raising as in other activities. The Humphrey campaign, for instance, had key people working out of Washington, New York, and Minnesota, although two or three of those in the central command knew what was happening financially and managed to coordinate some efforts.

McCarthy's campaign was the most decentralized in modern American history, yet it managed to raise substantial sums: there were a small number of extremely large contributors, few of whom had given in such large amounts before; a large number of small contributors, including voluntary services; but only a small group of contributors in the $100 to $1,000 category. The contrast in contributors was matched by split views on strategy. Some large contributors favored television campaigning; others saw McCarthy's greatest strength in the grass roots and in the sudden outpouring of the young. They thought the emphasis should be not on TV, but on encouraging popular and especially youthful political development through participation in personal political activity.

Decentralization plus strategy differences produced intrigues, espionage, and sabotage in McCarthy's financial operation. Door locks were changed to prevent access by deposed managers;

scores of different bank accounts were set up by influential persons to further favored projects; bootleg bank accounts were used to fund activities discontinued or no longer in favor; mailbags were captured to divert contributions to favored accounts; programs were cancelled by refusals to replenish funds; certain large contributors were persuaded to support only favored activities. As groups and individuals operated independently, jealousies among various finance or campaign managers accentuated differences on policy or strategy. The major personalities in the campaign were in competition among themselves for power, prestige, and the candidate's favor.

Expenditures ran to almost $9 million, without counting states where most of the campaign was financed locally. An estimated expenditure breakdown follows:

```
Washington:
    Headquarters* ......................................... $1,600,000
    Supplemental Accounts* .......................      400,000
New York:
    Headquarters* .........................................      950,000
    Supplemental Accounts* .......................      200,000
Television, network .....................................      250,000
M (McCarthy) Day .....................................      300,000
Convention .................................................      190,000
Debts ...........................................................    1,000,000
                                             Subtotal    $4,890,000
8 Major primary totals* .............................................    3,706,000
                                                  Total    $8,596,000
        *Adjusted for transfers of funds from national ac-
    counts to primary states, so as to avoid duplication.
```

A little more than one-third of McCarthy's total national expenditure went into the major primaries. In addition to the $2.3 million used in the five direct contests with Kennedy, about $280,000 was used in New Hampshire, $500,000 in Wisconsin, and $700,000 in New York. Most of the money spent in the New York primary was raised within the state.

In Pennsylvania, the primary campaign, for the most part financed locally, cost $430,000 on all levels. In New Jersey, over $100,000 was spent locally by the statewide organization in addition to money sent elsewhere. In Connecticut, where delegate contests were mounted in the major cities, at least $119,000 was spent locally. Massachusetts expenses for McCarthy were $269,890, mostly but not exclusively for the primary.

After the Chicago convention, a McCarthy finance manager sent a simple form to finance operatives in each state to request financial information. Returns came in from only 18 states, and their figures reflected mainly statewide expenditures because amounts raised and spent locally were unknown to the state treasurers. The amounts reported ranged from $125 in Arkansas to $48,800 in Washington. Considering the gaps in information about other state activities and about local activities in most states, hundreds of thousands of dollars must surely be added to the accounting, enough to bring the McCarthy funds well above $11 million.

For the national campaign, it is believed about $2.5 million was raised from about 50 large contributors. Key finance operators still do not always know the actual sources of funds in certain accounts, whether they came from personal contributions of fund raisers or from funds collected by them from others. Numerous loans, some of which were repaid or forgiven, further complicate the task of learning precisely who gave how much. Many lenders of large sums received payment in early 1969.

Contributors were no doubt attracted by McCarthy's stand on the Vietnam issue and by his courage in taking on first an incumbent President, a wealthy Senator whose family name and record are legendary in American politics, and an incumbent Vice President. Of course, McCarthy also attracted money that was anti-Johnson or anti-Kennedy, for whatever reasons. Both Humphrey and McCarthy supporters admit some Humphrey supporters gave money to help McCarthy in order to offset the appeal of Kennedy, particularly in Oregon and California; Mc-Carthy people claim to know of such contributions. Some say more was arranged for but was not forthcoming after McCarthy won in Oregon and the potential donors reneged.

McCarthy fund raising featured the usual dinners, luncheons, and parties, but McCarthy was also able to do what no other candidate but George Wallace could do: obtain large proceeds at rallies. "McCarthy Summer" saw outpourings of people in New York, Boston, Detroit, and Richmond, Virginia. Later, a series of rallies held in 22 cities linked by closed-circuit television, produced a net of hundreds of thousands of dollars. A zeal and contagion were evident at several rallies where barkers read off pledges and whipped up enthusiasm. At Madison Square Garden a $50,000 gift was apparently unpremeditated and spontaneous. Many McCarthy supporters gave repeatedly and in large amounts.

Most McCarthy money was ideological or protest-minded and less touched, it is fair to say, by selfish interest than usual in political campaigns. Although few contributors believed for long that McCarthy could be nominated, the money continued to arrive even at the convention. Still, the money flow was uneven as it was heavily influenced by events. The instability of the cash flow had a critical effect on the nature of the campaign.

Because resources were uncertain, the McCarthy campaign, especially at the start, concentrated on one state at a time, and incidentally demonstrated how a steady build-up could be achieved by a good showing in one primary after another. A truly national effort would have required a much larger budget. There soon came a point, however, when the McCarthy campaign waged in several states at once—Indiana, Nebraska, Oregon, California, and South Dakota, among others—strained its resources. The consequences of financial uncertainty could be seen in California, where much of the money arrived only after the Oregon victory. When money was available finally for TV during the critical last week of the California campaign, McCarthy forces discovered that good air time had been purchased by Kennedy and the Lynch slate. This was one reason why McCarthy newspaper advertising was relatively heavier than Kennedy's in California.

By September, 1968, the McCarthy campaign owed creditors as much as $1.3 million. All debts for $400 or less were paid 100 cents on the dollar; the rest were negotiated. Hotel-chain bills were aggregated, as were auto rentals, telephone, and other such bills from around the country, and negotiations took place with the national parent corporation. Individual companies were owed hundreds of thousands. Some received partial payments with the understanding that no more could be expected. Others negotiated settlements. On the average, settlements ran about 36 cents on the dollar—almost the same as the Kennedy campaign's 33 cents on the dollar.

Two short campaigns illustrate how it is possible to spend $50,000 or $100,000 in no time at all.

Senator George McGovern of South Dakota announced his candidacy August 10, barely two weeks before the Democratic Convention. The impetus for the McGovern campaign may have come from Kennedy supporters, but rumors of Kennedy money backing McGovern seem unfounded. The net $74,000 total was supplemented by considerable volunteer assistance.

The major costs were at Chicago, where a bloc of 40 rooms was rented, a hospitality suite operated, and a luncheon held for Mrs. McGovern. At the Amphitheatre, a switchboard was installed and a room partitioned. Between $35-40,000 was raised; the remaining $27,000 constituted debts which the DNC assumed.

An even briefer campaign was waged on behalf of Governor Lester Maddox of Georgia. Maddox announced as a conservative candidate about 10 days before the convention, but managed to spend $50,000. Most of the costs were at the convention; some would have been incurred by the Georgia delegation in any event. Other costs entailed travel to the convention and a few newspaper ads in Georgia for fund-raising purposes.

It is said that winners pay their bills and losers negotiate. Debt settlements by the Humphrey, McCarthy, and Kennedy campaigns may lead many creditors to reexamine policies on political campaigns. Public utilities must provide service, but only broadcasters insist on payment before the service. The experience of 1968 may lead more firms to demand pre-payments or large deposits (as utilities sometimes require), or to levy excessive charges to anticipate settlement for a fraction of the bill later. When debts are settled at a discount, the corporation, in effect, is contributing indirectly to the campaign. Some companies may do so willingly as the price of doing business, but when corporations do so, they may be open to suits by stockholders or customers who must pay full rates or to sanctions invoked under laws governing political spending.

By 1971 it was clear that campaigns for the Democratic Presidential nomination in 1972 had begun in earnest by the time of the mid-term Congressional elections. Senator George McGovern officially announced for the 1972 nomination in January 1971, and a half-dozen other candidates had significant headquarters operations going by the same time. The pace of activity quickened rapidly, and cost overruns began to occur almost as soon as budgets were adopted. Legislation was proposed in 1971 to limit media expenditures, but few provisions in the bill would have much effect in keeping other election costs down. The prospect of up to 27 primaries made cost estimates unpredictable. As 1972 approached, some relief in sight was related to the fact that none of the aspirants were themselves wealthy. Their financial limitations might have some dampening effect upon spending, as would their inability to raise sufficient funds from supporters, but intense competition for the nomination could attract money enough to erase such handicaps. In a move against such competition, Democratic aspirants for the Presidency met with the Chairman of the Democratic National Committee and agreed to refrain from criticizing one another and to restrict their primary spending. If the agreement holds, an important precedent could be made.

6

THE PRICE OF THE PRESIDENCY

The fog that obscures preconvention finances lifts slightly after the nominations.

The Federal Corrupt Practices Act, in effect until 1972, required that any political committee seeking to influence the general election campaign for a federal office in two or more states file reports with the Clerk of the House of Representatives. Republican and Democratic National Committees, for instance, were vehicles for the Presidential effort, and national citizens groups like Citizens for Nixon-Agnew or Volunteers for Humphrey-Muskie also filed reports of their receipts and expenditures. Some such groups reported with less than perfect candor, but their accounts did provide a rough guide to the financing of a Presidential campaign.

Still uncertainty remained. The law did not require reports from Presidential candidates on their personal outlays, and more important, it did not require reports from campaign committees which confined their activities to a single state.[1] A citizens' group backing a Presidential candidate only in New Jersey, for example, did not need to report. Hence figures reported by the central headquarters of Presidential campaigns did not reveal all.

Despite intense national concern with the Presidential contest, the campaigns are remarkably decentralized. There is seemingly no limit to the number of organizations or the diversity of political interests in a Presidential campaign. A party's national committee is a permanent nucleus—often ill-financed and understaffed—with each candidate's personal organization and staff loosely allied. A new national chairman literally may not know his way around the headquarters. A national volunteer organization flowers in thousands of clubs across the land[2] and competes for funds with the regular party committees in every state. A multi-million dollar operation is run by a collection of amateurs and professionals, family and friends, specialists, job-seekers, old Washington hands and new faces, party bureaucrats, statesmen and hangers-on. Budgets may be non-existent or disregarded. No commercial firm could operate so loosely and show a profit. Yet this casual, mercurial protean outfit is devoted to the serious business of winning the most powerful elective office in the world, the Presidency of the United States.

The rise in all political spending has significantly outpaced growth in population and economic indicators since 1952. Presidential election spending has followed the same pattern. The table below[3] covers spending by national-level political committees reflecting primarily spending on Presidential elections:

	Millions		Millions
1912	$ 2.9	1940	$ 7.8
1916	4.7	1944	7.7
1920	6.9	1948	7.8
1924	6.4	1952	11.6
1928	11.6	1956	12.9
1932	5.1	1960	19.9
1936	14.1	1964	24.8
		1968	44.2*

*Almost one-third of 1968 increase caused by inclusion of $7 million spent by George Wallace committees.

Although the numbers voting in national elections grew from 15 million in 1912 to 73.2 million in 1968, the actual cost per Presidential vote remained remarkably stable until the 1950's. Between 1912 and 1928, the outlay per vote stayed at 19 to 20 cents while the price level rose 40 percent. By 1952, the amount spent per vote for President was still only 19 cents,[4] but in 1960 it went up to 29 cents, in 1964 to 35 cents, and in 1968 to 60 cents.[5]

These increases reflect a combination of new methods, inflation, and increased appreciation of the value of the Presidency. The steadily increasing importance of the federal government and its chief executive has come to be realized as ever more people feel the direct effects of Washington in the lives and the economy of the entire world. The more at stake in the Presidency, the more dollars seem to focus on this election. The use of television has proved so valuable in these contests that Presidential broadcast expenditures in the 1964 general election were double the 1956 level and then some. In 1968, expenditures almost doubled again. The total broadcast expenditures for Presidential aspirants (including primaries) in 1968 were $28.5 million, almost one-half of the $58.9 million spent by all candidates for political broadcasts during the year.

Other techniques that have sharply increased Presidential campaign costs, public opinion polling and air travel, have become standard practice since 1960. John Kennedy had a passion for massive polling. Richard Nixon reveled in the flights that enabled him to stump Portland, Maine, Tallahassee, Florida, and San Diego, California the same day.

Chartered campaign jets require not only flight crews but radio and telephone operators to keep in touch with headquarters. Replete with equipment like duplicating machines, they are in effect jet-offices. Every speech, every activity requires planning by the candidate, his campaign manager, his headquarters, advisors, advance men, research team, speech writers, publicity men, communication specialists, cleanup men. On the travelling staff of Senator Kennedy in 1960 were a speech professor to teach the candidate voice control, a psychologist to evaluate the size, composition, and reactions of campaign crowds, an official photographer, and a two-man stenographic team to transcribe every public word of the candidate so that transcripts were available to reporters within minutes after a speech. In 1968 public opinion polls and survey work for the Nixon electoral campaign cost $384,102 (including both conventional panel polling and heavy telephone polling); Humphrey's polls and surveys cost $261,521.[6] Nixon's campaign listed travel costs of $1,837,416. Subtracting the $492,000 reimbursed by media travellers leaves $1,345,416. Humphrey's much leaner campaign spent $875,000 on travel, net.

The cloud of helicopters moving the candidate and his aides may tend to overshadow the groundwork below but both entail considerable expenditures. Rallies and parades are not spontaneous demonstrations of affection for the candidate but well-planned affairs with a large investment in public relations, telephone calls, buses, and other means for summoning crowds.

How much political high jinks—old and new—are really

necessary is not easy to say. Some appear to be pursued simply because one side is spending lavishly, and the competition feels it must keep abreast, but those engaged seriously in trying to win do not wittingly indulge in fiscal foolishness. They have sober political reasons for what they do. Financial prudence is not their guiding rule. To the contrary, keeping close track of money might deflect energies from the main business at hand. What seems extravagant may prove so only in defeat. Nevertheless, politicians need dollars more than debts.

Recent Republican Presidential campaigns have been especially successful in financing and, consequently, in elaborate electioneering. Though Goldwater lost the 1964 election decisively, he emerged with a modest surplus. The Nixon campaign of 1968, spending 67 percent more than Goldwater, raised practically all the money needed but hardly changed Nixon's relative position (if poll standings are to be credited) from Spring to November.[7] The late trend, in fact, was toward Humphrey.

Nixon in 1968 inherited a financial surplus from the excellent preconvention Republican performance. Adding Convention Gala funds to the cash balance, his campaign had more than $1 million in August, before post-nomination fund raising began. No borrowing was necessary. Campaign fund raising consisted of three main elements: a mail drive utilizing the large base provided by the RNC Sustaining Fund and supplemented with lists of the Nixon prenomination contributors; a large gifts drive that was a dazzling success; and a series of 22 dinners held on September 19, linked by closed-circuit television, the only dinner held in Nixon fund raising in the entire year.

The financial position of Hubert Humphrey in contrast to Nixon's was down at the heels and patched at the elbows. Whereas the outcome at Miami Beach was so far anticipated there was no serious rancor or disunity after the Republican convention, the Chicago Convention brought such political and financial chaos to the Democrats it was called a disaster. The disturbances created bitterness, disaffection, and disunity. Humphrey's prenomination campaign was in debt. As the convention was late in the year, the Democrats had too little time to heal wounds or gear up to raise money. Moreover, Humphrey's prospects were considered by many to be far weaker than they proved to be. President Johnson's assistance, for whatever reasons, was hardly that ordinarily expected from an incumbent President. Worst of all, Humphrey had no clear plan for raising the required $10-$15 million. For lack of a plan, his already grave troubles were compounded. The gap in advertising spending suggests how disparate were Democratic and Republican campaign efforts. The categories are generally comparable though more detailed in the Humphrey campaign.

NATIONAL-LEVEL NIXON AND HUMPHREY ADVERTISING EXPENDITURES, GENERAL ELECTION, 1968

	Humphrey	Nixon
Time and Space		
Television	$3,525,000	$ 6,270,000
Network	2,151,000[1]	
Regional Spot	1,374,000	
Radio	425,000	1,870,000
Network	123,000	
Regional Spot	302,000	
Newspapers	429,000	880,000
Refund	—150,000[2]	_____[3]
Total Time and Space	$4,229,000	$ 9,020,000
Media Production		
Radio and Television	1,043,000[4]	
Newspapers	62,000	
Refund	—45,000[2]	_____[3]
Total Production	$1,060,000	$ 1,980,000
Agency Fees	378,000	
Refund	—125,000[2]	_____[3]
Total	$5,542,000	$11,000,000

[1] Divided approximately $1 million for programs and $1.1 million for spot announcements.

[2] Details of the $320,000 in advertising agency refunds are: $45,000 for overestimated production costs; $150,000 in rebates for network time ordered and paid for but where local station clearances could not be obtained; the remaining $125,000 was from advances to the agency bank accounts and could not be categorized.

[3] The Nixon campaign had some refunds but details are not known.

[4] Including about $300,000 spent on preparation of film biographies.

These disclosures, which relate time and space charges to production costs, are lower than the FCC data used in the discussion of political broadcasting (Chapter 14). The FCC figures reflect all network and station charges, including those for broadcasts placed by state and local committees not controlled by national headquarters.

The advertising agency the Democrats used, a unit of Lennen and Newell, Inc., worked on a fee basis rather than charge commission fees, because a commission on a seven-week campaign of such volume would have run up an inordinate charge. The item listed as time-buying charges was basically the agency fee, covering costs for about 68 workers in New York and 6 in Washington. Of the production costs, about $300,000 was spent on preparation of film biographies. Production costs in normal agency commercial work run only about 7 percent of time and space charges, but a 20 to 50 percent charge for production is not unusual in politics because of the crash nature of campaigns, overtime, new issues demanding urgent response, and a high rate of rejection or cancellation of material.

The major Nixon advertising costs also were in TV. Productions costs were almost $2 million. Election eve telethons, consisting of a two-hour network program and a two-hour West Coast telethon, including production, cost about $450,000. Nixon's television campaign featured nine live regional hour programs, telecast with citizens in a studio asking the candidate questions. Production charges for these varied from $11,000 to $27,000, mostly to build the set and to interconnect various stations.

While television made the principal dent in the Nixon treasury, there were substantial outlays for campaign staples. At a cost of $1.3 million, a special projects unit organized a national campaign center that designed, ordered, warehoused, supplied, billed, and controlled all the major items used in the campaign. A catalogue was prepared for nationwide use and kits were collated for servicing 116 rallies with custom-packaged materials. (A breakdown of items and costs appears on the next page.)

Buttons (20,500,000) $300,000
Bumper strips (9,000,000) 300,000
Balloons (560,000) 70,000
Posters and placards (400,000) 70,000
Straw skimmers (28,000) 30,000
Brochures (30,000), speeches
and position papers (3,500,000) 500,000
Paper dresses (12,000) 40,000
Jewelry 50,000

There was some income from sales of items to state and local campaign committees. The printed materials figures do not include many items handled by the press secretary or the costs of two books of speeches and papers: *Nixon Speaks Out* and *Nixon on the Issues,* published by campaign committees.

Among the figures available from the Nixon campaign are some which detail fund-raising costs. Expenses of running the finance office were $340,423. Direct mail costs were $1,566,117, including costs of acknowledging contributions. Costs to the national campaign for a series of dinners on September 19 were $216,705. National fund-raising costs came to more than $3 million, a small investment for the $25 million actually raised.

While the Nixon campaign set a new record in spending, there do seem to be limits on what can be spent on specific items like television. The Humphrey advertising budget was close to Goldwater's in 1964 (although the total budget was about 25 percent less). Total Democratic expenditures in the general election in 1968 were at about the same level as for Johnson in 1964 and Kennedy in 1960, in the $10 to $12 million range, and not much below the 1964 Goldwater total of $14 million. This suggests that costs may be leveled or plateaus maintained if necessary. In 1968 the Democrats would have liked to spend more and would have if they could without going deeper into debt. As it was, two weeks of spot television and 25 percent of network television had to be cancelled for lack of funds.

One special item of more than $1 million in connection with the 1968 Presidential election warrants mention. For the first time, federal funds for the transition period between election and inauguration were available and used in the Johnson-Nixon changeover. A total of $900,000 was appropriated for 1968, divided as follows: $375,000 each for the incoming and outgoing President; $75,000 each for the incoming and outgoing Vice President. The Republicans used their $450,000, mainly for salaries and expenses connected with preparations to assume office on January 20, 1969. The transition cost the party an additional $500,000 not covered by government subsidy,[8] but the party raised this money at a Republican Victory Dinner in 1969. There was an undercurrent of Republican criticism that half of the transition appropriation went to Johnson and Humphrey but no public debate ensued. The Republicans could have used the full appropriation or more themselves.

Candidates for Presidential office generally prefer to leave the raising and spending of money to subordinates or managers, partly so as not to be bothered and partly perhaps to remain ignorant of gifts that possibly could be embarrassing. Sometimes candidates lay down general rules for fund raisers, which those operatives may choose to observe, forget or forgive. In 1960, John F. Kennedy personally ordered that all important campaign contributors be specifically warned that no commitment, for jobs or otherwise, was implied by acceptance of their checks. Candidates may also refuse to accept contributions from dubious sources. The fact that they do not only speaks well for the candidates but also is evidence that some contributions are intended as bribes.

In addition to the large contributions in the prenomination activities, there were many large contributions to both the Nixon and Humphrey post-convention campaigns. At least seven individual contributors or family groups are known to have given $50,000 or more to the Nixon post-nomination campaign, the top one being W. Clement Stone, who gave at least $153,-916.[9] Three others gave between $31,000 and $41,462 each.

The Humphrey campaign had at least one $100,000 contributor; six who gave between $50,000 and $60,000; and three who gave between $30,000 and $45,000. Humphrey actually drew more large contributions on the record than Johnson in 1964 or Kennedy in 1960. In addition, Humphrey benefitted from loans aggregating more than $3 million, made by 43 or so persons, many individually lending sums ranging from $5,000 to $240,-000.[10] If some loans are forgiven and counted as actual contributions, since they may not be repaid, several individuals could have given more than $300,000 to the Humphrey campaign in the general election period alone. Presumably some of these persons also gave in the prenomination period.

Of 93,195 Democratic gifts in the September-December period, 88,596 were in amounts less than $100. Of the others, over 4,000 were from $100 to $999 and about 250 for $1,000 or more. Television appeals obtained the greatest number of gifts, but with less than $5 million raised from all sources, the Humphrey budget was tight, especially in its plans for advertising.

The campaign had to be financed in substantial part by loans. The DNC officially reported $6,155,000 in contingent liabilities assumed by it to various individuals. The DNC assumed liability because most of the loans were made to ad hoc citizens committees which would expire after the campaign. There was some double borrowing; that is, borrowing to repay short-term loans, so the effective total debt is not certain. Some few loans were repaid during 1968 and 1969.

The party reported $3,125,000 in itemized loans from 43 persons, by name, address, amount, and date of the loans. No individual loan of more than $5,000 was extended to a single committee.[11] There were, for example, two lenders of $240,000 each on the record, but these were itemized as 48 different loans of $5,000 each to 48 committees. Some of the receiving committees had no funds other than loans. Normally, borrowed funds were transferred to operating committees which spent the money. In addition to the two lenders of $240,000 each, there were 19 lenders of $100,000; one of $95,000; four of $70,000; four of $50,000; two of $37,500; eight of $10,000; and three of $5,000. Some were also substantial contributors.

Some of the loans were distributed by an attorney. To avoid having to write a number of $5,000 checks, the lender could send the entire sum to the lawyer who, because he was not considered a political committee, was not subject to the apposite federal law. The lawyer redistributed the loan in $5,000 lots to appropriate committees. Some lenders borrowed the money themselves, individually; others borrowed the money from a major bank which acted as grand lender (purportedly lending as much as $4 million of the total).

Though the reporting of loans in this fashion was unusual, there were elements of secrecy in the procedures followed to explain the discrepancy between the $6,155,000 in money borrowed and the $3,125,000 in loans actually itemized. This was accomplished in the official filings of one of the Humphrey committees, named Citizens for Humphrey-Muskie, which carried two notations. One, a single item listing $2,800,000 in receipts, was explained as "Received constructively from various local, state and national committees when obligations contracted for by this committee were liquidated in whole or in part by direct payment of this committee's obligation in the above amount." The other item, a listing of $2,800,000 in expenditures, was described as: "Disbursed constructively by this committee when various obligations contracted for by this committee were paid in whole or in part by various local, state and national committees in the above amount."

These notations mean that $2,800,000 was received in loans or contributions by state and local committees not reporting under federal (or some presumably under state) law; and that $2,-800,000 was spent by these committees on behalf of the national Humphrey campaign. Democratic officials admitted that some campaign bills were paid directly by individuals or "non-reporting" committees because some donors did not care to be known. Some of them may have been the same ones openly disclosed as lenders or contributors but who did not wish to be recorded as lending or giving as much as they actually did. The practice of concealing names is not unusual. It can be accomplished easily through committees in states without reporting laws.[12] These committees receive and disburse money in secrecy at the command of the national campaign headquarters: thus the requirements of federal law—that name, address, amount, and date of contributions or receipts of $100 or more be itemized— could be evaded. What was unusual about the Democratic reports was the admission that such activity occurred and the disclosure of the total amount. The notations were useful both in documenting the practice and also in disclosing the total amounts of receipts and expenditures controlled by the national campaign.[13]

For the Humphrey campaign, the implications of borrowing

were clear. Borrowed money financed the media campaign. Without it, Humphrey's use of the media would have been crippled. Previously lending had at times been reported in a less frank manner; for example, one item might have specified a $1 million loan from a named bank.[14] This procedure would not have disclosed the co-signers of the loan nor told of repayments.

The big contributor or lender persists as a prime source of campaign revenue if only because of the deficits that so often face parties at the end of campaigns. The Democratic deficit of $3.8 million in 1960 set a record. This debt was paid off by 1963, mainly through large gifts. In 1964 there were conflicting accounts of the size of the deficit from the Johnson campaign, but DNC debts were additionally incurred in 1965 and 1966. By 1967 there were rumors that the Democrats owed as much as $4 million, but they claimed to have paid most of it off. The Humphrey post-convention debts were a record $6 million, and the Democrats did not control the White House as they did following 1960 and 1964.

Whether the Humphrey people inherited a debt when they took over the DNC is a matter of dispute. Johnson associates had commitments to pay off all bills but apparently some of the money was hard to distinguish from campaign funds that came in. There can be no doubt that Humphrey inherited a moribund National Committee. It had been criticized between 1965 and 1968 for failure to pursue small contributions and for too much emphasis on the President's Club and program advertising books.[15] After President Johnson withdrew as a candidate, the committee did not do much. The President's Club, as will be shown in Chapter 7, was the main source of Democratic money. It, too, was inactive after March 31, and the Sustaining Fund, or $10 per year membership program, was not promoted with energy either.

In view of this financial vacuum, it was an unusual move, particularly in a losing campaign, for Robert Short, the treasurer of the DNC, to propose in January, 1969, that the DNC assume responsibility for one million dollars each for the Humphrey and Kennedy campaign deficits. He reasoned that with a DNC deficit of $6 million from the general election campaign, there was need for united action to raise funds. Since

Hubert Humphrey and Senator Edward Kennedy, two stellar attractions at dinners, could be expected to assume responsibility for the Humphrey and Kennedy prenomination debts and would not otherwise devote their talents to helping the party wipe out its debts, Short therefore asked the DNC to combine all three deficits into one. By the time Short's proposal was advanced, most of the McCarthy debts had been settled and his workers were concerned that their creditors would seek to reopen negotiations on the chance they might win larger payments if his debts also were pooled. However, their creditors mainly remained quiet, and McCarthy people were not eager to turn to the party regulars. The Democrats will be strained financially for years to come, especially when they add the 1972 campaign load to the debts outstanding.

While in office, a successful Presidential candidate needs political funds, too, as Richard M. Nixon has learned. As leader of the party, he must help it to pay off his own campaign debt. He must build a fund for mid-term Congressional elections or for his own re-election. He also likes to have money to help favored candidates for strategic or personal reasons. The White House staff has been called a continuing campaign organization, and it is. The burden of staff salaries is on the government, not the party, but the political implications of what the White House does are always prominent, even when the motives are non-political.

The Democratic President's Club was born of the need to pay off the large 1960 campaign deficit while also preparing for the 1962 elections. It became the main financial arm of the Democratic Party nationally. During the 1964 campaign, one group supporting the Johnson candidacy was called "Friends of LBJ." The nomenclature is meaningful because most contributors were indeed the President's personal friends who raised the fund for his use in the campaign. Of course, friends of any President may direct spot funds to candidates he suggests. During the 1970 Congressional elections, personal friends of President Nixon contributed to certain of his favorites among Congressional and gubernatorial candidates, as will be seen.

Outgoing and former Presidents, too, must concern themselves with political fund raising. In 1960, President Eisenhower participated in several rounds of dinners to benefit the Nixon campaign. Closed TV circuits linked 83 simultaneous dinners in as many cities on Dinner with Ike Night; later a campaign dinner similarly linked 36 separate affairs. The 119 dinners grossed about $7.7 million, of which the national party netted about $4.3 million. After leaving office, Eisenhower took part in numerous fund-raising events and opened his Gettysburg farm to Congressional Boosters Club members in an out-party equivalent of the President's Club.

Defeated Presidential candidates cannot escape the fund-raising circuit either. Adlai Stevenson devoted much time to helping to pay off deficits from his campaigns. From 1960 to 1968, Richard Nixon proved indefatigable in speaking at party affairs.

Presidents, former Presidents, and defeated candidates alike have found the knife and fork to be mighty implements in fund raising.

The 1968 campaign of George Wallace had no pre- or post-nomination periods. There was no national convention, though the Wallace command studied the idea of holding one to obtain free television coverage. There was, therefore, a legal question of whether the Wallace campaign should be filing official fund reports. One had to assume, once it became clear that no nominating convention would be held, that Wallace's electioneering was pointed toward the November election. Therefore, by this interpretation, the Wallace campaign would not be exempted from reporting. Because it was attempting to influence the election of Presidential and Vice Presidential electors in two or more states, it would be required by law to file. The argument was raised when the pre-election filing dates came in October; the Wallace campaign did file reports going back to February 7, 1968, but protested that filing was voluntary.

In addition, federal law required a political committee to have a chairman and a treasurer. but there was no admission that a political committee was filing. The reports came only from "The Wallace Campaign." Federal law prohibited a political committee from receiving or disbursing more than $3 million, but the first Wallace filing reported more than this. Interpretation turns, then, on whether the reporting body was a political committee.

The Wallace campaign was the costliest third party effort in American history. In comparison, the national expenditures of three Henry Wallace committees in 1948 were $1.1 million,[16] and those of the Roosevelt Progressive Party in 1912 were $665,420.[17] From February 7, 1968, the George Wallace campaign reported expenditures of $6,985,455; receipts were reported at $6,713,524. In addition to the national total, two Western-based Wallace committees raised and spent $258,000, indicating that thousands of state and local Wallace committees throughout the country must have spent additional hundreds of thousands, if not millions.

The Wallace campaign commenced seriously in mid-1967. Considerable money was spent before the period covered by the national campaign. In California the drive to get on the ballot took place in the Fall of 1967, and the campaigners admitted it cost at least $500,000. Campaign officials also estimated that during 1967-68 the organizational and legal efforts to get Wallace on the ballot in the 50 states—preparing petitions, signatures, legal fees, etc.—cost $3 million of the total. The campaign was inseparable from the task of seeking ballot qualification (which began as early as February, 1967) because Wallace would spend time in the state, to attract attention and to whip up enthusiasm, in order to get enough signatures to qualify. Qualifying was a major drain on the treasury, and managing to attain ballot status in all 50 states was a prodigious legal precedent, perhaps the most lasting and beneficial achievement of the Wallace campaign.

Wallace undoubtedly had more individual contributors than any candidate during 1968, pre- or post-nomination. A total of 900,000 contributors was mentioned, but a responsible Wallace worker estimated 750,000. The best returns came from direct mail and television appeals, but there were also collections at rallies, a series of $25-per-plate luncheons, a few dinners, and substantial sales of jewelry and campaign materials.

A total of 498 individuals or husband-wife combinations gave $500 or more for a total of $458,753; more than one-third of these large contributors were Alabamans. Texas and Florida were the only other two states with significant numbers of large contributors.

Apart from the South, only Indiana, California, and Pennsylvania yielded large contributions totalling at least $10,000. The large contributors became members of the Patriots Club; Charter Members were those contributing $1,000; Distinguished Members, $2,500; and Lifetime Members, $4,500. However, most of the large contributions were for $500, and only a handful qualified as Lifetime Members. There were 4,032 persons who contributed from $100 to $499, for a total of $508,625.

Most significantly, and in contrast to the sources of funds of the two major parties, contributions of less than $100 accounted for $5,090,861—75 percent of the total receipts.

In April, 1968, a civil suit brought in Federal District Court in Montgomery alleged that State Finance Director, Seymore Trammell, who served as campaign manager for Wallace, was a party to a conspiracy to limit competition, set prices, and demand campaign contributions from companies seeking to sell asphalt to the State of Alabama. The Finance Director was in a position to do this since he controls purchasing and disbursement of money by all state agencies. Independent of the court case, the press carried allegations of kickbacks in the form of campaign contributions demanded of those who sold liquor to Alabama through its Alcoholic Control Board. The asphalt suit was settled out of court after Wallace's wife (and successor) had died. Her successor as Governor, Albert Brewer, permitted new bidding by the company that brought the suit, but the allegations were documented in the press and questions persisted as to the sources of certain Wallace campaign funds.[18]

Another suit, brought by an Alabama state representative, accused Wallace and other former state officials of using public funds in the Presidential campaign. Frequent charges were made both in 1964 and 1968 regarding Wallace's use of state officials in his campaign while they were on the state payroll. One charge had it that, excluding state troopers, the annual pay of officials working for the Wallace campaign exceeded $175,000. Eventually some of the challenged officials took leave of absence. The issue receded after Mrs. Wallace died and several accused officials left their state jobs. Other charges related to use of state airplanes, autos, credit cards, and such. The legislator's suit was dismissed in Federal District Court. Its fate was left to the state courts.[19]

Were Presidential campaigns financed on a four-year budgetary cycle, deficits incurred during the year of greatest spending would be seen as normal debts to be repaid in fat years. Party deficits would be accepted as Americans accept deficits in corporate, government, and personal finance, to be reduced in time. The Democrats were forced into deficit financing, unfortunately, at a time when purses were snapping shut. Money is especially hard to raise in non-Presidential election years by the party out of power. However, a Republican surplus in 1964 permitted attention to details of party organization and certainly contributed to their 1966 and 1968 showing, while Democratic deficits since 1968 have tended to demoralize the party faithful.

NATIONAL PARTY FINANCES:
CONTRAST AND CONFUSION

Party finances are enmeshed in a set of complex relationships with no neat formulas for gathering money for the national organization.

Political funds may flow along two basic routes. Money may rise from county to state levels to the national party according to a quota system, a method praised by political scientists who consider it an example of responsible party procedure. Money may be raised directly by the national party organizations, a way of contributing that has been attracting large gifts in recent years because of the nationalization of American politics and the focus on federal policy.[1]

A national party finances a multitude of functions—publicity, the planning of strategy, research, and issue-development, as well as electoral, financial, and organizational guidance for candidates and for state and local party committees. The party helps finance campaigns for the Presidency, and, through Congressional campaign committees, it helps provide money and services for Senate and House candidates.

The parties collect money at both ends, national and local, at various times. Never does all the money flow upward or downward, nor do national, state or local organizations ever gain complete control. A national party may be tempted to give extra help to candidates and party organizations that share its policies and goals, but it will compromise on policies to secure friendly Senate and House seats. It will try to mollify a local organization that is willing to help elect the party's Presidential candidate even when the local candidates have views that strongly oppose the national platform. State and local organizations in turn know that their individual contributions to the national party cannot control national party policy. National policy must reflect a broad consensus of views while tolerating a broad diversity of views as well if the party is to win and hold national power.

Direct national fund-raising weakens the power of state and local organizations to the degree that they cannot claim credit as the chief source of the party's wealth or the federal candidate's resources. At the same time, national funds may relieve Congressional candidates of some of the narrow, parochial pressures that can come with dependence upon local money. When national funds are ample, only the power of the ballot remains as the bastion of local power.

Raising money is something many Americans know how to do well (universities, health organizations, charities, religious groups). With notable exceptions, however, when political parties ask for money they are rarely systematic or efficient. They do not often have the means or the time to ask enough people to give, nor do party practices or campaign organizations readily lend themselves to United-Fund-type drives. The result has been that each party develops its own techniques and own styles. As spiralling campaign costs have challenged the parties, an examination of the Democratic and Republican Party finances in the 1960's may tell how they responded to that challenge.

"Frenzied" is a word commentators have applied to Democratic fund raising. The characterization does not seem unjust. At least on the national level, the party has found itself in debt from the campaigns of 1952, 1956, 1960, 1964, and 1968. One might have thought that after 1960, when the party recovered the Presidency, its financial woes would pass, but deliverance did not come. The party continued to be plagued by deficits, increasing reliance on large contributors, and associated sorrows. Even in 1964, with the stunning Democratic victory, the Republicans raised more money, and Democratic confidence led to overspending in 1964 and 1965. President Johnson's illnesses and long recuperations in 1965 and 1966 cost the party expensive postponements of fund-raising events. By 1967, when the Democrats claimed to erase their debt, the President's Indochina policy had begun to cut into the party's appeal. Whatever the political significance of 1968 for the Democrats, the $6 million campaign deficit represented a new financial nadir. Their fortunes sank still lower when Humphrey and Kennedy prenomination debts and some subsequent operating losses brought the total deficit to $9.3 million.

During the 1960's the search for cash left the Democrats little time to improve their broader-based solicitations (Dollars for Democrats and the Sustaining Fund). A strategy of appeal for large sums used such tactics as the President's Club, program advertising books, expensive galas and dinners. Each device proved productive financially, but also provoked controversy. Defense contractors or government employees or someone was dunned to give because enough money in small sums was not forthcoming—indeed, was not vigorously sought. The Democratic Committee's attempts to help Senatorial and Congressional finance campaign committees, undertaken in the Kennedy days, met with reverses in Johnson days both because of petty jealousies and insufficient dollars. Many program books raised as much fuss as money.

No Democratic program was more successful, or raised more questions, than the President's Club, begun in 1961. A variation of the political-dinner formula, combined with the sustaining fund concept of annual membership, the Club was patterned on the Democratic 750 Club organized to help wipe out a $750,000 deficit from the 1956 Stevenson campaign. The goal to attract 750 contributors paying $1,000 each was not achieved until 1960. The President's Club reached 4,000 members in 1964, a remarkable increase from the upper limit of only 750 considered possible less than a decade before. Even the 2,000 members claimed for 1965-67 represented a notable increase since the 1950's.

Although not explicitly stated, a major attraction of President's Club membership was the idea that members would have an occasional opportunity to meet the President and might even be invited to the White House. Membership also helped to open doors and gain access to power centers in Washington. To the extent that laws allowed, the names of Club members were secret;[2] Republican members, for instance, clearly preferred not to be listed publicly. Barring the press from Club functions provided at least the illusion of privacy and intimacy with top political officials. This inside-dopesterism, Club officials admitted, was a major attraction, along with the chance to attend social affairs at the White House (although as membership grew that chance diminished). Club apologists suggested such minor genuflections to political snobbery were a small price for assuring large donations.

Between 1961 and 1963 President Kennedy appeared at President's Club affairs at which a total of $1,950,000 was raised. President Johnson's first political activity, many weeks after President Kennedy's death, was to appear at a Club luncheon in New York City, February 6, 1964. A total of $2,271,000 was raised in 1964 through Club events where Johnson appeared. In total, the President's Club accounted for at least $6,371,000, or almost one-third of the $21,849,500 raised at all Democratic fund-raising events across the country at which either the President or Vice President appeared between 1961 and the end of 1966.

The Club offered a wide variety of dinners and special events. Under one format a Presidential speech was scheduled at a $100-a-plate dinner, with an exclusive reception or after-dinner buffet for members of the Club with the President in attendance. From 1965 to 1968 Vice President Humphrey and other high officials led seminars in such places as New York, Cincinnati, and Dallas; these included brief speeches, with question-and-answer periods.

An annual President's Club cycle developed across the nation including a New York seminar in January, and a New York Ball and a Texas dinner-dance in mid-year. Such events brought the Texas contingent to 600 in 1966, about the same number claimed by New York. A 1967 dinner at Los Angeles grossed $475,000 suggesting the approximate size of the Southern California Club. The District of Columbia President's Club was a unique one, with membership of perhaps 200 extending into Washington's Maryland and Virginia suburbs and consisting of many government officials, lobbyists, and members of Washington society.

The President's Club developed its own state chapters in areas of concentrated wealth: New York City, Chicago, Southern and Northern California, Texas, and Minnesota. Each bargained for its own division of funds with the national leadership.

The Club spared no effort or money to give members a good return for their money. One member from California claimed his $1,000 in 1964 was the best social investment he ever made. He and his wife went free to a dinner dance and another event in California. While attending the national convention in Atlantic City, he was invited to a special event for members each day: on Sunday night a cocktail party with music and hors d'oeuvres; on Monday, a brunch at a choice of two hotels and an exhibition golf match in the afternoon; on Tuesday, an old-fashioned clambake; on Wednesday, a day at the races, followed by cocktails and dancing in honor of the next Vice President of the United States; on Thursday, a birthday party for the President followed by a buffet supper-breakfast. The author was a guest of a member at several of these affairs and can testify to the bountiful food and drink. Other benefits of membership for the Californian included an invitation to the Inauguration, the Inaugural Gala and Dinner, and a dinner at the White House—all for $1,000.

The Club created an elite financial constituency that bypassed traditional channels for funds. In some states, President's Club leaders supplanted state leaders with respect to patronage and other matters. State and county committees contributed to the Club so that their leaders could attend club events, and numerous union political committees paid $1,000 to purchase membership for their leaders. Some local Democratic managers complained that the Club drained off local funds to Washington, adding to problems in soliciting money for state and local candidates.

The secrecy and snobbishness surrounding the President's Club irritated some and prompted others to ask sharp questions. Three months before the 1966 fall elections, the Treasurer of the Democratic National Committee, Clifton C. Carter, resigned—a "fall guy," it was said, for a series of revelations about the President's Club.

The Republicans had learned that certain officers of the nation's largest brewery, Anheuser-Busch, Inc. of St. Louis, had contributed (with their wives) a total of $10,000 to the President's Club only weeks before the Justice Department dropped an antitrust proceeding against the company. There were denials of any connection between the events, but suspicions deepened with the discovery that, during an airlines strike, Vice President Humphrey and Donald Turner, the Justice Department's antitrust chief, were flown to St. Louis in the company's private plane for the All-Star baseball game and a pre-game luncheon of the President's Club.[3] If it is assumed only that a series of odd coincidences occurred, it is clear that high-minded persons, a Vice President with reformist leanings and an antitrust chief who is a former Harvard Law School professor, can get trapped, innocently and unknowingly, in a system of political financing that relies upon large contributors. The system leads inevitably to suspicion if not to corruption.

Republicans subsequently reported other oddities about the President's Club. In May, 1966, the House of Representatives voted against supplying funds for Project Mohole, a scientific study that envisaged drilling a hole in the earth's crust beneath the ocean floor. Three days later, members of the family of George R. Brown contributed $23,000 to the President's Club. Mr. Brown was the chairman of the board of Brown & Root, a Texas firm serving as a contractor to Project Mohole. Mr. Brown was also a friend and supporter of President Johnson and a past contributor to his campaigns. Within days, President Johnson urged the Congress to restore the funds, which the Senate did, but the House refused.[4] Again there were denials of influence. The President dismissed the Republican allegations as "periodic political charges." [5] There may well have been good scientific reasons to urge continuance of Project Mohole, but again, the system caught its victims, one of them the President of the United States.

An antipoverty contract was awarded to Consolidated American Services, Inc., a company whose senior vice president was a member of the President's Club. The company won the contract although it was not one of the four firms originally recommended by program officials.[6] Again, the administration found it necessary to issue denials.

A tip from an employee of the Veterans Administration put the Republicans on the trail of VA contracts awarded to architectural and engineering firms in California and Texas whose officials and families had contributed a total of at least $30,500 to Democratic committees in the 1964-66 period. The *St. Louis Post-Dispatch* then reported a VA award of a design contract to a Georgia architect who later contributed $10,000.[7] It was revealed that one of the California contractors who contributed was a member of the John Birch Society and a former Republican functionary. Most contributors, caught in similar circumstances, would plead that the money was contributed in support of President Johnson and the Great Society programs but it was unlikely that a Birch Society member would contribute to the President's Club for reasons of ideology or to enjoy White House invitations.[8] Suspiciously, in several cases the amount contributed by different contractors from the same industry was identical, $12,500.

These revelations about the President's Club came when Washington tongues were wagging about Bobby Baker, and they added fire to criticism of another questionable means of raising funds, principally used by the Democrats, the program advertising books. Federal law prohibiting corporate contributions contains a section making it illegal to sell goods or commodities, including advertising, if the proceeds aid a candidate for federal office. These laws were eroded, however, by court and tax agency decisions sanctioning deductions of reasonable corporate expenditures for ads in journals and programs of political parties if the ads had a relation to business activities.

Until 1964 both national parties had published advertising books every four years for distribution at the Presidential nominating conventions, with ads costing about $5,000 a page. In 1964 the Democrats published their convention book as a memorial to President Kennedy with ads at $15,000 a page. The advertisers were mostly corporations doing business with the federal government or under federal regulation. The estimated book profits of $1 million were used, said the party chairman, John Bailey, for educational purposes or to defray convention costs. It seemed unlikely that the Democratic convention deficit came to $1 million as claimed, and the only educational expense which came to light was $50,000 given to the National Council for Civic Responsibility, a nonpartisan group which sought to combat the broadcasts of rightwing groups.

Sources later indicated that a major portion of the surplus profits was spent in registration drives in heavily Democratic, including Southern Negro, areas. Under law, however, no official accounting had to be made and none was. The secrecy was prompted by the federal law prohibiting the use of corporate gifts or advertising revenue for partisan political purposes, as opposed to legitimate use for convention costs. The secrecy was probably also prompted by practical politics: Southern white elements of the Democratic Party would have screamed at the reported use of the funds to register Blacks.

The 1964 Democratic convention book was so successful that the Republicans published in 1965 a program book called *Congress: The Heartbeat of Government,* which charged $10,000 a page for ads and raised about $250,000. Not to be outdone in the quickening race for publication, the Democrats came back in late 1965 with *Toward an Age of Greatness,* with ads again running at $15,000 a page for a profit of at least $600,000. This one was prepared for distribution at fund-raising movie premieres for Democratic Congressional candidates in 1966.

The political connections of many advertisers were shown by the activities of their officers. United Artists, which took a full page in the 1964 and 1965 Democratic programs, was headed by Arthur Krim, the chairman of the President's Club. The secretary of the President's Club in 1964 was the late Neil J. Curry, who was chairman of the Executive Committee of the American Trucking Association and a political coordinator for trucking interests. He arranged for 16 pages of public service advertising in the 1964 program at a cost of $240,000, sponsored by 114 trucking companies. Curry was also a director of Avco Corporation, which bought one page at $15,000 and the inside back cover at more than $15,000. An active member of the New York President's Club, Francis S. Levien, was president of the Universal American Corporation, which had a page ad in 1964. Levien was also a director of Paul Hardeman, Inc., a subsidiary of Universal American, which also had a page ad; another subsidiary of Universal American, the Young Spring and Wire Company, also bought a full page ad. Avco and Universal American advertised again in the Democrats' 1965 program book. By means of these ads, Democratic fund raisers were able to employ the resources of the corporations for political purposes.

Not only national but state and local Democratic and Republican committees had come to rely on program books. A 1966 survey showed 31 Republican state committees had published them as a source of funds. In California, Democrats admitted that 65 percent of state committee income derived from program books. The books were viewed by many as flagrant attempts to extort funds from government contractors. Certainly some corporate officials agreed to give Democrats tax-deductible corporate funds while they reserved personal nondeductible contributions for the Republicans.

Toward an Age of Greatness killed the golden program goose. The reaction in press and Congress was instant and hostile. Republican Senator John J. Williams of Delaware led a protest which culminated in the Williams Amendment prohibiting corporate tax deductions for advertisements in programs or books with a political connection.[9] Technically, corporations could still place ads if the costs came from their profits after taxes, but then, as Senator Williams pointed out, they could be subject to stockholder's suits for unwarranted distribution of profits. Although officially dead in national politics, the program books were revived in 1968 by an act of Congress which set forth specific and controlled conditions for their exclusive use to help finance the 1968 and future national nominating conventions.

After the Williams Amendment was adopted, the Democrats decided to let the dust settle before using the $600,000 or more profit from *Toward an Age of Greatness*. Accordingly, the money was placed in a bank savings account, and there it stayed and stayed. Since the money was hot in 1965, it was put on ice under control of at least one trustee who was associated with a public relations firm doing work for the Democrats. Hubert Humphrey wanted to use it for his financially starved 1968 campaign: since the money had originally been planned for use in registration and voter education drives, there was reason to spend the money early. Following President Johnson's withdrawal, and before the convention, it was objected that the funds could be spent in ways that might he interpreted as aiding one aspirant for the nomination over the others. After the convention, the Humphrey people tried to spring the money loose, without success. The attorneys for the trustee raised substantial legal questions as to the conditions under which the money could be released and how it could be spent.

Humphrey operatives seeking to spend the money for registration and election day expenses were turned down. Columnists Evans and Novak[10] charged that President Johnson was refusing to release the money to the Humphrey campaign as a means of keeping Humphrey in line on Vietnam. Both the White House and the DNC denied this. Despite protracted negotiations, the money was not freed during the campaign. As yet, lawyers have been unable to secure release of the money, now estimated at more than $700,000.

One of President Kennedy's less fortunate appointees was Richard Maguire, first as Acting Treasurer in 1962, then Treasurer of the Democratic National Committee. Maguire had been with the Kennedy organization in Massachusetts in the 1960 campaign. While on the White House staff, he handled political activities for the President. Unconfirmed reports alleged that he participated in staff work on government contracts and suggested that contractors show their appreciation by contributing to the Democratic Party. When Maguire joined the Democratic Committee staff, he strengthened President's Club operations and then pushed the idea of the allegedly nonpartisan program books.

Maguire remained in office after Kennedy's death, expanding his power when Johnson men were slow to grasp the reins of the national party. Rather than change Maguire's policies, they encouraged his aggressive program to attract large contributions to the neglect of small ones.

For all practical purposes Maguire virtually eliminated whatever frankness there had been about Democratic finances. He was largely responsible for a credibility gap in the public information policy of the Democratic party before the phrase hit the Johnson Administration. He was so secretive that even other top officials of the Committee did not have an accurate picture of their financial condition or the nature of many party transactions. Though the Committee's members constituted the legal governing body of the party, they were not given statements of receipts, expenditures, assets, or liabilities. Even in official reports filed with the Clerk of the House there were many peculiarities, such as the listing of names of contributors by first initial rather than full name, without street addresses.[11] No reports of the New York and California President's Clubs were filed in Washington at all (California law at that time did not provide for detailed disclosure of such a committee.) During 1964 cash was used excessively at the DNC. The Democratic party was thus treated as a closed corporation accountable only to the White House, not as a public institution. Contributors did not seem to care how their funds were being used, and most national committeemen appeared oblivious to the way their trust was misused.

During 1965 filings by the Democratic Committee provoked other questions. From January to June, official reports showed $1.3 million more was spent than received. Where the excess funds came from was a mystery, since 1964 filings did not show excess income. No loans or transfers from state or other committees were itemized to account for the excess. Months later it was admitted that money had been borrowed, but loan sources and amounts were not cited in filings for fear reporters would ask who the co-signers were; officials obtained co-signers on promises that their names would not be divulged.

Secrecy also surrounded the deficits at the end of the 1964 Presidential campaign. Immediately following the election, John Bailey stated that there was no deficit. When members of the National Committee met in Washington in January, 1965, they were given no financial report for the election year or on the party's postelection financial status. The only clue was one sentence in Chairman Bailey's report, that the DNC had wound up the election year "with a great vote surplus and a sort of little financial deficit." Maguire said only that the auditors were "hard at work" trying to determine the extent of the deficit. If they told him, he never told the National Committee. One source said the deficit had been $1 million.

By summer, 1965, reports were leaked to the press that the deficit had really been $2 million. At the end of 1965 Maguire submitted his resignation. His successor in the treasurer's slot, Clifton C. Carter, a longtime Texas associate of President Johnson, further confused the picture by saying early in 1966 that the 1964 deficit actually had been $3 million. And by May 1966, discussions with DNC officials brought out the contention that the "sort of little deficit" Bailey had talked of after the 1964 election had been an unprecedented $4.1 million. Yet the Democrats claimed a few months later, after incurring all the expenses of the 1966 mid-term election, that they had reduced the debt to $1 million. If the $4.1 million debt figure claimed a year before had been true, much of it must have resulted from excessive expenditures in the operations of the DNC during 1965-66.

After the losses suffered by the Democrats in the 1966 election, there were serious recriminations from Democratic governors and Congressmen about the lack of a functioning national committee. Some journalists attributed the trouble to the President's conception of politics, Texas-style, personal instead of party. If sufficient funds had been available, the DNC might have avoided trouble, Johnsonian attitudes or no. As it was, only big contributors were courted, the program books were no longer a source of even indirect revenue, and the President's Club was not enough to carry the party. Several plans to broaden the base in 1966-67 failed for lack of ardor. At the beginning of 1968, the Democratic National Committee was far from ready for the coming election.

The divisiveness of the 1968 nomination struggle and the loss of the Presidency, with all accompanying recriminations, further enervated the Democratic Party. Borrowing for Humphrey's election campaign and previous debts, combined with operating deficits in 1969 and part of 1970, found the Democrats in the 1970's whistling for courage.[12]

Instead of using their eight years of White House power and prestige to build a solid financial structure with hundreds of thousands of party supporters, the Democrats had turned to a handful of rich contributors, White House social patronage, and corporate advertising. Not sufficient either was money from newly wealthy entrepreneurs or from traditional Democratic friends in the entertainment industry. Those sources were inadequate, even in the affluent years of 1961-68, to support the party, much less energize it. Money attracted because a party is in power is not the kind that pays the bills when the party is out.

Preoccupied by national and international events, Presidents

Kennedy and Johnson, though theoretically the party leaders responsible for raising funds, found little time to strengthen party financing. They sanctioned the President's Club and the program books but neither gave real leadership to increasing the number of supporters. Both Presidents, as a result, were under financial pressure as party leaders—fatal pressure for Kennedy. One of the reasons Kennedy went to Texas in November, 1963, was to attend a fund-raising dinner in Austin.[13]

After 1968 the Democratic Party was a shadow of its former power and affluence. Without the power of the White House, with a weakened Congressional majority, with immense debts, with party dissension and a disturbed, elusive, and uncertain constituency, the party seemed to be on the way to bankruptcy. Moreover, there was no evident leader capable of rallying the ranks. Chappaquidick at least temporarily destroyed Edward Kennedy's value as a fund raiser. Humphrey found that many former friends would not help to pay off debts from 1968. The Democrats lacked resources even to finance their reform commissions (in delegate selection and participation, on convention management, and on financial organization) at a time when their greatest need was to restore confidence in the organization and reactivate its members.

In 1970 new leadership at the DNC—Larry O'Brien as Chairman and Robert Strauss as Treasurer—began a welcome policy of financial candor. They put the DNC on a pay-as-you-go basis. While they were unable to reduce the debt, they won pledges from about 700 persons to contribute regularly, some as much as $100 per month, to finance current operations. Meanwhile, with seed money to begin mailings large enough to build the $15-a-year Sustaining Fund, they harvested 45,000 contributors by the end of 1970. In early 1971, the Democrats found it easier to muster financial support. An April dinner grossed $900,000, and there was gratifying cooperation from Congressional leaders who helped to sell tickets by visiting major cities where cocktail parties were held in their honor. Some Congressional leaders, such as Representative Wilbur Mills, participated for the first time in raising funds for the party. With newborn confidence, in early 1971 the DNC dropped its pay-as-you-go policy and negotiated new loans to finance still broader direct mail appeals. At the same time, half a dozen aspirants for the Democratic Presidential nomination, by raising funds for their own campaigns, inevitably tapped sources needed by the national party. Democratic financial difficulties are rooted partly in the fact that their usual constituency, scattered through the country's suburbs and cities, on small farms, in universities, and in the ranks of organized labor, are harder to reach than the pantheon of corporation executives and professionals who favor the Republicans. At the same time, it is ironic that a party with as large an electoral base as the Democrats has not been able to tap its constituents for large sums in small packages. Part of the failure seems to be a consequence of apathy, a tendency to take the easy route (the President's Club), and lack of seed money to develop programs. Part results from independent efforts of labor and other movements to raise money for causes which the national party neglects. President Kennedy showed his awareness of the need for a broad financial base when he said to a gathering of major contributors, "The day will come when we will let you go." [14] That day is not yet in sight.

Democratic and Republican fund-raising methods differ in manner, tone, and structure, rather than technique. While Democratic vote getting and fund raising are combined in one organization, the Republicans separate fund raising from spending.

The Republican National Finance Committee coordinates the financial policy of the National Committee and the Senatorial and House campaign committees. The politicians of these committees, however, are free to decide how the money is shared among candidates. Most Republican State Committees have separate finance committees to raise money for them and there are separate finance committees in large cities. The system is business-like. It frees politicians from tiresome, time-consuming tasks. Different markets are blocked out for different appeals, to reduce competing solicitations. Finance committees have their own staffs and their own volunteer crews. Often they have separate headquarters and are usually directed by specialists in finance, a professional service which the Democrats usually assign to amateurs. Republican financial organizations work year around, in election and non-election years, seeking steady and reliable income for the party.

While Democrats increased their dependence on large contributors, many of them businessmen, the national Republican Party has begun to palliate its past image as the favorite of the "fat cats." The RNC has learned to attract small givers who have helped to avoid the deficits which have plagued the opposition. The Republicans, moreover, accomplished this feat in the face of the divisive party factionalism of 1964. Goldwater supporters often preferred to give directly to Washington to avoid state channels which would share funds with moderate candidates. Moderates, not anxious to support the Goldwater campaign, gave directly to local candidates.

Following the election, there were threats from the Goldwater and right-wing splinter groups to withdraw their funds if the national party took a moderate course. Two major Goldwater campaign committees did withhold surpluses from the RNC. The Citizens Committee for Goldwater-Miller refused to part with its $309,000 surplus; it used the money, under a new name, Citizens Committee for Conservatives, to support conservative contenders in GOP races, mostly in 1966. Another group, the National TV Committee for Goldwater-Miller, finished the 1964 campaign with a $506,534 surplus. Some went to unsuccessful projects like a conservative television pilot film which the RNC refused to sponsor. The post-Goldwater era also witnessed the emergence of several right-wing splinter organizations which tried to exploit lists of contributors attracted by 1964 Goldwater appeals. One group, the misnamed United Republicans of America, was attacked by the regulars for using the name "Republican" in its title.

In 1965 Ray Bliss took over as Republican National Chairman and General Lucius D. Clay as Finance Chairman. Bliss had run a remarkably unified fund-raising effort in Ohio and was anxious to repeat the performance on a national level. Under Bliss and Clay, the Republican impulse toward coordinated fund raising began to reassert itself. Their new national financial structure stressed direct fund raising by the national party and de-emphasized quota payments by state committees. The system had two tracks—personal solicitation for large contributors and mail solicitation for smaller ones. An auxiliary track is used once a year for a Congressional dinner; in campaign years a separate Senatorial dinner and a Congressional gala may be held.[15]

The new financial structure was based on the phenomenal success of the Republican National Sustaining Fund, started in the spring of 1962 on the basis of $10 per year per contributor. The Fund produced $700,000 its first year but seems to have reached a plateau.

1962	$ 700,000	1966	$3,300,000
1963	1,100,000	1967	3,500,000
1964	2,369,000	1968	2,400,000
1965	1,700,000	1969	2,125,000
		1970	3,040,000

The Republican Sustaining Fund is built by mail solicitations conducted by professionals. The cost is seen as seed money. About $1 is spent to collect $3. In 1968, for example, the cost of raising the $6.6 million in the Sustaining Fund and campaign mail drive was about $2.5 million, or about 38 percent. With 22 million letters mailed, the response rate was about two percent, a normal return. A total of 450,000 contributors responded in 1968 to the Republican mail drive alone, compared to the Republicans' claim of 651,000 individual givers in 1964 in response to all appeals.

In 1968 fewer new contributors were attracted by the mailings, but the 1968 base of known contributors was greater than in 1964. In dollar amounts the $6.6 million collected in 1968 compared with the $5.8 million in 1964. In the postconvention period, Goldwater drew $4.7 million whereas Nixon drew $4.2 million. The difference was mainly in the preconvention period, when the RNC Sustaining Fund in 1964 received barely $1 million compared with $2.4 million in 1968. Another difference was that the average gift in 1968 was larger than in 1964.

The income from the Republican sustaining fund was sufficient by 1966 to cover day-to-day costs of the National Committee, enough to release large contributions to pay for party-building programs like the Republican Coordinating Committee, the Big Cities program, the Republican Governors Association, and a college youth program. Since 1968, the Republicans have had even more money for organizational and promotional programs.

A similar separation of financial functions is found in the Republican Congressional Campaign Committee (RCCC) whose operating costs are paid by 50,000 contributors through $25-a-year subscriptions to the RCCC Newsletter. Large contributions derived from the Gala or paid directly are used for campaigns by incumbent House Republicans. Nonincumbent House candidates receive assistance from still another source, the Republican Congressional Boosters Club. As in the President's Club, members pay at least $1,000 each, and the funds go to candidates as contributions. Some candidates receive as much as $15,000 in contributions from the Boosters Club. Such financing helped Republicans gain a combined net of 56 Congressional seats in 1966 and 1968 elections. Finally, the receipts from the annual Republican Senatorial dinner paid for aid to Republican Senate candidates as well as operating expenses of the Senatorial Campaign Committee.

The Republican Associates, another club for $1,000 or more per year contributors, was organized in 1959; since 1965, its fundraising activities have sometimes been carried out jointly with the Republican Congressional Boosters Club. It is conceived as "enlisting a group of dedicated Republicans who can provide counsel and leadership in helping to strengthen the Republican party," according to a party brochure. A 1966 brochure described the benefits of membership for Associates (and Boosters):

• "You will be invited to participate in private regional and national conferences with the Republican leaders.

• "Your advice will be solicited on key issues.

• "You will receive a private bulletin each month to keep you advised on Washington and campaign developments.

• "For national Republican activities (conventions, etc.) you will receive priority on tickets and credentials.

• "Above all you will share the satisfaction of knowing that you are making possible the very survival of our two-party system. Accordingly, your membership in the Associate-Booster Program will be a strategic investment for our timetable in 1966."

Since the Nixon Administration came to power, such promises as item #2 are no longer advertised publicly, but a newer brochure still admonishes the reader to "Invest in Your Own Future."

The financial value of the Associates Program to the Republicans has been less significant than the President's Club was to the

Democrats. In 1968, for example, the Associates provided only 13 percent of Republican preconvention funds, while the Sustaining Fund brought in 43 percent. General election figures for the Associates in 1968 are not available, but figures for 1969 and 1970 are as follows:

REPUBLICAN INCOME, 1969-70

Source of Funds	1969	1970
RN Associates	$1,112,363	$ 2,542,038
Sustaining	2,125,286	3,040,072
Speaker Commissions	6,254	402,384
State Payments	67,037	9,698
Special Projects and Misc.	102,711	26,266
Congressional	1,284,107	2,109,359
Gala Dinners	2,024,000	1,707,947
Boosters	482,416	874,550
Total	$7,204,174	$10,712,314

The remarkable combination of mail drives and personal solicitation permits the Republicans to obtain the bulk of national income without depending on state organizations.

In a sense, the development of systematic direct fund-raising by the national parties should be welcomed by state parties, which have labored under various quota systems aimed at getting them to undertake a fair share of national expenses. Local operatives have mixed feelings: they want to free state collections for exclusive state and local use, but they like national speakers as their fund raisers, and they want the national party to provide services.

By 1967 the Republicans had evolved a new credit system based on a four-year average of the responsiveness of each state to national mailings, and a two-year average of total performance, mainly in Booster-Associates appeals. The states pay only small speakers' commissions (the Democrats take larger percentages for providing national speakers) and the rest is credited from actual contributions to national appeals. In 1968 only 17 of the 53 states and territories had met their Republican quotas, though nationally the quota was 97 percent fulfilled. The systems in both parties are best described as efforts to gain state cooperation with direct national fund raising rather than as quotas in the conventional sense.

Though the Republicans have been successful in recruiting a

large number of givers, much emphasis in both parties still focuses on the means of attracting contributions. Since the 1930's, both parties have been eating and drinking their way toward solvency with the political dinner (or breakfast, brunch, lunch, or cocktail party). Matthew H. McCloskey, Philadelphia contractor and longtime treasurer of the Democratic National Committee, is credited with having invented the $100-a-plate dinner in 1934 when he established a "100 Club" in Montgomery County, Pa., consisting of 100 people who would contribute $100 each to the Democratic party's effort that year. He signed up 100 in four weeks and held a luncheon to celebrate. In the ensuing years, the Jefferson-Jackson Day Dinner, the Lincoln's Birthday Dinner, and other fund-raising events became national institutions.

Both parties rely so heavily upon fund-raising dinners that they are said to be financed on the "cash and calorie" plan. No one appears to have invented a better way of dunning businessmen, sympathizers, lobbyists, office-holders, and favor-seekers who are reluctant to imperil their standing by refusing to buy tickets. Still, fund-raising dinners are over-worked, as the diners will testify and as many fund raisers will admit.

With growing affluence (and inflation), the price of tickets to political dinners has risen, too. The standard fee is still $100 a ticket, though there are many for less at local levels, but it is no longer unusual to charge $500 or $1,000.

In 1966 the annual Republican Congressional dinner cost per ticket rose from $100 to $500, while the Democrats increased their equivalent from $100 to $250 and then to $500. Party functions at $1,000 per ticket are now frequent. With prices like these, even a fall-off in attendance brings greater receipts. In New Jersey, Democrats claimed they couldn't find dining facilities ample for all the faithful willing to pay $100, so they upped the price to $250 a plate—and grossed more dollars. In 1967 the New York Republicans raised the price of their annual dinner to $150 and had the largest attendance ever.

In preparation for these dinners, guests at cocktail parties are urged to buy entire tables, not single seats. The admission price of $100 or $500 per ticket thus becomes $1,000 or $5,000. The donor either sells the tickets to others or passes them out to friends, business associates, and party workers.

Instead of the usual chicken and speeches, the event may provide entertainment—music, dancing, or movie premières—virtually any device to give the ticket purchaser some gratification. Some have attracted as many as 6,000 or 8,000 persons.

President Nixon has rationed his public fund raising appearances carefully. He has spoken at the annual spring dinner in Washington and at an occasional dinner in Chicago or elsewhere, but he has not traveled for fund raisers as often as Presidents Kennedy and Johnson. He assigned much of that role to Vice President Agnew. For the Washington dinners, the Republicans used the location to protect the names of those who bought tickets. In the District of Columbia, public records were not required; contributors remained unknown. At the 1969 dinner, the largest single dinner of its kind, grossing $2.6 million, President Nixon was presented with the sole copy of a leather-bound book listing the ticket purchasers. Since the Republicans would not release a seating list, the public could not know who attended.

During 1969 Vice President Agnew became a major attraction at Republican fund-raising affairs. By 1970 he was the prime party orator. In that year, he spoke at dinners estimated to have grossed more than $5 million. In a seven-week period alone prior to the 1970 elections, he spoke at affairs that snagged $3.5 million. About 10 percent of the gross went to the RNC to defray his travelling costs. Agnew's rhetoric was so well-received that the Republicans issued a recording, "Spiro T. Agnew Speaks Out," and offered copies to sustaining members.

Dinners and similar events do widen the base of candidate and party support.[16] They give the votaries a chance to mingle and exchange ideas and information with party and public officials; they give the passive partisan an opportunity to contribute; they serve to inspire enthusiasm; they give local citizens and party workers a chance to observe political leaders in person, off camera. Mainly, however, dinners are a source of political funds; it is hard to imagine politics without them.

Many object to the frequency of dinners, the escalating prices, and the pressure to buy tickets. A few object to the class stratification—the members of the President's Club who paid $1,000 enjoyed special attention and did not mingle with the $100 rabble. A dilemma for harried finance managers is that in order to be solvent they have to spend so much time in staging money-raising events that too little is left for seeking better methods, methods to reach the vast majority who cannot afford to share in the political process at $100 a plate.

The extent of the parties' continued dependence on large contributions is unknown. During 1969, for example, the public could not know the sources of certain funds that appeared on official Republican campaign fund reports. The March filings revealed that 6 different committees in Illinois transferred funds amounting to $268,610 to 11 national committees. Each Illinois committee conformed with federal law by contributing no more than $5,000 to any national committee. Inquiries in Washington and Chicago brought little light on the sources of the funds. In Illinois, which has no disclosure of political contributions, party officials said they had never heard of the six committees in question. Some claimed the money was surplus from the 1968 campaigns, but that was denied by 1968 Nixon officials in Illinois. Most likely all or most of the money came from one source, one of Nixon's financial supporters in Chicago, and the committees were mere fronts to channel funds to Washington anonymously. In any event, Republican credibility, usually good on financial matters, was damaged.

Another example of concealment occurred during the 1970 elections. A unique fund-raising operation funnelled millions into the campaigns of selected Republican candidates. The chief functionary was Jack A. Gleason, a former assistant to Maurice Stans, Nixon's director of fund raising during 1968. Gleason later became a White House aide but resigned to work in the 1970 campaigns. From an office in downtown Washington, Gleason, according to one account, boasted that his efforts for Republican candidates had raised more than $12 million, no doubt an exaggeration.[17] Among the known beneficiaries were Richard L. Roudebush, U. S. Senate candidate in Indiana, who acknowledged receiving $114,000, and Raymond J. Broderick, candidate for Governor of Pennsylvania, who admitted $83,000. Others, particularly candidates for the Senate, received funds, but exact amounts are unknown. Gleason filed no reports. The data mainly became available when filed under the state laws.

The contributors to the Gleason fund are unknown. Some may

have been the same who contributed to the Illinois committees in 1969. Some may have been among seven American ambassadors listed as large contributors to Republicans running in Maryland, Florida, California, Texas, and Ohio. Two of the ambassadors' contributions in Maryland and Florida were officially listed as having been sent "care of Jack A. Gleason." [18] On record, the seven ambassadors gave $28,000. The pulling power of the White House was evident in both the ambassadorial gifts and in the Gleason activities. The Gleason project also exposed the weakness of the laws which permitted fund raising in the District of Columbia to go unreported.

With the federal government's pervasive role in American life, it seems logical that direct fund-raising drives at the national level will continue. In the short run the Republicans may continue to take advantage of their success in the direct mail, Newsletter, the Associate and Booster campaigns, and large contributions as in the Illinois and Gleason operations.

In the short run, the Democrats may fail to broaden their financial base unless they obtain sufficient seed money. They need to negotiate their debt and transform remaining individual loans into contributions. Possibly they will have to resort to austerity and prayer for deliverance, unless they produce winning issues.

In the longer run, sustaining funds probably cannot be expected to provide for much more than the annual operations of the national committees. Indeed, the Democrats would be gratified with that accomplishment and since 1970 have made some progress in that direction. Sustaining funds have not supplanted other sources and may never do so. Neither is there much prospect for expanding memberships in President's Club, RNC Associates, Boosters, Sponsors, or other high priced coteries. Levels of affluence and motivations of large givers will not keep pace with demands for political spending.

The economic dip in 1969-71 hurt both Republican and Democratic fund raising. Many contributors reduced their gifts, and some refrained entirely. The Democrats suffered more because many of their contributors were locked into a sagging market or were confined to disturbed industries such as movies, electronics, computers, or aerospace. Republican links to well-established families with diversified investments, coupled with their hold on the White House, kept them in funds. In 1968, at the national level, the Republicans reported spending more than twice as much as the Democrats, while some Democratic spending used borrowed money. In 1969 the disparity between Republican and Democratic spending at the national level favored the Republicans more than three to one. In 1970 the Republicans maintained a three-to-one edge. Although the Democrats had won the Presidency and maintained control of the Congress for much of the time since 1932 despite heavier spending by the Republicans, lack of money hurt but did not defeat them. Now, however, the disparity is even greater if the Democratic debt and efforts like the Gleason operation are taken into account. To redress the balance, the Democrats need support from labor and associated movements. As will be seen, there is an intimate relationship between Democrats and labor that is, in form but not in substance, far different from the historic relationship of the Republicans with elements of the business community. As a party, the Democrats probably may not emerge from deficit financing until they again win the White House or enact legislation to reduce their financial handicaps.

8

LOCAL PARTIES AND
THE CONGRESSIONAL LINK

Ideally, an integrated party financial structure would collect funds locally through systematic mass solicitation, for sharing with state committees and the national party. Such a system would free the national parties from dependence on large donations and money-raising gimmicks, while energizing neighborhood party units needed to organize collections. Though a system in which money flows upward from mass solicitations by the local party seems logical, it is not likely to materialize despite compelling arguments for more local financial responsibility.[1]

The most effective solicitation is face-to-face, and that tactic can reach large numbers only through local volunteers, literally millions, who would solicit friends, colleagues, and neighbors. The most that national and state committees can do for such a system is to initiate and guide the drive for funds and provide materials and kits. The possibilities are limited also by the weak discipline in voluntary organizations and the often forceful reasons that inhibit local committees from extending help to state or national bodies.

Yet there are possibilities of local financing despite fitful but real signs of increasing nationalization. The trend toward direct national fund raising, examined in the last chapter, is balanced by the conviction that, given our institutional arrangements, the basis of political organization in the United States is and will remain local; that a satisfying, reliable foundation for a strong financial structure within the parties could be based on small contributions obtained by local solicitations; and that the search for a rational financial system should begin locally. The search must overcome three major hurdles. The first, in broadening the base of political contributions, is where there is substantial resistance or inability to change from traditional sources; the second is friction in the process of funnelling money to higher party levels; and the third is in the competition for authority or power

117

in coordinating fund-raising efforts and centralizing responsibility in the handling and use of funds.

Many, perhaps most, local organizations do not feel a duty to squeeze the ward for money to export to the capital. Certainly most have not been conditioned to share funds except where quota systems operate, or where speakers are supplied by higher level committees for fund-raising events. Local leaders are not all impressed by promises of federal patronage; local jobs are more immediate. Many regard themselves as disbursers of money sent from angels above to be used to deliver the vote. To raise significant sums, local leaders would be expected to recruit, organize, and deploy large corps of solicitors who would inevitably expect a piece of the action. Local party leaders reasonably fear that volunteers recruited to raise funds would soon be scheming to take over the organization offices. Even if local leaders were successful in controlling the fund raising organization, they might be reluctant to pass much money to state and national headquarters. The accounting and auditing of local collections and spending might not prove satisfactory, either.

"Local organization" is too grand a term to apply to some small party units. The local organization may be one man working at a secondhand desk under a bare light bulb in a cubbyhole upstairs over a store, with a pay telephone on the wall and the files in his hat. He may not keep books. His staff may be an idler hoping for crumbs. Communications may be handled in the mayor's office. The treasurer may be a clerk on the payroll of a contractor. If this "local organization" received a letter proposing mass appeals in a national campaign for money, the action would no doubt stop right there.

Certain other districts are poor prospects for financial support: low income areas; sparsely-settled rural areas; districts where a dominant party is a closed organization and the opposition has trouble finding a vote. For the present it is practical to think of launching massive drives only in carefully pinpointed, relatively wealthy neighborhoods.

Money is raised to buy political services because there are not enough volunteers. Directly or indirectly, money buys manpower. At the same time, raising money requires manpower, and the broader the solicitation, the greater the demand for volunteers. The arithmetic is revealing. There are about 176,000 election districts in the United States, (averaging few more than 400 voters per district in a Presidential election year). Only 10 solicitors per district for each of two parties would come to 3,520,000. Consistently, according to Gallup polls, there are actually more than 4,000,000 volunteer workers in Congressional election years and more than 6,000,000 in Presidential election years. Are these enough volunteers to handle both fund raising and other party work? Gallup reports 38 million adults claim to be willing to work as party volunteers, but no realistic politician dreams of such a turnout.

The party leader works with two scarce resources, money and manpower, and allocates them according to his perception of need. He considers manpower needs for registration drives, election day, putting up posters, sealing envelopes, and the rest. In his scheme, door-to-door fund raising may have low priority, particularly if he has reliable sources of funds. Moreover, he soon learns that many volunteers will gladly do anything but ask others for money.

Professional politicians have not emphasized grassroots work for fund raising in the precincts as they do registration and getting voters to the polls. Were they to ask precinct politicians to organize local solicitation, they would have to reconsider their techniques of campaigning before large constituencies, including wide use of TV and travel by jet and helicopter. These methods require more money, and parties need local workers to raise it, but enthusiasm for precinct work wanes as candidates rely upon publicity rather than organization, on expert professionals instead of district politicians. Reliance upon the media frees some volunteers for fund raising, but few have been asked to help with broad-based fund raising, and fewer have offered their services. Many are skeptical about the amount of work and the probable returns.

Reliance upon publicity is standard political practice in a society saturated by mass communications. Many believe that electoral success is won by an attractive leader with access to radio and TV. Incumbents in the White House or the governor's mansion have access to means of mass communication without much reference to party organization. For others, exposure costs money. These realities encourage reliance upon candidates who attract funds at dinners and other events. Consequently, not enough is done to build a solid organizational structure for fund raising. If the party were an effective vehicle for mobilizing workers, voters, and money, politics would be less chaotic.

Party organizations at the state level, like national and local structures, leave much to be desired. Independent of control of the governorship or strong potential for winning that control, few state party organizations have sound financing broadly based. With governmental control, the organizations tend to depend for funds upon contributions and jobholders. Other sources are rarely developed as a hedge against the event that the party will be out of power. Too often the staff has neither the talent nor skill of the professional money raiser. Too often the committees are in debt or have too little leverage to obtain funds from local committees. The state organizations are not so readily seen or defined as are the local organizations, nor are state officials as powerful as federal officials. Consequently large contributors and special interests tend to be the main financial constituencies of state political committees.

The parties, state or local, have not done much to modernize. They have been slow to adopt and adapt new techniques, partly for lack of money. As campaign priorities emphasize media, a party's organization and operations get less attention, but only modern organizational and administrative techniques can improve the utility of the state party as a fund-raising instrument.

State candidates do not have the permanent organizations to build up numbers of contributors; citizens' committees working for them disband after the campaign; crews of fund raisers are hard to recruit and lists of contributors are hard to find. Volunteers and lists of donors are produced for candidates usually at the expense of their party. Party organization, in contrast, is permanent and comprehensive. It can schedule times for recruitment and solicitation. Even though party organizational activity suffers to some extent between elections, when volunteers retire, and even though the organization may be reshuffled frequently, the party is in an ongoing position. Also, the party has a span of time to test responses to non-political mail lists. By comparison, the candidate, no matter how wealthy, has the weaker and more sporadic base for political action.

Local Drives

Door-to-Door drives for years have operated successfully and repeatedly in a few districts. Aaron Burr, in 1800, set up local committees to canvass for funds from house to house. In the 1950's Republicans designed a national Neighbor-to-Neighbor program; it is now run most successfully in Minnesota, particularly in Hennepin County, which contains Minneapolis. The Minnesota results are phenomenal, showing a growth from 46,717 contributors giving $216,000 in 1960, to 67,344 contributors giving $407,000 in 1970, with variations in between, of course, and relatively insubstantial decreases in non-election years.

Dollars for Democrats drives in recent years are nowhere so successful; for example, in Montgomery County, Maryland, one of the nation's wealthiest, about $44,000 was donated in 1964 compared with $27,000 in 1968. Montgomery County Republicans, on the other hand, have provided figures showing variable success, from $29,482 collected in 1963, to $50,637 in 1968, then dropping to $35,458 in 1969, and $26,042 in 1970.

The 1968 drive was the most successful. The 1,119 Republican workers received 7,088 contributions, and 65 precincts exceeded quotas. The 1969 drive with 740 workers received 5,485 contributions. The drive fell $9,000 short of quota but a two-week extension brought in $7,000. The 1970 drive did less well. From 6,632 homes called on, it netted 3,235 contributions. Only 22 precincts went over quota; 26 precincts turned in nothing.

One estimate is that the number of calls represented about 30 percent of Republican households in the county, leaving many others to be tapped. The repetitions and achievements in Hennepin and Montgomery Counties show potentials. Montgomery contains suburbs of Washington, D.C., but no known factors make Hennepin County any different from numerous other counties in the United States. The difference is in the will and in the management.

Good management requires that kits be issued to provide instructions, badges, receipt books, and literature, supplemented by mailings of newsletters and weekly reports. The Maryland Republicans offer awards to collectors (first to reach quota, highest percentage over quota, highest number of receipts, most money received) and to districts with the highest quota and household response. Firm deadlines discourage procrastination. Other party activities are held to a minimum during the fund drive. On 1968 awards night, the drive netted $19,562, a record. In 1968 the Montgomery County out-of-pocket costs of raising $50,637 were reported by the Republicans to be $2,121.[2] In comparison, mail drives cost from 30 to 50 percent of the amount collected, as noted.

Above all else, local collection committees need "affluence-voter profiles." Census data can pinpoint districts with the highest potential for fund raising. As in registration and election-day work, the strategy is to select and work districts in cities, suburbs, and exurbs where there is an ample mix of organizational skills, seed money, and enlightened leadership. A profile of motivations of persons who now contribute would be equally useful as a guide to information about the conditions which encourage donors to give.

A system for improving collections, however successful, can be frustrated for lack of fair means for sharing funds vertically or horizontally within the party. To rationalize the party system entails a sophisticated concept of central treasuries, crossing current organizational jurisdictions and candidate constituencies, receiving money from areas of affluence and allocating it to areas of need. The United Republican finance committees follow this concept but are curbed by current boundaries. Surmounting present boundaries carries implications for party loyalty, discipline, and obligations that hardly need be spelled out. How visionary is it to conceive of horizontal regional party groupings and metroparty structures allowing suburbs and centers of wealth to supply funds for their own districts and for low-income neighborhoods as well? Or to consider a tristate party grouping or compact including New York, New Jersey and Connecticut?

Could affluent districts send money up from local to state to national parties? The restraints on dollar flow within the party have in the past effectively choked off circulation from the local collection system to dispensaries with wider concerns. Some kind of pump is an obvious need. Many organizations levy a head tax on a portion of dues on local members and local chapters, but these systems apply in politics only in minor degree: e.g. favorable seats in a national convention could be made conditional upon delivering state quotas.

Obstacles to fund sharing are not constant nor consistent. Competing federal and state and local elections are not always concurrent. Prospects for urban fund raising may improve if city centers again attract affluent families. Strong interest in national party affairs and a sharp sense of context often stimulate changes in local leadership. Not all lower-level party committees are at odds with upper-level committees. Some local leaders are ideologically neutral or understand national financial needs and will cooperate. National party policy derives from a consensus of a majority of state and local committees which share and help create national interests and goals. A platform may be an armed truce between conflicting interests in the party coalition, but it also represents broad agreement. Those leaderships which share interests may also be willing to share funds, especially if ample funds are available.

The forces favoring national coordination of politics are on the increase. Modern technology and communications create greater interdependence, national consensus, and acceptance of common goals. Conditions that cause local organizations to modernize and retire old leadership are the same that strengthen party coherence.

An institutional pump for moving money from precinct to capital and back to precinct hardly is visible as yet. Its evolution depends upon local success in finding excess funds. It is a big order to call for enough money to support state and national elections when it is now a struggle to finance even local campaigns.

Broad party solicitation would have wide political effects. There would be a premium on organizational ability, the kind of ability marked by effective registration and election-day activities. It would systematize the handling of money and give leverage to those collecting and disbursing excess sums. Parties with sufficient funds could underwrite campaign costs for local candidates, with effects on party discipline, a candidate's obligations to the party, and even the nomination process. Indeed, ample party funds to finance general election campaigns for candidates could lead away from open primaries and return control of nominations to party leaders, themselves subject to primary election. The net result would lower campaign spending and reduce competition among candidates for funds. These gains would have to be weighed against the denial of popular voting for party nominees, which has visceral appeal to most Americans.

A byproduct of fewer primary contests could be an easing of burdens of political finance. Primaries put each candidate on his own, to raise what funds he can in competition both with the party and rival candidates. The system dilutes reliance on party leaders and encourages independence from party policy. Moreover, primary battles are often so bitter, it is hard to restore party unity for the general election.

In some states, run-off primaries add to political expenses. Where run-off primaries are held, nomination used to be tantamount to election, with few general election costs, but this may be less so where parties are well matched. The candidate who has won a primary has a major advantage: his long exposure to the electorate and continuity of organizational and media operations save expenses in the general election.

Even competition at conventions can be expensive if the potential candidate has to spend many months or years cultivating a following in a large constituency. A candidate from upstate feels he must spend liberally to become known downstate or in the metropolitan area where there are more votes.

The ability of the party to supply funds to candidates tends to reduce the temptation to nominate candidates who are wealthy or can guarantee the financing of their campaigns. In the prenomination stage, the disparity in the financing of candidates may be telling and the influence of money critical. Candidates in the prenomination stage also have the least prospect for tax-based public assistance because definition of "major" and "minor" candidates must be arbitrary.

The Congressional Link

Congressional campaigns suggest a perplexing yet promising

link between the national and local party interest. They are local campaigns shared by the national party increasingly, while the candidates remain highly exposed to local sentiment reinforced by financial dependence upon special local interests. As the national party raises the ante in dollars and services for Congressional campaigns, so do other national interests (including party factions) ease the Congressional candidate's campaign burden.

The Capitol Hill committees of each party (the Senatorial Campaign Committee and the House Campaign Committee) are long-established sources of assistance to Congressional candidates. The failure of Republicans to win control of Congress led to the organization of a major new party unit in 1964, the Republican Congressional Boosters Club, for the express purpose of raising funds for nonincumbent Republican candidates for House seats. The established Republican Congressional Campaign Committee tended to assist incumbents more than aspirants. At first, the Boosters raised funds independently, though for an interval they solicited jointly with the Republican Associates. Originally intended to fund only nonincumbent House candidates, the Boosters now fund nonincumbent Senatorial candidates, too. In 1970 selected House challengers (those considered to have a reasonable chance to win) received as much as $10,000 each while selected Senate challengers received $25,000 to $30,000 each. The Republican Congressional Campaign Committee, meanwhile, gave as much as $7,000 to marginal and freshman incumbents. Other incumbents received about $3,500. The RCCC provides each House member with an annual drawing account for public relations expenses connected with re-election; marginal and freshman incumbents could draw about $4,000 each in 1970 and $3,000 in 1971, while other incumbents could draw about $2,500 in 1970 and $2,000 in 1971. Incumbent Senators received between $20,000 and $35,000 for the 1970 campaigns and air travel credit cards for limited periods before the election, for trips between Washington and home. Whether in the House or Senate, incumbent or not, specific candidates received through these national party committees funds that were earmarked for them by contributors. George Bush of Texas received at least $110,000 from the Senatorial Committee and Boosters, possibly a record for funds channeled through a national party for a Senatorial campaign.

Regularly or not, committees for various Republican factions supply campaign funds to favored candidates for Congress. In 1964 moderate Republicans formed several groups to help candidates whose Congressional campaigns were weakened by hostility to the Goldwater candidacy. Under new names, several Goldwater committees still distribute money to conservative candidates. There is no lack of national party or factional committees to aid Republican Congressional candidates.

On the Democratic side, before 1960, the National and Capitol Hill committees were each out for themselves. None was affluent despite Democratic control of Congress. Following 1960, the Democrats consolidated fund raising but not spending. The DNC agreed to provide certain funds and, under President Kennedy, the party held no separate Senatorial or Congressional fundraising dinners. President Johnson permitted a revival of the separate dinners. During 1965 the DNC deficit and jealousies impaired the consolidation policy, and in 1966 it was abandoned. In 1965 the DNC undertook a Congressional Assistance program that included a staff of writers and publicists to help Congressmen prepare newsletters, press releases, speeches, and scripts, to coach Congressmen on media and public relations techniques, and to help disseminate materials to constituents by mail, teletype, and voice recordings. This program lost most of its support, but it indicates what national committees as distinguished from Congressional committees could and should do for their Senators and Representatives.

The Democratic Congressional Campaign Committee has not provided House candidates as many services or as large annual budgets for election-related expenses as has the Republican. In 1970 many candidates received sums in the $1,000 to $2,000 range, but few drew more, and many nonincumbents got nothing.

Another Capitol Hill committee, the Democratic Study Group, gives limited assistance to liberal House Democrats. Established in 1959 as a policy group to whip up legislative votes and concerted floor action, it took little part in the 1960 campaign. In 1964 it spun off its own campaign committee using the same initials and called Democrats for Sound Government. Originally supported by funds from the non-partisan Committee for an Effective Congress, the DSG raised only a few dollars itself. By 1968, however, it raised $180,000 and spent $140,000 in contributions and assistance; it repeated this performance in 1970. Some candidates receive a nominal $50 contribution from DSG, but a few receive as much as $2,500 to $3,500. The DSG is tolerated rather than approved by the DNC and DCCC.

The Democratic Senatorial Campaign Committee found a minimum of $5,000 each to give to needy incumbents in 1970 and issued some air travel credit cards as well. Nonincumbents usually receive little if any money, but in 1966 Robert Duncan, a Representative who ran for U.S. Senate from Oregon, benefited from at least $31,000, mostly earmarked through the DSCC by friends of President Johnson. This campaign seemed to some a test of attitudes toward American policy toward Vietnam, because Duncan lost to Republican Mark Hatfield, an early dissenter from the war policy. This race at least demonstrated the use of disguised party channels to finance a candidate favored by the Administration for reasons of national policy.

In 1970 Democratic finances fared poorly in comparison with the Republican: Democratic Senatorial candidates received $428,000 from party committees, compared with $956,000 for Republican Senatorial candidates; Republican Party committees gave their candidates for the House about $1.7 million compared with $344,000 for the Democrats.

This familiar disparity was accentuated by the success of the Republican Boosters Club. In late 1967, in an effort to upgrade the ability of the national party to help candidates for the House, the Democrats tried to establish a Democratic Congressional Finance Committee, but feuding and procrastination prevented its taking shape.

Campaign assistance by national party committees is not confined to election years; some incumbents draw help in nonelection years also. Help includes research and speech materials, outside speakers, field workers, ideas in fund raising, photos taken with leaders in Washington, and taping broadcasts for replay in the home district. These services traditionally have been available mainly to incumbents but are being extended to others, especially by Republicans.

In the Senate, Democratic and Republican leaders agreed some years ago to a procedure whereby four photographers, hired to snap pictures of Senators greeting constituents or at work, were transferred from employment by the two Senate Campaign Committees to the public payroll in the Senate, to provide photos impartially.

Another traditional government subsidy of political services permits Capitol Hill campaign committees to operate in the Senate or House Office Buildings rent-free. The Republicans in early 1971 dedicated the new Eisenhower National Republican Center on Capitol Hill, which now houses their Senatorial, Congressional, and Boosters committees in addition to the RNC. The Republican House Conference, a policy group with electoral overtones, continues to use free space in the Cannon House Office Building, as does the Democratic Study Group. The Senate and House both provide studio space for taping broadcasts to send to local stations, an activity not unrelated to politics.

Given the extent of national party assistance to candidates for Congress now, it is possible that there will be further national intervention in Senate and House campaigns. The established Capitol Hill committees of both parties will no doubt continue their services. Though their own leaders are sometimes at odds with their national committees, the financial interdependence of the National and Capitol Hill committees tends to draw the Executive and Congressional wings of the parties together, and the drawstring could be centralized financing. Given the principle of allotting equal or at least minimal amounts to each category of candidate (incumbent or nonincumbent), factional bias in distribution of funds could abate.

Factional leaders are always alert to bias in distribution of party money. In 1970 Senator John Tower of Texas, Chairman of the Republican Senatorial Campaign Committee, was charged with favoring conservative candidates and giving only token contributions to liberal candidates. Though a committee of Senators served with him, Tower responded that he personally made the decisions about the distribution of funds. He admitted they were judgmental but said his judgments were based on the best information available as to the candidate's prospects, the candidate's financial resources, and his opponent's resources. When Tower's term as Chairman expired, candidates for the position vied in promising evenhanded distribution of funds to conservatives and liberals alike.

Significantly more national party money reaches Congressional candidates than a decade or two ago. Even as a percentage of total campaign costs, the national party contributions to individual candidates are probably greater than a few years ago. The question really is whether ties to the national party are preferable to local ties. This question will be pursued in this chapter after consideration of Congressional financing by national interests outside the parties.

Congressional Candidates

The unique complexion of each Congressional constituency determines the electoral pressures that operate on its representatives. These pressures are closely linked to the amounts and sources of money required for political expenses. They are strong when the local party controls the funds and the votes. State Republicans in Ohio and Democrats in Indiana provide major financial assistance to candidates for U.S. Senate and House; in Indiana, party committees are structured to coincide with Congressional district jurisdictions. Candidates are expected to contribute to the state committee or are assessed fees as delegates to the state convention. In contrast, many candidates for Congress elsewhere receive little if any party money, but may even be expected to contribute funds to the party. Members of a party's Congressional delegation often are expected to sell or purchase blocs of tickets to party fund-raising events.

National party funds are especially welcome by incumbents, although Margaret Chase Smith hardly needs to spend more than the $5,000 she receives from the Republican Senatorial Campaign Committee, as her situation is exceptional. Strongly entrenched Senators like John McClellan return their allocations from the Democratic Senatorial Campaign Committee. As Southern Democrats in key leadership positions attract private contributions they do not need for their own campaigns, they relay them to the Senatorial committee or steer them to favored colleagues. In California, Jess Unruh built solid power by so channeling funds to other state legislators. Senator Russell Long has done the same on Capitol Hill.

Non-party committees such as political arms of business, labor, farm organizations, medical societies, peace groups, the National Committee for an Effective Congress, or Americans for Constitutional Action also contribute to Congressional elections. Special cause committees proliferated in the 1960's. With each campaign, new ones appear; in 1968 there were 37 labor committees, 36 business or professional committees, and 8 miscellaneous interest group committees, a total of 81 non-party committees directly contributing a total of $3.6 million to Senatorial and Congressional candidates. For 1970 the greatest increases came in the business or professional categroy; 16 new committees represented non-party interests from dairy farmers to bankers. In the miscellaneous category, there were 19 new committees, 12 of which were peace-oriented.

According to federal files, which are not free of error and understatement, the heaviest contributions from national-level party, labor, business or professional, and miscellaneous committees combined in 1968 were reported by Democratic Senator Wayne Morse of Oregon ($206,469) and Democratic Senatorial candidate from Ohio, John Gilligan (receiving $204,594), both defeated. These candidates conducted expensive primary campaigns. The figures reflect contributions to primary and general election campaigns and, in Morse's case, to a vote recount. For the election alone, Senator Birch Bayh of Indiana, with $108,045 received most among Democrats. Robert Packwood of Oregon, with a total of $60,010 from national-level committees, led the Republicans. Senator Everett Dirksen of Illinois was next, with $53,000.[3]

It appears that Republicans receive more dollars from national party sources than do Democrats, but certain liberal Democrats receive more dollars from all national-level committees, the bulk of them from labor and peace-oriented committees. Based on 1960-1968 data, certain Republican candidates for Congress have received as much as 70 percent of their national-level contributions from party sources, but others receive less either because of local resources or because chances of winning are slight. In either party, many candidates for the House receive $5,000 to $15,000 in campaign contributions from sources other than national party committees.

Several Democratic Senators from the Rocky Mountain states, where campaigning still is relatively inexpensive, have collected as much as half of their political funds from Washington cocktail parties, mainly in advance of the actual campaign. These Senators set up nondescriptive committees such as the Committee for Good Government, Committee for Civic Improvement, or the D. C. Montana Committee, which collect and then transfer funds to candidates' committees. Until 1972 the givers were not reported in official filings under the law. Funds from industrialists, lobbyists, and their national organizations in Washington, D.C. are their main sources because labor is not strong in those states, and local Democratic funds cannot match local Republican sources. Some Western candidates, often incumbents, also receive funds from parties held on their behalf by wealthy supporters outside of the District of Columbia.

One example related to the 1970 election is instructive. Senator Vance Hartke (D.-Ind.) received $80,000 in contributions from a fund-raising dinner held in his honor in Chicago more than a year before the election. Hartke is chairman of a Senate subcommittee handling rail and trucking legislation, and among those attending were various leaders of the railroad and trucking industries. But Hartke also received at least $61,000 in national-level labor contributions during the 1970 campaign, including money from railroad unions and the Teamsters, the counterparts in the concerned industries.

The task of raising funds for campaign purposes falls to national-level committees, party and non-party, and the candidate himself, with occasional help from local party units. Given a choice of two systems, which would local politicians prefer? In one the national party has sufficient money, either from its direct fund raising or through quotas collected through the party system, to pay most campaign expenses. In the other, local party units have ample funds received from broad solicitation. Given a choice between directly financing Congressional campaigns themselves (along with other local campaigns) or sending quota funds to the state and national committees in expectation of a flow back to assist local candidates, there is little doubt which choice most local parties would prefer. If they value control or influence over their candidate, why let the national party take over at local expense?

Funds from electoral interest groups other than party complicate this choice in actual practice. Candidates sensitive to the public interest may find it difficult to choose between national or local labor funds or funds from a national trade association as against funds from local business men. Either choice may be contrary to the public interest. One would assume that the national American Medical Political Action Committee (AMPAC), for instance, may be more enlightened than many of its state affiliates, if only because it is more open to political pressures and public scrutiny. On the other hand, a state medical group in New York or California may be more progressive than the officers of the national body, the American Medical Association.

Such are the alternatives in the present system of financing politics. Unfortunately there are few desirable sources of funds other than small contributions.

Baker and Dodd Cases

The abuses invited by present methods of political financing were publicized by charges against Senator Thomas J. Dodd and former Senate aide Robert G. Baker, mentioned earlier. Other relevant activities to surface include the $18,000 disclosed in 1952 as contributed to Senator Richard Nixon [4] and a $2,500 "contribution" offered to (and refused by) the late South Dakota Senator Francis Case to influence a vote on a natural gas bill, as he himself disclosed voluntarily on the Senate floor in 1956.[5]

The Senate Ethics Committee found, and the Senate agreed, that from 1961 through 1965, Senator Dodd or his representatives received at least $450,273 from seven fund-raising events and that he authorized the payment or used at least $116,083 "for his personal purposes." [6] A jury decided that Baker, who had been Secretary to the Senate majority, had received some $99,600 in political contributions and had retained for personal purposes about $80,000.[7]

The techniques in the game of giving and influencing are infinitely variable. During an exchange in his trial Baker was charged with asking California savings and loan officials for campaign funds for Senate candidates of either party. According to the prosecutor, Baker had told one executive that the savings and loan industry had not been making political contributions "commensurate with its importance" and had asked, "Why don't you get on the bandwagon so you will have friends in Washington?"[8] There were also published reports that Baker had set up a "cinch amendment" adversely affecting the tax status of the savings and loan industry, to imply that, with appropriate campaign contributions, the amendment would be killed. Baker may not have been alone in creating "cinch amendment" situations to attract campaign money, nor in his ability to have legislation dropped in response to contributions. In one situation, legislative muscle is flexed to extort funds. In the other, funds are volunteered to obtain favorable legislation.

The Dodd case revealed comparable practices, exceptional or not. Dodd's office compiled a list of potential contributors among businessmen and constituents who have received favors. A fund raiser was hired on a commission of 25 percent of every dollar he raised. The Senator's personal staff and staff of a subcommittee he chaired were used for personal political purposes, a practice not uncommon on Capitol Hill. It has been suggested that Dodd received contributions from members of industries his subcommittee was investigating and that certain investigations were set up as "cinch amendments" have been, to be toned down or called off when contributions arrived. Forgetful and uninquisitive treasurers were appointed to his political committees.[9]

It has been widely commented that even if Dodd and Baker were innocent of diverting political funds to their personal use, there is something terribly wrong when businessmen and constituents customarily fork over large sums and Senators and staff employees presumably are willing to accept them. The inescapable implication is that the contributors expect something for their money. The $99,600 collected by Baker came wholly from the officials of savings and loan companies in California concerned with proposed legislation that would have increased their taxes. Eight Senators named as the supposed beneficiaries of the funds successfully denied receiving the money, which averaged above $12,000 per Senator from one industry in one state. The "cinch" legislation, sponsored by the late Robert S. Kerr, himself a multimillionaire, was shelved. Baker's defense attorney sought to imply, without being explicit, that the money may have gone into Kerr's pocket as a political contribution. Whether or not that was true—the jury decided it was not—the fact remains that a small group of businessmen were able to mobilize almost $100,000 in cash and, presumably within the bounds of legality, hand it over as a political contribution directly related to a specific legislative decision. The brown envelopes used to pass the money were off the record. No public accounting was required.

Beyond question, the public tends to believe that what has been disclosed in the Baker and Dodd cases is only the visible edge of common practice in political financing. There exists, particularly in the Dodd case and in the 1952 Nixon case, a shadow land in which no fixed rules determine whether contributions are for personal or political purposes; even the Internal Revenue Service found it impossible to establish this distinction in a suit against former Governor William Stratton of Illinois.[10]

For an elective public official, separating the personal from the political is difficult. For an ambitious politician, every act may have political significance—whether a regular newsletter is mailed, how many Christmas cards are sent, what affairs he attends, whom he entertains. Two uses of money from the 1952 Nixon Fund illustrate: the need to send 10,000 Christmas cards and employment of a maid at home for baby-sitting and entertaining. For an ambitious, rising politician, as Nixon was then, who can say that his actions overstepped moral bounds; without personal wealth or going into debt, how else could his political cost be assumed except through a fund set up by supporters? How else could he compete against wealthier rivals? Even wealthy candidates rely on such support.[11] For a candidate, politics is a business, yet political costs are not deductible on income tax forms as are business expenses.[12] In this expense-account society, there is strong temptation to use a political committee as an expense account for semiofficial purposes.

One Congressman recalls that Bobby Baker insisted on hand-ing cash to Senators in person, even traveling to their states with cash rather than send a check. Whether or not he worried that checks provided a record, the personal touch was a form of influence in which Baker persisted, perhaps in expectation of future favors. Large contributors use similar tactics.

Public service provides ample psychological rewards, but some feel the financial rewards are insufficient. Public elective or appointive office is for many both a financial and personal sacrifice. Sufficient remuneration, if it did not attract better candidates, would at least lessen the need or temptation to seek outside income while on the public payroll. Members of Congress from distant states do not have enough travel funds to touch home base as often as they may want to. Long-distance telephones and jet planes have eased communications with their districts but at substantial cost which a challenger back home is spared.

The Dodd case prompted the proposal in 1966 of reforms requiring disclosure by candidates of personal income, gifts, and honorariums, as a means of bringing financial influences into the open air whether in the form of gifts at testimonials, fees, or whatever. Of the few members of Congress who voluntarily disclose their income, some report actual dollar amounts including assets; others report in general terms, listing the companies whose stock they hold without noting numbers of shares. Former Senator Paul Douglas made annual disclosures which were helpful in understanding the exigencies of political life. Douglas lived quietly in Washington, yet reported he could not have met expenses without income from lecturing and writing. He also revealed the political contributions he felt impelled to make to campaigns other than his own.

Senator Douglas' expenses for 1966 reveal heavy election costs. From personal income he spent $3,413.31 for radio and television time; $2,156.47 for entertainment of constituents and others; $1,505 in contributions to political organizations and candidates.[13] This was a frugal budget. In 1961, Senator Jacob K. Javits recounted how he augmented his Senatorial salary to fulfill what he considered the requirements of office; to supplement salaries of assistants, $8,000; travel, $3,500; petty cash, including non-official mail not enjoying franking privileges, taxis, dinners for staff members working late, $2,000; telephone in excess of allowance, $1,200; contributions to county, state, and national politics, $2,500; to print and process 350,000 copies of an annual report (mailed under frank), $4,000; newspapers and periodicals, $500.[14] His budget was relatively modest. While some of these expenses may appear to be frills, they are necessities for a conscientious or ambitious Senator.

If members of Congress cannot be insulated completely from personal or political pressures, should the public be denied knowledge of financial practices that may corrupt government or favor powerful interests excessively? Would personal income disclosure make officeholders second-class citizens, as some maintain? There is no obligation to enter public or elective service if a person is unwilling to disclose his economic interests. A Gallup Poll, conducted after the Baker and Dodd exposures, found nearly seven of ten citizens felt members of Congress should file a complete statement of assets and holdings every year.[15] Service in Congress is not a part-time activity. The day of "citizen-legislators" is past, as it is also in many state legislatures, but remuneration, both salary and expenses, is not commensurate with the responsibility and the costs of political life.

Congressional campaign financing attracts extra attention because eyes focus readily on Washington, on the large number of candidates every two years, on exposures like the Baker case. Still Congress resists legislation affecting the members' personal and political lives. Presidential elections are easier to reform than elections of 535 members of Congress, who create administrative difficulties simply by their numbers. Though Congress is slow to reform itself, a salutary improvement in national political life could serve as a model for reform of elections to state legislatures.

THE POLITICS OF SPECIAL INTEREST

In a pluralistic, democratic society like that of the United States, it is natural that individuals and groups with abundant economic resources will try to use their wealth to influence the course of government. While money is a common denominator in shaping political power, other ingredients are vital as well: leadership, skill, information, public office, votes, public opinion, legal maneuvers. The wealth of one group can be matched by the human resources or electoral power of another. The interests of various segments of industry, labor and agriculture vary widely. Both major parties find supporters in every industry and interest group. Monied interests need to enlist the support of other constituencies. The demands of wealth must be tempered to demands that are politically and electorally viable. The fact that a minority representing wealth must get a majority on its side by constitutional means, means that this minority can lose to the majority in the same way, as it often does, despite high levels of political expenditures.

Representative government is built upon three constituencies: the electoral, the financial, and the organizational, which in turn are composed of three basic sources of political power: numbers of people, resources, and social organizations.[1] Thus numbers of persons, situated in electoral constituencies, find political expression through their elected representatives who are grouped according to political party. The power of social organizations, or interest groups, stems from the combination of two factors, people and resources. Resources are brought to bear upon the political process in many ways, through many available channels.

When wealthy persons seek to translate their economic power into political power, one of their tools may be money contributions. The translation of individual or group demands into public policy occurs in various ways, mediated in part by ideological references and by group alignment. Since policy preferences are in competition with conflicting claims for political action, individuals or groups with wealth use it to achieve policy goals by promoting nominations or elections of candidates with views congenial to theirs. Between election campaigns they cultivate the sympathies of public officials and the public. In this process, the initial advantage usually lies with monied interests.

National income for both parties has been heavily dependent on large contributors, defined as those who contribute in sums of $500 or more. The proportion of such sums contributed to selected committees for national campaigns from 1948 to 1968 varied between 74 and 28 percent, more often nearer to the higher figure. In 1948, while Democrats were in power, 69 percent of the totals contributed to them by individuals came in sums of $500 or more; in 1956, while Republicans were in power, the proportion was 74 percent; the Democrats in 1964 were again at 69 percent.[2]

In contrast, in 1964, the Republicans derived only 28 percent from contributions of $500 or more, because of the large outpouring of small contributors to Goldwater and the loss of large contributors to President Johnson.

Despite the continued success of Republican small contribution drives in 1968, the percentage of funds coming from small gifts was substantially less than in 1964 because the large contributors had returned.[3] Analyses for 1968 show 47 percent of the dollar value of individual contributions to the Republicans came in sums of $500 and more. The large Democratic contributions dropped slightly to 61 percent in 1968, but if their figures were to count loans, the percentage of funds gained in large chunks would be much higher.

These figures for 1960, 1964, and 1968 are derived from data in the files of the Citizens' Research Foundation. Its data has become more comprehensive in each succeeding Presidential year. For 1968, a computer printout contains listings of about 15,000 individuals who made a total of about 21,000 different contributions, each in sums of $500 or more. This is an even larger collection of large contributors than the official compilation of the Gore Committee in 1956 [4] or the Heard compilations for 1952 or 1956.[5] The list includes every contribution of that amount contained in reports filed with the Clerk of the House of Representatives and the Secretary of the Senate, as well as available information from selected major states and from other special lists.

In the analyses to follow, data do not include contributions for less than $500 from these sources, even if several gifts in the aggregate might exceed $500. Contributions to state and local campaigns for offices other than President were included as available but not in comprehensive form; in other words, donations to Congressional campaigns, more fully reported to the state authorities than to Washington, as many were, are incomplete. Except for the McCarthy and Romney campaigns, data do not include contributions to prenomination campaigns not covered under certain state laws. These exclusions mean that many who made contributions of $500 or more for primaries or for state and local campaigns might have contributed more than shown on the Presidential record. Some information received in interviews was added to printout totals. Where precise amounts could not be verified, minimal known amounts are given with a sign (+) to signify that contributions were probably larger than indicated. Yet the following analyses are based on the best available data, and within their limitations, offer comparability with other election years as far back as 1956.

For 1968, of the 15,000 donors listed, 424 gave reported sums aggregating $10,000 or more for a total of $12,187,863+.[6] Of this lot,

> 250 gave $10,000 to $19,999 for a total of $3,284,535+;
> 85 individuals gave $20,000 to $29,999, for a total of $2,020,131+;
> 89 individuals gave $30,000 or more, for a total of $6,883,197+.

As to party preference, 232 gave to the Republican cause and 135 to the Democratic, while 53 contributed to both major parties or to a major party and the American Independent Party. Several contributed to miscellaneous nonparty committees as well, and others contributed to miscellaneous committees exclusively; the amounts are included in the totals.

In 1956 the Gore Committee selected for study twelve family groups: duPont, Field, Ford, Harriman, Lehman, Mellon, Olin, Pew, Reynolds, Rockefeller, Vanderbilt, and Whitney. The rec-

ords available since then indicate the following distribution for
the twelve family groupings:

	1956	1960	1964	1968
Republican	$1,040,526	$548,510	$445,280	$2,580,785
Democratic	107,109	78,850	133,500	149,700
Miscellaneous	6,100	22,000	24,146	35,651
Total	$1,153,735	$649,360	$602,926	$2,766,136

The total amounts contributed by members of these families
in 1960 and 1964 were only about half as much as they had given
in 1956; in 1960 and 1964, their gifts to Democratic committees
and candidates increased proportionately to the total but in
1968, they reverted with respect both to totals and to disparities
between the major parties.

In these compilations for 1968, the Rockefeller family contributions include the massive contribution of Mrs. John D. Rockefeller, Jr. to Nelson's Presidential prenomination campaign, which
in itself adds $1,482,625 to the total and thereby distorts com-
parison with other years when such information was not available. Nevertheless, in 1968, without Mrs. Rockefeller's gift included, the various family totals increased dramatically over
1960 and 1964 and returned to close to 1956 levels.

These family selections do not reflect certain other families
recently active in politics—the Dillons, the Watsons, and others;[7]
nor do they reflect certain new wealth such as the Frawleys,
the Salvatoris, and others,[8]—largely originating in the South-
west, engaged in oil, cattle, and real estate. Some of this latter
group helped to bankroll the radical right, and some were active
in the Goldwater campaign in 1964. They helped to create means
for challenging the moderate Republicans who had controlled Republican Presidential nominations at least since 1940.

The Olin and Pew families are the only ones strictly Republican for 1956, 1960, 1964, and 1968. Alexander Heard reports
that for many years the duPont family stood out for its political giving, not solely because of its wealth but because of its
size. In 1960 and 1964 the duPont contributions diminished
while the Mellons and Pews came to the fore. In 1968 donations
increased from all three families. Some families, like the Leh-
mans, drop down the scale when the most politically active, a

patriarch like Herbert H. Lehman, dies. His survivors do not have the same imperatives or alliances and can more easily refuse to give. Certain families suddenly turn up with Democratic members after years of straight Republican giving. In general, Democrats have improved their position with these families, while Republicans suffered in 1960 and 1964 but recouped in 1968.

In 1957 *Fortune* interviewed 50 out of at least 250 Americans who possessed personal capital of at least $50,000,000. About two-thirds admitted to being campaign givers. *Fortune* also listed 76 persons with wealth estimated to exceed $75,000,000, two-thirds of whom are known to have been contributors to politics.[9]

In 1968 *Fortune* listed 66 individuals each with wealth of at least $150,000,000.[10] Their rate of contribution is very high; 46 (70 percent) are known to have given funds in 1968. These 46 individuals account for $1,138,502+[11], more money than any other group analysed in this chapter. Of course, as the wealthy are most visible, their political behavior merits attention. They are most likely to be asked to contribute and are most able to give.

What are their motives and those of other large contributors or special interest groups supplying money to politics? How effective are they in achieving their ends? Do they have an unfair advantage in the competition for power and favors? What are the relationships between those who give and those who receive?

In most large contributors, motives are mixed and complex. Often the contributor admits giving only to further the principles or ideology of the party or candidate he supports. Often he says he gives simply because he is asked and can afford to do so. The contributor probably does not know how much of what he says is rationalization and how much truth, nor does anyone else. Certainly, the contributions earn some return, some gratification in party or governmental influence or in personal prestige or ego-satisfaction, although occasional donors may feel cheated.

Some factors which impel men to give can be sorted out. First, there are goals that are extraneous to the party or candidate. Among these are belief in the two-party system, a sense of responsibility, feelings of duty, patriotism, or a desire for good government, and friendship with non-political motivation. Such goals might include ego satisfaction or even exhibitionism. (One donor at a rally carried a check between his teeth, saying, "I put my money where my mouth is.")

Second, there are goals that result in moving the party or candidates or some faction of the party into power. These may consist of ideological identification with faction or party, or the belief that the party's or candidate's accession to power will in some way create direct or indirect benefits.

Third, there are goals that result in political, legislative, judicial, or administrative action. These consist of moving agents into positions of authority in party or government, or into contact with those in the high ranks, for purposes of personal gain, power, prestige, or deference. The goals are not mutually exclusive, and usually are mixed.

Diverse strategies and interests are reflected in patterns of giving. Certain individuals give only to the party and others only to candidates; some give annually but more give only in election years or on special occasions; and some at times give to both parties. Some give to sure losers, others only to probable winners. The mode of giving varies according to individual sympathies, reasons for giving, available money, and who the candidates are.

Some political donors give anonymously to promote a cause. In 1966, for example, Republican Edward Brooke of Massachusetts benefited from Democrats who wanted to aid the election of a well-qualified Negro to the U. S. Senate. Other large contributors who normally favor Democrats sent donations to Republican U. S. Senate candidates in appreciation of their views on Vietnam. Gov. Mark Hatfield of Oregon and Charles Percy of Illinois, for example, benefited by opposing Democratic candidates who took a harder line on the war. A generous donor sent them campaign funds through channels that would not reveal his name; he did not care to admit in New York, where he is active in Democratic party politics, that he was aiding Republicans. The contribution in Oregon, where his company had a plant, served a double purpose; the donation was made through the local plant manager, with the effect of being principled and self-serving at the same time.

Some donors give publicly to promote causes or candidates. Perhaps the most prominent is Stewart R. Mott, son of one of the founders of General Motors, who has compiled and made available lists of his large contributions to liberal candidates since 1968. That year he itemized his political gifts, a total of $364,700. In 1969, his contributions amounted to some $55,000, and his 1970 total of $49,319 is itemized in Appendix B. When the CRF published its listing of contributors of $500 or more for 1968, several listed donors informed the Foundation that they had contributed much more: one listed at about $17,000 claimed he had actually contributed $50,000, and one listed at about $30,000 claimed he gave about $25,000 more. While neither gave a complete listing, at least they owned up to more than on the record. One was indignant that his full total was not published. Not only are their motives varied: large contributors are not all secretive and some are even candid about their gifts and their reasons.

Mary W. Lasker, a generous but practical woman, determined years ago to promote federal spending in the fields of health and medical research. Realizing that her entire fortune, large as it was, could not make much of a dent in the total need, she decided to use political contributions and lobbyists, both professional and volunteer, to stimulate government action. Through judicious campaign contributions, perhaps $25,000 to $50,000 per election year, she succeeded in tapping a gusher: hundreds of millions of tax dollars were spent on biological research and hospital programs at her urging.

Other idealists contribute out of principle or party loyalty to hopeless candidates, perennial losers, or extremist groups that have little influence or hope of winning elections. Yet without the staying power of such donors—Republicans in the Solid South in the 1950's or wealthy Democrats in the 1920's—the political system would be far less competitive.

Other contributors are interested in politics for the purpose of social climbing. They are satisfied by small favors such as low-numbered license plates, an invitation to the Governor's mansion, sitting on a dais during a speech, or purely honorific government appointments. In the Kennedy-Johnson Administrations, numerous financial supporters received what have been called "political non-jobs," defined as bestowing "the status symbols of high office without the job itself." [12] These honorary positions range from membership on White House commissions to serving as special Presidential representatives at foreign ceremonial functions or being honored members of inspection tours at missile ranges—"jobs" requiring only a few days at a time. One fund raiser reports that he is amazed at what people will pay to be in a reception line, or even to go through a line if the person at its head is the President. Many were attracted to the President's Club by this motive.

Appointment to public office is an honor coveted by others. In 1957 President Eisenhower appointed Maxwell H. Gluck, the owner of a dress shop chain, the United States Ambassador to Ceylon. When Mr. Gluck was called before a Senate committee for confirmation, he could not give the names of the Prime Ministers of India or Ceylon. Neverthless, he was confirmed by the Senate and served for a year. Few doubted that the appointment was based on his $26,000 in contributions to Republican causes in 1956.

Edward J. Flynn reports that after the 1932 Presidential election, a small, informal committee of those close to President-elect Franklin D. Roosevelt was formed to consider federal appointments for what Flynn called the 34 original "investors" in Roosevelt's campaign. This group became known as "FRBC": "For Roosevelt Before Chicago" (site of the 1932 Democratic nominating convention). Said Flynn, "There was a more or less tacit understanding that whenever possible they should be taken care of."[13]

Such incidents support the legend of contributors in effect buying government posts. That system may not be as undesirable as some think. As one of the master politicians of modern times, James A. Farley, has testified: "The patronage is a reward to those who have worked for a party victory. It is also an assistance in building party machinery for the next election. It is also—and this the public usually forgets—the test by which a party shows its fitness to govern. Every bad appointment comes home to roost eventually . . . As . . . a politician I would reward those who have worked for the Democratic party . . . Realizing that party success is largely dependent on party unity, I would fight to see that patronage was equitably distributed. I would try to diminish envy and rancor by giving rewards to ability." [14]

It is also true, however, that the increasing complexity of government and the increasing rewards of private enterprise have tended to diminish the number of wealthy persons seeking appointive office. Those rich enough to make large political contributions are sometimes unwilling to make the sacrifices demanded by government jobs: drastic reduction in annual income, residence away from home, and conflict-of-interest laws that may require selling income-producing securities. In fact, some observers are less concerned that too many jobs are given to political contributors than that too few competent administrators among them are willing to take appointment to responsible posts.

Although some spots still are filled by political appointees who are not qualified, civil servants cannot and should not fill all policy-making positions. Many posts can and should be manned by intelligent citizens who can execute the policies demanded by the electors. That a citizen is wealthy, or has contributed or solicited money, should not disqualify him from holding high position.

One obvious recourse has been appointment of professors, technical experts, professional and defeated politicians, and career public servants, most of whom cannot afford large contributions. Many diplomatic appointments go to career officers, who are not allowed to contribute. Some key posts go to members of the opposition party—even to their heavy contributors. The prime example is C. Douglas Dillon, appointed Secretary of the Treasury by John Kennedy even though he and Mrs. Dillon had contributed $26,550 to the Republican party and the 1960 Nixon campaign. In 1964, while Secretary of the Treasury, Dillon was one of the largest Democratic contributors. (In 1968 he supported Nixon again.)

In the 1960's ambassadorial posts awarded large contributors were relatively few. Of the first 27 non-career Chiefs of Foreign Missions appointed by President Kennedy, only 7 had made recorded contributions of $500 or more. Of some 35 similar appointments by President Johnson during 1964-65, only 10 went to large contributors. Of some 34 such Nixon appointments, 15 had contributed a total of $251,675, much more than in the Kennedy or Johnson administrations.

Major contributors have not accounted for many other major appointments in recent years. Of 253 major appointments made by President Kennedy through mid-1961, 35, or 14 percent, were found to have contributed at least $500 or more in the 1960 campaign, and a few had actually given to the Republicans. Under President Johnson, only 24 of 187, or about 13 percent, major appointees through September, 1965, had given $500 or more in the 1964 campaign. Other appointees, of course may not appear in the analysis because they either stayed in the same job or may have contributed less than $500. Even when Nixon became President, the trend continued; few of Nixon's major appointees were large contributors. Of 345 major appointments confirmed as of December 12, 1969, 34 appointees (or about 10 percent) contributed $500 or more each for a total of $326,975—more than twice the total amounts given by appointees in either 1960 or 1964 but still a low contribution rate. The only Democratic contribution was from a split contributor: John D. J. Moore, who gave $1,000 to a Nixon committee and $500 to a Humphrey committee, was appointed Ambassador to Ireland.[15]

Many wealthy contributors give for what is the most obvious reason—someone has asked them. This someone is a business associate, a social friend, another rich person, in other words, a peer. The elite fund raiser, generally himself a volunteer, serves as a significant link between the party system and wealthy segments of the population. He is a power broker, with knowledge of and access to the financial community, and he often becomes a strong force in the process of making decisions; he influences the character of an administration or the results of a legislative session by making known his attitudes and those of the contributors he has come to represent.

One of the most influential roles played by a party's financial constituency affects party nominations. The fund raiser may be asked which potential candidate will attract the most money. The contributor, in turn, is asked whether he would contribute if one or another possible nominee is named.

Members of the financial constituency are often national committeemen and women for their state party organizations, convention delegates, or members of platform committees. Of Republican and Democratic National Convention delegates answering a questionnaire in 1964, about 80 percent in each party were contributors of cash, and between 19 and 22 percent had contributed at least in sums of $500 or more in 1960 and 1962.[16]

Another type of giver may have no current or prospective concern with government but feels that the day may come when he can use a friend in court. What these contributors buy, writes Heard, "is not as tangible as its often supposed. Mostly what they buy is 'access.' Politicians who get the money, along with solicitors who raise it and contributors themselves, state invariably that in return for his funds a contributor can get, if he seeks it, access to the party, legislative or administrative officials concerned with a matter of interest to him. Other lobbyist call it 'entree' and another called it 'a basis for talking.' Access may not give the contributor what he wants, as the number of disgruntled (and talkative) contributors indicates. And if he is eligible for what he wants, a government contract or a job, he will often get it anyway. The main result of access, said a former national treasurer noted for his persuasion with the fatter cats, is to 'speed things up' . . . Access can be obtained through any type of political service, and many politicians argue stoutly that campaign work at the right level produces greater influence. But large contributions pave a sure road to the decision-making centers of government for those who want to present their case, which is often all they need . . ." [17]

Access, however, is not open to all. It may be granted automatically to some and denied to others; it can be a means to political power and influence or it can be squandered. Deference tends to be accorded those who have achieved high status or positions of leadership and wealth—social characteristics of many members of the elite financial constituencies.

Today, the political climate is not friendly to blatant purchasing of outright favors or high pressure collection tactics, though always there are exceptions. In the Bobby Baker and Thomas Dodd cases, the motives of givers and takers were rightly impugned, but money is not often used this directly, often does not need to be. Rather the atmosphere has become one in which it is hard for legislators and top government decision makers to distinguish between their honest convictions and their concord with financial sympathizers and supporters. The congenial attitude, the similar frame of reference, the comparable point of view—these are as responsible as any other factors, and this is why the key influence through money contributions is applied in assisting candidates for nomination or election whose views are congenial. No special pressure is necessary when it is possible to predict how elected officials will decide on given issues.

In recent decades, there have been no publicly known cases in which a Congressman was convicted of accepting a campaign contribution made for the express purpose of buying his vote on a particular issue. One case did arise in 1956, when a lobbyist offered Republican Senator Francis Case a $2,500 campaign contribution (which he rejected) in order to influence his vote on a natural gas bill. The uproar was notable, and eventually President Eisenhower vetoed the legislation on the grounds that "acceptable standards of propriety" had been violated.[18]

Of course, a gift to a candidate does not guarantee that he will agree with the giver or, if he does at one point, that he will not change his mind at another. When he moves to higher office, a politician may adapt his views to suit a new constituency. Robert Griffin takes a much more moderate position as a Senator with a Detroit constituency than as a Representative of a conservative upstate Michigan district. Charles Goodell went further in a similar direction once he moved from an upstate New York seat in the House to the Senate. In most parts of the country, the moderate politician is preferred; no amount of reactionary money, for instance, could cause him to adopt rightwing views contrary to his convictions if the price would be defeat at the polls.

Elected officials normally try to avoid going against consensus of community leadership or against the interests of a large industry in the community, regardless of contributions made or offered. Politicians have their own concepts of the public interest, most do have principles, and on most issues do follow conscience. The "payment" they receive for favors performed is most often interpreted simply as an expression of gratification from a friend or a supporter for a good turn, for helping a party, or for a host of reasons unrelated to personal gain.

Clearly, most politicians do not consciously sell their votes no matter how much money is offered. Many politicians, on the other hand, who do what they honestly think is right, never realize that they are mere spokesmen for their financial supporters. A legislator can avoid a conflict of interest by investing in government bonds, but he cannot change the conditioning that leads him to believe that what is good for his former company or present backers is good for the country.

The complex tapestry of political contributions and power is not a pattern of simple generosity or selfishness but more often a blend of both. Quite as individuals give money with a variety of motives, so do special interest groups—business, labor unions, trade associations, and other organizations of persons banded together for ideological as well as selfish motives.

Groups, like men, are moved by principle as well as by interest, and interests are easily rationalized into principles. Individual and group action are often fused, but each represents a form of political articulation inherent in the American system. Usually the organized pressure groups, rather than individual contributors, are the powers able and willing to mobilize enough economic resources to influence public policy by whatever means. Still there are occasions, especially in the action-laden avenues of government leading to large economic rewards, where an individual contributor can head the parade. When it refrains from actions that conflict with other powerful interests, individual influence can be profitable, particularly in affairs of low visibility which the public neither knows nor values.

The leaderships of interest groups have attributes similar to those of elite fund raisers: they have access to wealth among members, they can collect money from each member, and can convey it in amounts tantalizing to politicians.

When two strong interests collide, as they often do, the legislator may do a balancing act on the fence. The president of an auto company in Michigan can get access to political leaders there and in Washington, even if he has contributed to the opposition party, but the automobile industry does not always speak with a single voice. Companies differ on government policies. Management and labor, of course, have conflicting interests. A Democratic legislator from Michigan may favor labor and owe his election to labor's political backing, but he will at least try to steer a course designed not to hurt the auto industry and its payroll. When opposing interests are at odds, as they frequently are, the politician may have to choose a distasteful course of action which one side or the other considers harmful. Then the large contribution may tip the balance.

Fortunately, the concept of "the public interest" and public opinion can counter special interest pressures backed by massive campaign contributions. Henry Ford was one of the largest Democratic contributors in 1964, but he could not overcome the influence of Ralph Nader and his book, especially after the General Motors investigation by Nader aroused the public and moved the Congress to act on automobile safety legislation in 1966.[19] All the contributions of all the managements of all the companies in the automobile industry could not change the vote for safety regulations. Of course, industry pressure influenced safety standards once the program proceeded.

The concept of public interest is so broad that no organization appears to have the omniscient wisdom to serve as a "People's Lobby" persistently and on a sustained basis. Without such pressures the needs of the consumer, the small taxpayer, the poor, or the public at large may not be voiced at all or only insufficiently. Under these circumstances, the entrenched special interest holds the aces as well as the trumps. The ideal is to build an alert populace and a body of public officials independent of special interests; this is the aim of disclosure laws concerning political contributors, lobbying, and the income of elected officials. The media which are dependent on advertising and are owned or controlled by wealth cannot be depended upon to champion public interests except as the public good coincides with theirs. In recent years, public officials, often at the prodding of public interest law firms and allied organizations, have made gestures to strengthen representation of the interests of women, labor, the poor, minorities, and children. Common Cause is perhaps the best-known organization that claims to serve as a people's lobby. Some such organizations have political arms, such as the League of Conservation Voters, and contribute funds to friendly candidates. Such activities should be applauded and encouraged.

Politics are graced also by a variety of contributions in kind. A billboard company may provide a candidate with free 12-sheet space during his campaign. When a bill regulating that industry comes to the floor, beneficiaries of such largesse find it hard to vote against the interests of the outdoor advertising lobby.

The ability of the wealthy to win tax concessions or to prevent tax reform has led insiders to refer to the "Coca Cola clause," the "oil depletion clause," or the "speculative builder clause." The "Louis B. Mayer Amendments," added to revenue bills by friendly Congressmen, provided a personal tax windfall of about $2 million, for which no one except Louis B. Mayer happened to be eligible. Tax legislation benefits or hinders many special interests, not only through setting rates but also (and sometimes particularly) by creating loopholes and complex special provisions.[20] A member of the Senate Finance Committee, asked why he uncharacteristically sponsored several tax amendments that would favor a particular industry, explained in an unguarded moment: "That's the way we finance our campaigns. Hell, I wish there was a tax bill every year." (In most recent years there have been major tax bills.)

Contributions come after election, too. Many a Representative or Senator has received congratulations after his election from the spokesman of a group with an offer to help pay off his campaign debts. Bobby Baker, then secretary to the Senate majority, was reported to have conveyed such an offer to newly-elected Sen. Thomas J. McIntyre (D.-N.H.). McIntyre refused.

Fears of scandal as well as principle make politicians circumspect about accepting gifts, while public concern with the role of cold cash tends to ignore how mass-based interests wield political power with little or no money. Heard studied mass member organizations that rely chiefly on the size of their following as a source of political strength—labor, veterans—and found few or no contributors among their leaders, although agriculture and labor organizations spend liberally on political campaigns. Even the data on campaign giving by business in the past several years suggests that the cash influence of special interest groups may be overrated.[21] It is easy but simple-minded to exaggerate their role. Several indices lead to this conclusion.

In 1956 the Gore Committee analyzed large gifts ($500 or more) to candidates and campaign committees from the lists of officers and directors of 13 trade associations and special interest groups.[22] A continuation of the analysis through the 1960, 1964, and 1968 elections showed a decrease in giving by these individuals.[23] There was some revival in 1968, but in none of these Presidential election years did more than 18 percent of officers and directors of these combined groups contribute to campaign funds personally, not a large number in view of the wealth and interests involved. Admittedly, the percentages among the 13 groups are brought down considerably by the large number of non-contributors among the top leadership of such groups as the National Association of Real Estate Boards and the American Bar Association. The ABA figures are especially revealing for members of a profession that commands such influence and that consistently provides so many candidates for major public office; in 1968, among 297 members of the ABA House of Delegates, only 17 were found to have contributed an aggregate of $13,500. Despite the attention of the medical profession to the issue of Medicare, the leaders of the American Medical Association did not appear as important contributors in either 1960 or 1964 when the issue was prominent.

The legal and medical professions and the real estate interests are so dispersed, with interests on state and local levels, that their campaign contributions could have been made at lower levels not reporting for the record. Also the practice of the American Medical Political Action Committee is to seek contributions of lesser amounts that are not used in this analysis, and it is the practice of physicians to support financially state affiliates of AMPAC not appearing in the CRF listing of contributors.[24] The medical lobby at any rate has a strong influence through the family physician of the legislator. As one physician said, "A politician can be quite attentive during a physical examination."

The highest percentages of recorded contributors are among the membership of the Business Council, which has been called the elite of business and finance. Of the Council's membership, about 58 percent were listed among large contributors in 1968, 53 percent in 1964, almost 65 percent in 1960, and 45 percent in 1956. The contributions from 69 contributing members increased in 1968 to a record of $367,213. There were 67 contributors to Republican candidates and committees totalling $280,913, and 5 to Democrats totalling $83,000. Three of the five gave to both parties.[25] Compared to 1964, when 36 gave a total of $87,100 to Republicans and 33 gave $135,450 to Democrats, the switch is remarkable. Aggregate amounts of contributions decreased between 1956 and 1964 at the same time that contributions to Democrats had been increasing. The Goldwater campaign of 1964 turned many members toward President Johnson. The 1968 pattern reverts to Republican dominance, but with Democratic amounts at still higher rates than in 1956 or 1960.

The record of the American Petroleum Institute shows that from 1956 to 1964 its board members and officers appeared to reduce their contributions but in 1968, this trend reversed: 59 of 175 members and officers gave $461,639, of which only $30,-606 went to Democrats.

Contributing patterns of officers and directors of groups such as the National Association of Manufacturers, the Chamber of Commerce of the U. S., and the Iron and Steel Institute show fewer contributors and less money than might be expected. For 1968, $154,211+ was derived from 45 out of 168 associates of the NAM, and only $20,500 went to Democrats. For the Chamber of Commerce in 1968, 9 of 61 contributed a total of $40,000, all to Republicans. The Iron and Steel Institute analysis revealed 12 of 36 contributing $25,500, also exclusively to Republicans.

The numbers contributing and the amounts revealed are not outstanding. If any group would seem to have special reasons for making significant contributions to the party in power, it would be persons associated with defense industries receiving a large share of federal contracts. Similar analyses were not done for earlier years, but for 1968 alone analysis was made of the contribution patterns of officers and directors of the 25 largest Pentagon contractors, the largest contractors of the National

Aeronautics and Space Administration (NASA), the 25 largest
with the Atomic Energy Commission (AEC), and the 25 largest
industrial corporations on the *Fortune* magazine list.[26] The patterns are shown in the following:

	Pentagon	AEC	NASA	*Fortune* *Industrial*
Total Number of Officers and Directors[1]	856	700	856	1,013
Number of Individual Contributors	176	105	163	228
Total Contributions	$779,753	$306,201	$626,103	$837,239
Republican				
Number of Contributors[2]	161	93	142	212
Amount of Contributions	$664,252	$270,200	$496,602	$698,839
Democratic				
Number of Contributors[2]	22	13	27	26
Amount of Contributions	$110,000	$ 30,050	$129,000	$132,150
Miscellaneous				
Number of Contributors[2]	2	6	1	6
Amount of Contributions	$ 5,501	$ 5,951	$ 501	$ 6,250

1. For each of the four groups, certain individuals were officials of more than
one company within that group. They and their contributions have been
counted only once.

2. Due to the presence of individuals who gave to more than one party or
cause, the number of Republican, Democratic, and Miscellaneous contributors is
larger than the total number of individual contributors given at the top of
each column. The first total gives the actual number of individuals.

Some overlap occurs because certain corporations appear on
several lists. The Pentagon and NASA lists are especially con-
gruent. There are actually only 70 companies on the four lists,
contributing an aggregate of $1,478,935 as follows: Republican,
$1,250,284; Democratic, $216,200; and Miscellaneous, $12,-
451.[27] Despite limitations of the lists of contributors against
which the names of officers and directors were matched, the
data offer evidence of the extent of contributions in sums of $500
or more representing managements of the elite of the military-
industrial complex. The few companies on the *Fortune* list
which are not among the 25 largest on the other three lists are
mainly oil companies which also benefit from military and de-
fense-related activities.

Total contributions of officers and directors of the Pentagon list are less than contributions from individuals with fortunes more than $150,000,000 as listed by *Fortune*. As noted, major oil companies not among the largest defense contractors—Standard Oil Company of California, Mobil, Texaco, Gulf, Shell, and Standard Oil Company (Indiana)—make the significant difference on the *Fortune* industrial list, with a total of $186,300 in contributions. Of this total, however, $65,000 was contributed by Richard K. Mellon of Gulf Oil, who was also on the Board of General Motors (Pentagon and NASA).

Of the companies studied, Litton Industries was the corporation with the largest aggregate contributions: $156,000 (151,000 to Republican committees and $5,000 to Miscellaneous committees, and none to Democrats). It is remarkable, that for a company fourteenth on the Pentagon list, no officers or directors made any contributions to Democratic candidates or committees. The Democrats, after all, were in power in 1968 and were still awarding contracts. Litton had grown to prominence during years of Democratic dominance in the 1960's. Moreover, the two largest individual contributors were directors, not company officers; these were Henry Salvatori, who with his wife contributed a total of $95,000, and Vernon Stouffer, who with his wife contributed a total of $27,000. As directors may be wealthier than officers and have interests quite divergent from those of the company they serve, the data may exaggerate company financial participation in politics. For example, a director of an industrial firm may be a banker or a lawyer or a financier, and the question is, how are his other interests to be distinguished from the company interests? How can anyone determine whether any vested interests governed his contributions and, if they did, to what extent?

Of the five largest Pentagon contractors—General Dynamics, Lockheed, General Electric, United Aircraft, and McDonnell Douglas—officers and directors contributed a total of $122,677 but split with $119,677 for Republicans and only $3,000 for Democrats. McDonnell Douglas and United Aircraft had no Democratic contributors, and the others had only one each. Is this a true index of the financial involvement of the military-industrial complex in politics? The disparity in contributions suggests that if the complex has political ties, they are mainly Republican, and that the Democrats were unsuccessful in forming the right connections.

Certainly in the face of these data no simplistic explanation will suffice, not even the assumption that businessmen's contributions do not appear on the surface or that the Citizens' Research Foundation compilation is insufficient. These data are incomplete, but not to an extent that would alter the main findings that, at the national level at least, not much money was contributed by corporation executives; that most of the contributors with business ties were directors, not company officers; and that not much of the money on the record (sums of $500 or more) went to Democrats despite their control of the White House and the Congress in 1968.

One sure sign that men of wealth try to control politicians would be reports of numerous "split" contributors, persons who hedge their bets by buying a stake in the campaigns of opposing candidates. At times, of course, one executive of a corporation will contribute to one party and another executive to another, but it could as easily be surmised that the executives simply differed in their political views as it would be to say that the corporation had instructed its top echelon to buy a share in both parties. One of the few records of deliberate "split" spending in 1962 concerns a group calling itself "James H. Lum, a Political Committee for the Nov. 6, 1962 Election." Lum reported spending $11,929 to support various candidates, ranging from liberal Democrats to conservative Republicans. James H. Lum was assistant to the president of the Monsanto Chemical Co., and all the contributors were high Monsanto executives. Lum told reporters that the candidates they supported had been picked on the basis of their ability. Asked why the group gave both to Sen. Edward V. Long (D.-Mo.) and Crosby Kemper, Long's Republican opponent in that year's election, Lum said, "It's one of those things." [28]

On the national level, the number of individuals giving to both Republican and Democratic causes over the past few years has not been great. For example: 86 persons in 1952, 35 in 1960, and 255 in 1968. A few of the "split" contributions represented husbands and wives contributing to different parties.

In the years 1956, 1960, and 1964, all but a few of the split contributions went to candidates for different offices, not to directly opposing candidates or committees. The split contributions were scarcely ever large enough (say more than a couple thousand dollars) to obtain for the giver more than the usual access. In 1964, it was noticeable that individuals were giving to the Democratic Presidential candidate but also to moderate Republican Senatorial candidates. In contrast, in 1968, 95, or 37 percent, of split contributors gave to both the Nixon and Humphrey campaigns. The large increase in the numbers of split contributors and in the number of same-level contributors in 1968 cannot be explained except possibly by the improvement in the compilation of large contributions. Another possibility is that Nixon and Humphrey were more nearly matched than were Johnson and Goldwater.

The evidence suggests that while undue influence may be wielded by large contributors as a result of their campaign gifts, the financial elite of the country, themselves often sharply divided in political sentiments, are not investing in politics and politicians to the extent one would consider necessary for serious influence. Data do not reveal the degree to which rich contributors channel money through family members (other than wives), friends, and business associates. The lists omit the bulk of financing for primary campaigns, for Congressional candidates, and for state and local offices. Still, it is doubtful that a detailed accounting of the real sources of the $300 million spent on all politics in 1968, would demonstrate by any one set of data overwhelming financial dominance by the wealthy or by the business or professional elite or excessive hedging or contributing to both sides. What emerges most clearly is the Republican financial advantage over the Democrats; considering the lop-sided Republican support from multimillionaires and the party's advantage in smaller sums, too, at least at the national level, the disparity is cause for more concern than the occasional use of money to obtain favors. The true stake is political control of society to support well-established economic control.

In earlier days Jay Gould of the Erie Railroad was candid indeed when he said: "In a Republican district I was a Republican; in a Democratic district, a Democrat; in a doubtful district I was doubtful; but I was always for Erie." [29] Today, too, wealthy businessmen and companies with huge investments need police, fire, and regulatory protection. Gould said that "the politics of business" called for contributing to the locally dominant parties. Today, the robber baron and his mustachioed agent with the black bag of money have gone mod. In their place is the discreet lawyer who is perhaps a former member of Congress, the trade association executive, or the sophisticated company representative or public relations expert. So delicate and subtle are their maneuvers that, without a scorecard, you can't tell the offense from the defense.

Some contributions are made in the name of an entire industry to candidates and committees of both parties on a regular basis in an obvious effort to influence particular members of Congress in key strategic legislative positions. To choose an outstanding example, in the mid-1960's, hundreds of truckers were asked to send contributions through state trucker agents to a millionaire trucker, the late Neil J. Curry, who acted as national political agent for the group. Curry collected the checks, many of them for less than $100 so that they would not have to be listed individually on campaign fund reports. He periodically turned the collection over to the House and Senate campaign committees of the respective parties or to individual candidates, including both Democratic and Republican members handling transportation legislation. In 1968 efforts of a political action committee by then in operation, the Truck Operators Non-Partisan Committee, backfired. An enterprising journalist found that $29,000 had been given in the last three years to key members of Congressional committees which were processing a bill to permit larger and heavier trucks on interstate highways.[30] The adverse publicity was sufficient for House leaders to fail to call up the bill on the floor, and it died in the House Rules Committee. The House Committee on Standards of Official Conduct was asked by a members of Congress to look into the matter, but it did not choose to start an investigation.

The device of channeling money through Senate and House campaign committees can be used to conceal from the electorate the origin of the funds. Candidates are informed of the true source of the earmarked funds, but, if they report at all, they report the contribution as coming from the party committee.

The single contribution does double duty. The party leadership controlling the campaign committees knows the origin of the money, and the candidate knows it. The *Wall Street Journal* reported that executives of the R. J. Reynolds Tobacco Company, grateful for Congress' action in prohibiting Federal Trade Commission interference with cigarette advertising, contributed $10,490 in 1966.[31] Eight top Reynolds executives were reported to have contributed a stated percentage of salary plus fringes. They left the job of specifying how their money should be distributed to former Senator Earle Clements of Kentucky, head lobbyist of the American Tobacco Institute. Most of the money was divided among Democratic members of the House Commerce Committee who had helped to enact a less stringent cigarette labeling bill.

Labor unions also give to individual candidates of both major parties but not to two opposing candidates. The Teamsters' DRIVE consistently gives to many Republican candidates for Congress as well as to Democrats. The Seafarers International Union contributed in 1964 to six House Republicans, four of whom were members of the Committee on Merchant Marine and Fisheries. The chairman of that committee and a staunch friend of the Seafarers, Rep. Edward Garmatz (D.-Md.), received at least $17,000 in 1966, $5,500 in 1968, and $3,000 in 1970 from the same union. The Bankers Congressional Committee, an offshoot of the National Associated Businessmen, gave in 1964 to nine House members, eight of whom were on the Ways and Means Committee, four of whom were Democrats and four Republicans. Their one contribution on the Senate side was to Harry Byrd of Virginia, then chairman of the Senate Finance Committee, hardly in a marginal race.

On occasion, political leaders are the conduits for contributions. Apparently, the late Senator Robert Kerr of Oklahoma, one of Bobby Baker's mentors and a high-ranking member of the Senate Finance Committee, acted as a channel for oil money. Senator Russell Long, presently chairman of the same committee, has also been said to funnel oil money to candidates. He was widely reported to have called all his credits with other Senators when in 1965 he won the position of Democratic whip in the Senate, but when he lost the position to Senator Kennedy in

1969 it seemed clear that other factors were more relevant. An appraisal of the role of large contributions in American politics must also evaluate countervailing power. The form of power may mean less than the way it is exercised. Restraints on the use of financial power either may be self-imposed or forced by vocal opposition. Only when many wealthy contributors and groups coalesce on a major policy against the public interest do they tend to undermine the democratic process as we have known it.

If he shuts his door to the common people, the politician may find his job at risk. Entrenched Congressional leaders have been defeated—some in primaries and some in general elections—for having closed minds, the equivalent of being excessively selective in allowing access to their offices. For this reason, a contribution to gain admission is not always necessary or helpful.

Many observers belittle the contribution of money as a means of influence. Professor Lester Milbrath found that Washington lobbyists themselves do not think political contributions are particularly effective.[32] Many Washington lawyers advise clients having business with the government not to contribute for the purpose of seeking special consideration. On the other hand, numerous lobbyists apparently feel they can best guarantee their lines of communication to government by purchasing tickets to Washington fund-raising dinners and by being seen at them; but contributing is only a small part of their activity.

Whether or not the lobbyist is the "right person" or wealthy, there are many alternative paths to political influence, both direct and indirect. The long-range strategy is to nominate or elect candidates with congenial views. Another is to persuade policy makers or lawmakers by a combination of personality, information, logic, and persistence. Another is to enlist public opinion in order to indirectly influence the decision maker. Resorts to demonstrations, violence, threats of violence, or even threats of reprisal at the polls may backfire but they have been tried and will continue to be used as a substitute for lobbying, personal petition, or campaigning in the traditional sense. Demonstrations and instruments of violence may gain for dissenters the attention — much of it free — that they cannot afford to buy. These tactics, however, seldom match the cogency of day to day consultation and counselling with legislators in the intimacy of a club, a dining room, or a private office, or the leverage of naked political or economic power.

Lacking the tenacity, information, poise, money, or votes to pursue a long-range strategy, protestors who feel frustrated by the calm indifference of politicians feel they have little choice but act out their grievances with any device from a peaceful parade to a bomb. They can expect more mileage by inviting a TV news crew to cover 25 pickets at the White House than by filing their 25 signatures on a petition to a Congressman. For the organizers, demonstrations come relatively cheap—letters and calls to summon the dissenters, a few placards, paint, a bullhorn—but the consequent disruption can prove expensive for society, even disastrous, not only economically but politically. Witness Chicago in August, 1968.

To the extent that the parties depend upon large contributions from special interests or persons seeking favors, they consider the views of the interests somewhat more carefully than those of the demonstrators. The system is predisposed in any event to succumb to institutional obstacles and centrist pressures. Consequently a claimant's perception of the limitations within regular channels may lead him to an activitism outside the party processes.

An incumbent has a forum in the White House, in the State House, in the legislature. Most of what he says and does attracts attention. Established or wealthy interests have resources to propagandize or lobby. To the alienated or dissenters, with access neither to a governmental forum nor to funds, there seems little choice but to take to the streets for an audience, if not on TV or in the papers, at least in the courts. This formulation is not meant to recommend decisions to go beyond the regular political processes but merely to explain their causes and costs. Their eventual effects are unpredictable.

Once opposition to official Vietnam policy was channeled into established institutional processes by the candidacies of Senators Eugene McCarthy, Robert F. Kennedy, and George McGovern, the costs of effective dissent mounted. About $20 million was spent on these three campaigns, much of it from wealthy sources.

The 1968 campaign of former Governor George Wallace represents much the same phenomenon on the right-of-center. Even small contributions from labor union members represent vested interests such as the jobs of those who fear the effects of "equal employment" programs or unemployment.

In other words, the general direction of political change is not necessarily determined by the size, source, or pattern of political contributions. Unfortunately, there is no way of measuring the degree of restraint on change or responsiveness engendered by the present system of financing politics, nor is there any way of rating the influence of money in relation to the influence of voters, the anticipated reaction of potential voters, or other forces in the constituency, although money surely reinforces any political trend it favors.

As a rule, candidates and parties do not move so rapidly that they run away from their bases of support. Before they act, they consider how decisions will affect relations with financial or other supporters. A law of "anticipated reactions" is at work. Politicians learn to estimate the boundaries of acceptable behavior. Some have an intuitive ability to circumscribe their behavior even before potential supporters have expressed commitments. The chronic need to continue and expand fund-raising appeals limits the pace as well as direction of change.

The role of money or wealth in the political process is a legitimate issue for political debate: the ties between public policies and private interests are always at question. (Public bureaucracies, incidentally, contain vested interests no less than private enterprise.) As all interests participate to some degree in partisan politics, the sources of financial support for both major parties come to be questioned especially by those who assume that money for politics is supplied primarily by government contractors, large contributors, labor unions, and financiers. It is easy to impute motivation on the basis of surface information. When a person identified with a large corporation makes a large contribution, and his company gets a large government contract, the conclusion is drawn that A caused B, although it could have been that the bids were open and unrigged, that the company was competent, and that it had received contracts from the opposing party without contributions.

John M. King, who gave the Nixon campaigns in 1968 perhaps as much as $250,000, later was charged by the Internal Revenue Service with tax liens totaling more than $5 million. Influence from his political contributions, if there was any, did not prevent this action, nor did it prevent the Justice Department in 1968 from charging discrimination in the renting of apartments by Samuel J. Lefrak, a $10,000 contributor to the Nixon campaign. If these examples are exceptional, so too may be examples of influence and favoritism.

"The inherent power of immense concentrations of wealth in a nation," as Dr. Heard has pointed out, "exists without regard to the particular ways political-party and candidate activities are paid for. People who have money will spend it to get what they want. If the system of campaign finance appears to offer a way of doing this, it will be one of the channels through which money is spent. If different arrangements are obtained, the inherent power of concentrated wealth would still manifest itself in other ways, as it does at present. It becomes an incredibly difficult task to distinguish between the impact of political gifts that emanate from large and small pools of wealth, and the impact of the other means of influence that such concentrations of economic power inevitably command . . ." [33]

Even in socialist economies, special interests attempt to influence and exploit government for what they consider their needs. No form of government can avoid this. So long as a private system of financing politics is valued, part of the price for it is the influence of private contributions. The political system survives by rewarding or serving its supporters. If the system engenders favoritism, it is unlikely to correct itself from within. A democracy permits, indeed should encourage, articulation of interests. The challenge is to give all groups fair opportunity and fair representation. Certainly society's disadvantaged —the poor, the minorities, the young—too seldom receive fair consideration in America's ruling circles. In contrast, large contributors and their allies, usually get a sympathetic hearing if they want it. Whether redress can be had and a balance of interest achieved is considered later.

THE ROLE OF BUSINESS AND LABOR

The roles of corporations and labor unions in American politics can scarcely be overstated. Misused, their power can pervert the democratic process. Channeled properly, it can constitute a wholesome influence.

Considering the dimensions of corporate and union political activity and the stakes, the regulatory laws and court decisions are singularly ambiguous: generally, federal law defines what corporations and unions must not do in terms so sweeping that the courts, mindful of Constitutional rights of petition and free speech, have been unwilling to interpret it literally. The result has been a tendency to ignore both letter and spirit of the law.

In 1907 Congress, reacting to disquieting disclosures of corporate money flowing into political campaigns, declared it illegal for corporations to make "money contributions" to campaigns for federal office. Later this law was expanded to forbid contributions, defined as "anything of value," such as free billboard space provided by a vendor.

The labor vote was an early factor in American politics, but it was not until the 1936 election that unions engaged significantly in financing national campaigns. That year they spent eight times as much as the American Federation of Labor had laid out during the preceding 30 years.[1] In 1943 the ban on direct political contributions by corporations was applied to labor unions by the Smith-Connally Act. No sooner had that expired, in 1947, than the Congress wrote into the Taft-Hartley Act another ban on contributions by labor unions and corporations, extending the prohibition to political expenditures as well as contributions.

Under Taft-Hartley provisions, still in effect, unions and corporations are forbidden to make contributions or expenditures in connection with candidacy for federal elective office, or in connection with primaries, conventions, and nominating caucuses held to choose candidates for federal office, or in general elections. An additional provision of the law, applying only to a small segment of business (national banks and the few corporations organized under authority of federal laws), forbids participation in elections or primaries for local and state offices. All unions and most corporations, however, are free to make contributions and expenditures in local and state elections, unless prohibited by state law.

Thirty-one states forbid corporate contributions to local and state campaigns.[2] Most of these laws were passed early in the century. Only four states (Indiana, New Hampshire, Pennsylvania, and Texas) forbid unions also to give directly to local and state campaigns. The imbalance can be explained by the fact that in some states organized labor was so weak there was no need for restrictive legislation, whereas in others it gained strength quickly enough in the 1930's and 1940's to be able to fend off passage of such legislation. "Right-to-work" laws, rather than prohibition of union contributions, have preoccupied some state legislatures in recent years.

For many years enforcement of the federal prohibitions was marked by frank failure to press for indictments or to convict those under indictment. There have been 18 or so convictions of corporations under such laws, mostly in 1969 and since. A few indictments were brought against labor unions following the Taft-Hartley prohibition, but no conviction has been upheld upon appeal. The Justice Department and the courts have been mired in the sticky task of interpreting what actually constitutes an "expenditure" to aid a political candidate or party and determining how strictly the law may be interpreted without abridging First Amendment guarantees.

Aside from constitutional questions, the law involves tax considerations, matters of equity and of equality, and definitions of terms such as contribution and expenditure, direct and indirect, partisan, bipartisan, nonpartisan, education and propaganda, and internal and external (what is intra-corporate or intra-union and what is an outside political communication).

Also the law contains glaring inconsistencies. For example, when broadcasting corporations, under Section 315 of the Federal Communications Act, make available time to political candidates, they are giving something of value, contrary to Section 610 of the Federal Corrupt Practices Act, the federal prohibition against corporate contributions. Such contributions by incorporated newspapers or broadcasting stations are nevertheless part of the corporation's "normal organizational activity," though that distinction is not stated in federal statutes.

The phrase, "in connection with" creates a question: are unions and corporations prohibited from making contributions or expenditures in years in which no federal elections are held, or in election years before candidates announce or get nominated? May contributions go, as they may under some state laws, to intra-state political committees that support the party ticket, including federal candidates?

Corporations enter the political process through the activities of corporate managers and by the use of corporate resources. Among the many ways corporate funds percolate into partisan politics, one uses expense accounts to reimburse employees for political spending. Another provides free use of company goods and services and equipment, ranging from furniture and typewriters to airplanes and office suites or store fronts, to parties or candidates. Complimentary travel in company autos and airplanes is common even when no campaigns are going on.

One businessman managing a campaign for the mayor of a large city gave postage stamps instead of cash: the value of the stamps, charged to his company, could be deducted from income as a business expense. Unlike cash, the contribution could not be traced though its aid to the campaign was as good as money.

Other corporate aids come in the form of pay raises and bonuses provided with the understanding that the recipient will make political contributions in proportion.

Corporate payments to business and professional organizations, such as trade associations, are marked for political purposes. Some of these organizations are mere bank accounts established to collect and disburse campaign funds: they render invoices to the corporations for dues and subscriptions which ostensibly are legally deductible business costs for the contributing corporations.

Corporations also keep officials and their secretaries on the payroll while they work full-time in a campaign. This technique also is widely used by labor unions whose officials work on political campaigns. Payments to public relations firms, lawyers, and advertising agencies regularly used by the companies make it possible to lump political costs with charges for business as usual.

So common is this lumping technique that, in 1968, the Internal Revenue Service undertook a broad inquiry into the practices of corporations which deduct political payments concealed as legitimate business expenses.[3] The investigation led to the conviction of corporations as diverse as savings and loan associations, a brewery, a liquor wholesaler, a manufacturing company, a real estate firm, a packing company, and several advertising agencies, shipping companies, and banks. All were fined, but no corporate officer was penalized. One advertising agency had a secret code to distinguish political bills from business services. Four of the companies, units of the late Howard F. Ahmanson's financial empire, pleaded guilty to contributing illegally a total of $50,026 to an unnamed Presidental candidate in 1964.[4]

Some of these investigations were begun by the Johnson administration and continued under the Nixon administration. They led Randolph W. Thrower, Commissioner of Internal Revenue, to cite illegal corporate practices in politics and to deplore the conspiracies found "where cynicism and disregard for law are so flagrant that businessmen invited to a group meeting are openly briefed upon the plan for concealing the true nature of the contribution and deducting it as a business expense." He further complained of violations of the tax law by "some of the very people on whom we would normally rely heavily to establish a high standard of compliance." [5]

Institutional advertising also uses corporate funds for political purposes. In the 1956 Presidential campaign, the Minneapolis *Star and Tribune* published as a full-page ad in six other newspapers around the country a reprint of its endorsement of President Eisenhower, but denied the ads were political: they were merely institutional advertising.[6] Strong political implications, liberal and conservative, appear in institutionally-sponsored news stories, documentaries, features, lectures, and dramas, distributed by press and radio broadcasters at the expense of corporate advertisers seeking public good will. Several companies controlled by Patrick J. Frawley, Jr., including Eversharp and Technicolor, have engaged in widespread "rightwing" propaganda activities in recent years, both through direct contributions to tax-exempt groups and by sponsoring publicity programs.[7] In contrast, Xerox and others have supported liberal oriented public service programs on educational networks. Whenever a corporation undertakes such programs, the costs can be deducted as a business or charitable contribution and the government, in effect, pays 52 percent of the bill. Those who receive the money, such as an educational TV station, may themselves be tax-exempt.

An earlier chapter noted that political debt settlements by corporate lenders or others in effect yielded indirect assistance to candidates and parties. Long-term credit, without charging interest, is a similar method of corporate contribution. Short-term extension of credit by corporations is common. An advertising agency carrying a national account had an arrangement to be paid by the campaigners every Tuesday. It found, however, that it often needed cash on Wednesday or Friday to pay for a broadcast commitment. As it would not be reimbursed until the following Tuesday, the agency once found itself in debt for $500,000 for almost a week. Without an advance to cover commitments, the agency had to carry the financial burden. Because the agency wished to do a good job, and because its executives were sympathetic, the credit was arranged at agency expense, in effect a weekly contribution of hundreds of dollars in interest.

In an earlier chapter, the Williams amendment was said to dry up corporate contributions to program advertising books except on a bi-partisan basis for the national party conventions every four years. The Williams amendment at least focused attention on the need for money from individuals, by stimulating politicians to spend less time and effort in selling corporate advertising and presumably more on obtaining individual contributions. After the restriction on corporate advertising, one plant manager of a large corporation related that he received a call from the local county chairman, asking what the party could depend upon now that advertising books were not feasible;

corporate counsel told the plant manager to say that no corporate resources could be expected. The plant manager was boxed in between his counsel's advice and his desire to help the party. He resolved the problem by agreeing to make personal contributions and to persuade a few top colleagues to join him.

To the extent that the Williams amendment may have turned corporate officials to underground assistance to politicians, or to other devious ways of channeling company money into politics, it fails to serve the need to find fair and legitimate ways of financing politics. As with Prohibition, political restrictions lead the prohibited to seek new channels for converting corporate resources to political advantage.

In addition to advertising in program books every four years, business firms still may help cities pay the costs of nominating conventions.[8] Hotels, restaurants, and travel lines servicing the host city have for many years made direct contributions—legitimate business expenses—to nonpartisan committees established to guarantee bids for bringing national nominating conventions to their city. Such funds help pay for holding the political convention. Many companies provide free goods or services, forms of indirect contributions, to the national conventions. Car dealers provide autos with chauffeurs free. Soft drink companies give away soda. Scores of corporations cooperate in ways that must be considered partisan, even though contributions are usually funnelled through nonpartisan committees; they help only one party, because both parties seldom hold conventions in the same city in the same year. The highest political leaders in the country, the Presidential candidates, have winked at the practice which by strict construction must be considered contributing "something of value." Of course, corporations contribute to convention bureaus to bring nonpolitical conventions to town, and some also provide free goods and services as advertising to the benefit, for example, of the American Legion. Should a political convention be considered differently?

Like corporations, labor unions have learned how to be active in politics without violating the law against direct contributions. They have formed political auxiliaries, such as the previously mentioned COPE, which are free to raise funds from union members and to expend the money directly for political campaigns.

COPE was formed in December, 1955, when the AFL and CIO merged. Predecessors like the CIO's Political Action Committee had already made their mark on U. S. politics. In addition to COPE, which is the largest labor spender at the national level, reporting $1.2 million in 1968 and $969,000 in 1970, most national unions operate political arms. Expenditures of $7.1 million in 1968 and $5.2 million in 1970 were reported by national labor committees.[9]

Labor gathers political money from union members' voluntary contributions. A strong union may also use means, not the least of which is simple social pressure, to persuade members to "volunteer." The funds thus gathered are not union dues funds and can be used legally for direct assistance to candidates which labor feels are helpful. Labor gifts generally favor Democratic candidates.

Besides these "free funds," there are three clearly established channels by which labor money can flow into politics:

• *Non-Federal Contributions:* The sums spent where state law permits contributions by labor unions to election campaigns for state and local office. Studies have shown labor consistently provides 10-20 percent of funds of major Democratic candidates in some states[10] and is the largest single organized group in Democratic circles. In some places labor support keeps the two-party system alive.

• *"Educational" Expenditures:* Money taken directly from union treasuries to be used for such technically "non-political" purposes as registration drives, get-out-the-vote campaigns, or printing of voting records of legislators. COPE and other unions distribute millions of copies of Congressional voting records every election year to indicate how a Congressman voted on selected roll calls by labor's standards. Organized labor's registration drives may be of more value to the Democrats than direct money contributions. In 1968 COPE spent more than $1 million on registration alone, concentrating on marginal Congressional districts. Local and state labor organizations tried to match this national outlay. Labor's registration drives, naturally, are carried out selectively in heavily Democratic precincts.

• *Public Service Activities:* union newspapers, radio programs, and the like, financed directly from union treasuries. As in corporation newspapers or broadcast programs, a sharply partisan point of view may be expressed.

The latitude currently enjoyed by organized labor in politics is illustrated by Supreme Court decisions holding that federal prohibitions on union political activity did not cover the use of general union funds (money from members' dues) for a wide range of purposes.[11] Among these are the purchase of radio and television time, even to advocate the election or defeat of particular candidates; the endorsement of particular candidates in union publications, even when extra copies are circulated to other than regular subscribers; and compensation to union employees and others while rendering services to political candidates. Such activities are in addition to public services "buried" in public relations or manpower assistance to political candidates.

These decisions have been based on the majority opinion that a union has a right to advise its own membership and to relate the political climate to the union's economic goals. The Supreme Court has expressed the "gravest doubt" about narrowing constitutional rights of speech and association. Understandably, the rulings have been read by unions and corporations alike as giving them license to use funds to influence members or stockholders, with appreciable fallout among the general public an added bonus. The political necessities of business and labor alike approach the restrictions of the present law as a flood enveloping a feeble dike.

Normally, organized labor spends far less on Presidential campaigns than on races for Congress. By comparing some national labor committees which list the gifts to candidates with selected state sources, it is possible to gauge the proportion of support some candidates received from labor. In 1964, Senator William Proxmire of Wisconsin received at least $51,000 from all national and state-reported labor sources, about 25 percent of his reported expenditures.[12]

As noted earlier, the largest gifts in dollars from labor committees were reported in 1968, for the campaigns of Senator Wayne Morse (D.-Ore.) and Democratic candidate for the Senate from Ohio, John J. Gilligan. For both candidates, the recorded labor contributions supported primary and general election campaigns, including $29,000 contributed to Morse's election recount expense. Various national political committees of labor reported contributing a total of $178,944 to Gilligan's campaigns in 1968 and $137,496 to Morse's campaigns. These amounts do not include funds and other assistance received from state and local labor organizations. Some national committees (such as COPE), until 1972, clouded the extent of aid to individual candidates by transferring funds to state affiliates which in turn relayed gifts to the chosen. This decentralized process served other functions (such as decision-sharing), but until 1972 it also escaped the requirement to file a federal report telling which candidates actually benefited and how much. In states where disclosure laws were inadequate, the labor gifts of the state organization could not be traced officially. This practice was adopted also by the Political Action Committee of the American Medical Association. AMPAC officials privately acknowledged that the chief reason they placed all gifts from their national committee through state affiliates instead of directly was to spare the candidates possible embarrassment. Even if this practice is followed under the Federal Election Campaign Act, such money cannot escape disclosure in federal campaigns.

The support for Morse and Gilligan indicates the potential for labor financial assistance in selected campaigns. Labor may not be able to donate so much in many Senate contests but, in selected contests, funds in these ranges are mustered. Without labor support, numerous Democratic candidates would not be in office.

Sometimes a single union will participate heavily in Congressional campaigns. The Seafarers International Union in 1968 disbursed more than $500,000 to candidates, more than any other union committee except COPE—and the COPE money cannot be calculated for reasons noted. According to one account, since 1965 the SIU made campaign gifts in at least 150 Congressional districts.[13] Moreover, the SIU has an educational apparatus that sponsors luncheons at which speakers, mostly members of Congress, receive substantial honorariums.

In national campaigns, labor-Democratic relationships, financial and otherwise, are intimate, though not without friction.

Normally the organizations coordinate registration drives and financial matters, including allocation of funds to candidates for Congress. Some craft unions tend to be Republican, and some state and local groups occasionally favor moderate Republicans. The Teamsters tend to be more bipartisan than most strong unions, but the national labor bodies generally aid the Democratic ticket.

The labor movement early grasped the need for strenuous precinct work, with all the drudgery of registration and fetching voters to the polls, at times in militantly hostile settings. Still, the cash labor puts in politics tends to be if not overestimated at least overrated. The sums sometimes contributed to candidates by labor are the gifts of many union members. A single rich contributor may give as much to a given candidate, say $1,000 or $5,000, as an entire international union. Since 1950, labor money has accounted for about 10 percent of reported gross disbursements of national political committees. Not all of that reaches candidates because some goes for expenses. No one knows how much more labor committees spend at state and local levels, but labor is not monolithic and not well-organized in every state. Yet when labor can muster the money to contribute 10 to 30 percent of a candidate's expenditures, its strength is obvious and its influence likely to be strong, not only when the candidate is in office, but also in determining campaign strategy. Labor's promise to contribute can influence both nominations and policy directions. Politically-oriented labor leaders complain that too few of the rank and file contribute. They maintain that gleaning voluntary political dollars from members is largely a matter of organization and zeal and that many locals, where the money is collected, provide neither. Still, where successful in raising political money, labor's techniques bear imitation. The labor structure provides a ready collection system through constant communication and personal contact. After the 1966 Congressional elections, when many labor-backed candidates suffered defeat, COPE proposed to undertake more intensive political education, with special appeals to young inexperienced members. Another idea was to develop local COPEs on a community basis in order to "go where the members live," increasingly in the suburbs, to offset diminishing concern with labor's political objectives among rank-and-file members.[14]

Labor has performed a constructive function by increasing participation in elections. In some areas, COPE has pilot projects that rely on computers to coordinate registration and get-out-the-vote campaigns. The programs contain pertinent information on each union voter and voting-age family member and compose so-called walking lists to facilitate door-to-door canvassing and transportation to the polls.

Theodore H. White has commented on labor's role in 1968: "The dimension of the AFL-CIO effort . . . can be caught only in its final summary figures: The ultimate registration, by labor's efforts, of 4.6 million voters; the printing and distribution of 55 million pamphlets and leaflets out of Washington, 60 million more from local unions; telephone banks in 638 localities, using 8,055 telephones, manned by 24,611 union men and women and their families; some 72,225 house-to-house canvassers; and, on Election Day, 94,457 volunteers serving as car-poolers, materials-distributors, baby-sitters, poll-watchers, telephoners." [15]

The value of the manpower is immense. While much of it is volunteered, some is paid for by political action funds of unions when, for example, on election day workers take off from their jobs and are recompensed by the union. Ironically, some of this political work is financed by employers who sign labor contracts providing election day as a paid holiday.

The role of labor in 1968 is particularly difficult to assess. According to numerous observers, labor ranks were as badly split as the Democratic coalition as a whole. As noted, labor dissipated much of its punch in intra-party contests for Presidential nomination, when perhaps it should have saved its resources for the general election. The inflexible loyalty of George Meany to the White House Vietnam policy also hurt. Yet labor mounted a massive drive for Humphrey when George Wallace was making inroads among elements of the rank and file, and the steady but tardy upturn in Humphrey's fortunes must be credited in part to labor leadership.

In some respects 1968 was a chastening experience for labor. Labor leaders spent a good deal of money and effort in directions opposed by many members who favored Robert Kennedy or

George Wallace, yet it may have been labor's single-minded determination to fight Wallace that brought Humphrey so close to victory. Certainly 1968 exposed the moral issue of leadership using political money voluntarily contributed for purposes or candidates opposed by substantial numbers of the givers but, since the role of leaders is to educate and lead in political as well as in economic affairs, the issue is not clear cut. Rank-and-file confidence in the leadership on bread-and-butter issues often seems to assure support of leadership decisions on political issues, too.

Labor faced a similar dilemma with respect to candidates for Congress who were solid liberals but differed with labor on the Indochina war. Although John Gilligan and Wayne Morse in 1968 were vocal opponents of the Vietnam line supported by AFL-CIO headquarters, they still received generous support from that source.

Labor's growing sophistication in politics has also served to spur the employers' opposition. Countering labor's drive for mass individual contributions, the National Association of Manufacturers made an initial grant in 1963 for a new organization, the Business-Industry Political Action Committee (BIPAC), whose avowed purpose is "to provide financial support to Congressional candidates who support the principles of constitutional government." BIPAC spent $568,000 in 1968 and $539,000 in 1970, derived from voluntary contributions of individual businessmen. BIPAC encourages contributions of $99 to avoid individual listing by name in campaign fund reports and has a separate bank account, corresponding to COPE's educational budget, which is financed directly by corporations. This portion of the BIPAC effort concentrates on year-round activity.

For a few months before a national election, all BIPAC operating expenses, including headquarters operation and staff salaries, are paid from voluntary rather than corporate funds. This contrasts with COPE and other organizations which pay for operations and staff year round from unions' educational funds even though much of the activity is partisan.

In 1968 a new Exchange Firms Campaign Committee reported income amounting to $187,000 from the securities industry. As the federal prohibition against corporate contributions does not apply to partnerships, contributions of $5,000 each were received from such well-known firms as Reynolds and Co., White Weld and Co., and Loeb, Rhoades, and Co. Stockbrokers acknowledged openly that their political activity was triggered by a toughness among federal regulators regarding brokerage commissions, use of inside information, and mutual fund management fees. Almost $147,000 was distributed, mainly to candidates for Congress from both parties, in amounts as high as $5,000.

Another new committee in 1968, innocuously named the Effective Government Association, raised and spent $6,000 and was found to be mainly a political fund organized by officers and employees of Merrill Lynch, Pierce, Fenner, and Smith. It contributed to candidates for Congress and to both the Nixon and Humphrey campaigns—more to the Nixon campaign. Many such committees exist and are as neutrally named: the Committee on American Leadership is an acronym for the coal industry it represents; the Committee for Action represents certain construction contractors.

The technique of giving political money is important, as noted in Chapter 9. Rather than pay the candidate or his campaign committee directly, some give to the Senatorial Campaign Committee and earmark the funds for the favored candidate. This creates good will with the members of the Senatorial Campaign Committee and the Senate leadership as well, and the candidate, of course, learns the source of the money. This is known as "triple scoring." An additional advantage is that the candidate's campaign fund report shows only a gift from the party committee, not from the actual source. Some who earmark funds by this route are themselves special interest political committees—labor or business—which use this channel so that the candidate will not need to report receiving funds from sources which could be attacked by his opponents.

As some of these committees, such as COPE, contribute lump sums to state affiliates to redistribute to designated Senatorial and Congressional candidates, beneficiaries or patterns of contributions of some major lobbies could be completely reviewed until 1972 only if states required comprehensive reports. In 1968, COPE transferred about $710,000 to state affiliates for redistribution to candidates, while AMPAC transferred almost

$584,000 to its affiliates. In 1970 COPE transfers to state affiliates amounted to $637,340; AMPAC transfers totalled $634,-500. In an unusual move COPE also gave $63,908 directly to eleven Senatorial candidates in 1970.

Political money flows according to strategy designed to have the most effect with the fewest dollars. As the Senate is relatively liberal and visible and has power in foreign affairs, Senate contests are of interest to groups such as the National Committee for an Effective Congress or the Council for a Livable World. On the other hand, since the House tends to be conservative and often can exercise an effective brake on liberal legislation, conservative groups such as BIPAC or AMPAC send "veto dollars" to legislators who are in key positions to block or revise bills. (The authors of the Constitution expected the Senate to act as a brake on the House, but political processes have reversed their intended roles.)

Though their political methods have sometimes seemed to verge on the devious, corporations and unions are major social and political as well as economic forces. Their stake in the political process is such that it is naive to suggest, as existing laws do, that they divorce themselves from political work.

Instead of deploring the potential evils of corporate and labor activity in politics, there is reason to emphasize their potential for the public good. Corporations and labor unions have natural constituencies with large blocs of voters, political money, and volunteers for political service. Many authorities agree that the present prohibitions are unenforceable, undesirable as public policy, and perhaps unconstitutional, and that some or all of the restrictions should be removed.

A move to extend the rights of unions and corporations to engage directly in political action enters unexplored terrain, but there are a few guiding principles:

• Few would oppose a policy that encourages business and laboring men to participate in politics. Corporations and unions may well be the chief agencies to do the encouraging; constitutionally, they cannot be barred from doing so.

• It seems proper to restrain both corporations and labor unions from direct political activities, to place at least a strict limitation on direct contributions. Few would want the raw economic power or political potential of either corporations or trade unions to dominate American politics. As Steffens has explained, political parties serve as a countervailing force against dominant economic powers.

• At the same time, it is unrealistic and probably unconstitutional to prevent political expression through institutional advertising, sponsored commentary, and other means. The distinction between prohibiting speech and prohibiting an expenditure for speech is not substantial. As as effective speech today may require use of expensive mass media, the expenditure can hardly be denied.

• The rights of stockholders who disagree with company management and union members who differ from their unions's political point of view are to be respected and must also be protected by the First Amendment. Voluntarism should be emphasized even while certain types of political activity are encouraged. Compulsory assessments and the like should be discouraged or prohibited.

• For protection of the dissenting members of both corporate and union communities as well as the public at large, an effective law could enforce disclosure of all uses of corporate or union money, including personal funds of officials, used directly or indirectly for political parties or candidates, including educational and registration activities carried on in the name of citizenship.

• Government could encourage, by every means possible, the bipartisan programs of several corporations to collect small contributions from employees.

Corporations are well-situated to support such nonpartisan programs as fund-raising and voter registration drives and appearances by political candidates on plant and office sites. The President's Commission on Campaign Costs recommended in 1962, "individuals and private organizations including corporations, labor unions, farm organizations, civic societies and other appropriate groups—[should] be encouraged as a matter of good citizenship to make expenditures for *bipartisan* political activities." [16] The Internal Revenue Service concurred, ruling that reasonable costs for such activities are deductible expenses. (The IRS also permits deductions for corporate sponsorship of joint appearances of candidates on radio and television and of "battle pages" in newspapers and magazines. Corporations have been slow to pick up the idea but should be encouraged to do so as long as the efforts are nonpartisan.) [17]

In bipartisan fund raising, corporations do and can support activity consistent with the goal of broadening the base of financial assistance for politics. It has been demonstrated that the stimulus to contribute can be applied without intrusion of company pressure or preference. The most successful method permits periodic payroll deductions for the amount of the contribution.

In a properous America, the prospective harvest from this technique is dazzling. In 1968 three firms—Aerojet General, Hughes Aircraft, and Thompson Ramo Wooldridge, Inc.—reported combined employee contributions of more than $300,000. If a thousand corporations could each mobilize that average of $100,000 in election years, no less than a hundred million dollars would be amassed, much of it in small sums—an unparalleled source of funds. A collateral effort by labor unions would add to this potential, although admittedly one system of collecting would cut into the other in some instances. In 1968, there were 18 million labor union members and 11 million employees in the 1,000 largest corporations.

The longest-term effort occurred at Aerojet-General, where the most far-reaching in-plant solicitation has reached the workers paid by the hour. Since 1958, when $24,000 was raised for parties and candidates, collections yielded $60,000 in 1960, $97,000 in 1962, $136,000 in 1964, $82,200 in 1966, and $90,815 in 1968. In 1968 70 percent of the firm's personnel contributed an average of $8.27. The contributions went to 107 candidates and committees throughout the nation. The financial condition of the company caused it to abandon the program in 1970.

Hughes Aircraft Company undertook an Active Citizenship Campaign in 1964. Hughes employees probably established a national record for first year contribution programs with $86,053. In 1970, $154,100 was raised with contributions by one of every four employees. They designated four political parties and 150 individual candidates in 28 states. All contribution deduction forms were coded to prevent identification of contributors by the employer.

Thompson Ramo Wooldridge, Inc., conducted a Good Government Program in 1968 which raised $111,816. A cash carryover from other years brought the fund to $148,686. Of this sum $117,372 was disbursed as follows:

To political parties (local, state, and national)	$47,525
To candidates, partisan and nonpartisan	55,247
To special fund-raising activities	8,000
To Democratic and Republican Congressional Campaign Committees	6,600

In 1970 about $140,900 was raised and contributed, but no breakdown was made public. Contributors in the TRW program can designate the party or candidate to receive the funds. Alternatively, donors in higher ranges can earmark their funds for the TRW Good Government Fund, which is administered by a disbursement committee that apportions funds for all four of the purposes listed above. A payroll deduction system is used.

The Democratic State Central Committee of Michigan has issued summaries of employee citizenship participation programs in that state since 1964. Ten to twenty companies have organized programs with approximately 1200 employees contributing. Democratic committees and candidates have been receiving between $24,000 and $34,000 each year, including non-election years.

In California in 1966, ambitious organized efforts were made to enlist more companies in bipartisan solicitation programs, pioneered earlier in Southern California. Both state party chairmen cooperated and leading businessmen gave the program their time and seed money. The California Good Citizenship Committee held luncheons for corporate executives to tell the story of the bipartisan solicitation drives. Companies undertaking programs for the first time were guided in their efforts by workshop sessions. In all, 55 firms employing nearly 500,000 workers participated. Political contributions totaled $276,266. In 1968 companies employing 600,000 workers produced at least as much. During 1967 efforts to start a similar program in New York state failed. As some point, as motivations increase, the establishment of such programs can become a "national story." A national, prestigious, bipartisan organization could certainly accelerate the movement.

So far, bipartisan corporate programs have been most successful in the aerospace and electronics industries, which relatively speaking, have high percentages of well-educated, white-collar employees, but not many companies even in these industries have acted. It appears that for generating enthusiasm among employees, candidate rallies are the best means. For this reason large companies with many employees scattered in many branches are not as productive as those with hundreds or thousands in one location with the facilities for mass meetings.

Where operable, corporate bipartisan programs have the advantage of providing a channel for direct solicitation where an employee can contribute without going to the trouble of writing out a check or hunting the right address. The collections cost candidates and parties nothing, and the expenses of collection are deducted from the companies' income for tax purposes. Such methods help to reduce the number of diffuse and competitive appeals and spare candidates or committees the need to solicit each prospect individually. Solicitation can be focused on the whole political process at the same time in a way that permits the employee to determine the beneficiary of his choice.

To be sure, either management or unions may object. Some companies think it prudent to keep out of politics, even nonpartisan activities. Some want only their top management to participate, in behalf of the "right side." Some labor unions, usually among the largest, prefer to raise contributions from their members exclusively for political leverage. Understandably, they do not care to add muscle to the corporate influence, and besides they fear corporate fund raising will cut into their own. Still, many levels of clerical and secretarial workers and middle and upper management, untouched by union appeals, can be reached by vigorous corporate bipartisan programs to the net gain of parties and candidates.

Public distrust of bipartisan solicitation is based on the assumption that both labor and management will try to coerce givers. Nevertheless, successful use of fair bipartisan programs in corporations could lead to similar programs in banks, universities, and government agencies, although government participation would require a reexamination of the methods of enforcing necessary restraints on political influence in the civil service.

Bipartisan drives among government employees could be handled in ways that would do no violence to career public servants, federal or state.[18] For example, commercial banks could act as trustees of withheld funds so that government employees would be free to contribute to the party or candidate of their free choice with only the bank knowing to whom they gave. Trustees then distribute lump sums directly to the beneficiaries without naming donors. There need be no compulsion on anyone to give.

American governments at all levels list more than 11 million employees. The penetration of government by nonpartisan programs, if widely endorsed and publicized, could stimulate similar action by business, labor, and other organizations.

The list of what could be done by unions and industry to encourage participation in American democracy is by no means exhausted. Unions and corporations could work together without sacrificing identity or freedom of thought so long as programs are nonpartisan. "Contracting out" systems, rather than "contracting in," could develop in both corporate and labor programs. Corporations might be allowed to match employee contributions specifically earmarked for registration and getting out the vote. Corporations could reward donors with inexpensive favors, box lunches, or banquets. Unions and corporations could make available to both parties names and telephone numbers to be checked against registration lists, and registration booths could be set up in plants.

There is no good reason why corporations should not be given tax deductions in return for providing on a nonpartisan basis automobiles and buses to take voters to the polls or for paying workers for time lost to register. Financial accounting of such nonpartisan programs should include information on services supplied as well as money contributed. There are indeed myriad ways of helping Americans to participate in their political system, and big organizations—unions, corporations, universities, governments—can lead the movement.

11

THE STATE OF THE LAW

Federal and state laws relating to political finance have been predominantly negative. Their primary purpose has been to prohibit, limit, and restrict ways of getting, giving, and spending. Most of these laws were devised to remedy or prevent flagrant abuses at a time when it was evidently assumed that honest politicians could afford to pay their expenses with their own money or "untainted" gifts. The major federal law until 1972 was the Federal Corrupt Practices Act of 1925, which in large part reiterated enactments of 1910-11.

Efforts to free candidates from dependence upon any one person or interest group usually took the form of restricting or prohibiting contributions from presumably dubious sources. Moreover, arbitrary ceilings were set to prevent excessive spending. The rationale was that such limitations would prevent money from dominating elections and tend to reduce undue advantages of candidates and parties with the most funds.

But as quickly as restrictive laws were passed, new methods of getting, giving, and spending came into existence. When the civil service movement prohibited assessment of government employees, attention turned to contributions from corporations. When corporate contributions were prohibited, gifts from wealthy individuals, including many stockholders or officers, increased. When direct contributions from the wealthy were somewhat curtailed, program books, fund-raising dinners, and special events found more donors. Throughout the legislative efforts, until federal tax incentives were enacted in late 1971, few positive measures were passed to replace traditional or undesirable sources of money or to assist in fund raising.[1]

Legislative enactments at the federal and state levels have taken five basic forms:

• To meet the problems of rising costs and the disparities in funds available to various candidates, laws set ceilings on expenditures. The federal government and 23 states limit the amount that candidates can spend on campaigns. Until 1972 federal law did not permit political committees to spend more than $3 million—a limitation easily evaded by creating numerous committees, each eligible to raise and spend $3 million. As funds accumulated, committees divided like amoebas.

• To spare candidates from obligations to special interests, federal laws have prohibited contributions from certain sources and, until 1972, have limited the size of individual contributions. Corporations, national banks, and labor unions are prohibited from contributing, but corporate executives may and do contribute funds out of their own pockets. Through political action affiliates, labor unions may and do collect contributions for election campaigns; they also expend funds for educational or nonpartisan political activities. Federal law limited individuals to $5,000 in gifts to any one national candidate or committee, but one could give $5,000 to many different candidates or committees. In effect, a Presidential candidate could be supported with an individual's gifts to fifty state committees or as long as the money lasted.

• To provide the public, both during and after campaigns, with knowledge of monetary influences upon elected officials, and to help curb excesses and abuses by increasing risks for engaging in sharp practices, statutes have required certain candidates and committees to make specified disclosures of information about contributions and expenditures. The federal government and 41 states have some form of public reporting requirements.

• To prevent "spoils system" practices under which government workers are forced to support political campaigns, legislation like the Hatch Act was enacted to protect civil service employees (generally excepting those in top policy-making positions) from pressured solicitation.

• To prevent partisan domination of the airwaves, federal law obliged a broadcaster to yield rival candidates equal amounts of free time on the air. Use of the mails by incumbents has also been restricted.

To the extent that the existing laws are negative, frequently unenforced, and generally unenforceable, they invite public cynicism. This cynicism inhibits political giving and volunteer work by the average citizen and forces parties and candidates to seek funds from questionable sources. Inevitably public attitudes find even more reason to be cynical.

There are good reasons why laws on political finance, both federal and state, are seldom enforced: difficulty in producing evidence, lack of respect for the law, self-serving partisanship, reluctance to open a scandal that may do more harm than good, and fear of reprisal if the culprit is a member of the opposing party. Since administrative and enforcement chiefs receive appointment or nomination through party processes, they are cautious about blowing the whistle on violators. Judicial relief is seldom sought; even losing candidates rarely care to spend time and money on litigation. Apart from other considerations, they are reluctant to be considered "sore losers."

In any event, many state and federal laws are unenforced because they are unenforceable: the statutes themselves are vague and perforated with loopholes. Prior to the 1972 law, spending limitations applicable to candidates for Congress were a good example of this. Unless state laws prescribed lesser sums, the ceiling for House candidates was $2,500 or 3 cents for each vote cast for the office in the last general election, with a $5,000 maximum; the ceiling for Senate candidates was $10,000, or a larger amount determined by the 3 cents formula, with a $25,000 maximum. The limitations did not, of course, apply to expenditures by a committee on behalf of a candidate, nor to a candidate's personal expenses prior to nomination. Moreover, expenses of filing fees, travel and subsistence, telephone and telegraph, distribution of literature, stationery, postage, and printing (other than newspaper and billboard advertisements) were all exempt from the limitation. Such exemptions tend to make restrictive laws irrelevant. Millions of dollars spent in prenomination and convention activities were not reported under federal law.[2] Such expenditures included, for example, the cost of waging primary campaigns and influencing convention delegates. Certain of these costs were reported in some states, but not uniformly.

Under federal law, a political committee included any group which handled funds for the purpose of influencing federal elections in two or more states. The law covered the national party committees, the Congressional and Senatorial campaign committees, *ad hoc* interstate committees, and all branches and subsidiaries of these groups, including branches operating in only one state. Specifically excluded from coverage were state and local party committees although their activities necessarily benefited federal candidates.

One clear evasion of the intent of the reporting law was the practice of organizing a committee in one state to sponsor a fund-raising dinner on behalf of a federal candidate, because under federal law the committee was intra-state and needed not report in Washington. The net proceeds from the dinner were then transferred in one lump sum to the candidate or one of his reporting committees. It was not then necessary to report names and addresses of contributors or the amounts given of $100 or more, as required by law for interstate committees. Committees sponsoring fund raising dinners or galas on behalf of the national, Senatorial, or Congressional committees of the major parties were usually organized in the District of Columbia, where as noted, reporting was not required either.

There was no law requiring consolidated accounting of all expenditures for a candidate, and neither the party nor the candidate himself was required to exercise full control over finances, and that hardly seems practical in any case. While a candidate and committees organized on his behalf may work side by side, each with its own funds, the candidate often does not know who is working for his election or with how many dollars. Although federal law required that the candidate for the Senate or House report what he spent in a campaign and also whatever was spent on his behalf with his "knowledge and consent," the candidate was invariably backed by intra-state committees which did not have to report to any federal authority, nor to the candidate.

The candidate did not report his committees' spending because of a neat fiction: since he had not *asked* for the information, he did not have specific knowledge of funds spent in his behalf. He may have appeared on a television show paid for by the committee, and he may have known in a general way what it cost, but, because he did not have exact knowledge or had not given specific consent to the spending, the law was not violated. There also could be expenditures which his supporters would not admit even to the candidate.

The Senate reports were made available to the public for six years (a full Senate term), but access to those in the House was closed after two years. After six years, the Secretary of the Senate sent reports to the National Archives, while the Clerk of the House could keep the reports on file for an undetermined period.

Few provisions assured interested citizens easy access to the reports. Hours of availability (especially when Congress was not in session) and working space were restricted. Use of typewriters and adding machines was prohibited. Photocopies were not obtainable. Such conditions hindered close examination, analysis, and summarization of reports. In mid-1967 it was revealed that the policy of the Senate's Secretary was to withhold from public inspection filings of campaign committees not directly attached to candidates' "personal" campaign fund reports. After some prodding, the policy was abandoned, but it serves to illustrate how arbitrary was administration of the law. (Many of these inadequacies were corrected in the 1972 law, as Chapter 17 shows.)

The receiving agents (the Secretary of the Senate and the Clerk of the House) were not even directed by law to ensure that required statements were filed, although they do notify delinquent candidates or committees. Even so, the receiving agents were not required to audit reports regularly or to notify investigatory or enforcement officers of violations. The lack of statutory provision for regular audits bred irresponsibility in campaign bookkeeping and a corresponding lack of confidence in the accuracy and completeness of reports. Audits may not catch all omissions, but they will uncover inaccuracies and provide grounds for investigation. From 1925 to 1972 these conditions existed at the federal level.

Like the federal laws, state reporting laws often have many loopholes and exemptions. In Tennessee and Arkansas, statements of expenses for statewide primaries are filed with the chairman of the party executive committee, not with a state official, and the reports are not available to the public. It is hard to imagine how the law could be enforced if only the party chiefs have access to the facts.

The unenforceability of laws on campaign financing is compounded by the inconsistency and frequent incompatibility be-

tween federal and state laws. Many state laws actually conflict with federal statutes and candidates tend to obey the laws
more convenient to their needs and strategies. Most recent
federal bills propose to give federal laws priority over state laws
and to encourage states to accept federal reports as meeting
their requirements. A copy of the report deposited in Washington would be filed with the Secretary of State in the candidate's
home state to ease local access. Meanwhile in most states conditions resemble those described by the *St. Louis Post-Dispatch*
in a four-part series on campaign laws:

"Missourians are electing men to govern them under a set of
campaign laws that at best are complicated, muddled and
ignored, and at worst encourage candidates for public office to
cheat to win election . . .

"The study shows that election expense reporting is frequently ignored by party committees; that spending limitations often
are exceeded; that loopholes permit the intent of the law to be
skirted, and that those charged with helping to enforce the
statutes often are unaware the laws even exist." [3]

After the series appeared, the *Post-Dispatch* commented edi-
torially: "If it took *Post-Dispatch* reporters three months to
learn how much four state-wide office-seekers spent in the last
general election campaign, how on earth is the public expected to
know anything about campaign expenditures?

"The obvious answers are that the public is not expected to
know anything and does not know under Missouri's present
Corrupt Practices Act. The law is unenforced because it is unenforceable. It is unrealistic as to spending limits and full of
loopholes as to reporting procedures." [4]

A Massachusetts study also revealed the status of reporting requirements. In 1962 a blue-ribbon committee recommended a
new Corrupt Practices Act, and the proposal subsequently was
enacted into law.[5] After the 1962 election, with the new provisions in effect, a Greater Boston Junior Chamber of Commerce study revealed, among other things, that loans to candidates were not fully reported; that candidates delayed the reporting of debts; that disclosure was avoided by persons who paid
candidates' bills rather than undergo the publicity of making
donations directly; that several candidates concealed types of

expenditures and names of payees by channeling large sums to advertising agencies for undisclosed uses; and that cash contributions were not fully reported. The study showed if nothing else how difficult it is to frame the laws to meet all contingencies and how well-intentioned administrators may find themselves helpless to correct omissions or errors in campaign fund reports.

In the American system, in theory and sometimes in practice, the states can serve as laboratories for public policy experiments. But most states have done little better than the federal government in promulgating election laws.[6] Some states have not done as well. Where federal-state powers are divided, state inactivity is understandable, but in a housekeeping function like elections, where the states have basic jurisdiction under the Constitution, there is no explaining the states' failure to demonstrate concern, imagination, or resourcefulness. For example, reapportionment, forced upon the states by the federal courts, should have been demanded by the voters years ago.

To improve laws on corrupt practices or public reporting does not require large appropriations. Tax incentives for political activity at the state level are relatively inexpensive, yet only nine states have adopted them. Minnesota alone encourages political leadership by permitting candidates for specified offices and certain party officials to deduct from their gross state income tax limited parts of campaign expenditures or personal political costs. Few such innovations have found acceptance in other states.

Some degree of disclosure of political finances, with predictable inconsistency and variation, is required by 41 states: exceptions are Alaska, Delaware, Georgia, Idaho, Illinois, Louisiana, Nevada, North Dakota, and Rhode Island. Only 9 states require candidates and committees to file reports, detailing sources of funds and types of expenditures, before and after the primary and general elections. In most states, municipal contests are excluded. Even if all the disclosure laws were complete and consistent, there would still be a gap between the reporting of the information and public knowledge of political funds. Only 2 states, Oregon and Kentucky, go the necessary step beyond disclosure by publishing at state expense for public distribution a summary of the total reported receipts and expenditures of every candidate and committee for both the primary and general election periods.

The number, form, and timing of reports are important. Many states require reports only after an election has been held. If damaging items are not revealed before voting, disclosure will have little immediate effect; public memory is notably short unless it is jogged by the competition in the next election. The ways of listing contributors and specifying expenditures may enhance or obscure critical details: for example, listing a contributor without full first name deters identification, and permitting statements of payment for "services rendered" camouflages the purpose of the expenditure. Of the states with reporting requirements, only 17 require public notice of delinquent reports, only 11 specify that the receiving officials inspect the reports, and a mere 13 require the receiving official to report excessive or illegal expenditures to a prosecutor.

As a first step to effective regulation, officials need statutory responsibility to determine whether reports have been filed or whether items are properly reported; whether the limits are observed; whether reports are complete. They must have statutory responsibility to report infractions to enforcement agencies. While such provisions would not often lead to successful prosecutions, they would at least provide a basis for serious regulation. In Maine, for example, a Campaigning Reports Committee, composed of five state legislators, reviews the fund reports and has investigative power. This committee may fine candidates $5 per day for failure to file. If the fine is not paid, the candidate may be disqualified. This system has stimulated prompt filing.

Probably the most controversial issue related to campaign laws and proposed legislation for reform is the limitation on expenditures and contributions. The difficulty of enacting limitations which are realistic and enforceable has turned legislators away from that tactic. Between 1965 and 1970 eight states repealed laws limiting campaign expenditures. Only one state, Florida, adopted an expenditure limitation law during that period. The net total number of such laws is 23. The Florida law, more realistic than most, allows up to $350,000 for campaigns for either nomination or election for governor or U. S. Senator;

$250,000 for such campaigns for statewide offices; $75,000 for campaigns for U. S. Representative; and $25,000 for local contests. Federal experience in 1970 and 1971 indicates a strong tendency to confine restrictions of expenditures to advertising, particularly television advertising, to be discussed later.

Another approach to control of expenditures is to indicate what kinds of political activities are lawful or legitimate; 20 states specify acceptable campaign expenses, although these provisions do not limit the amounts which may be spent. The lists vary in their applicability and content. Oklahoma, for example, approves expenses for transporting ill, poor, or infirm voters to the polls; the transportation of healthy, vigorous voters is apparently illegal! Florida, recognizing modern customs, permits campaign expenses for public opinion polls and for baby-sitting service.

Under Florida law, both last-minute and post-election contributions are prohibited, in theory to prevent saturation campaigns in the closing days while also discouraging commitments in expectation of future payments. The flaw is this provision, especially when coupled with a limitation on total spending, is that it also may prevent a candidate from raising money to answer last-minute charges. Campaign debts are prohibited, a restriction not likely to be adopted elsewhere nor complied with anywhere. Without incurring debts, many qualified candidates could not contest for office let alone win election.

Several states limit individual contributions, with ceilings from $1,000 to $5,000. These limits generally are interpreted to apply to gifts by one person to any one candidate or committee. Donations up to the maximum usually can be made to any number of separate committees, which may all support the same candidate. In Massachusets, individual contributions in each year are limited to $3,000 to one candidate, $3,000 to one party, and $3,000 to nonelective political committees which support no specific candidate. In Florida, limitations apply collectively to the primaries and general election and are set at $3,000 for statewide office, $2,000 for Congressional office, and $1,000 for countywide, multi-county, or state legislative office. (These limits do not apply to amounts contributed by a candidate to his own campaign.) In some states, direct expenditures by individuals on behalf of candidates are prohibited. Iowa forbids the use of contributions from nonresidents.

Several states have enacted laws which attempt to close the federal loopholes. For example, they have centralized financial responsibility by using the legal doctrine of agency, which puts the obligations to report a complete tally of receipts and expenditures on the candidate or on a small number of designated agents. The agency system is most advanced in Florida: under its pioneering campaign disclosure law enacted in 1951 the state demands appropriate publicity for all receipts and payments, including services or goods. In addition to the general limitations on contributions, Florida flatly prohibits gifts from operators of utilities or race tracks or holders of liquor permits. All contributions must be channeled through a responsible campaign treasurer or deputy treasurer (agent). Direct campaign expenditures by private citizens are forbidden unless authorized by the candidate or his agent. Contributions must be deposited in a designated bank within 24 hours of receipt by the candidate's agent or subagent and written authorizations are required for disbursal of all funds. Florida also requires weekly financial reports by candidates for governor and U. S. Senator, while other candidates must file monthly summaries.

The validity of a law that prohibits expenditures on behalf of a candidate unless the funds are channeled through a designated agent or treasurer is questionable. The Wisconsin Supreme Court invalidated a similar provision in 1916 on the grounds that it prohibited independent persons from spending money to urge their views on government practices. "If this is not an abridgment of freedom of speech," the Court said, "it would be difficult to imagine what would be." [7] The Florida Supreme Court, to the contrary, upheld the state law as an acceptable exercise of legislative power designed to curb corruption in elections.[8]

The requirement that candidates authorize all expenditures raises another question: how can a person be drafted for nomination if money cannot be raised without his consent? The question came up in Massachusetts in 1964 during Republican campaigns for both Barry Goldwater and Henry Cabot Lodge before either had announced his availability. Also, how can the candidate ascertain the existence of all supporting committees or whether they are reporting all they should?

An alternative to the agency approach is a system for registering all committees (or individuals) handling campaign funds. A registration system is designed to achieve early disclosure of political affiliations of committees without the constitutional or political difficulties that inhere in the agency system and without putting responsibilities on candidates for activities which they cannot control. The federal registration system enacted in 1972 requires any committee that expects to handle more than $1,000 on behalf of federal candidates to file a notice of intention and identify committee leaders and favored candidates.

A registration system should disclose many sources that otherwise would not be known. An information center can distribute to the press and public lists of all registered committees supporting each candidate. With this foreknowledge, those interested can follow the activities of committees and the subsequent publicity should stimulate self-regulation. A registration system is a likely method of achieving full disclosure and publicity without infringing on either constitutional rights or political practices. The disclosure and publicity would raise public confidence in politics and contribute toward enlightenment of the voters. Of course, the penalties for failing to register would have to be severe and enforced, if the system is to work well. Kentucky has both registration and an independent Registry of Election Finance which publishes campaign fund report data, both before and after both primary and general elections.

Constructive legislation aimed at easing political costs or encouraging many small contributions has been tried in only a few states. In 1955, Minnesota pioneered a tax deduction system for individual political expenses, on the theory that, for some, politics is a business and deserves tax consideration like any other business. Candidates for public office and national committeemen and women in Minnesota are allowed to deduct from their gross state income tax liability part of those campaign expenditures or political costs which they have paid personally. The amount ranges from $5,000 for a U. S. Senatorial or gubernatorial candidate to $150 for county chairmen. For most other public offices, the deduction is one-fourth the annual salary of the office.

In eight states, individuals computing their personal state income taxes may claim deductions for contributions to primary and general election campaigns of political parties, candidates, and causes; Minnesota, California, Missouri, Arkansas, Oklahoma, Iowa, Utah, and Hawaii permit deductions ranging from $25 to $100.

In 1969 Oregon became the first state to enact a tax credit plan for individual contributions to political parties. The credit is allowed for contributions either to any candidate whose name is listed on an official ballot in any election held in Oregon or to committees and associations organized to campaign on proposals on the ballot, or both. The credit is for 50 percent of the contribution, to a maximum of $5 on an individual return and $10 on a joint return. An official receipt must be submitted with the tax claim. (A credit is deducted from an individual's tax liability, in contrast to a deduction, which is subtracted from gross income before the tax is computed. A credit yields substantially more to the taxpayer than deduction of a like sum. These tax incentives are discussed further in later chapters.)

Tax incentive programs encounter the objection that they reduce revenues. Oregon's credit program began so recently that the number of claims remains to be seen. Of eight states with a deduction system, data could be obtained only from California. The State Franchise Tax Board estimated that tax deductions for political contributions in 1966 were claimed on 75,000 taxable returns, approximately 2 percent of the total, for a revenue loss of $250,000. During the 1967 legislative session, as the tax structure was changed, it was estimated that for 1968 about 100,000 returns would contain the deduction. The projected revenue loss, about $500,000, was one-half of one percent of California's total 1968 revenues, $9.3 billion.

Direct subsidies for political campaigns have been almost totally neglected by the states. Colorado made one attempt more than 60 years ago when it provided subsidies to parties based on the number of votes received in the last gubernatorial election. Before it had been operative, the law was declared unconstitutional by the state supreme court and repealed by the legislature in 1910.

The Commonwealth of Puerto Rico has had a subsidy plan

since 1957: political parties which participated in the last election or which qualify by petition receive yearly allotments from an election fund in the Treasury. Up to one-half the yearly subsidy may be deferred for election years, when additional amounts are available. In 1968 $1,662,615 was alloted to five political parties.

Some states allow indirect subsidies by providing sinecures and "no show" jobs or by permitting those in real jobs to draw salary while working for the party in registration drives or on election day. Indiana goes further than most states by openly indulging job patronage and state employee contributions.[9] About 8,000 of the state's 22,000 employees are patronage employees who are expected to belong to the Two Percent Club, which requires them to contribute two percent of their net salary to the state committee, according to the political affiliation of the incumbent governor. The party out of office receives nothing from this source. The state committee has a personnel director who fills the jobs and, with the aid of a subtreasurer in each state agency, collects the contributions. The money is channeled through the state committee and is available to the governor, who consequently gains political leverage. The system is defended on the grounds that it is better for money to come from government workers than from other special interests. Some seriously contend that political parties are quite as interested in hiring qualified employees as a nonpartisan civil service system and even more eager to perform creditably.

Indiana has another unusual system of indirect political fundraising: all motor vehicle registrations and drivers' licenses are issued in branches which are awarded on a political basis to the county chairmen of the governor's party.[10] The franchise permits each branch to collect a service fee of 50 cents per license, of which four cents goes to the state committee. Branch expenses also are paid out of the service fee. The system awards jobs to party faithful while filling the party coffers. Obviously, such "party capitalism" only favors the party in power.

Such methods of filling a party's treasury aggravate public cynicism about campaign financing. If the political system is to be funded properly, the states, as well as the federal government, must encourage contributions from sources known and accepted by the public and must enact and enforce realistic laws against undesirable methods of raising, sharing, and using political funds.

The American system of law relies to a great extent upon action initiated by aggrieved plaintiffs. In elections, both the defeated candidate and the voters may be aggrieved by violations of election or campaign financing laws. A 1946 Massachusetts law permits five or more voters to request permission of a state superior court justice to file to void an election if they have reasonable cause to believe a corrupt practice occurred; the suit is heard by a special three-judge court. New York has a similar law. In neither state, however, have any such suits been filed. Under an Oregon law which provides for disqualifying the election of anyone found guilty of violating the state's elections laws, the defeated candidate for attorney general brought suit in 1968 on the grounds that the winner had overspent a $2,000 limit on a candidate's spending from his own resources. The circuit court ruled in favor of the challenger, but within a few months the state supreme court reversed the lower court with a ruling that the admitted spending was not deliberate or in "reckless disregard" of the law.[11]

The Oregon case raises the critical question of the appropriate penalty for an election winner who has violated the campaign law. On one hand, it is cogently argued, the will of the people as expressed at the polls should prevail even if they elect a criminal; on the other hand, law is not respected if it is not well enforced. One could argue that usually the people would not know that the candidate had violated the law at the time they were voting: charges of election or financing fraud almost invariably arise after an election. Perhaps the courts could declare the office vacant and order a new election.

Undoubtedly the best policing is a self-policing system in which all contenders, the press, and interested individuals and organizations, as well as the official auditing and enforcement agencies, play important roles. Professor Louise Overacker has said:

"Too often private citizens who suspect violations are not in possession of sufficiently definite information to be willing to bring charges. Too often violations of the law do not outrage the sensibilities of private citizens sufficiently acutely to spur them into action. A vicious circle is created in which public indifference has an unfortunate reaction upon prosecuting officers, and the indifference of prosecuting officers has an equally unfortunate effect upon the public." [12]

A catalyst is needed to spur interest in clean, honest, and fair elections. Several have been suggested. One proposal would allow any voter to bring a private right of action against parties engaging in illegal financial transactions. (This is similar to provisions in the Securities and Exchange Act.) In order to encourage such actions, the law could provide that the plaintiff be reimbursed for all legitimate expenses if any violation is proved. Another proposal would allot the successful plaintiff his expenses plus a monetary recovery. In order to insure that suits are not mere harassment, a bond could be required of the plaintiff. Liability for all costs if a violation is not proved may in itself be a sufficient deterrent to spiteful or frivolous actions. Two other proposed incentives to citizen action are finders fees for individuals or payment of triple damages to the plaintiff or injured party.

Effective legal procedures to stimulate enforcement and serious penalties will discourage abuses or violations of campaign laws. Enforcement, with penalties sufficient to deter abuse, is the key, but, given the facilities for mutual surveillance, publicity may be penalty enough.

CHAPTER 12

THE HISTORY OF REFORM

Official apathy toward serious reform of political finance has been a Washington tradition. From the years 1904-07, when Theodore Roosevelt in Congressional messages successively proposed disclosure laws, the corporate prohibition, and government subsidies, until 1961, several Presidents went on record for reform but took no vigorous action. President Kennedy showed serious concern on the issue by appointing a Commission on Campaign Costs which started a chain of promising events. His death interrupted the momentum; President Johnson did not offer his own program until 1966, and he faltered again in 1967. President Nixon took no public action until his veto of the 1970 political broadcast bill, a negative move. In 1972, however, the issue finally resulted in new legislation described in Chapter 17.

The Congress had not acted on political reform from the date of the Hatch Act, 1940, until 1966. (The 1947 Taft-Hartley Act related only peripherally to the basic law regulating public reporting and corrupt practices in that it codified the corporate and labor prohibitions. Until 1972 the basic law dated back to the Federal Corrupt Practices Act of 1925 and major parts were unchanged since 1910-11.) Even the 1940 date is misleading, because the Hatch Act merely added limitations to amounts that could be contributed and that political committees could receive or spend.

In 1966 two statutes were enacted without White House intervention. These were the Williams Amendment, affecting corporate advertising in program books, and the Long Amendment, providing a tax subsidy for Presidential election campaigns. The Williams Amendment was partially rescinded in 1968, and the Long Amendment was repealed before it became operative. And in 1970 a political broadcast bill was enacted on Congressional initiative and vetoed by the President. Neither the executive nor the legislative branch could claim credit for major electoral reforms from 1925 until 1972.

The first federal legislation relating to money in politics took the form of protection against political assessment of federal employees in 1867. This provision was later extended and broadened in the Civil Service Reform Act of 1883, which not only forbade assessment of government employees but also restricted the employees from soliciting other government workers.[1] Through a series of enforcement actions, court decisions, and rulings by the Attorney General, direct assessments of federal civil service employees were almost extinct by the end of the nineteenth century. The Hatch Act, passed in 1939 and amended in 1940, extended the restrictions on political activities by civil service employees to all except the highest-level appointed officials in the Executive branch.

As the electorate gained awareness of federal powers and influence, contributions to politics came under fire. In 1904 it was charged that corporations were pouring millions into the Republican campaign to elect Theodore Roosevelt. Charles Evans Hughes disclosed that several life insurance companies for years had been contributing heavily to the G.O.P. (which later nominated Hughes for President and appointed him Chief Justice). Banks, utilities, oil companies, and other industries also were in politics at all levels.

After the 1904 election, a move for federal legislation to force disclosure of campaign spending took shape in the National Publicity Law Association, headed by a former New York Representative, Democrat Perry Belmont. Associated with Belmont were Hughes, William Jennings Bryan, President Charles William Eliot of Harvard, and Samuel Gompers. In 1907 Congress cracked down on corporate giving by prohibiting national banks and corporations from contributing in elections of federal officials.

Congress passed the first federal campaign fund disclosure law in 1910; an amendment the following year required primary, convention, and pre-election statements and limited the amounts that could be spent by candidates for the House and Senate. The law was contested in a famous case in 1921. A federal court convicted Truman Newberry for excessive campaign expenditures in his successful bid for a Senate seat from Michigan in 1918. Newberry had defeated Henry Ford in both the Republican

primary and the general election. (Ford had taken the precau-
tion of running in both parties' primaries, and he had won the
Democratic contest.) Newberry's campaigns allegedly cost
$100,000 between December 1, 1917 and November 5, 1918, with
the bulk of the spending in the prenomination period. Newberry's
conviction was based on the 1910 law which, together with the
Michigan law, limited Senatorial candidates' expenditures to
$3,750 (excluding certain exempted expenditures). The trial
court judge had instructed the jury to find Newberry guilty if
they found that he had campaigned with full awareness that
illegal expenditures would be needed. The U. S. Supreme Court
overturned the conviction on Constitutional grounds, ruling that
Congressional authority to regulate elections did not extend to
primaries and nomination activities, and most of the questionable
expenses in Newberry's campaign had preceded the Republican
primary. This narrow interpretation of Congressional authority
was rejected in 1941 in *United States v. Classic* (in a case
relating to federal-state powers), but Congress did not reassert
its power to require disclosure of campaign funds for pre-nomination campaigns until 1972. Other federal provisions such as the
prohibition against corporate, national bank, and union political
activities and against members of Congress soliciting or accepting money from federal employees do apply to primary elections
and have been sustained by the courts.

Relevant federal legislation was codified and revised, albeit
without substantial change, in the Federal Corrupt Practices Act
of 1925, the basic law until 1972. Essentially, the law required
disclosure of receipts and expenditures by candidates for the
Senate and House (not for President or Vice President) and by
political committees which sought to influence federal elections
in two or more states. Spending limits on Senate and House
candidates were derived from the 1925 legislation. The Hatch
Act of 1940 also limited to $5,000 gifts an individual could
make to a federal candidate or to a committee in a single year
and set the $3 million limit on committee expenditures. A more
significant factor than the $5,000 ceiling in limiting individual
contributions has been the federal gift tax, imposing progressive
tax rates on contributions of more than $3,000 to a single candi-
date or committee in any year.[2] The bar on corporate giving that

had been on the books since 1907 was temporarily extended to labor unions in the Smith-Connally Act of 1944 and then reenacted in the Taft-Hartley Act of 1947.

The post-World War II years witnessed a series of Congressional gestures, usually no more than Committee reports, toward reform of political finance.

In 1948 and again in 1951, special House committees on campaign expenditures reported that substantial revisions were needed in the Corrupt Practices and Hatch Acts. The 1951 House committee took the stand that it was "patently impossible for a candidate to conduct a Congressional or Senatorial campaign" within existing limits and that "present unrealistic limitations on campaign contributions and expenditures are an invitation to criminal violation." [3] The committee also recommended that reports of primary campaign finances be required, that political organizations be precluded from receiving or spending funds for a candidate without his written authorization, and that the prohibition against election activities by government employees be eliminated or liberalized. The report produced no legislation. Not for more than 10 years would another House committee show interest in the subject. During his tenure as House Speaker, Sam Rayburn of Texas opposed any legislation placing primaries under scrutiny. In his day, a Democrat in Texas who won the primary nomination was certain to win election.

In 1953 the Elections Subcommittee of the Senate Committee on Rules and Administration proposed that the limit on spending for national political committees be increased from $3 to $10 million a year, together with increases in permissible spending for Congressional campaigns. The Senate did not act. In 1955 Senator Thomas Hennings of Missouri, the new Subcommittee chairman, introduced a comprehensive bill requiring all committees active in campaigns for federal office to file financial reports, even if their activities were confined to one state. He also proposed raising the spending limits for Congressional candidates and national political committees. The Subcommittee and the full Committee reported the bill, but it never reached the Senate floor.

The February, 1956, disclosure by Senator Francis Case of South Dakota (noted earlier) that he had been offered a $2,500 campaign gift if he would vote for the Harris-Fulbright Natural

Gas Bill [4] led to three Congressional investigations. The Senate majority and minority leaders, Lyndon B. Johnson and William Knowland, introduced a compromise election reform bill with the co-sponsorship of 83 Senators. It was not reported out of committee. Of several views about the reason for its demise, the favorite was that, with so many sponsors, the bill would have to be passed if it reached the floor.

Shortly after Senator Hennings became chairman of the full Rules and Administration Committee in 1957, he succeeded again in having his reform bill reported favorably out of committee, but again no floor debate was scheduled. Three years later he did secure floor debate. The bill became the first major piece of Senate business that year.

Faced with formidable opposition in committee to a strong bill, Hennings agreed to report a relatively weak measure, with the intention of adding strengthening amendments on the floor. With the assistance of Senators Kenneth Keating and Estes Kefauver, Hennings added several key provisions during the Senate debate: candidates for federal office would be required to report their expenditures in primary campaigns; state and local committees would be required to report if they spent $2,500 or more in federal campaigns; an aggregate limit of $10,000 on the amount an individual could contribute for political purposes in a single year was provided; ceilings on expenditures by Congressional candidates would be raised to more realistic levels; candidates for President and Vice President could spend up to 20¢ for each vote cast in any one of the three preceding Presidential elections. With these amendments included, the Hennings bill passed the Senate by a vote of 59 to 22. Landmark that it was, the measure received a quiet burial in the House.

The cause of clean elections suffered a setback with the death of Senator Hennings, the most able and persistent advocate of reform. The chairmanship of the Rules and Administration Committee went to Senator Mike Mansfield, who as majority leader became too busy to give it much attention. When he relinquished the post to North Carolina's B. Everett Jordan two years later, the chairmanship of the key Elections Subcommittee went to Senator Howard M. Cannon of Nevada.

Public hearings were held on the various reform proposals by

Cannon's subcommittee in the Spring of 1961, but the final result, rewritten and reintroduced as the Cannon bill, was a minimal reform, lacking most of the substantive improvements approved on the Senate floor the previous year. As floor manager, Senator Cannon took a different course than had Hennings, offering no strengthening amendments and in fact arguing for the weak bill on the ground that the House would not accept anything else. The bill was passed by voice vote in the Senate, but still the House failed to go along.

Post-war Presidents all have voiced concern about the methods used to raise money to pay for political campaigns. President Truman favored government subsidies, though, like President Eisenhower, he later endorsed the recommendations of President Kennedy's Commission on Campaign Costs for tax incentives. President Dwight Eisenhower succinctly pointed to the problem: "It does mean, in effect, that we have put a dollar sign on public service, and today many capable men who would like to run for office simply can't afford to do so. Many believe that politics in our country is already a game exclusively for the affluent. This is not strictly true; yet the fact that we may be approaching that state of affairs is a sad reflection on our elective system." [5]

During his years in Congress, John F. Kennedy had expressed much concern about campaign financing, and his book *Profiles in Courage* is sprinkled with references to the subject. He was a member of the Senate Special Committee to Investigate Political Activities, Lobbying, and Campaign Contributions, one of the committees formed after the Case disclosure in 1956. Kennedy was sensitive to the advantages wealth gave one in politics and also was aware of the public cynicism, having himself been accused of buying public office.

Even before his inauguration, Kennedy, his concern heightened by the Democratic deficit of $3,820,000 from the campaign, set in motion activities which led to the creation of the Commission on Campaign Costs in 1961. In announcing the Commission's appointment, Kennedy forthrightly expressed his worry about the undesirable influence that might be wielded by those who put up the campaign cash. "To have Presidential candidates dependent on large financial contributions of those with special interests is highly undesirable," he declared. ". . . The financial base of our

Presidential campaigns must be broadened." [6]

Kennedy asked the Commission to recommend suitable ways to finance Presidential general election campaigns and to reduce costs of running for the Presidency. By restricting the Commission's jurisdiction to Presidential and Vice-Presidential campaigns, Kennedy was pointing an example but not telling Congress how to regulate its own campaigns. Later, when he submitted legislative proposals based on the Commission's report, he invited Congress to extend the proposals to all federal offices. The bipartisan Commission had been designed to give broad support for the objective of reform, and every effort was made to achieve unanimity in developing the recommendations.

Submitted to the President in April, 1962, the Commission's unanimous report was heralded by the President at a news conference. Among those who endorsed the report were the Chairmen of the Republican and Democratic National Committees, former Presidents Truman and Eisenhower, and Messrs. Nixon, Stevenson, and Dewey—all the living Presidential candidates of both major parties in the last quarter century.

The Commission stated its belief in a strongly organized and effectively functioning two-party system, in widespread citizen participation in the political system, and in the desirability of voluntary, private action wherever such effort is sufficient to meet needs. It sought to increase public confidence in the ways campaigns are financed and to instill public respect for the legal system regulating political finance.

Five of the twelve recommendations in the Commission's report[7] were major. They advocated:

• That individuals, business, labor unions, and private organizations be encouraged to take part in and to make expenditures for voluntary *bipartisan* political activities, such as registration and fund-raising drives, and that the reasonable costs of such activities be declared deductible for tax purposes.

• That tax incentives be tried for an experimental period extending over two Presidential campaigns, allowing either: (a) that individual political contributors be given a credit against federal income tax of 50 percent of contributions, up to a maximum of $10 in credits per year; or (b) that contributors be permitted to claim the full amount of their contributions as a deduction from taxable income up to a maximum of $1,000 per tax return per year.

The only contributions eligible for these benefits would be gifts to the national committee of a party (on the ballot in ten or more states), or to a single state political committee designated by such a national committee in each state.

• That the unrealistic and unenforceable ceilings on individual contributions and on total expenditures by political committees be abolished, and that an effective system of public disclosure be instituted instead, requiring that the principal sources and uses of money in Presidential campaigns be reported to a Registry of Election Finance. The proposed system would require that periodic reports be submitted by all political parties, committees, candidates, and other campaign groups raising or spending $2,500 or more on behalf of federal candidates, showing a total income and outgo, and itemizing certain contributions and expenditures.

• That the Congress provide funds for the reasonable and necessary costs of preparing and installing in office new administrations during the transition between the election and inauguration of a new President.

• That a temporary suspension of Section 315 of the Federal Communications Act be enacted, as in 1960, to permit broadcasters to make their facilities available on an equal basis to the nominees of the major political parties for President and Vice President without the legal requirement to do the same for all candidates for those offices.

Taken as a whole, the report presented a model and comprehensive program for reforming the financing of the political system, covering not only federal legislative remedies but also bipartisan activities, certain party practices, and state actions. There was little innovation in the report's recommendations; most of the proposals had been aired before. The purpose was more immediate: to get things moving in the field by detailing a comprehensive program of reform of political finance—disclosure, publicity, limitations, corrupt practices, tax incentives, and political broadcasting. To that date, there had been many isolated proposals, but none was comprehensive or related part-to-part for specific elections. The report accomplished its purpose.

The report was significant, too, in giving official voice to certain ideas, such as the position that ceilings on campaign spending are not enforceable or desirable and may be unconstitutional. Through the years, the notion that ceilings could be made effective has been shared by many observers, even though almost every study of this issue had concluded otherwise. The report also gave official sanction to original concepts that Congress had not considered seriously before such as the suggestion for a Registry of Election Finance to receive, examine, tabulate, summarize, publish, and preserve reported data on campaign funds.

The Commission's failure to suggest more about registration and election-day expenses was regrettable. Registration is a concern of government rather than of political parties in all mature democracies except the United States.

One innovation submerged in the report, and purposely not lifted to the level of a firm recommendation, was the statement that if tax incentives were tried and failed, and if further consideration were given to developing a greater federal share in bearing campaign costs, a new approach should be examined: a scheme the commission called a "matching incentive." Under it, contributions of specified amounts (for example, $10 per person) raised by designated political committees would be deposited with the U .S. Treasury, where the money would be matched by a like sum from appropriations. The combined total would be available to the committee to meet authorized types of costs, direct payments being made by the government to sellers of goods and services. Such a plan would give political organizations a powerful incentive to solicit private contributions. It would encourage voluntary financial support of the parties by masses of small givers and would reward party success in obtaining financial support from its own adherents.

Only one Commission proposal drew opposition within the Kennedy Administration. The Treasury Department would have preferred a subsidy to tax incentives, since it favored income tax reform and simplification and was not anxious for a new and complicated set of tax proposals. The President decided to follow the Commission recommendations for tax incentives but, in submitting the proposals to Congress, reduced the amount of the tax deduction from $1,000 to $750; the proposal for a tax credit was left unaltered. Kennedy decided that the good which would come from tax incentives outweighed other considerations relating to tax reform.

Kennedy accepted all other Commission recommendations, and one was carried out promptly by the Treasury Department. The Internal Revenue Service authorized taxpayers to deduct from income their expenditures in connection with federal, state, or local elections, if the money was used for the following purposes: for advertising designed to encourge the public to register and vote and to contribute to the political party or campaign fund of a candidate of their choice; for sponsoring a political debate among candidates for a particular office; for granting employees time off with pay for registration and voting; and for maintaining a payroll deduction plan for employees wishing to make political contributions.[8]

The IRS ruling is a form of encouragement too often overlooked. To this day, not many realize that joint appearances of candidates on radio and television and "battle pages" in newspapers and other print media can be sponsored by corporations and counted as a business expense.

The Commission recommendations on new legislation were included in the President's proposals to Congress in May, 1962,[9] but it was too late in the second session of the 87th Congress for serious consideration, and Kennedy renewed the proposals to the new Congress in April, 1963.[10]

The recommendations were less than enthusiastically received on Capitol Hill where certain members of Congress were distrustful of a Presidential initiative in a field traditionally considered a legislative prerogative. The Commission had not included any members of Congress. Although several key Senators felt they should have been actively consulted, the Commission had decided that consulting with Congress would have exposed it to efforts to obtain the lowest common denominator of agreement, contrary to its wish to contrive a model independent of tactical compromise. The Commission assiduously informed key Congressmen of the purpose and progress of the Commission and gave them advance copies of the Report but failed to attract much Congressional sympathy.

The lack of political appeal in the issue should have been no surprise. No blocs of voters were concerned. The only major industry substantially affected was broadcasting, and it lobbied almost exclusively with respect to Section 315 of the Federal Communications Act. The Committee on Campaign Contributions and Expenditures, a citizens' group which had been formed by William H. Vanderbilt, the former Republican governor of Rhode Island, in the mid-1950's, made one mailing to members of Congress urging consideration of the Commission proposals. Made up of about 75 prominent members of both major parties, Vanderbilt's Committee had neither staff nor headquarters. William L. Clayton of Texas succeeded Vanderbilt as chairman, but its mailing on the Commission Report and proposals was the committee's only public effort.

Press comments on the Commission Report and on subsequent submission of President Kennedy to the Congress were universally favorable. With a few minor objections but no serious opposition, hundreds of constructive editorials were published in papers and magazines.

The response from other quarters was less enthusiastic. The Chamber of Commerce of the United States was concerned that the tax incentive features would erode the tax base. The labor movement, led by the AFL-CIO and the UAW, objected to proposals on public reporting and tax incentives.

The combined tax credit and deduction had unanimous agreement in the Commission. It was felt the combination would draw maximum Congressional support. But labor observed that deductions would give greater advantage to those in higher tax brackets and wanted the tax credit alone to apply to all political organizations at any level, with an immediate 90 percent refund to the claimant. The former Chairman of the Commission, Alexander Heard, has summarized both sides of the argument:

"The lack of positive support from labor leaders for the President's tax incentives may be because contributions to labor political committees would not be eligible for such benefits. And if the money-raising capacity of the parties is improved, the relative importance of labor's help to Democratic candidates could diminish, thus weakening its tactical position.

"Opponents of the tax-deduction proposal, moreover, point out that well-to-do contributors would gain an unfair advantage.

Given the graduated income tax, the net cost of a political gift would go down as the taxpayer's income went up. In contrast, people with smaller incomes taking a standard tax deduction would gain no benefit at all. On the other hand, opponents of a tax credit fear it would give a powerful weapon to leaders of mass organizations who could use it to dragoon their followers into making campaign contributions. In both cases, the threat of a shift in political power is sensed." [11]

Contrary to expectations, the credit and deduction combination was resisted by those opposing either the credit or deduction, aligned with those opposed to any form of tax benefit.

Eligibility for the proposed tax benefits was another concern. The Commission prescription was that eligibility be limited to the national committee of a defined political party and one committee in each state, with the national committee choosing that committee. This would keep the number of eligible committees to about 100. The Treasury Department favored this limitation, which would ease the load of administration and validation. Under this formula, contributions to labor and other non-party committees would not be eligible for tax benefits. Labor leaders foresaw a disadvantage to their political funds. They pointed out, moreover, that the proposed eligibility factor would give a tax advantage to party committees controlled by anti-labor machines. The counter-argument was that, since American politics was splintered enough, broadening eligibility would give official sanction to the proliferation of political committees. The price of restricted eligibility was a loss of funds for labor and other non-party committees and, in some states, financial benefits to racist politicians.

Limiting eligibility to party committees would preclude financial help through tax incentives in the prenomination period when candidates must run without benefit of party resources. Possibly a party, confident of its financial resources, might indirectly support a party regular against the challenge of a reformer. Both situations would further limit the responsiveness of entrenched parties to new voices.

Labor objected also to a provision that would have required reporting of bipartisan expenditures of $5,000 or more, accounting in detail for receipts and expenditures regarding educational or citizenship activities.

Actually, labor's opposition to tax benefits hurt the Democrats as well as the Republicans. From the start it was unlikely that the Congress would enact a deduction for more than $100 per claim, which would benefit Democrats as well as Republicans. Though labor is quick to condemn businessmen for their political influence, labor has not helped a great deal to provide disinterested sources of funds for parties or candidates.

Congress is often blamed for its failure to enact electoral reforms. Vested interests may be behind Congressional inactivity, but it is also true that some Congressmen resisted legislation that would advantage the party organization with funds which might be denied to them as candidates. Congressional reluctance plus labor's opposition resulted in the major reform bills being introduced for the record only, with the understanding that the White House would not push hard for them. Hearings were not held on the major proposals for improved disclosure or for tax incentives.

President Kennedy's interest in political finance continued after the Commission expired. He engaged its Executive Director, the present author, as a White House consultant to deal with legislation pending in 1962 on all aspects of political finance. There is no department or agency of the federal government with that responsibility. The Justice Department deals with corrupt practices and enforcement. The Treasury Department deals with tax incentives, directly or through the Internal Revenue Service. Any subsidy scheme would be administered in part by Treasury or in part by the Comptroller General. The Federal Communications Commission, an independent regulatory agency, deals with political broadcasting. As the Executive Office of the President keeps an eye on all legislation, the responsibility devolved upon the author, in cooperation with White House staff, for seeing legislation introduced and moved through the mill. Rather than risk a backlash from Congress, the White House cautiously refrained from inciting public pressure.

As in the executive branch, legislative responsibility also is fragmented; no one committee of the Senate or House covers all aspects of political finance. When President Kennedy proposed separate bills covering public reporting, tax incentives, political broadcasting, and transition costs, each bill went to a different committee in each house, each attempting to deal with separate aspects of the same subject and none able to consider the whole. Such dispersal of responsibility makes it easy to delay or defer action. Comprehensive legislation could be enacted during floor debate by adding amendments, but this tactic does not often lead to well-considered legislation.

Lack of Congressional response to the Presidential recommendations led to a re-evaluation during 1963. A three-point program proposed by the author was designed to broaden the base of financial support for the 1964 elections. President Kennedy agreed to the program shortly before his death. Several of the so-called Irish Mafia on the White House staff, reputedly hard-boiled, professional politicians, helped to promote the program and ease the way for its execution. The program consisted of the following:

• *A White House Conference on Campaign Finance to be held in March, 1964.* Preliminary talks with Republicans were held. Former President Eisenhower would have been invited and President Kennedy would have attended. A full day of sessions would have drawn 300 persons representing major political and private groups. A meeting was scheduled to draft the Executive Order for the Conference on November 22, 1963, the day an assassin's bullet intervened. The Conference would have stressed responsibility of citizens to participate financially by contributing to the party or candidate of their choice, encouraged bipartisan activities to raise political money, and announced the two other elements of the contemplated 1964 program.

• *Fund-raising exhibits of the major parties in the United States Pavilion at the New York World's Fair.* Numerous party committees around the country were to man booths at state or country fairs, both to bring in money and to win friends for the party. As the World's Fair was to be held in a Presidential election year, it offered an opportunity to reach 40 million persons with a bipartisan appeal. Both parties were interested, but in the transition period, the project lacked needed White House support.

• *An inter-party competition for small contributions.* A contest would have been held to determine which party nationally, under rules agreed upon, received the larger number of small contributions. Talks with Republicans had begun and, had the project gone forward, a day-to-day tally, publicly announced, might have spurred competition for small gifts. (In 1963, the Republican advantage in attracting small gifts was not as great as it was later.)

Understandably, the new Johnson administration had other priorities. By the time the White House was ready to consider the program, it was too late to meet the schedule. In April, 1964, with no program on which to consult, the author resigned.

Two of President Kennedy's proposals met little opposition in Congress. One was the bill to suspend the equal time provision of Section 315 of the Federal Communications Act for the Presidential and Vice-Presidential campaigns of 1964, a repeat of the 1960 bill which had made possible the "Great Debates." The feeling was widespread that the broadcasting industry needed periodic Congressional scrutiny and thus only a temporary suspension was warranted. This bill passed both Houses of Congress, in slightly different versions, by large margins in 1964. By this time, President Johnson seemed to have decided that he would not debate Senator Goldwater. If the bill passed, pressure for debate would build. Accordingly, the leadership saw that the bill was not reported out of the Senate-House Conference.

The other bill, largely noncontroversial, was to provide government subsidies for the President-Elect and Vice President-Elect from Election Day until Inauguration Day. The purpose was to provide for an orderly transition of political power following an election. In 1964 the two chambers agreed on the bill, and President Johnson signed it. In 1964-5 Vice President-Elect Humphrey drew less than $75,000 from this fund to cover some staff expenses, permitting him to resign his Senate seat early to give a bit of seniority to his appointed successor, Walter Mondale.

(The total amount of $900,000 was used in the 1968-9 transition; it was divided as follows: $375,000 each for the incoming and outgoing Presidents, and $75,000 each for the incoming and outgoing Vice President. In addition to their $450,000, the

Republicans spent an additional $500,000 or so not covered by government subsidy.[12])

In his first two years in office, President Johnson failed to support any legislative reform of political finance and ignored representations from former members of the President's Commission. The program on political finance was one of the few Kennedy creations to suffer seriously in the transition to the Johnson Administration. It must have been considered the most expendable of ideas with a strong Kennedy imprint, for while other Kennedy programs may have been downgraded or changed in emphasis, this one was cut out. The White House Press Office later boasted about saving the few thousand dollars it would have cost per year.[13]

Arguments were advanced that President Johnson should have been especially attentive to electoral reform in view of comments about Texas oil money and Bobby Baker. Perhaps the Baker hearings turned him against further airing of the issues. From a pragmatic point of view, it appears that President Johnson elected to protect his advantage in public sympathy and popularity in 1964. He may have believed that reform would impair the money-raising activities of the President's Club. It is pertinent, too, that he had learned practical politics from Sam Rayburn.

The White House gave the subject no public attention until 1966 when a crescendo of criticism about the President's Club, the advertising books, secrecy about Democratic Party finances, and incomplete filings of required reports reached the President's ears. In his State of the Union address, the President stated his intention to submit an election reform program, but proposals were not transmitted until late May, too late for passage in the 89th Congress.

Between 1962-63, when Congress ignored most of the proposals of President Kennedy's Commission, and 1966, when it received the Johnson package, the cause on Capitol Hill was nearly dormant. Late in 1963, the Senate Finance Committee offered an amendment to the pending tax reduction bill to permit tax credits for small political gifts. The amendment was rejected, but a substitute was offered, changing the benefit to a deduction of up to $50 a year for individuals (or $100 for married taxpayers filing joint returns). The Committee approved the deduction with solid Republican support, and the bill passed the Senate with little discussion, but when the bills came to conference, the deduction hit a snag. Anticipating a loss of revenue, the Treasury Department opposed the amendment because it would apply to all candidates and committees at all levels, not merely to Presidential nominees. Representative Wilbur Mills of Arkansas, the conference chairman, also was opposed. Only personal intervention by President Johnson could have saved it. The conference voted the amendment out of the bill.

With the death of the deduction in 1964, Congress seemed to relapse into its usual cataleptic posture on reform of campaign finance, but events led to unprecented activity in 1966, sparked by Senator Williams.

Delaware's Senator John Williams (R) qualified as a zealous opponent of waste and corruption in modern American politics. He was among the first to demand investigation of the relationship between Sherman Adams, Assistant to President Eisenhower, and industrialist Bernard Goldfine. His one-man study of Bobby Baker had led to Baker's resignation in 1963, the subsequent Senate investigation, and indirectly to Baker's conviction in 1967 for several violations of the law, although the investigation was charged with sidestepping Baker's connections with political money. Williams' disapproval of the 1965 Democratic program book, with ads at $15,000 a page, had led to passage of his amendment outlawing tax deductions for ads in political literature.

As the gap in money raising left by the Williams amendment had to be filled, Congress took fresh interest in ideas previously considered suspect. President Johnson proposed in 1966, among other recommendations, a tax deduction for political contributions. Similar to the defeated 1963 proposal, it would have applied to taxpayers whether they took the standard ten percent deduction or itemized deductions. It would have allowed a deduction up to $50 for a single taxpayer, $100 for husband and wife. Other recommendations of the Johnson Administration's bill sought to plug the two largest loopholes in the law by extending reporting requirements to primary elections and by requiring reports by committees working in a single state in behalf of federal candidates. The bill fell short of the ideal by leaving responsibility for receiving campaign fund reports in the hands of the Secretary of the Senate and the Clerk of the House, without provision for their review for violations of the law. The President broke new ground, however, in suggesting that members of Congress make public their income from personal services and gifts over $100.

In the past Congressional inaction on political finance seemed rooted in part in the procedures of Congress; the seniority system had tended to freeze committee control in the hands of southerners or others from districts dominated by one party, men having little interest in the needs of candidates in competitive districts. In the mid-1960's, with mounting Republican competition, campaign finances became much more important to southern Democrats. For this reason, if not others, the proposals of Lyndon Johnson received relatively sympathetic treatment, at least in the House.

Congressional activity was stimulated from other directions, too. In 1965 and again in 1966 the Republican Coordinating Committee released reports urging legislative action. By 1966, the new House Republican leadership constructively worked up a progressive reform bill and pressed the Democrats for action.

After years of quietude, the House Subcommittee on Elections held four days of hearings and produced the bipartisan Ashmore-Goodell Bill, the most comprehensive bill considered in Congress to that date. Sponsored by Robert T. Ashmore of South Carolina, the Democratic chairman of the Subcommittee, and Charles Goodell of New York, the ranking Republican on the Subcommittee, the bill was a mixture of the strongest portions of the Johnson and Kennedy proposals, the Republican bills, and ideas of subcommittee members and experts. The author, a consultant to the Committee, believes the bill went as far as feasible then; many of its improvements were enacted in 1972.

Most importantly, the bill called for a bipartisan Federal Elections Commission to receive, analyze, audit, and publicize spending reports by all candidates and committees in federal elections. Like the Administration bill, the Ashmore-Goodell bill also abolished ceilings on spending by candidates or committees, included primary and nominating convention coverage in disclosure requirements, and made it obligatory for committees to report if they intended raising or spending $1,000 or more to influence federal elections. A registration system for defined political committees was provided.

One feature of the bill barred trade associations, as well as unions and corporations, from using their regular funds to support the staff and administrative expenses of any of their political subsidiaries in partisan activities. The provision was not intended to affect use of corporate and labor dues funds in nonpartisan activities, including registration and other citizenship or educational activities (such as publishing a newsletter), but labor opposed. Rather than attempt to get the offending section modified or deleted, labor opposed the bill in its entirety. Many liberals, dependent to a greater or lesser extent on labor support and funds, were understandably anxious about affronting labor. Some thought, however, that once reform legislation reached the floor, the liberals might find themselves in an awkward public position if they opposed it. The problem was to get it to the floor.

The Ashmore-Goodell bill was reported out by the subcommittee too late for 1966,[14] but in June, 1967, it was revived and moved forward in the committee with an additional provision prohibiting members of Congress or Congressional candidates from using, for personal purposes, funds raised at political events. The new provision was added only a few days after the Senate had censured Senator Dodd.

In contrast to the House, the Senate Subcommittee on Privileges and Elections, chaired by Senator Cannon, refused to schedule hearings on the Administration proposals. Cannon's action was not unexpected. Nevada is one of nine states with no campaign disclosure laws. Cannon felt little pressure from home to play the reformer's role. In 1962 Cannon had been asked and had refused to introduce President Kennedy's election reform bill except by request; this meant he would not manage and fight for the bill as his own. In 1963 he would not introduce the bill at all. In neither 1960 nor 1968[15] did Cannon undertake a Senate investigation of campaign costs, as Senator Gore had done for the 1956 election. In 1966 neither Cannon nor any other ranking member of the Senate Rules Committee or Cannon's subcommittee would introduce President Johnson's bill. Its eventual sponsor was Senator Joseph Clark of Pennsylvania, a critic of the so-called Senate establishment. No hearings were held. Cannon persuaded both the subcommittee and the full Senate Rules Committee to report out a weak bill which he offered year after year and which was no more than a restatement of existing law. The editorial storm this raised, however, led Cannon to promise to hold hearings later on President Johnson's bill.

In 1967 Cannon introduced President Johnson's latest bill, a weakened version of the Ashmore-Goodell bill of the previous year. Why the Administration returned a weaker bill is unknown, but it was a tactical mistake, for its unanimous passage by the Senate indicates that a stronger bill surely would have passed. The Administration bill had been watered down to require that reports should continue to be filed with the Secretary of the Senate and the Clerk of the House—two offices that could hardly be expected to insist upon full and accurate reports filed by Congressmen—rather than to a Federal Elections Commission or other single repository. The President's bill required more disclosure, but it would have flooded the two filing offices with reports without ever facing the need for a mechanism separate from Congress to distill the data and to help publicize violations.

Pushed by criticism and events, Senator Cannon guided the Johnson bill without significant change through the first Senate hearings on election reform in six years. Both Cannon and the Senate, however, refused to support an amendment submitted by Senator Joseph F. Clark which required that reports be submitted to a single repository. Also failing support, although by a surprisingly slim margin, was another Clark amendment requiring a form of personal disclosure of finances similar to the requirement for disclosure of gifts and honorariums in the Ashmore-Goodell bill. One amendment which was adopted tightened restrictions on the solicitation of government employees. Senator Williams of Delaware had long sought to relieve government employees of pressure to buy tickets to partisan fund-raising events, a source of particular irritation in the Washington area.

The Senate amazed observers by voting 87-0 for the full bill, including the Williams amendment. No doubt the Baker and Dodd cases were significant factors in forcing the Senate to take this first step toward real reform.

Another factor was pressure growing out of extended debate over the Long Act. While the other proposals were under consideration, Senator Russell Long of Louisiana, Chairman of the Senate Finance Committee, introduced and managed the passage of a major bill providing a federal subsidy for Presidential election, a plan which contrasted sharply to the Administration's tax incentive plan. The act was important because it stimulated thinking on the issue, though it had one of the shortest gestation periods on record, June 15 to October 22, 1966, and a comparably short life. On its own, the act would no doubt have faltered; it passed as an amendment to an unrelated bill, without reference to an elections or appropriations committee in either house.[16] No hearings were held on the House side, and the bill passed on the last day of the second session of the 89th Congress without visible support from the public, the press, or opinion leaders.

For more than a decade, public support had been mounting for tax incentives for political contributions. Government subsidies for elections, however, had few supporters; this subsidy passed on strength of support by a persuasive speaker, a skilled and wily parliamentarian, a determined and powerful advocate: Senator Russell Long. As the President had not proposed the measure, the Administration was caught off guard and, at the last hour, chose to help pass the bill and shelve its previous recommendation for a tax incentive.

The statute, with its narrow form and broad implications, provided for a combined tax checkoff and subsidy only for general election campaigns for President. The act provided that every taxpayer who filed a federal income tax return showing $1 or more of tax liability for the year could designate that $1 be paid into a Presidential Election Campaign Fund. Married individuals filing joint returns would both be eligible. Designations could first be made on 1967 tax returns, filed in 1968. In each Presidential election year the Treasury would pay major and minor parties according to a formula based on their performance in the last election, although total payments to a political party could not exceed the amounts actually spent. Each political party whose Presidential candidate received 15 million or more votes in the preceding Presidential election would receive an amount equal to $1 times the number of votes received by the candidates of all such parties in the preceding Presidential election, divided by the number of such parties, less $5 million. (The two major parties would have received about $30 million each in 1968.)

A minor party whose candidate received more than 5 million but less than 15 million votes in the preceding Presidential election would receive $1 times the number of votes in excess of 5 million received by such party's candidate in the preceding Presidential election. No provision was made for payment to a new party in any current campaign, so the act would prolong the life of a minor party for four years to the disadvantage of a new party.

If the amounts in the Presidential Election Campaign Fund were insufficient to make the payments to which political parties were entitled, the payments to all parties would be reduced pro rata and the balance remaining would be paid when sufficient monies were in the fund. Surpluses would be returned to the Treasury general fund after the bills were paid. The plan would be supervised by the General Accounting Office, which could issue regulations and conduct investigations. An advisory board to assist in administering the plan would consist of two representatives from each major party and three independent members selected by the party representatives.

The act clearly aimed at equal subsidization of the two major parties only. Those two parties would presumably always maintain the advantage of major party status. Even in the lop-sided election of 1964, the losing candidate, Republican Barry Goldwater, received 27 million votes. Only later did George Wallace come close to receiving the 15 million votes needed to qualify for sharing in the pool of funds for major parties. The minor parties would not receive any subsidy until they could win 5 million votes. Ascending the steep threshold into major party status would require, of course, the mobilization of resources outside the federal subsidy. Although the major parties were treated equally under this plan, the minor party's subsidy was based on the number of votes cast for its candidate rather than the total cast. As Senator Albert Gore (D.-Tenn.) warned, the plan would protect the interests of the major parties but discriminate against minor parties.

When the bill had passed the Senate, to the surprise of all, it survived House-Senate Conference in only slightly amended form. The Long formulation, essentially a means of getting off the hook with regard to tax incentives, passed the House readily but was almost filibustered to death when it came back to the Senate. Led by Senator Gore, opponents put up a strong fight, relenting only to the demands of Congress to go home for the elections, which were less than three weeks off.

The new law received an unfavorable response, partly because it projected a subsidy without achieving fundamental reform; partly because of constitutional and practical questions of fair treatment of minor parties and of taxpayer earmarking of money through the checkoff; and partly because there were no guidelines as to what expenses could be reimbursed. As enacted, it could have changed the balance of power within the major parties by infusing large sums of money at the top of the party structure. The advantages this could give to the Presidential wings of the parties did not pass unnoticed, particularly by Democratic liberals then at odds with the foreign policies of the Johnson Administration.

After much lobbying, pro and con, the President signed the bill. Labor finally supported it and called for extension of subsidies to Congressional campaigns. *Broadcasting,* an industry trade magazine, editorialized that the Long Act had much to commend it, particularly since it would probably take pressure off the "unconscionable demands that are being made for free time," [17] but the reaction was generally negative. Editorials in *The New York Times*[18] and *The Washington Post,*[19] among others, urged the President to veto the Foreign Investors Tax Act because the Long Amendment was attached to it. Few laws have received such universal adverse reaction before they were operative.

President Johnson, on signing the bill, announced that Professor Richard E. Neustadt, Director of the Kennedy Institute of Politics at Harvard, would head a bipartisan group of political scientists and experts to "see how the promise of the new Presidential campaign fund law can be fully realized and to review the problems of election reforms and campaign financing in non-Presidential elections.[20] The group's recommendations were never made public but were exclusively for White House use in formulating the President's 1967 election reform proposals to Congress.

The 1967 proposals were late in going to the Congress, and as a result the White House lost initiative in modifying objectionable features of the Long enactment. In the meantime Senators Gore and Williams had announced their co-sponsorship of an amendment to repeal the Long Act entirely. Evidently realizing the amounts the Long Act would offer to the Democratic Party for the 1968 elections, the Administration then made valiant efforts to support Senator Long in defending the bill. Senator Williams accused the White House of seeking support from the business community against the Gore repealer on grounds it was attached to the Investment Credit Act, a bill in which business had a stake. The Senate response was to adopt the Gore repealer by a vote of 48 to 42 in May, 1967.

The vote was interpreted in the press as a defeat for the Administration, rightly so in view of its massive effort to save the measure. No Republican voted for it. But Senator Long refused to accept defeat; he undertook dilatory parliamentary tactics, at times abetted by the Administration, that were to require more than a month of debate and five more inconclusive votes before the Act was finally doomed. Senator Gore argued that comprehensive reform, not piecemeal patching, was desirable and could not be accomplished on the floor of the Senate in amending the Long Act. The debate wearied the Senate and the public, but its length more than made up for the years of neglect of this subject.

Undoubtedly one of the reasons for strong Republican opposition to the Long Act and other subsidy schemes was the Republican advantage in fund raising. The effects of a subsidy would have been to equalize the campaign funds for 1968 at a time when the Republicans had demonstrated their pulling power for small as well as large contributions and when the Democrats were ostensibly not in a position to perform as well.

Although discredited, the Long Act was the first positive legislation to help relieve campaign financial pressures, if only in elections for President. And it did prove one thing: almost half of the United States Senators would vote for a subsidy. The Long Act swung Congress from consideration of tax incentives to consideration of subsidies.

It was not until the debate was over, with the Long Act repealed, that President Johnson sent his recommendation to the Congress.[21] The President's bill, which was introduced by Senator Long himself, proposed that funds be provided by direct Congressional appropriation, rather than by individual tax checkoff. Public funds would be used only for expenses essential to bring the issues before the public, such as radio and television, newspaper and periodical advertising, the preparation and distribution of campaign literature, and travel. Private contributions for major parties could not be used for expenses to which public funds could be applied. The percentage of funds received by a major or minor party that could be used in any one state would be limited to 140 percent of the percentage of population of the state in relation to the national population.

The Johnson recommendations were reviewed in extended hearings before the Senate Finance Committee, with other proposals. It was agreed that positive government action was desirable. The hearings ranged over all of public policy, with wide criticism of most forms of subsidy. Testimony supported tax incentives more than any other reform, but there was little consensus on the form. Republicans were unanimously for tax deductions, and several prominent Democrats, including Senator Robert Kennedy, favored tax credits.

In September, 1967, the Senate Finance Committee ordered reported to the Senate a substitute for the Long Amendment[22]— an omibus bill providing a tax credit for political contributions, federal financing of Presidential and Senatorial campaigns, and the text of the Election Reform Act of 1967 that had unanimously passed the Senate shortly before. This report was never debated on the Senate floor, and nothing came of the action until late 1971, when the Democrats revived the tax checkoff, this time providing the money to nominated Presidential candidates, rather than to their parties as in 1966. Again, the bill was attached on the Senate floor as an amendment to a tax bill. This time, with President Nixon's threat of a veto, the checkoff was accepted by Senate-House conferees in principle, but deferred in operation until 1973 (a story recounted in detail in Chapter 17).

Back in 1967 the repeal of the Long Act considerably slowed forward movement on reform.

The Ashmore-Goodell measure had been stalled in the full House Administration Committee for almost an entire year. Certain liberals, seemingly taking their cues from labor lobbyists, succeeded in modifying the bill by making small changes in section after section. Then there was an organized effort to kill the bill by failing to provide quorums in committee whenever the bill was up for consideration, a tactic which played into the hands of southern conservatives who had never been convinced about the legislation, but who might have gone along with Congressman Omar Burleson, a Texan and chairman of the committee, and Congressman Ashmore.

Some Republican pressure was exerted to get the Ashmore-Goodell bill reported out. Finally, an agreement was apparently reached among Democratic House leaders to remove the section obnoxious to labor and have the House Administration Committee report the bill out[23] in deference to public pressure but with the intention of bottling it up in the House Rules Committee. By that time, since the session was nearing an end, only the most urgent legislation could go on the calendar. Congress adjourned for the 1968 elections without further action, except to prepare for new maneuvers in 1969.

Congress did find time during the 1968 session partially to undo the Williams Amendment prohibiting business tax deductions for corporate advertising in political program books. With the Long Act subsidy dead and facing the enormous expense of a Presidential election year, the parties prodded Congress to exempt corporate advertising in program books published for the national nominating conventions every four years.

In 1966 the Congress had passed a subsidy and in 1967 made it inoperative; in 1966 the Congress passed the Williams Amendment and then in 1968 made a major exception, a consistent but rather confusing record of both dilution of principle and the effects of political pressures.

While the Long Amendment repealer was on the Senate floor and at the time the Senate Committee on Standards and Conduct submitted its recommendation for censure of Senator Dodd, the House voted unanimously to establish a separate House Committee on Standards and Conduct. Unlike the House committee, the Senate one is a select committee which can recommend action but cannot legislate. The Dodd case was thrust upon the Senate committee soon after it was organized, following the Baker disclosures and before it could propose a guide for standards and conduct. Both committees worked up guides for conduct simultaneously, with reference to conflict of interest, disclosure of personal income, lobbying and other matters relating to ethics. The main thrust is more in these directions and less toward codifying procedures for raising and spending campaign funds or testimonial funds, though these topics receive mention. Both have moved cautiously; neither has faced up to the issues of campaign funding.

The Dodd censure was not unexpected, even though censure is unusual in either House. There have been only five in the history of the Senate. In the 1920's the Senate three times acted in cases relating to campaign contributions.[24] Truman Newberry, as noted earlier, was seated but condemned for excessive and illegal expenditures in a primary. Frank L. Smith was denied a seat for accepting, contrary to Illinois law, funds from officers of public utility corporations, including more than $125,-000 from Samuel Insull. William S. Vare was unseated because of excessive expenditures and on grounds of corruption and fraud in a primary. It is worth noting that although the Senate was ambiguous about Congressional power in regulating primary elections, it disbarred two Senators-elect whose primary campaigns did not conform to what it considered sound public policy. The Committee action on Dodd was unanimous. Senator Long stated publicly he would oppose censure, at a time when the Long Amendment repeal was hanging fire on the floor. He was quoted in the newspapers as saying that the Ethics Committee had made a "scapegoat" of Senator Dodd, and that "half of that committee couldn't stand the investigation Senator

Dodd went through." In talking with newsmen later, Senator Long raised the estimate to "half of the Senate," [25] though he later publicly apologized for exaggerating. Long was almost alone in defending Dodd.

In 1968 many major committees of the Nixon campaign failed to file official reports required prior to the general election. These late October filings are supposed to give some notion before the election of who is giving and spending how much. The failure to file on time attracted considerable press attention, in view of the amounts of money spent and the lapse in usual Republican efficiency. By the time Nixon won the election, only 5 of the 20 reports were in; only one filed on time. Some Democrats thought the Republicans purposely withheld reports so as not to divulge names of contributors—whom the Democrats could have solicited on grounds that Humphrey was gaining and was a possible winner. Some thought that the Republicans were reluctant to admit their high spending, but Republican officials had already given public indication of the gross amounts. Others charged the Republicans with failing to live up to the principle that laws should be obeyed, a violation of their campaign pledge to "law and order."

For the first time in the history of the law, the Clerk of the House of Representatives sent to the Attorney General an official notification of the Republican violations and a violation by one Democratic committee. The Justice Department ordered the FBI to investigate reports of 21 late-filing committees, ranging from 9 to 23 days late, but the investigation was still going on when the Republicans took control on January 20, 1969. As noted, the matter was not raised by the Democrats at the Senate hearings on nominations of Nixon's campaign manager and finance manager to the Cabinet.

Republican explanations of the late filings rationalized the infractions. Apparently, a computer made some mistakes by double listing some contributions, and a decision was made to favor accuracy over timeliness. Some reports were prepared on time but not filed until others could be submitted simultaneously; others were notarized before the election but not filed until later; and some were held up in the mails. There was some truth to the statement of one Republican official that he was too busy raising money to worry about meeting the deadline; Republican reports filed in January, 1969, showed at least $6 million reported received between November 1 and December 31, much of it barely before Election Day.

At the same time the Clerk of the House referred to the Justice Department the names of 65 House candidates who had not filed at all and 42 candidates who had missed filing deadlines in 1968. The Justice Department ignored these cases, and it is fair to state it was not a new phenomenon for Republican and Democratic candidate filings to be late or forgotten. The Justice Department finally decided there was no precedent for prosecution for either non-filing or late filing in the 45-year history of the Federal Corrupt Practices Act. To no one's surprise, it dropped the cases.

In 1970 the Clerk of the House put candidates on notice that all violations would be reported. The House Special Committee to Investigate Campaign Expenditures then recommended that the Clerk transmit to the Attorney General the names of candidates who failed to file pre- or post-election reports,[26] and about 30 such cases were certified. At this writing there is no Justice Department determination, but the decision is complicated by one case on the list. Dennis J. Morrisseau, who ran as the Liberty Union candidate in Vermont for that state's lone seat in the House of Representatives, publicly refused to comply with the disclosure law on grounds that it was unenforceable, unenforced, and provided no control over campaign spending. Morrisseau said that his action was to protest the "empty procedure for reporting" and that he was aware of the penalties for noncompliance. The House Clerk tried to persuade him to cooperate, but he refused. The Department of Justice seemed wary of prosecuting Morrisseau because it would then have to follow through on others as well or explain why not. In testimony, Deputy Attorney General Richard Kleindienst agonized about how difficult it would be to achieve "fair" enforcement of current laws, and admitted reluctance to prosecute. After nearly five decades of nonenforcement, the precedents of 1968 and the warnings of 1970 could have served as a basis for prosecution, but old attitudes were unchanged.

By 1969 several new conditions made the future of reform of

political finance uncertain. The first was the natural tendency of the Congress to await the views of the incoming Administration. Such views were not apparent for almost two years when the Political Broadcasting Bill of 1970, initiated in the Congress, was vetoed by the President. (Chapter 14)

The second uncertainty arose from changes in leadership in the key House Administration Committee in 1969 and 1971. Chairman Burleson moved to Ways and Means and left the chair to Congressman Samuel N. Friedel of Maryland, who took no action. When Friedel was defeated in 1970, Congressman Wayne Hays of Ohio became Chairman. Congressman Ashmore, who as a conservative had taken enlightened action, did not run for re-election in 1968, and the chairmanship of the Subcommittee on Elections passed to Congressman Watkins Abbitt of Virginia who seemed unlikely to initiate serious action. In 1971, Hays and Abbitt introduced a bill which in some respects was worse than current law and which was considered by many to be an indication of lack of serious intent as well as an obstacle to a better reform measure passed by the Senate. (Chapter 17).

Still another uncertainty was brought about by efforts to enact the Political Broadcast Bill. These moved the center of action from the Rules Committee and the Finance Committee to the Commerce Committee. Senator Cannon and other Senators felt with some justification that action on disclosure legislation taken by the Senate in 1960, 1961, and 1967 had not produced similar action in the House, so they questioned the value of continuing to produce legislation that would never become law. This rather defeatist attitude overlooked the alternative of the Senate passing good legislation year after year and thereby putting increased pressure on the House to act.

The crucial issues of disclosure and public reporting are central to reform, relating both to sources and amounts of funds and expenditures. Disclosure sharpens judgment of right and wrong by creating awareness. The purpose is not to expose or punish evil but to provide opportunities to evaluate conduct in the court of public opinion. The Dutch give the same reason for having no curtains on their windows: they say they have nothing to hide. Disclosures must contain information in a form which permits the public, the media, and scholars to use them easily and well, without putting undue burdens on candidates and parties whose main tasks, after all, are not bookkeeping and accounting but campaigning.

As noted earlier, proposals that reduce political funds rather than increase them have been characteristic of reforms in the past 50 years. Politicians are understandably reluctant to approve new regulations that might dry up the flow of funds or give undue advantage to opponents. A deterrent to disclosure and publicity is that certain funds come from interests that do not want their contributions advertised. Publicity might cut off this money or drive it under the table. Disclosure would be less important only if there were to be enough small contributors or subsidies so that large ones could be discounted as an influence.

Practicing politicians, however they feel about the public advantages of a given bill, also consider its effects on their re-election or on their party. They have relations with interests that may distrust proposed reforms. Labor's role in the reform legislation of the early 1960's was no worse than the usual stand of businessmen. Labor felt threatened and reacted predictably. The business community does not forcefully advocate remedial legislation: it passively enjoys the advantage of present laws. In its own way, business protects its interests as actively as labor has, when it sees the need. No President, under these circumstances, sees election finance reform as a major legislative priority, nor does Congress.

In January, 1971, in an unprecedented effort to challenge the enforcement of federal laws on limitations by litigation, Common Cause filed a suit to enjoin the Republican and Democratic National Committees and the Conservative Party of New York from violating or conspiring to violate two sections of the Corrupt Practices Act. Common Cause is a citizen's organization headed by John Gardner, a Republican who served under President Johnson as Secretary of the Department of Health, Education and Welfare. The suit charged that these committees were encouraging and assisting the formation of multiple committees on behalf of single candidates, in order to accommodate individual contributions in excess of $5,000 and the making of expenditures on behalf of a single candidate in excess of $3 million in a year, in alleged violation of the intent of the law.

This suit is the first class-action in the field. The defendants' responses all asked for dismissal of the complaint on grounds of lack of standing, lack of court jurisdiction, and other technical legal matters. At this writing, the judge refused to dismiss, designated the case properly a class-action, and plans were made for pretrial depositions. Clearly, the suit was filed with more than judicial relief in mind. It has had great publicity value both for Common Cause and for the issue. It may have acted as a prod to the Congress to act, as it did, before 1972 because a Presidential campaign could not have been waged if the $3 million limitation were enforced.

The action of Common Cause gives rise to speculation about suits on other grounds: failure of the Attorney General to enforce the laws; failure to administer properly; failure of candidates or committees to comply; interpretations of law in obvious violation of legislative intent; the right of the voting public to know the facts about political financing; or the public character of political parties and campaigns. On any of these grounds, the suits could present real difficulties to the parties, candidates, and to the law enforcement agencies before the courts.

Some of the efforts to regulate political money have moved from the legislative front to the judicial. Although the suits may not be resolved for a long time, the courts have affected other electoral issues, among them reapportionment, voting rights, and the 18-year-old vote.

Few are content with present practices; the present ferment and experimentation indicates the desire for better ways to finance and regulate politics. The search for legislative and judicial remedies for long-standing deficiencies will continue. The next chapter discusses goals of reform.

CHAPTER 13

THE ISSUES OF REFORM

Recent proposals for reform of political finance have ranged from tightening disclosure requirements to major changes in the electoral system. Comprehensive plans have been proposed by the President's Commission on Campaign Costs,[1] the Committee for Economic Development,[2] the Twentieth Century Fund in its two reports, *Voter's Time*[3] and *Electing Congress*[4] and the Association of the Bar of the City of New York.[5] Harry T. Ashmore, executive vice president of the Center for the Study of Democratic Institutions, has suggested complete overhaul of the electoral process[6] and Philip M. Stern, author and president of the Stern Fund, has proposed a comprehensive subsidy program.[7]

Authorities generally agree that prior limitations on campaign spending were unrealistic and that the disclosure requirements were only partially effective. The most commonly advocated reform was the broadening and stiffening of disclosure laws to cover candidates and committees in prenomination as well as general election campaigns and any intra-state committee raising or spending more than $1,000 in support of a federal candidate, and that was accomplished in 1972.

Electing Congress further proposed that candidates be required to designate a single official campaign committee. All specialized committees would be subsidiaries of the official committee, which would file and so assure full disclosure. With no limitation on expenditures (or on contributions), there would be less incentive to finance independent campaign units. To preserve constitutional rights, truly independent committees could support any candidate without authorization, but their expenditures would likely be minor.

The argument for taking the lid off contributions or campaign spending requires explanation. The case in favor of imposing limits on spending is simplistic, not realistic: it avers that money denies equal opportunity for public office, that the man of little wealth finds it difficult to enter public life, that the well-financed candidate may win with a media blitz, that the candidate with little money of his own is less favored to win nomination or may obligate himself to special interests in order to meet wealthy competition or heavy campaign costs. All these arguments are valid to some extent. In theory, limitations on political spending would reduce the imbalances, the need for funds, and the need or temptation to accept contributions with conditions, explicit or tacit.

The arguments against limitations are relatively complex and subtle. Their brunt is that if limitations are not effective, they are illusory and breed disrespect for law, but if they are effective, they may inhibit free expression.

The President's Commission on Campaign Costs in its report, *Financing Presidential Campaigns,* asserted its belief that limitations were unenforceable and that full disclosure is a better way to moderate both contributions and expenditures. The Commission stated: "The imposition of 'realistic ceilings' or 'segmental limitations,' the latter designed to limit expenditures for certain purposes, e.g. broadcasting, which has been urged by some, would only create a false impression of limitation. Moreover, there is doubt whether individuals could be prohibited from making certain expenditures instead of contributions if the latter were effectively limited, in view of constitutional guarantees of freedom of expression." [8]

This position was joined by the reports of the Committee for Economic Development and by *Electing Congress.* Most bills introduced in the Congress in the 1960's would have abolished limits on spending but retained them on contributions. In 1970, partial limitations applying only to the electronic media were introduced and were enacted by the Congress but vetoed by the President, and in 1972, legislation was effected to extend limitations to nonbroadcast advertising media as well.

Enforcement of limitations on all spending would be difficult even for strong and fearless enforcement agencies. The regulation of political finance has been marked by unrealistic limits and by legislation that invited evasion or avoidance. It has been marked also by lack of serious enforcement. There seems little point in replacing one defective law with another.

Partial limitations on spending, particularly as applied to broadcasting, are readily enforceable through the Federal Communications Commission if candidates certify that each purchase of time will not exceed the limit, as required in the ill-fated 1970 federal legislation, discussed in the next chapter. What a candidate or his supporters spend on newspaper ads or bumper stickers, however, cannot be so easily policed. Segmental limitations mainly are untried. We do not know whether they will reduce expenditures or divert spending to other categories, such as mailings—a major omission because it can cost as much as $20,000 to reach a Congressional district. The limitation might give only a false impression that advertising spending was controlled. It could be false economy, too, to limit activities such as radio or TV broadcasting, which are relatively efficient and effective methods for reaching certain constituencies.

The amount of allowed spending must be specified arbitrarily (e.g. 10¢ a potential vote) because political exigencies change: what was spent in one campaign in one year or place may be inadequate for another. With so many variations in regions, campaign practices, and costs, uniform limits cannot be fair. If limits are low, they invite evasive tactics like financing committees that speak against the opponent rather than for the candidate.

Low ceilings on spending fail to recognize political necessities. Campaign costs are particularly high where party identification is weak, where voters tend to split tickets or switch sides. Gallup polls show that between 25 and 30 percent consider themselves independents and that as many as 54 percent split tickets.[9] Many voters now take their political views less from traditional sources, such as family or party allegiances, than from the media, particularly the broadcast media, in the form of both news and advertising. Many modern campaigns, especially those of challengers in primaries, are won mainly by advertising the candidate on the air. To limit such broadcasts artifically is to handicap the challenger.

Paid or published endorsements by labor unions or other groups or individual supporters presumably would fall within the candidate's spending limitation. Limitations might be politically offensive, because a candidate would have to tell potential supporters they could not campaign on his behalf when he approaches his ceiling. Effective limitation would thus restrict free speech. If, in support of a candidate, a committee proposes to broadcast its endorsement, the courts could rule that to prohibit an expenditure for speech is substantially a prohibition of speech itself. The broadcast is considered necessary to speak effectively to a large constituency.

The same theory may apply to an individual as to a committee or other group. The constitutional issue here is how far the Congress may go in protecting the purity of elections without abridging freedoms. The judicial presumption could well be against enforced surrender of rights unless restriction is justified by "clear and present" danger to the public interest. Would the courts find the use of money in elections sufficiently dangerous to justify, in effect, giving the candidate discretion to prohibit speech or even to limit the candidate's own effective uses of media?

Admitting that Congress has the authority and duty to protect the electoral process, is there not also a duty to prove that restrictions on spending damage the integrity of the process? How could such evidence be presented to the courts?

If the political system is to be open and responsive to challenge, limitations are undesirable because they tend to favor the status quo. The percentages of challengers who are successful against Congressional incumbents are low, not more than 15 percent in the Senate and 8 percent in the House in the past 16 or so years.[10] One key goal of the political system should be intense competition because that helps to make the system more responsive. Limitations tend to reduce opportunities for voters to learn about candidates and issues. Periodic electioneering helps to structure and politicize society—an essential to the functioning of a democracy. Reducing expenditures reduces opportunities for voters to learn that the political season is on, that an election is coming.

Of course, the option of the challenger to spend is only theoretical unless he has the bankroll, but leaving the possibility of spending open is an essential safety valve to permit challenges when entrenched interests or policies become intolerable, to assure the right of anti-establishment, peace, Black, or other candidates to challenge complacent indifference to public distress.

To oppose limitations is not necessarily to argue that the sky is the limit. In any campaign there are saturation levels, a point where further spending no longer pays. Common sense dictates that benefits from unlimited spending may be less than marginal. As for limiting disparities or dubious sources of funds, self-restraint is encouraged by disclosure and publicity. Historically, disclosure has been inadequate, but even improved disclosure laws covering prenomination funds and intra-state campaigns and emphasizing pre-election reporting will not suffice unless a publicity office isolated from political pressures, with clear statutory responsibilities to receive, examine, tabulate, audit, summarize, publish, and preserve the reported information, provides the press and public with easy access to full accounts.

The constitutional arguments against limiting campaign spending also apply against limiting contributions; specifically, it is the right of an individual to spend his money to support a congenial viewpoint, provided the process does not restrict expression by others, for example, by preempting all broadcast time or advertising space. Some views are heard only if interested individuals are willing to support financially the candidate or committee voicing the position. To be widely heard, mass communications may be necessary, and they are costly. By extension, then, the contribution of money is a contribution to freedom of political debate.

The President's Commission, the CED, and *Electing Congress* all recommended removing limitations on political gifts by individuals provided that disclosure be required of individual gifts in excess of stipulated amounts, and provided that direct expenditures also would be reported. Other current proposals would maintain some limits on individual contributions, although all would change the present law. For example, one proposal would limit the aggregate amount of contributions to a single candidate to $5,000 in connection with any campaign, nomination or election and would apply the limit to the aggregate given to the candidate and any committees substantially supporting the candidate. A contributor could give $5,000 to a candidate for the U. S. Senate but could not also give to the Senatorial Campaign Committee of that candidate, because the committee would be substantially supporting the candidate. Whether the contributor could give to the State Committee of that candidate's party if the committee were supporting the candidate is uncertain, as the State Committee would be supporting an entire ticket. The meaning of "substantial" in this context is ambiguous.

Other proposals would raise the limits on contributions: $50,-000 for a Presidential campaign, $35,000 for a Senatorial campaign, and $25,000 for a Congressional campaign. (This formulation survived in the Federal Election Campaign Act of 1972.)

The urge to restrict undue influence of any individual or interest in any campaign is understandable. In an ideal world, political needs would be supplied by big money in small sums. Until options other than large contributions succeed, however, two immediate implications of spending limits need consideration. If effective limits apply to individual contributors, they should apply also to what candidates spend from their own pockets to campaign. *Congress and the Public Trust* suggested a $25,000 limit on the candidate's own spending;[11] otherwise, the law would restrict a candidate opposing a wealthy rival without also restricting what the rival could spend. The second implication is that a limit on gifts or spending in any calendar year would encourage elected officials to spread fund raising over an entire term. An annual $5,000 limit could become a $20,000 limit for a four-year term. Annual limits would encourage continual fund raising by incumbents and pre-announcement campaigns by non-incumbents lasting for several years.

To counteract the advantages of incumbency or wealth, rather than enact ceilings legislators should establish floors, minimal levels of support for all legally qualified candidates. Floors could guarantee broadcast time, mailing privileges, or other subsidies that assure candidates exposure to voters. Tax incentives, while not assuring support for any candidate, at least may help develop sources of finance that will reduce a candidate's reliance on contributions from self, family, or special interests. Various combinations of reforms can move toward guarantees of funds for qualified candidates.

Congress seemed unlikely to enact a tax benefit for more than a $100 income deduction (possibly $50 per individual or $100 on a joint return) or a $10 or $25 credit (per return). Tax deductions in contrast to credits generally favor persons in the higher tax brackets: a $100 deduction may save small taxpayers only $15 in taxes, but a wealthy taxpayer could save more than $70. Moreover, the deduction is applicable only to taxpayers who itemize personal deductions. Taxpayers who take the standard deduction (about 50 percent do) would recover nothing from a political donation.

A tax credit, as noted earlier, is subtracted from the tax rather than the income. Whether the tax bill is $1,000 or $1 million, the donor could subtract from his payments a specified portion of his contributions up to the maximum.

Tax incentives are versatile. They can be readily extended to few or many offices and to prenomination as well as general election campaigns. They help to persuade potential contributors to give. They also have the smallest side effects upon the political structure because donors choose the recipients, without arbitrary legislative determination of who gets the money in what amounts. Moreover, incentives do not require annual appropriations as subsidies do.

No one knows how much revenue would be lost by tax incentives. There is no experience with the number of federal claims that would be filed. The revenue loss would vary from year to year. Some estimate the total loss to the Treasury at $200 million over a four-year period.

Numerous doubts apply to tax incentives. There is no way to place statutory limits on the aggregate revenue loss; direct subsidies, in contrast, would have specific dollar limits. Tax incentives would exclude those who pay no federal income taxes but who might contribute a nominal amount to a campaign.

Opponents of tax incentives fear they may further encourage special tax consideration for other purposes, such as college tuition. Incentives could be abused with relative ease; for example, a contribution of $1,000 in cash would permit finance managers to distribute 100 bogus receipts for $10 each as a reward to volunteer workers who then could claim the tax benefit.

The Internal Revenue Service has found that charitable deductions tend to be overstated by 15-20 percent; political contributions also would probably be overstated. Other studies have shown that deductibility of charitable gifts has little effect on the level of donations except in the high tax brackets. Instead of increasing political funds tax incentives may merely oblige the Treasury and its tax-paying constituency to share the cost of gifts others donate for personal reasons.

Another option for putting floors under candidate funds is a government system of direct subsidies. The most comprehensive set of proposals for subsidies has been put forward by Philip Stern, whose plan calls for direct federal financial assistance to candidates for President, Senator, and Representative in the primary and general election periods. Assistance would be based on prior election votes cast for that office at a given amount per vote, with half that much available for primary elections. To protect against misuse of federal funds, the assistance would be channeled through drawing accounts in the Treasury. The candidate would send certified invoices for goods and services which the Treasury would pay directly to the purveyor. Minor and new parties would be eligible for partial aid by petition or prior vote record. The plan also calls for a limit of $50 per private contribution per contest; a tax credit up to $50; a limitation on the candidate's spending equal to twice the amount of the subsidy; reduced rates for radio, television, and newspaper advertising; and full disclosure, including daily reports by purveyors of goods and services.

A subsidy of this kind has a certain flexibility. Subsidies can be restricted to specific amounts of money, confined to specific elections, or extended to cover either or both pre- and post-nomination periods. A subsidy formula, if based on the number of registrants or voters, might induce the parties to encourage broad participation in elections. Subsidies can be conditional upon the recipient meeting a requirement, for example, that private funds spent in a campaign be limited, or that the receipient not accept private contributions of more than a specified sum.

Another limitation of subsidies was contemplated by the 1967 Senate Finance bill. Candidates choosing subsidy payments would receive them for all expenses for 60 days before and 30 days after an election, up to the defined subsidy limit, with complete prohibition of private giving during that period, when spending would be confined to the amount of the subsidy.

Other conditions can be required. A portion of the subsidy can be withheld pending filing and review of required audits and reports. To shorten the final election campaign, one bill would have withheld subsidies unless the party held its national nominating convention after September 1.

Despite advantages, a subsidy system warrants serious criticism. If the amount of the subsidy is based upon previous votes received by the candidate's party, incumbents would receive more money than challengers, who are already at a disadvantage for other reasons. (Under 1966 and 1967 Senate Finance Committee formulas, the parties or candidates qualifying as "major" would receive equal subsidy assistance.) Subsidies require formulas that raise difficult questions as to what is a "major" or "minor" party and why a party is so classified. They also bring up the issue of what is a "qualified candidate," particularly in the pre-nomination period. Eligibility by petition on a nationwide basis presents problems of validation of signatures and possible harassment by challenging petitions. If subsidies base eligibility on the vote received by a party in the previous election, new parties would not qualify until two or more years after they have organized. To subsidize a minor party after its political activity has peaked could prolong its uselessness; otherwise it might fade away.

Under the original Long Act, the subsidy formula, based on the previous (1964) vote, would have allotted each major party national committee about $30 million, more than twice as much money as the parties had at the national level in 1964 and more than either spent in 1968. Senator Robert Kennedy pointed to the potential power that control of such a subsidy could give to the national chairman. Many other Senators found subsidies to be distributed by the national committee unacceptable for two reasons. In the prenomination period, the chairman could promise a state delegation certain funds and deliver them for use in the election if that state helped a certain candidate win the nomination. Through control of election funds by the party chairman, a President could silence critics from his own party. Moreover, if the national party worked solely through the state and local party committees, traditional voluntarism by citizens committees could fade away to yield to a tightly disciplined machine. If, in 1968, the Democratic National Committee had had the $30 million promised by the Long Act, it would have had decisive leverage in the nominating campaign. There can be no doubt that partisans loyal to President Johnson would have used this leverage to quiet their critics and try to control the primaries.

If a Senator is interested in building a state party, or seeks to maintain his independence from national party policy, he may oppose national party power, as many have done. Even those predisposed to strengthen the national party seemed concerned over who would control subsidy funds. In 1967, many liberal Democrats who concluded they would not have control voted against the subsidy.

Alexander Heard has cautioned about confining assistance to federal candidates exclusively, arguing it could widen the breach between the national and state parties. He has warned of a possibility of fostering rival systems within each of the present major parties by struggles for control of national funds.

To satisfy the arguments of those who did not wish state organizations to be eclipsed or enslaved by subsidy-dispensing national committees, formulas were proposed to guarantee funds for state organizations, but it was argued that any such formula would interfere with campaign strategy for spending disproportionate amounts in key states with large numbers of electoral votes.

The 1967 Senate Finance Committee bill proposed bypassing parties entirely, giving money directly to candidates and extending coverage to Senatorial as well as Presidential candidates. All subsidies have the effect of reducing or eliminating a candidate's dependence upon the parties for financial support. Such a step could increase candidate independence and weaken party cohesiveness, discipline, and effective execution of national policies and campaign pledges.

Eligibility for subsidy in the original Long Act was restricted to Presidential campaigns in the general election period only. Experimenting at the Presidential level, where abuses are least likely, would allow problems to be ironed out before subsidies were extended to any other campaigns. Major party Presidential candidates, however, are least subject to the influence of special interests because the constituency is so wide, the pressures so diverse and diffuse, and the campaign directed at so large an electorate. One way subsidies may be extended to Congressional campaigns is for government money to go directly to the Capitol Hill committees for allocation to individual candidates. This system might help to create some candidate obligations to the national party, but many find the national Senatorial and Congressional committees unacceptable as agencies to determine the use of funds on the ground that their leaders may favor factional control.

Congress and the Public Trust questioned the formula devised by the 1967 bill for requiring the candidate to choose between public or private financing because the choice created a bugaboo. A candidate choosing private financing could charge a subsidized opponent with feeding from the public trough. On the other hand, a subsidized candidate might charge that his privately-financed opponent was indebted to large contributors and special interests. Both candidates could campaign on this bogus issue.

In this bill, the candidate who accepts public subsidy in effect sets a limit on his spending, whereas the candidate preferring private funding can spend as much as he wants. As noted, limiting spending limits freedom to answer a scurrilous charge the weekend before election. At the same time, the limit could not stop the Liberal Party or the Conservative Party or labor unions from endorsing and campaigning for the candidate. The limit might lead to proliferation of minor parties to serve as fronts for the major parties. It could be unconstitutional to forbid such groups, and the candidate himself could not control their activity. If, on the other hand, the prohibition of private financing extends only to national campaigns, then uncontrolled solicitation and spending by local parties on behalf of Presidential candidates could thwart the intent of the upper limit of the subsidy to moderate spending.

It has been stressed repeatedly that a prohibition or limitation of private contributions might be unconstitutional. The power of the state to conduct elections, however, probably would permit ceilings on contributions from individuals, perhaps as low as $100. Stringent enforcement of ceilings on gifts would overcome constitutional objections and diminish some political objections. Ceilings are preferable to complete prohibition, because the latter tends to insulate representatives from their constituents and from members of their party.

Throughout the debate in 1967 it became apparent that President Johnson was interested in establishing the principle of government subsidy for campaign costs, but he was less interested in the way it was done. Some Congressmen, on the other hand, became intensely interested in the mechanism of a subsidy. So long as Republicans had an advantage in private fund raising, they seemed unlikely to vote for any subsidy.

One other option, a proposal by Senator Lee Metcalf, would offer political contribution vouchers, a form of scrip, to taxpayers who checked a box on their tax returns. Taxpayers would receive vouchers at the beginning of each campaign or year, each redeemable for one dollar when presented to federal authorities by candidates and committees. Congress would appropriate funds to cover the vouchers contributed to politicians by taxpayers. Unclaimed funds would revert to the Treasury. The plan would be automatic in operation. Eligibility could be applied easily to Congressional campaigns. If distributed early enough, the scrip could be used in prenomination campaigns. Scrip could be redeemed by politicians at banks, post offices, or through the Treasury.

This system gives no assurance that all eligible candidates would get enough money to provide a minimum floor of subsidies. It is assumed, however, that the scrip would diversify patterns of giving and would infuse considerable silent money into the political system. The costs of administration, distribution, and redemption might be large in relation to the donations, but this proposal has the virtue that it avoids arbitrary formulas for allocation of funds and permits citizen determination of where funds go.

Whatever the merits of the Metcalf scrip, the Stern subsidy, or other forms of direct government financing of campaigns, it is certain that there will be continued resistance on the part of Republicans and others who will want to measure the effectiveness of the newly-enacted tax incentives (Chapter 17). Both Congressman Wilbur Mills, Chairman of the House Ways and Means Committee, and Senator Russell Long, Chairman of the Senate Finance Committee, opposed tax incentives in principle over the years, but were willing to accept them as part of the price to get a tax checkoff. Now tax incentives are in effect, but the future of the checkoff is doubtful. In order to get the checkoff into operation, further Congressional action will be required before the elections of 1976. There is little prospect that budgetary pressures will ease over the next few years, and the urgent needs for domestic welfare, education, transportation and urban programs will surely continue. In these circumstances, many legislators will have a ready excuse to resist voting for what may appear to be self-serving subsidies.

Indirect forms of subsidy perhaps have a better chance of enactment than direct assistance. For example, free mailings by candidates or committees make sense, particularly in campaigns for Congress because incumbents already have the franking privilege. Though few abuse the frank for campaign purposes, some do. Free mailing would tend to equalize opportunities to reach voters. *Electing Congress* recommended that the national committees of the political parties be allowed to use the lowest postal rate available to charitable organizations, so as to encourage parties to expand direct mail solicitation for small gifts. The new U. S. Postal Service may be difficult to work with on free mailings or mailings at reduced cost, in view of its aim to cover all expenses. Any program of subsidies or cut rates for political mailings might require a special appropriation by Congress.

Electing Congress also recommended that the federal government provide postage for voters' information material prepared by each state. CED offered a similar idea. Presently, only Oregon and Washington provide candidate information pamphlets to voters. In other states, the League of Women Voters sends such information. There is no reason why governments should not assume responsibility for informing the electorate about candidates for office. The CED also urged that government subsidies be appropriated to expand the use of educational or public television outlets for public enlightenment on political affairs. Such services could be helpful in easing financial pressures on parties and candidates.

In recent years, several ideas for structural reforms in the political or electoral system have been offered. Some have been proposed expressly for the purpose of reducing costs; others, advanced for reasons of fairness, would incidentally have financial advantages.

Many would like to shorten campaigns, to save money and nervous strain. Advocates of short campaigns rarely consider that candidates might spend more money in less time for more impact. Given the number of candidates, there is a limit to the exposure possible in a short period. Prime time on desired stations is always tight at any price. Challengers or relative unknowns, for lack of exposure, would not be able to overcome the advantage to incumbents or individuals with well-known names. Short campaign periods might reduce boredom on the part of the campaigner and the voter, but, on the other hand, there would not be time to develop more than two or three campaign themes. Sloganeering is hardly in the public interest and shorter campaigns might condition the public to accept even less edifying politics. In a democracy politics, unlike baseball, cannot be considered seasonal: the voter needs entertainment less than continuing information.

The question of timing candidacy announcements is related to the period of campaigns. Early candidacy may amplify the effect of later action; as a candidate, a politician commands attention. Although a clear decision without vacillation or coy deferrals cuts early speculation, it helps to solidify support. In prenomination campaigns, the announcement may also squelch possible rivals before they can mobilize. On the other hand, an incumbent or well-known aspirant usually postpones announcement until the last minute in order to delay the application of Section 315. An unannounced candidate can continue to be available for guest appearances on radio and television and to disseminate weekly tapes to constituents without subjecting broadcasters to the obligation to offer possible opponents equal time. The undeclared candidate may also be invited to non-broadcast speaking engagements at conventions and other affairs which customarily bar active candidates. These advantages, however, accrue mostly to incumbents and raise questions about fairness to their opponents. In sum, short campaign periods tend to help incumbents and well-known candidates without necessarily curbing spending.

Another common idea is that long terms of office would ease campaign costs. In 1966 President Johnson proposed to the Congress a four-year term of office for U. S. Representatives.[12] This recommendation had some support in the Joint Committee on the Organization of the Congress, but White House endorsement was not sufficient for its adoption. The proposal is deceptive. A major argument is that campaign costs would be reduced if elections were held only half as often. Savings in some campaigns are possible but in others are doubtful. A four-year term would upgrade the office, make the stakes higher, and in competitive situations, might tempt candidates to spend more to win. Even where inter-party competition is minimal, the value of gaining nomination would increase. There might be some reduction of pressure between elections, but the reduction would probably be minor; Senators, with six-year terms, complain about the costs in maintaining their political position and ties between elections. Whether or not long terms would reduce costs, as the pace of change in the world accelerates, people need to have the opportunity to express their political judgments as often as possible.

The two most popular structural reforms are for nationwide Presidential primaries and for direct election of the President. The main argument for a nationwide Presidential primary is usually that the present patchwork system in the states—open conventions, closed conventions, preferential primaries, delegate primaries, and various combinations of these methods—does not provide each voter with an equal voice in determining his party's nominee.[13] While this is true, the cure may be far more dangerous than the disease.

The most obvious drawback to the proposal for a national Presidential primary contest is that it would require a candidate to have the financial resources, not to mention the physical stamina, for two nationwide campaigns within a year's time. Since a Presidential hopeful would have to raise vast sums before he could prove himself as a candidate, he would be no match for well-publicized or party-backed aspirants. In 1968, Eugene McCarthy could not have been a major contender in 50 state primaries. As an untested candidate, opposing an incumbent President of his own party, McCarthy initially could raise only enough money for the first primary. His success in New Hampshire attracted money sufficient for the Wisconsin campaign. That victory carried him along further.

The advantages of a succession of primaries work two ways: while they enhanced the McCarthy candidacy, they served to deflate Romney. Without the primaries, George Romney would have spent much more time and money in order to learn he was not a lively candidate.

Another advantage of the primaries is that they give candidates of differing appeals opportunities to appeal to sympathetic constituencies. In Oregon and Nebraska, where the law directs the secretary of state to put the names of all generally accepted candidates on the ballot, even dark horses, unannounced, or absent candidates have a chance to be voted upon. Not all candidates enter all the primaries (because of the cost and the physical strain of campaigning), and of course each chooses primaries where he expects to do best. The sum of these efforts usually does give the people and the party professionals a fair idea of the candidate's strengths and weaknesses.[14]

Elimination of the electoral college in favor of direct election of the President is another idea with cost implications. A "blue ribbon" commission of the American Bar Association recommended this change in 1967, and Congressional support has been widespread.[15] The advocates of direct election cite the one-man, one-vote principle; the opponents include those who think it dangerous to give up a system that has always functioned, and liberals who want to preserve the system because the edge it gives center city voters in the election of the President is some counterbalance to the domination of Congress and state legislatures by rural and suburban interests.[16]

The financial effects of direct election are not usually discussed. If a vote anywhere in the country were to count equally, the tendency would be for Presidential candidates to campaign directly to a nationwide constituency, primarily through television, rather than to capture key states with major votes in the electoral college. Another tendency might be to recruit new voters by intensive registration drives. The premium on getting voters in this way could help to strengthen state and local party organizations, whereas the opposite tendency would emphasize a national media campaign that could reduce interaction between voters and party workers on campaign issues. Direct election would also oblige third-party campaigning to go nationwide rather than concentrate on states where enough electoral votes might be gathered to give it bargaining strength. Third parties rarely have funds for a national campaign, although Wallace was an exception in 1968.

Some direct election proposals provide that if no candidate receives at least 40 percent of the popular vote, there would be a runoff election. The intent is to prevent minor party candidates from playing spoiler roles and to guarantee that one of the two most acceptable candidates wins. The provision would require candidates to spend more money for the runoff, not necessarily a negative feature but one to calculate.

Opponents of direct election of the President argue that national policing of elections would be necessary to assure honest vote-counting in 176,000 precincts.[17] If this were so, administrative costs would be immense, particularly if requisite voter and residence qualifications were uniform (as might be ordered by the courts in behalf of the one-man, one-vote rule). On the other hand, a federal election system could have salutary effects as to costs and suffrage. It is unlikely, however, that even with direct election the federal government would assume full control of federal elections.

If that day should come, Harry Ashmore's proposal would be appropriate to consider. Ashmore is "convinced that fundamental surgery is going to be required if the representative system is to survive." [18] His proposal for a federal election system is based on the assumptions that there should be federal standards and federal control of the election process, including primaries, for national offices; that the federal government should pay for a nationwide registration system, all costs of holding the primary and general election, and statements by candidates in the communications media; and that all but minor campaign expenditures by the candidates should be prohibited. All existing federal and some state campaign machinery would be replaced by a Federal Bureau (headed by an Overseer of Elections appointed by the President and approved by a two-thirds majority of both Houses of Congress), with an office of this Bureau in every Congressional District.

Ashmore favors a nationwide primary on the first Tuesday in June of even-numbered years to elect delegates to each party's (Congressional) District conventions at which the nominees for Representative and Senator would be chosen; Senators would be nominated by the votes of all the state's district conventions. In Presidential years, these delegates would choose delegates to the national conventions. Delegate candidates would have to indicate their Presidential and Congressional preferences, but the voters would not have a direct voice in nominations.

Between early March and the June primary election, and be-between the opening of the campaign period on September 1 and Election Day, every party would be provided one hour of television and radio per week in prime time on all broadcasting stations serving the district; two issues of a publication presenting the views of all candidates on the ballot would be sent to every registered voter; and sufficient newspaper space to advertise all party broadcasts and meetings provided. During the primary period, each party's time would be allocated equally among all qualified candidates. For the Presidential election, broadcast time would be granted on all radio and television stations. The Federal Election Bureau would provide funds for one public campaign rally per week. Travel and maintenance expenses for the candidate and his staff also would be paid by the Bureau, subject to the approval of the Overseer. The funds for this system would come from a one percent surcharge on the federal income tax.

The Ashmore proposal raises many constitutional, practical, and political questions, even though such a major change is unlikely. The constitutional question of prohibiting private expenditures for (political) speech is raised in this proposal. At the practical level the broadcast time requirements for a major city with 5, 10 or more Congressional districts, 5 or more television stations, and 20 or more radio stations might result in far more politics on the air than people like. Even if the practical details in the Ashmore proposal could be solved, the constitutional question and its political imperfections seem insurmountable.

Many proposals for political reform are applicable to state elections. In a few states, legislative or gubernatorial commissions have been established to recommend changes, but the results have been disappointing. The terms of reference too often concern limitations and publicity, to the neglect of laws designed to assist candidates and parties to raise necessary funds or reduce current expenses. In Massachusetts, a Governor's commission on electoral reform was allowed no funds. In New Jersey the legislature set up a commission which displayed no discernible results until given a deadline by the legislature. The latter then delayed a decision. In California efforts at reform by Governor Brown were defeated by key members of his own party in the legislature. In New York in 1967, a joint legislative committee held hearings, but the outcome was negligible.

Unusual success in Kentucky resulted from concerted efforts by numerous civic groups, a Governor committed to improvement, a Governor's Committee on Campaign Expenditures, the State Legislative Research Council, an influential press, and helpful broadcast coverage. The move was led by the Kentucky Government Council, an independent and nonpartisan group, but it could not have succeeded without the cooperation of others such as the Kentucky Farm Bureau Federation, the Kentucky and Louisville chambers of commerce, the Kentucky AFL-CIO, the League of Women Voters, the Kentucky Bar Association, the Associated Industries of Kentucky, the County Attorneys Association, and the Democratic and Republican State Central Committees. In few states do such disparate groups work together so effectively.[19]

Among prominent proposals at the state level is one that the government assume all registration and election-day expenses. The assumption is that the widest possible registration and voting are desirable goals; by extension, if government assumes the costs of counting votes, government also should assume the costs of making votes count. As noted earlier, the United States is the only mature democracy in which election costs are not paid by the government. Unfortunately, a party may discourage voter registration or turnout if its regular supporters are dominant. In some districts, of course, ethnic or racial bias has intensified such policies.

Few states can boast about their registration or election-day procedures. On the positive side, Idaho pays deputy registrars, one in each precinct, to keep registration rolls up to date, and door-to-door canvassing is authorized. California authorizes the appointment of large numbers of deputy registrars and permits counties to pay registrars up to 25 cents for each new registrant. North Dakota and Alaska do not require prior registration. A few other states permit mobile registration units. Permanent registration in several states assures voters of their continuing eligibility.

Most states fall far short of these desirable procedures. Accordingly, parties and candidates are subject to financial pressures and so rely upon labor organizations and other volunteers to register voters, help them travel to the polls, and guard against fraud, error, or other illegality. If volunteers are not sufficient, in some places the election district captain of each party may spend $100 or more for workers, watchers, and drivers. A study in New Jersey indicated a minimum of $440,-000 was spent on election day in a 1965 gubernatorial election.[20] In Philadelphia, each party committee distributes at least $100 in each of the more than 1,600 election districts, for a total of more than $320,000 spent on election day.

Two key recommendations of the CED related to registration and election administration. One was that all nonpartisan political costs should be borne by government. And the second (in this *Electing Congress* joined) was that there should be a simple federal registration system maintained by the government. The first would include poll judges and watchers in either a primary or final election. At present, poll watchers of either or both parties are unevenly distributed. Also, in some election districts collusion by the major party watchers discourages independents from challenging a vote. Were poll watching a nonpartisan function, as poll judging is, paid for by the government, the selection of independent observers would still be difficult without strong aid from the legal profession. Nonpartisan efforts, such as babysitting and car pools, to get the vote out could be conducted either by government or by independent groups.

As registration and election-day expenses are heaviest in local campaigns, the assumption of these activities by government would free local party money for other work. Since local election-day practices are frequently attacked for false counting and vote buying, government intervention might reduce such abuses. The states could undertake these duties, or the federal government could establish a matching grant system for states willing to meet federal requirements.

Two proposals for structural reform in state election procedures have received distinguished support. The Committee for Economic Development strongly recommended separation of state and federal elections. The point of holding major state elections in odd-numbered years, as is done by New Jersey, Virginia, and New York City, is to confine attention to state and local candidates and issues. This separation also could help state and local candidates raise funds because they do not compete for funds with federal candidates in odd years.

The second change often proposed—a major recommendation of the CED—is to reduce the number of elected officials at the state level. A huge number of local candidates contend for the eye and ear of the voter. Only Alaska, Hawaii, and New Jersey elect no officials other than a Governor for statewide office. With recent emphasis upon appointment of technical experts to state cabinet jobs, there is less reason to burden the electoral system with candidates the public can hardly be competent to select for their administrative abilities. With ten state officials on the ballot, the voter cannot know the qualifications of most, even when the candidates are visible, though these candidates do spend, as was shown in the 1970 statewide office survey, to make their merits known.

Executive appointment of judges, as in the federal system, has produced a respected bench. On the other hand, there are numerous stories of the purchase of nomination for judgeships. In New York State nominations for judgeships have been bought with contributions as high as $100,000.[21] Moreover, judge's clerks are often appointed as patronage of party organizations. Surveys have shown that half of the citizens who went to the polls in New York City in 1966 failed to vote on judgeships on the ballot.[22] Campaigners for election to the bench seek funds from fellow lawyers, which creates a climate favorable to the corrupt sale of justice. There are few valid arguments in favor of judicial election and many—apart from the costs involved— against.

Despite the presence of numerous political scientists as delegates and advisors at recent state constitutional conventions, the new charters of government have not significantly upgraded political parties or the electoral process (save for redistricting). In their need for funds, parties continue to compete in the dark, despite sanctions and restrictions, without the constitutional status that might help open financing methods.

The National Municipal League, the Committee for Economic Development, and the Twentieth Century Fund have all been concerned about political finance, but the Council of State Governments, the Citizens Conference on State Legislatures, uniform law groups, national conferences of governors, of secretaries of state or of attorneys general fail to pay attention, let alone take significant action. Whatever other institutional and procedural reforms result from the work of these groups will be inadequate until officials who are qualified for office are elected free of obligations to hidden persuasions by private donors.

Chapter 14

POLITICS ON THE AIR

All mass media are important in politics but broadcasting, by radio or television, is in a class by itself because of its ubiquity, intimacy, and immediacy. Though time on the air and production of commercials are expensive, it can be argued that they are a good value, at least for those who use them well. Federal regulation of broadcasters, in any event, facilitates control of costs of political broadcasts. More systematic information is available on political broadcasting costs than on any other category of campaign expenditures, because the Federal Communications Commission since 1960 has required broadcasters to report the costs and distribution of all time allotted for political purposes. Consequently, the costs, uses, and proposed reforms of political broadcasting can be considered separately from other questions of campaign financing.

Although the airwaves seem totally dominated by politics in the closing days of a major campaign, not many candidates go on the air. Particularly at the local level, campaigns are conducted much as they were two generations ago. For the office-seeker who does wish to use radio or television, access to the microphone may be difficult and chancy. He may or may not be able to pay for time. The broadcaster may not want to sell the time desired, and usually does not care to provide the time free, except when news values prevail.

Every candidate knows that the American habit of turning on radio and television sets presents unparalleled opportunities for making—or breaking—a political career. President Roosevelt used the "fireside chat" on radio to combat a hostile press. Radio helped Wendell Willkie become a nationally-known figure in only a few months' time. Television reordered the political campaign itself, with itineraries, speeches, and national nominating conventions now planned according to the dictates of prime time. Candidates are named on camera under flood-lights rather than in the murk of smoke-filled hotel rooms. Television reaches 95 percent of all households in the United States. The average viewing time per household, counting children, is more than 45 hours per week— a potential audience which politicians would rather not resist.

In 1952, television enabled Richard Nixon to save his career by answering charges about the "Nixon Fund," only to jeopardize it in 1960 in his four debates with John F. Kennedy. These 1960 appearances (not really debates) were seen by 115 million people, more than previous Presidential candidates had reached in an entire campaign. According to Elmo Roper, 57 percent of the voters said the debates had influenced their actions at the polls, with an additional 6 percent (four million people) reporting that the debates were decisive for them. Three-fourths of this 6 percent favored Kennedy, enough to account for his margin of victory,[1] which might have shifted to defeat with the realignment of a few thousand votes in close state contests.

Television helped relatively unknown Senator Eugene McCarthy to build a developing issue into a national political movement. It helped Milton Shapp win a gubernatorial nomination twice from an entrenched Pennsylvania Democratic Party organization. Television obviously expands political options and encourages the political system to be open and flexible. Television also provides a powerful amplifier for minority views or unfamiliar ideas. Its dramatic documentary reports invite popular judgment on prevalent policies. Even as it offers a forum for demagogic appeals or crass distortions of complex issues, it facilitates and stimulates political discourse; not enough, but more than ever before.

In 1968 Nixon's carefully programmed campaign called for noncontroversial television spots and live regional broadcasts which featured the candidate answering prescribed questions from a panel of well-rehearsed sympathizers. Humphrey's media campaign, under the guidance of consultant Joseph Napolitan, stressed imaginative commercials, once sufficient money was borrowed to purchase TV time. Nixon's television presence was an improvement over 1960, but he was hardly a TV smash. Humphrey, who otherwise talked too long in his gravelly voice, appeared at his best in filmed documentaries that were carefully photographed and edited; he did not appear in his com-

mercials. Both Nixon and Humphrey—like Johnson and Goldwater before them—were products of party, not of television.
Neither Vice Presidential candidate was chosen on the basis of
television appeal. Though other candidates with more tube-
appeal were available to both parties, party politics do not necessarily favor actors, and the power of party can still be decisive.
Glamorous candidates, such as a John Lindsay, under some circumstances may still lose to less stylish types, such as a John
Marchi, who do not even use television.

Talk may be cheap, but not on the air. Candidates spent $58.9
million for air time in 1968. This figure represents the total of all
network and station charges as reported to the FCC for both primary and general elections at all levels. In 1964 the comparable
figure was $34.6 million. While total estimated expenditures for
all campaigns at all levels increased 50 percent from 1964 to
1968 (from $200 million to $300 million), as noted in Chapter 3,
broadcast expenditures increased 70 percent. As a share of total
campaign costs, broadcast expenditures grew from 17.3 percent in
1964 to 19.6 percent in 1968.

Although broadcast expenditures in primary elections are not
available prior to 1962, general election expenditures at all levels
are known from 1952 on. The following table details broadcasting
costs for the last five Presidential election years.

DISTRIBUTION OF GENERAL ELECTION COSTS
FOR BROADCASTS BY PARTY AND MEDIUM
(in millions)

	1952	1956	1960	1964	1968
Republicans	$3.5	$5.4	$7.6	$13.0	$22.5
Democrats	2.6	4.1	6.2	11.0	15.4
Other	—	.3	.4	.6	2.5
Total	6.1	9.8	14.2	24.6	40.0
Television	3.0	6.6	10.1	17.5	27.1
Radio	3.1	3.2	4.1	7.1	13.3

Source: 1952, Heard, *op. cit.*, p. 22, 1956-68, FCC, *Survey of Political
Broadcasting*, 1968, table 3.

The increases for the four-year periods were never less than 45
percent (1956-1960) and ran as high as 73 percent (1960-1964).

The 1952-60 increase was 133 percent and the 1960-68 rise 185 percent. Broadcast expenditures for general election campaigns in 1968 were almost seven times higher than in 1952. The largest portion goes for the Presidential contests, and this is growing more rapidly than the increase for total broadcast charges. In 1964 the Presidential campaigns accounted for 37 percent of the total general election broadcast costs; in 1968, for 48 percent.

The spiraling costs of putting candidates on the air are evident also in non-Presidential years. Figures for both primary and general elections, below, include spending by minor parties and independent candidates. Total station charges for primaries and general elections increased by 60 percent between 1962 and 1966, and by 85 percent between 1966 and 1970. For the general elections alone, the increase between 1966 and 1970, from $19.7 million to $38.5 million, was more than 95 percent. The following table gives figures divided by party and broadcast medium:

DISTRIBUTION OF TOTAL ELECTION COSTS FOR BROADCASTS
BY PARTY AND MEDIUM
(in millions)

	1962	1966	1970*
Republicans	$ 7.5	$12.1	$25.5
Democrats	12.0	18.5	30.5
Other	.7	1.4	3.1
Total	20.2	32.0	59.1
Television	12.5	18.9	37.1
Radio	7.7	13.1	22.0

Sources: FCC, *Survey of Political Broadcasting*, 1962, 1966, 1970.

* The FCC changed the ground rules in its 1970 survey. In order to make the 1970 figures conform to those of other years, an adjustment was made to include the normal 15 percent advertising agency commission. This was done by dividing the 1970 FCC figures by 85 percent.

The end is not in sight. Aside from potential CATV costs, color TV is adding to costs of production. Production costs escalate as expensive studio techniques evolve, whether for spot announcements, live programs, or film biographies. As production costs go up so does the investment for a single spot or tape. Therefore it appears economical to broadcast a single message repeatedly both for emphasis and for making the most of the initial investment, once it is assumed the copy is effective.

The FCC figures represent only network and station charges. The full financial load of political broadcasting includes air time, production, and promotion. From 25 to 33 percent more may be added to the FCC figures for production charges for programs and spot announcements, and still another several million dollars for promotion, including "tune-in" advertising. A cost analysis of broadcasting for 1968, allowing 25 percent for production, would bring the total to $75 million, outside of political staff time, travel, or fund-raising costs related to broadcast needs. There is no doubt that the largest single factor in campaign costs is related to broadcasting.

While television wins the lion's share of the political broadcast dollar, the use of radio has increased even more sharply. Expenditures for radio were up 73 percent between 1962 and 1966, compared with an increase of 55 percent for television, and up 87 percent between 1964 and 1968, again compared with 55 percent for television. Radio has several advantages to the candidate: production and time costs are less and the man who fails to "project" on TV may do better reading a radio spot. There are times of day, especially during commuting hours, when a significant portion of the population can be reached at low per capita costs. In 1968 Richard Nixon used network radio to deliver a series of speeches on the issues. Such speeches attracted more attention from the press than the conventional papers issued by candidates. The radio time was purchased for less than $10,000 for 25 minutes.

Broadcast spending has by no means been uniform. Republicans generally outspend Democrats in general elections, but in primary campaigns the Democrats usually outspend the Republicans by a wide margin. In 1966 Democrats outspent Republicans $10 million to $1.4 million in primaries, while the Republicans outspent the Democrats $10.8 million to $8.5 million in the general election. In 1968 the totals the major parties spent for broadcasts were almost identical—$27,860,093 for the Republicans and $27,865,649 for the Democrats, but the distribution (in millions) differed markedly:

	Primary	General Election
Republicans	$ 5.4	$22.5
Democrats	12.4	15.5

The bulk of money goes for spot announcements, not program time. Both stations and candidates prefer spots as a matter of strategy and convenience: the stations because they fear losing audiences to others running popular entertainment, candidates because they know the attention span of the average listener is short. It is understood the viewer probably will not switch stations during a spot as he might for a short talk. Spot announcements now account for almost all non-network radio billing; in 1968, $19.7 million was spent for political spots and only $500,000 for program time.

Total non-network radio and television billing for announcements increased 83 percent from 1964 to 1968—from $24.5 million to $44.8 million—while the money spent for program time declined 19 percent, from $5.9 million in 1964 to $4.8 million in 1968. The trend has been the same in non-Presidential election years. From 1962 to 1966, total spot billings increased 83 percent while program time expenditures declined 13 percent. Candidates and their supporters spent almost three times more for spots than for program time in 1962, more than four times as much in 1964 six times as much in 1966, and ten times as much in 1968.

This preference for spot announcements shows a willingness to advertise a name with limited characterization and to identify a candidate's position with a slogan. Spots do not raise the level of political life, education, or sophistication. They serve, says Arthur Schlesinger, Jr., "to cheapen political discourse, steadily reducing its length, its substance and its rationality." [2] Observers are prone to criticize spots without recognizing that longer programs also can contain partisan distortion and exaggeration and without noting that less well-known candidates use spots like electronic billboards to make their names familiar. Recognition of the name is particularly important to challengers. For this reason, if the political system is to be open and flexible, curbs on broadcast time, either spots or programs, should be approached with caution. They are the most economical way for some candidates to reach the electorate.

As noted, candidates may settle for spots because broadcasters, fearing a loss of audience, will not make program time available even at standard fees. Broadcasters are not specifically required to sell or give time for political broadcasts, and some do neither, despite the fact that the Federal Communications Commission is required to grant broadcasting licenses with a view to the "public interest, convenience and necessity." The precise meaning of this phrase has never been defined, but it has come before the courts.

Several 1968 decisions by broadcasters tended to place commercial interests ahead of public service or candidate needs. NBC stressed the sale of one-minute network participations on television, while CBS stressed the sale of five-minute TV slots at the end of a regular program abbreviated to 25 minutes. NBC gave 50 percent discounts for the participations, and CBS charged at a reduced rate for the trailers—one-twelfth of an hour rather than the relatively expensive five minutes. NBC received favorable publicity for giving the discount, but rates on programs and on spots of other lengths—perhaps more to a particular candidate's liking—were not discounted. The politicians were grateful for any discount and the networks did not suffer because they were simply cutting back on entertainment fare. NBC did not curtail commercials to accommodate the spots; it chopped minutes off its shows. Such decisions to encourage certain forms of campaigning are not properly the domain of private broadcasters: Congress or the FCC should have this responsibility.

A peculiar relationship exists between those politicians whose business is communicating and those licensees whose business is communications. The broadcaster, in view of his government license, may be reluctant to antagonize the politician. On the other hand, the politician may court the favor of the broadcaster. A sizable collection of reforms dealing with the financing of political broadcasting enters into this delicate relationship. Costs and blood pressures mount while reform dallies in a legislative environment rich with proposals but poor in accomplishment.

Critics sometimes suggest that the relationship between broadcasters and politicians is far more substantial than a mutual desire not to antagonize each other, implying suspiciously that many Congressmen have strong financial interests in broadcasting, comparable to those of Mrs. Lyndon Johnson. Surveys of both the 90th and 91st Congresses (those elected in 1966 and

1968) revealed, however, that only about three percent of the Congressmen had direct or family financial interests in broadcasting.[3] The number of Congressmen with broadcast interests has declined since the early 1960's. Of the 16 Congressmen in the 91st Congress (9 Democrats and 7 Republicans) with broadcasting interests, 9 had minor family connections. Only 4 of the 16 Congressmen owned more than a 25 percent interest and held official positions in the business.

Section 315 of the Federal Communications Act, misnamed the "equal time" provision, more accurately called the "equal opportunity" provision, is at the heart of the complex issues in political broadcasting. Section 315 prohibits stations from selling or giving time to one candidate without offering an equal amount on the same terms to all candidates for the same office. The purpose, of course, is to prevent broadcasters from providing an unfair advantage to any candidate. In 1959 permanent exemption from the application of Section 315 was granted to certain kinds of newscasts, including interviews, documentaries, or on-the-spot coverage of legally qualified candidates.

On the surface Section 315 may seem fair, but it creates practical difficulties. Independent and minor party candidates, from Vegetarians to Prohibitionists, under present law may claim time equal with major candidates. Moreover, the equality provision applies to candidates for nomination, whether at primary elections or in convention. Large numbers of potential candidates, many virtually unknown, can claim the right of equal access to the air. Broadcasters are reluctant to grant free time to major party or other serious candidates when minority candidates are in the race. Some might declare purely for the right to claim the time and free publicity. One observer has depicted Section 315 as a "noble concept of law that has run afoul of mathematical practicality." [4]

Section 315 has worked least well in Presidential elections where there are invariably many minor parties. For this reason, Congress in 1960 authorized a temporary suspension of the equal time provision to clear the way for the Kennedy-Nixon telecasts. A similar supension in 1964 did not come out of Senate-House conference after President Johnson let it be known that he wished to avoid last-minute pressure to debate Senator Goldwater, and at the same time deny free time to the Republicans and force them (and the Democrats as well) to pay for whatever broadcast time was desired. In 1968, it was Republican strategy to bottle up suspension in the Congress. Partisan considerations both times prevented suspension, and in the process the public interest was neglected.

During the 1968 campaign the National Citizens' Committee for Broadcasting recommended that broadcasters circumvent Section 315 by arranging for two candidates to appear simultaneously on a news interview program, as in the McCarthy-Kennedy debate on ABC during the California primary, or in some other fashion classified under one of the exceptions to 315.[5] The legality of such a move is not certain unless exempt news programs are redefined to recognize the news quality of a program presenting major candidates as news without political bias. An amendment to Section 315 along these lines could give broadcasters scope to present major candidates in debates, back-to-back or in other ways, including programs presented in special series for the duration of a campaign. Candidates might not agree to appear, but if they did, they would have no more or less protection from reporters than when they are interviewed alone. Minor candidates would be equally eligible to appear if broadcasters considered them newsworthy.

Apart from free time or news coverage, the air is available only to candidates who can pay. For those who cannot, Section 315 often blocks off a major channel of communication. According to democratic theory, every candidate has an equal right to put his views before the electorate over airways belonging to the public. Such theory, as Anatole France said, gives the rich rights equal with the poor to filch their dinners from a garbage can. The ability to pay should not be decisive. Political broadcasting presents a classic case of conflict, however, between the democratic theory of freedom of political debate and the economic doctrine of freedom of the marketplace.

In debates over Section 315, broadcasters have argued for outright repeal. There should be no legal distinction between electronic and press journalism, they say. All communications media should be treated alike despite the fact that broadcasters are licensed by the federal government and are dealing with a limited commodity, time.

A crucial question is, how much free time does the industry give when there are only two candidates? In contests for the Senate or governorships, the record is not good. FCC surveys of Senatorial campaigns show that television broadcasters do not provide significantly more sustaining (free) time when only two candidates are running than when there are more than two.

In 1968 the number and percentage of television stations giving no free time was greater in Senatorial and gubernatorial contests involving only two candidates than for similar contests involving three or more candidates. Of twenty-five states with two-candidate Senate races, only 34 percent of the television stations provided any free time, while in the seven states with more than two candidates, 45 percent of the stations did so. In the twelve states with two-candidate gubernatorial races, 35 percent provided some free time; in the nine states with three or four candidates, 48 percent of the stations did so. (The amount of free time provided was almost the same in all instances, between 22 and 28 minutes.) A similar analysis for radio and television in 1966 showed that the average free time for major party candidates was about the same whether or not there was a third-party candidate. These examples do not support the broadcasting industry's contention that rights of minor candidates limit the amount of free time provided to major parties.

While broadcast expenditures increased steeply during the 1960's, radio and television stations increased the allowance of free time very little. In 1962 television stations provided 841 hours of sustaining time, and six years later the figure had increased only to 1,130 hours. Radio stations did somewhat better, going from 2,549 free hours in 1962 to 4,321 hours in 1968. In comparison with expenditures during the same period, however, the increase in free time is small indeed. In the table on the next page comparisons are separate for Presidential and non-Presidential years.

Networks have a record worse than the average individual station. In general elections the amount of free network time made available to candidates has actually diminished since 1960.

BROADCAST EXPENDITURES AND SUSTAINING TIME
PRIMARY AND GENERAL ELECTIONS, 1962-68

	Increases in Broadcast Expenditures	Increases in Free Radio Time	Increases in Free TV Time
1962-66	60%	28%	11%
1964-68	70	32	12

Source: FCC *Surveys*, 1962, 1964, 1966, 1968.

SUSTAINING TIME PROVIDED BY
RADIO AND TELEVISION NETWORKS
GENERAL ELECTIONS, 1956-1968*

	TV Networks (3)	Radio Networks†
1956	29:38	32:23
1960	39:22	43:14
1964	4:28	21:14
1968	3:01	24:17

Source: FCC *Survey*, 1968. *In hours and minutes.
†Four networks for 1956-64; seven networks for 1968.

Not much free time is prime time, and some proffered free time is refused by candidates who do not like the suggested format or do not wish their opponents to enjoy equal exposure. An example of a candidate's reluctance to accept free time with stipulations attached can be found in Richard Nixon's tactics in 1968. Despite the high cost of television, he used paid time that he could control in preference to free time that he could not control. He refused invitations to be interviewed as a guest on programs like "Meet the Press" from early 1967 until the last Sunday before the November 1968 election.

Broadcasters, too, have preferences about campaign usage. They do not like to give candidates time without structure. They prefer the drama of confrontation, as in debates. Practical candidates, especially incumbents, avoid debates as a prime element of campaign strategy: they see no reason to give their opponent exposure. To attract an audience, the broadcaster might want to attach to the free time conditions that might be unpalatable to candidates. Some candidates, for instance, might need time without interruption in order to develop their ideas adequately.

Candidates need opportunities to speak to the public for themselves on their own terms, and many feel a need for more exposure to public view than is provided through debates and interviews. While broadcasters have a proper concern with program form, they should not be in a position to decide for the candidate. Broadcasters should not be able to substitute their judgment for that of a candidate, as often happens when free time is offered. Should stations be allowed, as at present, to use their judgment? Or should the decision be made by the parties? Or by a public arbiter?

The main effect of the repeal of Section 315 could be that if one candidate refused free time, broadcasters would offer free time to other major candidate(s) but still keep minor parties off the tube entirely—something which the price of time alone does well enough. In such circumstances, the fairness doctrine alone might not redress the injury before the election. The obstacles to many kinds of political coverage by networks and stations appear to lie less with Section 315 than with the refusal of candidates to participate, the inconsistent boundaries of the constituency and the audience, and the program judgments of broadcasters.

One controversial suggestion for reform of political broadcasting is that stations should be required to give a certain amount of free time as a condition of licensing. To use the government's regulatory power in this manner would be a departure from present policy. It has been argued that this could even open the door to government control of other kinds of programming. Requiring stations to give their commodity—air time—is a condition American society exacts of no other industry, although it is also true that no other industry is quite so closely linked to the public interest. The free time presumably would be program time, not spot announcements. The candidate might still wish to buy spots, and to deny that right might not be either constitutional or good public policy. In many ways it would be easier to provide candidates or parties with funds and let them choose their own time and stations, but if stations were required to give time or if the time were subsidized, who would get it, and who would decide who would get it and at what hours?

Broadcasts cross political boundaries. New York City TV

stations reach 40 or more Congressional districts. One cannot imagine a single station, even on educational or public TV, willing to air 80 or more candidates. If several stations agreed to share the duty, they could be charged with collusion, subject to antitrust action, unless officially authorized. What stations would land the colorful candidates in the "silk stocking" or reform-challenged districts? What stations would be stuck with the one-party dominant districts where interest is low?

Because there are no VHF commercial television stations in New Jersey, a candidate from that state must buy time on New York City or Philadelphia stations. His message then goes primarily to viewers who cannot vote for him. Before he goes on the air, he has thrown away 75 cents of every dollar he spends on broadcast time. Should these stations be required to give double time to serve New Jersey as well as New York? Eventually, CATV wiring may permit allocations according to political (Congressional district) jurisdictions. Then all candidates could address only the voters in their constituencies.

In the 1970 general elections, there were eight Senatorial campaigns in New York, New Jersey, and Connecticut, and five gubernatorial in New York and Connecticut, all in the audience range of New York City stations, including the Conservative Party campaigns in New York and the independent candidacy of Senator Thomas Dodd in Connecticut. To give time for all three states in the general election alone (not counting primaries) a New York station would have to produce perhaps 13 half-hour programs. This might not be a great burden, but it raises questions of equity in comparison to stations serving only one state.

Should time be given to the parties and let them untangle the issue of what candidates at what levels should be given free time? If so, what level of the party would decide? How would it cope with the tri-state problem? If subsidies were given directly to the candidate, permitting him to spend the money where he thinks it would be most effective, then what candidates at what levels should receive them?

Reform proposals on political broadcasting by the Commission on Campaign Costs in the Electronic Era[6] deal with broadcast time and general finance separately. As to time, the Commission recommends that Presidential and Vice Presidential candidates of parties that qualify in three-fourths of the states be given limited broadcast time which would be paid for by the federal government at a discounted rate. This time would be devoted to programs that "substantially involve the live appearance of the candidates," that "are designed to promote rational political discussion," and that are "presented in prime evening hours simultaneously by time zone over every broadcast and community antenna facility in the United States." The amount of time offered would depend on the vote received by the parties in previous Presidential elections. Parties which ranked first or second in two of the three previous elections would receive six prime-time 30-minute programs within the 35 days preceding the day before Election Day with the provision that there be at least one broadcast in each seven-day period. Candidates of parties that received at least one-eighth of the popular vote in the preceding election would get two 30-minute programs within this time period with the provision that no more than one be broadcast in any seven-day period. Parties which meet the state-ballot criteria, but not the previous-vote criteria, would receive one 30-minute program within the 35-day period. Administration of the program would be the responsibility of the Comptroller General of the United States.

As to cost, the commission recommends that all commercial broadcasters be required to charge legally qualified candidates for federal office no more than 50 percent of the lowest charge to any commercial advertiser. Broadcasters may then, for federal income tax purposes, deduct as a business expense the dollar value of such discounts from total taxable income. That part of the proposal requiring discounts and offering a tax deduction to broadcasters helps spread the cost of political advertising among the government, the public, the candidates, and the broadcasters. The discount provision would cut expenditures for television in half or enable candidates to purchase twice as much time at present rates, while the tax deduction offers an incentive to broadcasters to yield more free time.

The Commission's proposals raise minor questions of definition and practicality and several major questions of impact and consequence. While seeking to avoid unnecessary detail, the Commission has unfortunately left much unexplained. It does not define such terms as "rational political discussion," "substantially live appearances," or "prime time." The Commission does not suggest a format for handling negotiations among the candidates for specific program time nor does it advance a formula for determining which candidates get which minutes. The Commission does not consider the practicality or the constitutionality of the requirement that political programs be presented simultaneously over every broadcast facility in the United States; it would, for example, be advantageous to have some stations present the program late for those who missed the early broadcast. The Commission, furthermore, does not explain why the Comptroller General has been chosen to administer this program or what initiatives he could take. Why is not the FCC the administering agency?

Beyond such questions of definition and structure, the Commission left unanswered several fundamental questions about the impact and consequences of its proposal. The most important is whether a party should have to meet such extensive qualifications for subsidized exposure. The Commission's proposals may bolster the two-party system, but diversity is sacrificed. Access to the political system would be restricted for those who would not qualify for free time. New voices could be stifled while the well-established ones might be amplified. The ability of George Wallace to get on the ballot in 50 states in 1968 may serve as a helpful precedent, but getting on the ballot in even three-fourths of the states is still difficult and expensive.

Any refinement of the proposal should give minority candidates for President reasonable access to the voters. Within the limitations set, even a refined system would not assist minor parties. Perhaps giving subsidies directly to parties or candidates, rather than to broadcasters would be desirable.

Broadcasters seem correct in saying that they already bear a relatively large share of political program costs and that it would not be equitable if the industry were asked to assume the entire financial burdens. Former FCC Chairman E. William Henry suggested one provision adopted by *Voters' Time,* that the Internal Revenue Code be amended to give added incentive to broadcasters to offer free political time by permitting them to deduct from their taxable income not only out-of-pocket expenses of free broadcasts (as they do now), but also to deduct at least a portion of the revenue lost.[7] One could add the stipulation: if ample free time is made available under standards set by the FCC or by law as in the *Voters' Time* proposal. In this way responsible broadcasters would not suffer financially by serving the public at election time.

In 1969, after careful study, the National Committee for an Effective Congress drafted and had introduced a complex bill affecting broadcasting.[8] It guaranteed to Senate and House candidates certain amounts of time that could be purchased at discounts from television stations located in their districts or in states which transmitted to a significant portion of them. By late 1970, through a predictably slow process of hearings and committee and floor consideration, a different bill evolved which was enacted by large majorities in both the Senate and the House. The bill would have limited the amount each candidate for President, the Senate, the House, Governor, and Lieutenant Governor could spend on the broadcast media to seven cents per vote received for the same office in the previous election and half that amount in the primary. Moreover, it would have permanently repealed the "equal opportunity" requirement for Presidential and Vice Presidential campaigns and required broadcasters to charge candidates the lowest unit rate for the time they purchased, equivalent to the lowest rate obtained by commercial advertisers (presumably those who negotiate special rates when buying large blocs over long periods of time). States would have been permitted to extend the bill's provisions to other elections.

For a while it seemed possible that the bill would be enacted in time to take effect for the 1970 general election. Delays occurred, but the bill finally passed on September 23. Two weeks later, to the surprise and consternation of many, President Nixon vetoed it. The bill, he said, was incomplete because it limited only television and radio, not all, spending. It would favor incumbents and limit the ability of challengers to get their message across, would discriminate against broadcasters, and put Congress in the business of setting rates. It did not deal with spending by committees and individuals not directly connected with candidates, the President said.

Generally, the Democrats and the press deplored the veto and called on Congress to override it. By this time Common Cause, a citizens' lobby organized by John Gardner, a Republican and former Secretary of Health, Education and Welfare, was lobbying actively for the override along with the NCEC, the DSG, and labor. The White House lobbied to sustain the veto, which irked some advocates because the Administration had not played any lobbying role in formulating the legislation. The outcome was touch-and-go until President Nixon sent a letter to Senate Minority Leader Hugh Scott promising to cooperate in devising acceptable legislation in the next session. The Senate failed to override by four votes, and the issue was put on ice for the next Congress.

The 92nd Congress saw an unparalleled spate of bills introduced on all aspects of the regulation of political finance. Major bills covered various approaches to reform of political broadcasting but also to disclosure of political funds, limitations, tax incentives for political contributions, and subsidies. Forward movement came early in the first session when the Senate Commerce Committee held hearings. The Administration did not testify, but a bill introduced by Senator Hugh Scott was said to be acceptable to the White House. When the Committee began to mark up the bill, contention arose over limitations on spending and contributing. The Democrats charged the Republicans with delaying tactics. Some Republican Senators asked to reopen hearings to consider new testimony, and this time the Administration requested an opportunity to testify. Meanwhile, President Nixon had publicly stated he favored expenditure controls, provided they were comprehensive and did not give incumbents an advantage. This upset some Republicans and embarrassed Senator Scott who thought he had Administration support for his bill, which had no ceilings on either expenditures or contributions. These events gave impetus to the strong Democratic drive for limitations on amounts that candidates and committees could spend on advertising, with particular emphasis on restricting radio and television spending. Most of their major bills would limit advertising to a certain number of cents per eligible vote, with half of that as a ceiling on expenditures in the broadcast media.

Richard Kleindienst, Deputy Attorney General, testifying on behalf of the Nixon Administration, proposed: (1) an aggregate advertising limit without distinction as to any particular medium, (2) extension of the lowest-unit-rate principle to certain non-broadcast media as well, and (3) repeal of Section 315 to apply to all candidates at all levels. He declared that any new legislation dealing with media coverage should not apply to Governor and Lieutenant Governor because there seems to be no constitutional basis for exercising such authority in contests for state office.

Throughout most of the legislative activity the role of the Nixon administration was mainly negative. President Nixon's sudden position in favor of limits appeared to be rooted in a belated judgment that action would be forthcoming, at least in the Senate, and the Administration should therefore participate more directly in formulating the legislation. Many critics claimed that the Administration was not interested in reform but in protecting the Republican financial advantage. With the Republicans nationally affluent compared with the debt-ridden Democrats, and with the Democrats still controlling the Congress, the Republicans may have thought their electoral opportunities would be greater without limitations on contributions or expenditures. When they saw that the Democrats would vote for limits anyway, they tried to fashion a bill acceptable to themselves. In the process, critics thought the Republicans were deliberately delaying action, especially as the reopening of Senate Commerce Committee hearings set the schedule back several weeks.

The original NCEC bill was refashioned by many hands during 1970 and 1971, but the most significant changes were made by Senator John Pastore and Congressman Torbert MacDonald, the chairmen of the relevant subcommittees of the Commerce committees of the Senate and House. They became floor managers of the legislation, taking the leadership from the elections subcommittees of both Houses. One effort to expedite the portions of the 1971 legislation dealing with disclosure and tax incentives (or subsidies) was to refer the omnibus bills jointly to the committees on Finance, Commerce, and Rules, with the condition that, as soon as one committee reported its relevant portion, the other two would have 45 days to complete action. The implication was that if the second or third committees failed to report out on time, they would lose the opportunity to influence the legislation in committee and any amendments thereafter would have to be introduced during floor debate or in conference committee between the two houses.

After the Senate Commerce Committee reported out the 1971 bill, the Senate Committee on Rules and Administration held hearings and reported the bill favorably, but not before making major changes that conformed closely to the Kleindienst formula and differed significantly from the Commerce Committee bill. However, a number of these changes were revised again when the Senate as a whole debated the bill. The Senate enacted a strong bill that set the spending ceiling at 10 cents for each person of voting age estimated at 139 million for 1972, of which not more than 6 cents could go for radio and television. The remaining 4 cent ceiling would apply to newspaper, magazine and billboard advertising. Time and space would be required to be sold at the lowest unit rate. The bill limited candidates for President, Senate and House, with the ceiling applying separately in campaigns for nomination, for runoff, and for election. The bill also repealed equal opportunity provisions of Section 315 for all Federal campaigns, not the Presidential campaigns alone as in earlier versions. Third, it deleted an earlier provision limiting the maximum contribution by an individual to $5,000, leaving no ceiling whatsoever. However, fourth, it placed a limit on the amount a wealthy candidate or his immediate family can spend on his own campaign: ceilings are $50,000 for a Presidential campaign, $35,000 for the Senate and $25,000 for the House. Fifth, the bill extended the disclosure provisions and established a Federal Elections Commission to receive and process the financial reports of candidates and political committees, which would be required to report comprehensively their receipts and expenditures in campaigns for nomination and election.

Proponents hoped to complete action before the election of 1972 brought on a competitive mood that might impair deliberations already fraught with partisan overtones. Action in the Senate was easier to achieve than in the House. It requires strong leadership by both Democrats and the White House to move election reform in the House. Considerable momentum for reform was carried over from 1970 by the press and such lobbies as NCEC and Common Cause, but Section 315 was a major sticking point in the House. Many of those who favor Section 315 at least welcome its removal from Presidential and Vice Presidential campaigns. Although the section is designed to protect candidates from discrimination in the use of the airwaves, it also protects broadcasters in decisions about political broadcasting for reasons already discussed. Apart from Presidential elections, repeal of Section 315 would not by itself do much to give candidates the time, form, or the stations they prefer, but in Presidential campaigns, with a dozen or more candidates, Section 315 inhibits broadcasters from giving time they might like to give to major candidates. At less than the Presidential or Vice Presidential level, outright repeal of Section 315 could subject too many candidates to too many uncertainties because there can be no equity for a candidate once he has lost. Scores of complaints and court cases are ample testimony to the varying interpretations of "equal opportunity." In contrast, there is little chance that unfair practices will hurt a White House candidate because Presidential campaigns are well-monitored and have the resources and knowledge to appeal to the FCC or the courts.

The principle of discounts for political messages, the major thrust of the NCEC bill, was transformed in the vetoed bill of 1970 and in the 1971 version into a requirement that broadcasters sell time at the lowest unit rate.

But objections to the discount principle at first were raised by the broadcasters themselves. They asked why their industry should be singled out to give discounts for political purposes. The answer was, of course, because federal regulation of the public airwaves permits a direct means to cope with at least one aspect of campaign costs. Later, however, when the discount principle was extended to other media, the broadcasters were agreeable. The rationale for this extension was that Congress can regulate sale of advertising in other than the broadcast media either as a reasonable exercise of its authority to regulate federal elections or under the commerce clause of the Constitution. Legislative precedent for lower rates with regard to all media is found in a few states that prohibit newspapers, as well as radio and television stations, from charging for political ads rates in excess of published commercial rates. Section 315 of the Federal Communications Act already prohibits excessive charges for political broadcasts but the provision has not been enforced.

The lowest-unit-rate proposals offer some possibility of controlling rising campaign costs because voluntary discounting by broadcasters has been unpredictable. Lack of uniformity in discounting creates special problems of competition and obligation. It seems desirable that some standard discount be applicable to all stations and eventually to all candidates. Otherwise, discounting may be an indirect form of political contribution from companies in an industry regulated by the federal government. If the discount rate is set by law, no special obligations to specific broadcasters are incurred and no specific considerations involved. Few if any Congressional candidates in the metropolitan areas find it economical to buy television time, given the small size of their districts to the total audience. Presumably, with lowest unit rate, most candidates still would not find television time worth the cost, but if more did, the popular station would be hit by the most requests for discounted time. Under some proposals they would have an affirmative obligation to sell some time at the lowest rates. While there should be an affirmative responsibility of broadcasters to sell or give time, candidate demands for program time at reduced rates could prove some hardship on the favored stations.

Conceivably, discounts may encourage campaigners to purchase extra time. Only experience can tell whether candidates will be induced by reduced rates to buy more time. Presumably there are limiting factors: a candidate fears backfire from overexposure; stations may not have or yield time for more political broadcasts. Political psychology and the power drive no doubt will move some campaigns to purchase more time, but others find ways other than advertising to spend money saved. There is no way of knowing what practices will evolve until lowest discount unit rates are tried.

The House diluted the strong Senate bill, but the Federal Election Campaign Act of 1972 finally passed and this time the enactment was not vetoed. (More detailed information is provided in Chapter 17.)

If a campaign subsidy is still a remote prospect—certainly for non-federal candidates—how can Section 315 be adapted to meet the needs of politics? At present, Section 315 protects the rights of major candidates to buy equal time for political broadcasts, as noted, without considering capacity to pay. But there is no guaranty of a right to broadcast for either major or minor candidates. One formula, called differential equality of access, would recognize two-party dominance and still give all contenders some chance to be heard. Differential rights of access need not prescribe a complex rating based on vote, membership, or petition. It states simply that major candidates are equal to major candidates, that minor candidates are equal to minor candidates, but that the two are not equal to each other. If a group grows or at the outset looks significant, it can jump to major status. Minor candidates might receive a quarter or less of the time offered to the ones from the dominant parties.

A comprehensive proposal applying differential equality of access to Presidential campaigns has been formulated by Professor Roscoe L. Barrow.[9] His proposal classifies candidates for President and Vice President as major, minor, and evolving. Major candidates are those who seek nomination or are the nominees of parties which polled at least three percent of the popular vote in the last Presidential election or who are supported by petitions signed by qualified electors numbering at least one and a half percent of that popular vote. Minor candidates must be either qualified candidates for nomination or, as nominees, qualified in at least three states. And they must be associated with a party which received one percent of the popular vote in the past Presidential election or be supported by petitions signed by qualified electors numbering at least one half of one percent of that popular vote. Candidates who do not qualify as major or minor are called evolving candidates.

Under this proposal, in each of the eight weeks preceding election day, free prime time would be granted by every network and station to Presidential candidates. Each week each major candidate would get one hour, each minor candidate would get one half hour, and each evolving candidate would get none.

The Presidential candidate, not the party, would receive the time, and he would be able to share the time with his Vice Presidential candidate as he wished. The networks and stations would be able to deduct from their taxable income one-half of the revenue lost as a result of granting the time.

Beyond the minimum free time, networks or licensees would be encouraged to grant additional free time or commercial time, or both. The broadcasters would be permitted to vary the amount of time granted to opposing candidates for the same office according to this formula: if time is granted to a major candidate, the station or network would not be required to grant any time to evolving candidates; if time is granted to a minor candidate, the station or network would have to grant equal time to other minor candidates and half time to major candidates, but would not be required to provide time for evolving candidates; if the time is granted to evolving candidates, the station or network would not be required to grant any time to minor or major candidates.

Under the Barrow proposal, any candidate denied time within the variables would be granted a cause of action in Federal District Court. Regulations would be administered by the FCC, to be enforced by court order or the licensing process. The system could be extended to state and even local contests by suitably redefining major and minor candidates and appropriately altering allocations of time.

Barrow's proposals attack a variety of shortcomings in a reasonable manner. The formula for classifying candidates is simple for the entire election period, and all major and minor candidates would appear on TV during each of the eight weeks preceding election. Tax incentives encourage stations to grant (or at least sell) time in addition to that required. Although awards are small for candidates who charge and prove discrimination, such cases at least would be actionable.

One flaw in Professor Barrow's proposal is his treatment of evolving candidates: conceivably they could get no time during the campaign, even though Barrow does allow stations to give these candidates time without incurring obligations to other candidates. A station could broadcast Dick Gregory without having to offer time to everyone else, and that is a positive advance that even the *Voters' Time* proposals do not make.

Still another proposal would broaden the definition of a news program to include joint or simultaneous appearances of major candidates as previously noted. If the formula worked successfully at the Presidential level, it could be tried for other contests, even for primary elections.

Another controversial aspect of political broadcasting is the built-in advantage to incumbents. Between campaign periods, there are bound to be imbalances in the presentation of Democrats and Republicans on network interview programs. Obviously the party in power will make more news; the opposition has no shadow cabinet in the American system.

It has been estimated that 70 percent of U. S. Senators and 60 percent of Congressman regularly utilize free time offered by stations back home. Although the costs of taping the broadcasts are assumed by the Senator or Representative, studios are available on Capitol Hill, operated by government-salaried technicians, providing facilities at the lowest possible cost.

The incumbency controversy never flares more brightly than when a President who is running for re-election takes to the air for a Presidential address. President Eisenhower did it in 1956 over the Hungarian and Suez crises—against Democratic protest. In 1964 Republicans sought to obtain free broadcast time equal to that provided by the networks to President Johnson when he reported to the American people on the Khrushchev ouster and the Chinese nuclear explosion. The FCC and the Federal courts ruled against these pleas. Following his 1964 defeat, Senator Goldwater several times alleged that the failure to receive equal time had put the Republicans at a severe disadvantage. The Republicans, however, capitalized on the denial of free time by making paid television appeals for funds to buy time to answer the President; they even utilized one free time period provided by NBC not so much to answer as to plead for funds to answer.

When a President speaks as the Chief Executive the presumption must be that he is addressing himself to matters of concern to all Americans. The President's posture should not be compromised simply because he is in a campaign. If the equal opportunity provision had been suspended in 1964, the networks would probably have given Goldwater time to reply for news value alone. Without suspension, the stations have a ready excuse that all the minor party candidates would demand equal time.

When President Nixon used television to present reviews of American policy toward Vietnam, Cambodia, and Laos and to announce troop withdrawals, the Democratic National Committee filed formal complaints with the FCC and took the issue to the courts to gain opportunity to reply. They appealed to the fairness doctrine and not for equal time since the Democratic spokesmen were not certified political candidates. CBS voluntarily offered to provide time on a continuing but irregular basis for a "Loyal Opposition" series. Democratic Committee Chairman Lawrence F. O'Brien was provided time to reply to a televised Nixon "Conversation" with journalists. When O'Brien's reply was unmistakably partisan, the Republican National Committee asked for time to reply to the Democratic answer. The FCC made a distinction between "party-oriented" and "issues-oriented" reply and determined that time for a rebuttal must be given to the Republicans. The Democrats and CBS then complained, and CBS changed its mind and withdrew its offer of a continuing series.

Other complaints followed, including one from 14 anti-war Senators asking for time to answer President Nixon's appearances on Vietnam policy. The FCC thought that the demand was valid, and the networks presented programs accordingly—some as answers, some as debates with proponents and opponents. In general, the FCC has rejected the right of direct reply on an equal time basis to opponents of the President, but when the record was so one-sided that the other side was not getting an adequate hearing, it ruled that the networks must strike a better balance, even when it is the President speaking as the President and not as a party leader.

Another open question is whether the networks must sell time for answers. Senator McGovern sought to buy time to answer the President after the move into Cambodia, and only NBC agreed; the others refused. McGovern's program, telecast jointly with four other Senators, asked briefly for contributions to pay for the $70,000 cost of the broadcast. A flood of contributions came in which eventually reached $480,000 from about 50,000 givers. Not all the funds could be attributed directly to the television appeal, but the direct response in numbers of dollars and donors was probably the best in history on an issue (not on behalf of a candidate, where the Goldwater record in 1964 still stands). The money was used to pay for a media campaign to generate support for the McGovern-Hatfield amendment calling for complete withdrawal of U. S. forces from Vietnam by mid-1971.

The fairness controversy is continuing, and the ultimate outcome will likely be a victory for more dialogue, inevitably incurring political costs for the President and monetary costs for the broadcasters. The sale-of-time controversy also continues. Both issues point up the fact that the opposition is watching and weighing events carefully and seems likely to complain and litigate until satisfactory rules and compliance are assured.

The Supreme Court in two related decisions handed down in 1969[10] upheld FCC regulations requiring stations to take the initiative in giving free time to any individual or group whose honesty, character, or integrity had been attacked. The Court declared that the free speech right of viewers and listeners, not the rights of the broadcasters, is paramount and reiterated the argument that scarcity of channels places broadcasters under different obligations than publishers of printed communications.

The rules at issue were regulations adopted in 1967 by the FCC to specify broadcasting obligations under the fairness doctrine. The rules require stations carrying personal attacks to send the person or groups attacked a script or tape or an accurate summary of the attack, notification of the time of the broadcast, and an offer of free time to reply. The same requirements apply in connection with the broadcasting of editorials. The rules do not apply to regularly scheduled news programs or commentaries contained within such programs, on-the-spot news coverage, or personal attacks made by political candidates during a campaign. Situations exempt from the specific rules are not exempt from general application of the fairness doctrine. The Court, in upholding the concept of fairness and the specific rules, noted that the First Amendment permits the FCC to go still further. The decision by Justice Byron White said the Amendment does not prohibit the government "from requiring a licensee to share his frequency with others and to conduct himself as a proxy or fiduciary with obligations to present those views and voices which would otherwise, by necessity, be barred from the airways."

Directly applicable to political broadcasting are the Court's findings that the most important rights are those of viewers and listeners, not of broadcasters and that, since there are not enough airwaves for everyone, "it is idle to posit an unbridgeable First Amendment right to broadcast comparable to the right of every individual to speak, write or publish." These statements would seem to permit some differential in time made available to various candidates while at the same time requiring some standard of differential equality.

The rise to prominence of Eldridge Cleaver, George Wallace, or indeed Eugene McCarthy also has important implications for treatment of minor parties or dissenting candidates by broadcast licensees.

Apart from occasional discussion-panel shows or open-mike shows, there are no continuing electronic soapboxes or the equivalent of an underground press, either to enable people to let off steam or to give audience to potentially important but submerged ideas or emotions. Educational or public television has so far not met this need and ironically some public stations are prohibited by state law from engaging in political broadcasting or even from airing controversial subjects.

This is why in a political campaign some minimal time for ideas beyond the depth of slogans, especially ideas of dissent and protest, would seem imperative. A responsive democracy can hardly demand less.

Other possible reforms suggest a central agency, such as a statehouse or public TV facility, to plan and distribute taped shows to stations in the candidate's constituency. The programs might be broadcast free in segments at the end of a regular news broadcast. If it is done for weather, why not for politics? Public television, though its audiences are small, could conduct useful experiments with political programs that might attract a new following. Public TV should be able to devise an electronic substitute for political tracts or voters' pamphlets. A televised version of candidates night, like those sponsored by The League of Women Voters with studio audiences asking questions of candidates, might be useful.

WMCA in New York City carries on an elaborate campaign to assist voter registration, but few stations give out registration and polling information by area, as any substantial newspaper does. How many radio or TV stations present voting instructions and sample ballots? Many newspapers do. How many stations have run bipartisan fund-raising campaigns with the cooperation of the political parties? The broadcasting media could share in powerful campaigns to motivate small givers. Stations are permitted to sell time to commercial advertisers, get-out-the-vote, and contributions drives, but none seems to try aggressively. Radio and television stations could also help to alert the public to political broadcasts, as a public service.

If television and radio have the potential to raise the level of political education and participation, they have demonstrated that power only fleetingly and sporadically. It is time for the industry, the political parties, Congressional committees, the FCC, and state governments to improve opportunities for political communication in the national interest. Democratic institutions depend on learning how to use radio and television sensibly as these media influence the views, attitudes, and behavior of nearly all Americans.

CHAPTER 15

THE PRIVATE SECTOR

American politics has failed to provide the motivation to find or develop effective collection cups for sufficient numbers of conscientious citizens who perhaps might learn to donate money to politics if properly approached. The importance of small contributions in a democracy warrants the time, effort, energy, and investment to round them up in large numbers.

The prerequisites for broad-based political financing are here. The funds are available. Collection methods are tried and tested. Political giving can rise relatively as rapidly as gifts for charitable and educational purposes in recent years—from $8.9 billion in 1960 to $18.3 billion in 1970, though not in such huge aggregate amounts.[1] The success in attracting individuals to charitable giving has not been a matter of accident or a spontaneous result of general good will toward organizations with good causes. Rather, it reflects a serious effort to educate the public to its responsibilities and to organize collection systems. Political responsibilities must be similarly learned.

The value of contributing small sums for political activity is not taught much in schools nor widely understood as an act of good citizenship, although voting is both honored and respected, at least in principle if not entirely in performance. The present challenge is to associate contributing with voting as a desirable act of citizenship, to telescope into a few years generations of education, to upgrade and dignify political donation, to gain for popular financing of politics the public approval accorded voting. Motivation for contributing can be awakened in citizens now skeptical or indifferent, intensified in those already interested, and expanded in time. From childhood, the connection between freewill political offerings and civic virtue can be assured if youngsters see that their peers are giving; if they learn how small amounts given for the right reasons outweigh large amounts given for the wrong reasons; if they observe that those who spend political money use it wisely and well; and if they find that dependable political income favors selection of qualified candidates without regard to their personal fortunes.

Actually, the number of givers now is almost sufficient to provide necessary funds to finance American politics by small donations, if they would share the money according to need.

The percentage who give has not increased as rapidly in the 1960's as in the 1950's, notably between 1952 and 1956, but in 1956, 1960, and 1964, from 10 percent to 12 percent of adults say they contributed at some level; with population increases, the number giving has grown—from 8 million in 1956 to 12 million persons in 1964. In 1968 the percentage dropped to 8, but this is still 8.7 million persons, as noted in the following table:[2]

Year	Amount (in millions)	Contributors	Average per Contributor
1952	$140	3,000,000	$46.6
1956	155	8,000,000	19.6
1960	175	10,000,000	17.5
1964	200	12,000,000	16.6
1968	300	8,700,000	34.5

Average numbers, of course, may be misleading. An average $100 gift may represent 90 percent in $10 donations and 10 percent in $1,000 checks. Small contributors can fund the major campaigns only if their numbers and gifts increase. Assuming political costs of $300 million in 1968, at the $15 sustaining fund level there would need to be 20 million contributors, rather than 8.7 million as in 1968.[3] In these dimensions, the aim becomes at least a doubling of the number of contributors.

At present, relatively small percentages of the voters back their preferences with cash contributions. Of more than 73 million voters in 1968, about 11 percent contributed. George Gallup points out that giving is generally a family decision; the 8.7 million contributors would represent as many as 30 million with positive attitudes toward political giving. This number is consistent with the high correspondence between those who were asked to give and those who did: of each 10 solicited, 4 to 5 give. Even if the 15 to 20 percent of Americans solicited are relatively prosperous, surely the other 80 percent could at least give something.

One Gallup series consistently shows that there are many potential givers as yet unsolicited.[4]

To achieve a goal of 20 million contributors would require at least 40 million solicitations but perhaps no more than 60 million. Some may be reached through radio, television, church, union, or corporate solicitation; some by mail, press, or counter display. As noted, the Republican national campaign sent out 22,000,000 mail solicitations in 1968, counting duplicates. Republican and Democratic efforts combined, including face-to-face appeals, could easily reach the target.

As further evidence of the possibilities,[5] about 75 percent of voters identify with one of our major parties, and for perhaps one-third of this group loyalty to party is strong and unchanging. Almost all who make political contributions are voters. A solid core, perhaps half of the potential electorate, vote regularly. It would seem reasonable to suppose that the solid core who identify strongly with a party are likely to give if properly approached.

The task is to reach them, but how?

Every fund raiser knows that a face-to-face appeal is the best way to obtain donations. This technique requires solicitors in proportion to the numbers to be solicited. The number of solicitors may be reduced by such devices as collection booths at street corners, banks, and supermarkets. Such booths are often used to pass out literature or ask for votes but rarely to raise funds. For a saturation drive, local leaders would recruit and deploy volunteers block-by-block.

Realistic arguments used against this form of money raising were described earlier. Nevertheless organization in the U. S., despite increasing centralization, is and will remain basically local; therefore, politics should eventually come to depend on local funds that local volunteers are best able to solicit. Properly managed door-to-door drives can, as shown, bring gratifying results.

Though some local leaders may disagree, Gallup Poll results consistently indicate that a solid reliable core of party workers is usually available and that these can be supplemented by irregulars for certain elections but not for others.

A survey by the American Association of Fund-Raising Counsel reported 43.2 million enrolled volunteers in 22 national organizations relying on volunteer services.[6] Many such individuals volunteer in several causes. If the political parties could tap even half that volunteer strength, they would be on the road to collecting big money in small sums. All depends on leadership. Attractive candidates will attract volunteers and sympathetic political managers will welcome them.

With enough volunteers, parties may need less money, but to attract either takes professional manpower, which requires seed money. Since, even with improvements, there may not be volunteers enough to reach all voters, politicians use the mails. Although a mail appeal must compete with dozens of such solicitations, political and not, to motivate the giver to write a check, perhaps address an envelope and affix a stamp, the Republican National Sustaining Fund has demonstrated that it can be done.

Television and radio appeals have both strengths and liabilities. They need full attention from those expected to note where to send money for whatever purpose. Some broadcast appeals have been remarkably effective, but others fail to bring in even the cost of the appeal. The Goldwater campaign in 1964 delivered massive mailings at the same time its appeals were on the air so that the different media would reinforce each other; e.g., the mail appeal provided a self-addressed postage-paid envelope which his supporters used in their response to television appeals.

A nonpartisan collection through the income tax system would reach most Americans of affluence, though not at an ideal time and out of political season. One Congressman has proposed setting elections on May 15 while tax returns are a vivid memory. The Long Act in 1966 was the first attempt to use tax returns to collect political money and the 1971 bill discussed in Chapter 17 was the second attempt.

No solicitation and collection system—whether door-to-door, union checkoff, payroll withholding, or mass mail—will satisfy financial needs of all candidates. Barring a system in which all money is contributed to and distributed by a party choosing all candidates, campaigners will continue to seek funds separately.

Their interest is to achieve efficient use of available channels for soliciting and collecting money.

Labor, trade associations, and corporate bipartisan fund-raising drives, and tax checkoffs have special advantages: they cost the parties or candidates hardly anything and the costs to the organizations are minimal. In comparison, mail drives are limited by inability to produce sufficient funds and by their costs. The costs take 30 to 40 percent of a good return and more than 100 percent of a poor one.

Economies of piggy-back appeals for special audiences may be gained by nonpartisan appeals through professional societies. Lawyers or academics can be solicited through their national organizations. Possibly with the endorsement of such organizations as the American Political Science Association, national headquarters of professional societies could consent to receive and distribute money to the party or candidate of choice. The money can be sterilized by using trust accounts or banks for the actual disbursement (as was suggested for governmental collection systems). Similar cooperation and endorsements could come from book clubs, record clubs, and other organizations with large mailings. Such organizations should be encouraged not merely to lend their address lists but to participate as a civic responsibility.

Although British parties conduct football totes and other gambling devices to finance their work, Americans mainly use bingo to collect funds from the sporting element for social purposes. Several states have elected to socialize lotteries or racing bets for revenue but the big gambling take for the most part has been the province of extra-legal entrepreneurs. Could not some gambling revenue be applied to politics? What stakes are higher than politics?

Both solicitation and collection systems need to conform to American political structure and practice: the federal system which the party structure reflects and supports is not likely to undergo fundamental change. Regulatory improvements—in nomination provisions, in shorter ballots—among other structural reforms may relieve financial pressures on the political system. It would help to have a system that encourages donors to use party channels for their contributions or to take steps toward a rational fund-raising structure encompassing the different requirements of campaigns and of parties for standard operations. The remedies differ as much as the requirements—yet the connection is close. Without improving means of party support, there seems to be small chance of improving campaign support.

While soaring political costs affect some candidates more than others, especially in federal and state contests, reforms of political finance ought not be isolated. Remedies need to be devised to embrace fund raising for the entire political system with collections serving all levels of candidacy and arenas of contention. Because bipartisan or nonpartisan collection systems can raise dollars for all candidates and districts through one appeal, their use, as an alternative to appealing for one candidate, faction or committee in one place at one time, sets a crucial frame of reference for the future.

Such campaigns could retail our politics, take them out of the clubhouse and onto the streets, into the living room, into the shop. Through storefronts, door-to-door canvassing, appeals at work and at play, well-known gathering centers, the word can be passed, followed up, and repeated until the message gets across and the participation of the citizen becomes habitual.

Private efforts—collecting and contributing—can be energized by the new system of tax incentives. Filing income forms and paying taxes are focal occasions on the national calendar when the connection between the purse and politics is vivid. Taxpayers might be especially responsive to a stimulative campaign that could be conducted by the government itself in a brochure accompanying each tax form. At least, a section conspicuous on every tax form will serve notice that political giving is approved national policy.

The bulk of political donations will always be around election time, when campaigns excite the electors. A Presidential election is an unparalleled educational opportunity too little exploited for enlisting party supporters. No event receives so much publicity; speculation about who will run starts really at mid-term. Massive fund raising synchronized with this event and its publicity could successfully compete with the fat cat contributions for influence.

No persistent nationwide attempts at wall-to-wall solicitations have been tried in this country, and the media have not been used in saturation doses along with simultaneous attempts by both parties to solicit broadly and improve the climate for giving. To work, a massive national campaign would need to be mobilized with the cooperation of public officials from the President on down. The media, service organizations, and others can urge the public to put its money where its political interests lie. As no other command post competes with the White House as a center for education and action, the President's policy will be decisive. Most efforts at mass solicitation have been one-shot affairs. The public is not habituated to give as it might be by massive educational appeals sustained through the years.

The prestige and support of the White House, combined with broad participation by private groups—political parties, educators, the League of Women Voters, the Advertising Council, business, labor, and other organizations—can go far toward awakening public interest. Public understanding of the problems of political finance could be greatly improved also if the networks produced more documentaries on the subject.[7]

A nongovernmental, federally-chartered nonpartisan foundation has been proposed to work full-time with the parties on political finance[8] with the twin responsibilities of encouraging broadly-based fund raising and assisting registration and election-day drives. As a byproduct, the organization could serve as a catalyst or a neutral meeting ground for joint undertakings—such as bipartisan appeals or competitions between fund-raising groups—either to encourage wider participation, to reduce costs, or even voluntarily to limit certain spending. The organization could finance internships that help train personnel for professional party work, leadership, and public service in politics. Candidate fellowships could assist those whose personal resources are necessarily limited and who could not otherwise take time from their usual work to run for public office.[9] Such an organization could be financed readily if the political parties tithed 1 percent of gross receipts each year, or if corporations and labor unions were permitted to contribute.

A foundation-sponsored educational and publicity program on the political processes could be prepared and operated over a five-year cycle, beginning and ending in a Presidential election year, for about $5 million. This sum is not large, considering that in a five-year period parties and candidates will spend more than $1 billion in political money.

A thoroughgoing effort to increase participation in the democratic process could not ignore the schools. Surveys of citizenship education in the United States report that education in the electoral process and in political structure and operations is negligible. In high school courses, the emphasis is on American history and the Constitution, with little attention to citizenship beyond voting, although pilot experiments go beyond these limits by focusing on education for citizenship.

A few colleges and law schools encourage political participation, without course credit, through volunteer activity, including programs to solicit contributions, as in the 1968 McCarthy campaign. The Young Democrats and Young Republicans could be agencies for these activities instead of being mere appendages of their parent organization. By default, they have let militant and revolutionary forces capture the energies of sincerely democratic, idealistic youth: they have far to go to overcome the alienation and disaffection so evident in youth today.

A Gallup Poll in 1960 reported that 45 percent of the population recognized a duty to make political contributions,[10] although many have never seriously considered giving. Typical negative responses indicate the need for a massive educational campaign: e.g., "The average citizen should not contribute because campaigns are too long," "Too much is already spent and wasted on politics," "The more given the more will be spent," "There are enough others who are willing to finance politics," "Giving does not benefit the small donor," "Elections should be decided on the basis of ability, not money," and "Most people make up their minds before the campaign begins."

Such negative feelings and half-truths must be countered if constructive attitudes are to flourish. The range of responses provides some clues to what a successful educational campaign must contain.

The negative attitudes which currently prevail are based on prejudices and misunderstandings about the way politics works. They also show that the public does not understand how much money is needed to run for public office, where the money now comes from, or what are desirable options.

Democratically-oriented political financing requires strengthening of organizational and fund raising mechanisms within political parties. If political costs are high, then the parties must allocate resources to fund raising, as the Republicans have at the national level.

In a national sample, county party chairmen rated fund raising as their third most important activity (immediately behind election day and registration), but the chairmen rated their performance in fund raising as the poorest of six types of activities.[11]

Party strength and fund-raising activity can be improved by careful planning so that each level will do what it does best. National and state committees can most effectively raise funds through special events and mail campaigns. Local committees, without star attractions at fund-raising events and without resources for effective mail campaigns, can most effectively carry on door-to-door drives for funds. In recent years, the Republicans nationally have raised $3 million or more annually in their sustaining fund but at a cost of perhaps $1 million. If that same $3 million could be raised locally by volunteers, the out-of-pocket expense of raising the money would be minimal.

The parties also need to devise, separately or jointly with a bipartisan mobilization agency, a system of incentives for party workers and rewards for solicitors. Recognition of successful volunteers could be a stimulus to a volunteer corps and a means of attracting a flow of new volunteers. Slogans like "Open Parties for an Open Society" could offset the notion that party organizations are closed clubs, if practice conforms to principle.

Open parties can recruit candidates who are attractive, political leaders who are enlightened, solicitors who are eager, but not by mere exhortation. Party prospects need to hear what to expect as candidates, as political leaders, as solicitors, as contributors. The party program must create conditions that appeal to varied political interests, tastes, and aspirations.

As noted earlier (Chapter 8), too many identify political success with an attractive leader with access to radio and TV; they concentrate on the candidate who can capture the White House, a Governor's mansion, or on money for the necessary access to means of mass communication, without much reference to party organization. The attitude spills over into fund raising, where reliance is placed upon the candidate to attract funds and little attention is paid to the need for building and operating a solid organizational structure with a broad base of finance. Party organizations, unlike those for candidates, are permanent and comprehensive, with recruitment and solicitation as regular functions.

Still, it is easier for parties to extol financial efficiency than to achieve it. In a political campaign, party income is irregular and unpredictable; advance planning is highly speculative. Activity lags when funds drop and erupts when freshets of new funds come in. The deployment of funds depends on the shifting moods of the candidate and his managers, who may be calculating or passionate, and on chance events.

In the heat of the campaign, efficiency is not deliberately rejected, but the difficulties in achieving it, considering other pressing priorities, are formidable. At a minimum, efficiency implies that the campaign be coordinated by the one permanent agency concerning itself with elections—i.e., the party committee; nevertheless, the 1971 enactment of the principle of the checkoff would give money exclusively to the candidate and cut off private contributions. This would, of course, affect the role of the national committee and reduce candidate reliance on it. Centralization in financial operations presupposes a high degree of coordination of fund-raising efforts with near-unanimous agreement on budgets and quotas, allocations to candidates, and transfers of funds among committees, to gain the benefit of orderly purchasing and spending and a pool of funds to satisfy creditors.

Despite personality conflicts, petty jealousies, and the competitive spirit, both party and nonparty committees by valiant effort often achieve real cooperation in financial matters. Joint spending for special purposes is one reason why so many transfers of funds occur among party and nonparty committees. Unusually large expenses, like fees for television time, often require joint spending.

The national parties will no doubt continue to pursue direct financing to offset dependence on quota systems but in the heat of the campaign, to help pay bills, they will probably turn to state party organizations for help. Quota systems may reappear but less extensively than in the past. One of the best financial tactics for the national parties is to give state and local party organs wide technical assistance in modern methods of broad-gauged fund raising so that when required, locals may know how to collect the extra dollars needed for a Presidential campaign.

In a sense, the new-found ability of the Republican national party headquarters to raise money enough for its needs should be welcome news to the state parties, but some Republican operatives in key states now report that, instead of freeing state collections for exclusive state and local use, the absence of regular quota systems with a national orientation has made it harder to raise unified funds for state purposes alone.

The national funds that enable the party to obtain the services of competent professional staff, that permit stress on party building, that encourage attention to "nuts and bolts," are well worth the trouble of raising. The national Republican Party has generally moved further in these directions than have the Democrats, because they have had the financial wherewithal to permit attention to details of party building.

A related activity that is desirable is the party conference on organization, registration, and finances. Few conferences relate wholly to finances but all give a chance to exchange ideas and hear "How to . . ." lectures on successful programs. The Democrats staged a "Dollars for Democrats" national conference in 1966 and received a pep talk from President Johnson. Since the low point of 1966, when the Democratic Party seemed to be falling apart, successful new efforts have repaired some of the structure. The Republicans have had an Association of State Chairmen. As state chairmen are automatically members of the National Committee, they help to pull the party together in organizational and financial matters, if not in ideology or policy.

Party committees limit financial reporting to bare conformance with statutory requirements. They do not provide their contributors and supporters with instructive analyses of their financial operations. It would appear that important creditors at least would demand the circulation of periodic financial reports, detailing the sources of funds, comparative performance among various party organizations, disbursements of funds, trends in giving and in costs, and similar information. The current party practices fail to match public disclosure by corporations, foundations, and other groups which depend upon public support and good will.

Wide dissemination of party financial reports over the long run would generate confidence among contributors, deepen public understanding of the financial aspects of politics and reduce popular misgivings about the financial responsibility of party management and candidates.

Such constructive reporting probably requires initiative and imagination as well as accounting, which cannot be prescribed by federal laws. In 1908, when there was popular agitation for disclosure and publicity of campaign funds—and before reporting was required by federal law—the national parties did voluntarily publish the names of all contributors of $100 or more, together with lists of expenditures. The Democrats even publicized their figures before the election.[12] With this precedent, if a national committee released an annual financial statement with sufficient fanfare, the opposition would be quick to follow. State and local parties might then join the parade. Disclosure as required by law does not provide information with details and interpretations required in the party interest.

So far, too little has been done in the search for financial and party responsibility. Morever, little has been done consciously to develop solicitation and collection systems using available means to reach all prospective givers. The parties, the candidates, business, labor, and other groups all have challenging opportunities to improve the financing of politics.

CHAPTER 16

OVERVIEW

The dissension, alienation, and violence characteristic of the United States in the 1960's and early 1970's can be related partially to the creaky workings of the political system and to a failure to enlist wide enough participation and competence for reforming and sustaining democratic processes.

Prospects for improving the financing of political processes cannot be tested until they are tried. Tax incentives are only now, in 1972, being attempted by the federal government. Matching incentives are untested anywhere. The Long Amendment of 1966 and its revival in 1971 established the principle of government subsidy of the election process, but the principle is yet to be applied in a form satisfactory to both parties.

Government subsidies alone will not save the political process. Much remains to be done beyond legislative halls. Private action is crucial because in the foreseeable future most campaigns and most political committees will continue to need private financing in large chunks and small. Private solicitation is still necessary now that federal tax incentives exist. Much needed is a massive campaign to promote use of the incentives. If subsidies are enacted, they will likely be partial or will affect only federal candidates or those in a single state. They may apply to general elections and not to prenomination campaigns. Certain legislation might inhibit mass contributions: people may think if the government is paying, why should I give? Thus there can be no end to the need for extensive educational and publicity campaigns on political giving and spending.

Though the American people are pragmatic, wrestling realities rather than theories, they have notably failed to experiment with ways to finance politics. True, there have been adventurous undertakings, both partisan and bipartisan, some successful, many relatively unsuccessful. The sustaining funds of the national committees have persisted. Other experiments (Dollars for Democrats and Republican Neighbor-to-Neighbor drives) were nationwide in concept but devolved into local programs spottily employed. Only one bipartisan mail drive, the Eisenhower-Stevenson Appeal, was nationwide. Not a single nationwide project has enlisted all means and all media.

The need for efficient and effective collection systems to tap available sources is manifest. Truly bipartisan appeals in corporations, governments, universities, and other large organizations could satisfy that need. Labor unions and the American Medical Association are now the major membership organizations collecting political funds. Other membership organizations could emulate them. Automatic collection, perhaps a tax-form checkoff, and, where possible, payroll deduction, could stabilize the flow and minimize the trouble and expense.

In broad-based solicitation, as observed in Chapter 8, eyeball-to-eyeball fund raising excels over direct mail solicitation, broadcasts, advertising, etc. With enough volunteers, it is also most economical and pays an extra dividend to the political process, as the solicitor participates in political discourse along with the contributor. Truly broad-scale solicitation, even carefully pinpointed in affluent areas, requires recruitment of swarms of voluntary solicitors, even millions, with little or no previous political experience. The block system used in charity drives provides a proved model for voluntary solicitation by political parties, the largest membership organizations in this nation, with more outlets than any religious, charitable, or ethnic group.

As observed earlier, mass fund raising will not be successful if based on advertising and exhortation alone. These provide a readiness and a willingness, but only organized solicitation triggers decision. People can be prepared to give and yet will not give unless asked in person. Through easily manned and readily accessible collection systems enough persons must be asked by sympathetic and motivated persons.

For a candidate, the struggle for election is essentially short-range and manipulative. The emphasis must be on the means, but the candidate needs to conserve his energy and creativity for raising issues rather than money. Once victorious, he cannot forget his political role or lose touch with his constituency, but the need for money is ever-present and the system of fund raising too demanding, and the personal or party pressures too great, to permit him time to develop fully the qualities necessary in political office.

The relationships between candidates and party organizations are as diverse as the number of candidates, and the impulse of many candidates is to balk at the acceptance of party dollars, if that means party control of policies and campaign tactics. Surely it will remain as easy to contribute to a candidate as to a party, but if the party could provide funds enough, it would be possible to determine at least by practical experiment which kind of allocation (to candidate or party) the public prefers and which kind of money (from the public or the party at what level) best serves the candidate. Greater party financial influence would no doubt bring greater party discipline, but the independent-minded candidate, the reformer, the maverick, all would by definition not be organization men and would still seek independent funding.

For practical reasons the task of raising money should go more to the party than its candidates. As it is, the numerous special committees raising funds for candidates, often tools of special interests, are outside of party control. Such committees exist because they fill a void the parties leave and hook contributors the parties fail to reach.

This does not mean that legitimate interest groups, labor unions, alliances of tycoons, or anti-vivisectionists, ought not to be financed by individual contributors. The diversity which pervades American politics is certain to be reflected in its financing; it is doubtful that nonparty groups can be prevented constitutionally or politically from participating. This book has suggested only the virtues of using collection systems within membership organizations of any kind, recognizing that as giving to the party becomes habitual, nonparty drives may become less appealing.

Although the financial system must accommodate the diversity of American politics, a rationalized party must govern to some extent the flow of funds to its components, as from points of surplus to points of deficit, and cut down the competition for funds among individual factions or dispersed elements.

It has been pointed out that restrictions on giving often run counter to the needs of large interests. There were good reasons not to enforce restrictions opposed by leading politicians, powerful interests, or community leaders who learned to operate under the present system and resisted change. Well-ingrained practices, such as corporate activities in politics, were prohibited rather than monitored. Statutes were perhaps intentionally ambiguous and subject to varying interpretations, leaving issues of constitutionality unclarified.

The present regulatory pattern has been based in large part upon sanctions rarely enforced. With what pattern of regulation would it be to everyone's political interest to stay within permissible grounds? The object is to reduce financial pressures on politics by providing alternative sources of funds or reducing party expenses. A search is on for means to raise big money in small sums from private sources, through tax incentives or matching incentives, or for acceptable formulas for subsidies, or some other combination of devices. Proposals for reducing party campaign costs include governmental assistance for registration and getting out the vote, mailing (at cut rates), free use of airwaves, voters' pamphlets, transition costs, recount expenses, or whatever else is deemed a legitimate public charge for the expenses of candidates or parties.

Politicians provided with acceptable alternative sources of funds will likely resist gifts that may obligate them. Politicians receiving government funds, accounted for to the government, or receiving most funds in small sums, will likely divulge their financial operations.

Because of the public or even quasi-governmental nature of the political system, the resources and machinery of government should be utilized in supplementing private contributions. Those parts of the political process that are primarily public rather than partisan, such as registration and election-day duties, can be financed in some degree by direct appropriation. Those parts that are primarily partisan rather than public ought to rely on contributions which, like tax- or matching-incentive gifts, subsidy vouchers or straight-line donations, still leave room for partisan preference by the giver.

It is widely agreed that money should be raised in small sums for politics. It is possible to raise more of it that way, but few have been willing to invest the time, energy, and money necessary for results affecting more than one isolated campaign or level of activity.

A workable system can be established through improved collection systems entailing massive political mobilization spurred by a series of practical incentives. To achieve this end through private means, either one of two conditions, or both, must be met: (1) sufficient motivation or incentive to citizens to contribute or ask others to contribute; (2) collection systems organized so that person-to-person requests for gifts are motivated by peer approval, and eventually, by habit.

It is proposed to provide incentives useful in broadening the donor base and extending the ability of the parties to raise money in small sums. Options, alone or in combination, include: tax incentives, to give some benefit to contributors; matching incentives, to give defined political committees encouragement to solicit broadly by matching with government funds each contribution up to an amount such as $10; personal incentives such as competition between candidates and committees for the largest number of small contributors; incentives for solicitors, by awards and rewards, psychic and material.

As incentives alone, even legislative incentives, may not be sufficient, limited government assistance may be required in other forms, such as subsidies of certain political expenses. Each of these proposals deserves public and legislative consideration.

In choosing among the options, the ruling objective is a system which encourages, not merely permits, voluntarism, spontaneity, and optimal citizen participation in the political process. Citizen participation is a requisite of a free society. The President's Commission extolled private financing in these terms: "Active, widespread political participation is the key to successful democracy in the United States and voluntary effort is the great sustaining force of our political parties." [1] How can politicians infuse new money into the system while permitting all donors a representative voice in deciding where the money is to go? How can they inject incentives to private giving and prod party organizations and others into organizing wider solicitation drives? These are questions that must be answered.

Both tax and matching incentive plans are desirable, but at present both would surely give advantage to the Republican party at the national level, where its contributors outnumber those of the Democrats in some years by as much as 10 to 1. The $10 matching plan, however, might encourage the Democrats to solicit contributors. The Republicans would benefit from a matching plan also so long as their present contributors do not reduce their gifts. Matching incentives found favor in the Treasury Department in the Kennedy and Johnson Administrations. Every dollar appropriated for matching would go to politics rather than present a windfall to those already giving, as tax incentives do.

Matching would encourage action by the most important collection system (party organizations), for even if eligibility were to be wider, party committees have an advantage in organizing small gift drives. Also, to the extent the party became an effective collection agent, competing appeals for funds could be restrained.

Matching incentives, like tax incentives, are not set by rigid formula, but benefits are determined by the contributing patterns of individuals. Neither, however, guarantees a floor or minimum for any particular campaign; those unsuccessful in seeking contributions will not benefit. Matching incentives, unlike tax incentives, can be set if necessary at an aggregate dollar limit per committee, so that the government can control the amounts of money it allows the political system.

Either tax or matching incentives could be used for prenomination campaigns. The matching plan particularly might spur contributions for primary contests. To learn which incentive works better, perhaps tax and matching incentives could be tried separately in different campaigns. Whether the same committees should be eligible to receive both tax and matching contributions is a policy issue for the Congress or state legislatures.

Tax and matching incentives in combination can be rationalized as desirable reforms because they require citizen volunteers to do the soliciting and because both incentives are designed to bring people into politics. Straight subsidies may discourage rather than encourage public participation. Would people who previously volunteered for work in campaigns demand to be paid? With no provision for financing the national committees between elections, presumably private financing would continue, but would people in the habit of contributing to sustaining funds do so if they knew government funds were available in campaign years?

Money is only one part of a complex political ecology where voting is the single most important individual act. Otherwise responsible and sophisticated persons who would replace private financing with government grants might succeed unwittingly in changing fundamental balances of the political system. Providing money for politics is only a means to improve the performance of parties and candidates. In raising money, citizens become immersed in the political process. Those who pay together are likely to vote together. Critics who minimize individual efforts overlook history: a system of free elections cannot survive without voluntarism. In whatever form or quantity elections draw upon government assistance, freely contributed money and services will, of course, still be needed. Moreover, there is nothing inherently immoral or corrupting about a corporate or labor dollar, no more than other private dollars. Whether or not open acceptance of the corporate and labor impulse to give or to match political gifts of employees or union members and provide the means of collection would sublimate the temptation to skirt present proscriptions, recognition of legitimate concerns of labor and management with public policy would add an element of realism to the regulation of political finance.

Congress now has Committees on Standards and Conduct in both houses, requires reports on lobbying and on political income and expenditures, and might at any time decide to require income disclosure. These mechanisms could be reinforced and supplemented by a federal agency empowered to receive, audit, and reconcile reports, enter them in the public records, and publicize them. A computer-based system could feed names of contributors into a repository daily and print current data on sources, amounts, and uses of campaign funds, as demonstrated by the Citizens' Research Foundation. State data could be processed separately or jointly with federal data. Such an auditing agency need not become an Inspectorate General so stern as to inhibit the political process. The right to a certain privacy in politics is as important as the secret ballot.

To restrict and ignore as in the past is not to solve and cure. If rational political financing obliges government to assist parties and candidates, then reductions of certain political spending may be feasible, specifically in political broadcasting, mailings, billboards, conventions, registration, and elections. As to more fundamental changes, there is little early prospect of reducing the number of elected officials (even in the judiciary), mandatory primary elections (even assuming the right to hold challenge primaries after party nomination), or nonpartisan elections (inevitably with too many candidates).

Traditionally, democracy offers a free market for ideas, but effective expression of views, even major party views, requires use of the mass media, which are so expensive as to suggest governmental subventions through regulations requiring broadcasters to give free time or through subsidization of a public network, or through free time on cable systems.

Enlarging the popular base of political finance is perhaps the most effective available means of countering privileged interests with public influence on the principle of "one-man one-vote one-dollar." As all segments of the population at times have interests at odds with the national interest, popular financing of American politics could encourage representation of many interests relatively free of dominance by the few with thick bankrolls.

The few with ample money obviously will attract voters to policies that favor their special privileges, as is their right. The Republican Party, despite its constituency in the upper-income brackets, took the lead in the 1960's in broadening its base, while the Democratic Party, hypnotized by its conviction that it serves the masses, has yet to learn to tap the small giver. Their financial practices may produce strange internal effects in national party positions. Financial disparities between parties are inevitable, even acceptable, as long as the relatively poor party remains competitive. Even the party embracing the destitute as its constituency ought to be able to sustain itself financially.

The rocketing of political costs in the 1960's occurred when federal affairs were under Democratic dominance. Had Democrats been out of power, their financial position would have been desperate. Without the Presidency since 1968, their accounts are rife with red ink. Public policy on political financing, once it recognizes that the less affluent party will sometimes be out of power, must assure basic support from year to year for party competition, with daily prayers that the competition be for public service and not for selfish advantage.

Citizen participation in politics, including pocketbook participation, is one way to baffle concentrated privilege. The citizen who feels that elites make all the decisions in public affairs throws in the towel before the bell rings. The citizen persuaded that only large contributors are needed has been doped before the race. Such copouts are not in the American tradition.

America cannot live with a closed financial system that does not permit or tolerate small voices or strange faces. Insurgent and reform candidates as well as candidates of protest depend on public policies that assure basic financial support for qualified politicians.[2] Their candidacies may never be on a financial par with established competition but, unless the competition is open, the shutout majority will turn against the system, as many young people already have.

Among the numerous sources of inequities in politics, money is merely one, though perhaps Number One. The advantages of incumbency, of personality, of newspaper endorsement are all familiar. To reduce imbalance to exact equality, in money as in other attributes, is impossible, but equalities of monetary resources or their equivalents are more readily remedied than most others.

One obvious inequality is that persons in favorable occupations, especially law, hold most elective offices, at least partly because they can afford to give the time without earning income. In Congress and legislatures in large states, legislators work full-time. The historic "citizen legislator" who devotes most of his attention to his own profession or business is a vestige of the past. Full-time legislators require appropriate salary, office, and travel expenses if legislative service is to attract outstanding persons without ample private income. Also, since campaign costs affect political recruitment for elective office, financial pressures upon candidates should be light.

The Congress in 1969 voted increases in salaries for its members. Assistance to politics is an allied issue. Although the common view is that legislators voting money for politics or for office expenses have their hand in the till, actually they may be voting for open compensation for normal representational costs. As they improve the political system, such open payments benefit the electorate no less than the politician. If Congress reduces reliance upon funds from special interests, politicians are the more likely to be responsive to the public interest, even though the financial independence of incumbents also increases the financial burden of their challengers.

It is true that there is no conspicuous evidence of widespread public demand for reform policies, but the tax checkoff was twice enacted without public approval, and its withdrawal did not result from mass protest. There is little vocal demand for tax incentives, but they have been enacted by the federal government and nine states.

Most telling is the lack of leadership from the pros in political work, the lack of will on the part of national party headquarters, and indifference or dignified detachment among groups which could take positive steps to lead toward financial reform. Government departments such as Treasury or Justice that would have to administer new programs move slowly. Apart from the broadcasting industry, there are no powerful, concerned industries. Church groups stay aloof. Service groups, the Lions, Rotary, and such, if tax-exempt, are forbidden to work directly for legislative reform, but they do not deploy their educative resources as they might. Labor unions logically resist fundraising mechanisms that will compete with their own efforts to collect political money for collective political bargaining. Business groups worry more about their spending, taxes, and budget balancing (about the things representatives do *after* they are elected) than about the integrity and effectiveness of the system that elects them. As for the champions of public interest in election finance, the National Committee for an Effective Congress and Common Cause can jog only so many elbows.

Concrete action to reform political finance has been relatively low in the scale of Presidential priorities. Congress has on a few recent occasions marched up the hill and begun to scout the ramparts but it has spent as much energy devising a line of retreat as in occupying higher ground. Many political leaders regard improvements in political finance as a subject they would rather drop.

So long as the party at the crest of popularity and power feels no impulse to give the opposition a leg up, the party out of power may be helpless to effect reform. Whether Republican or Democrat, liberal or conservative, the incumbent is instinctively cautious about changes that would alter the system which has served him well. When incumbents do not really know how or why they won—a common condition—they are anxious and insecure about re-election. "Why change the rules? What's wrong with tradition? Why risk the unknown?"

Most people agree that money should not determine who holds public office. Thoughtful citizens accept political costs as the price of two-party competition. People can recognize the need for realistic regulation of funds in order to avoid undue political influence by a few persons or groups. They can come to see the wholesome effect of disclosure of sources of political funds, wide publicity for such information, and requirements for disclosure of personal income of candidates and incumbents. Current trends of opinion in Congress augur sympathy for the notion that government should assist candidates and parties to meet legitimate campaign and political expenses. Much of the public might favor salary and expense allowance levels for public officials if clearly this money reduced the influence of a few large private contributors. Voters might agree that political parties should provide expense accounts or subventions to officeholders even if the government does not.

Some claim political influence is shifting from those who control the means of production to those who control or know how to manipulate the media of mass communications. There is some truth in the influence of the pollster, the broadcaster, the advertising or public relations agency, the media buyer, but the services of technicians are for sale and parties with ample money can buy services relevant to the shaping of political decisions. Many candidates rely upon such specialists to free them to devote their whole energies to campaigning. It is true that the professional communicators influence the electorate but not always as they intend. In any event, democracy is based on faith in the voter's discretion.

Freedom of the press is postulated upon the right of the public to know. The press aroused readers with reports of the Baker and Dodd cases, the program advertising books, and the President's Club, the late Nixon filings in 1968, and the Gleason operation. The press could do as well by publicizing campaign fund data.

The combination of the unsavory disclosures before the Kefauver Crime Committee and a thorough newspaper investigation was crucial in the development of the Florida election reform law of 1951, but the press does not often dig beyond campaign fund reports because investigation is expensive and speculative. Columnists, who on occasion disclose significant events, tend to mislead the public by imputing sinister motives to large contributors. The press has given strong editorial support to reform, though newsmen seem biased against political spending and long campaigns. The broadcast media have produced next to nothing on political finance.

A cynic might argue that it would be helpful to the cause of reform if a series of juicy scandals about political funds were to decorate the front pages, but there have been scandals enough. There is a point where scandal, instead of producing pressure for reform, wearies the public so that it turns away from politics in despair. The cumulative effect of past scandals and studies has brought the beginnings of political response. Reforms in both federal and state politics simply await leadership.

Clearly, time is needed to bring changes. At most, only a generation of effort has gone into broadening the base; only a decade of effort has gone into mass drives for political funds; less than a decade of effort was expended in nationwide campaigns of the American Heritage Foundation-Advertising Council; only a few years of attention and effort at the Presidential level have gone into reappraisal of new political forces; even fewer Congressional years have been seriously devoted to objective study and debate of legislative proposals.

In perspective the chief task is to accelerate the process of learning the stubborn facts so that the need to direct resources toward improving American political life will be clear.

The major premise is that political financing in the U. S. is potentially undemocratic and corrupting to the extent that parties and politicians depend on large contributions of money by special interests. Fear of this potential has not been enough to incite reform. The system has functioned so far because it generally has provided sufficient competitive funds. Today the system is faltering not only because of financial bias but because it is not uniformly providing enough money for party competition.

Until now, we have not been willing to make the investment of time and thought and effort and money to put into operation collection and regulatory systems we know how to design and know we can build. It is hardly to be recommended that we indulge further the time-honored democratic habit of waiting until matters get worse. There is always a campaign coming up. There is really no necessity of financing many more the wrong way.

CHAPTER 17

EPILOGUE: NEW HORIZONS

Years of effort to reform our antiquated system of political finance came to a sudden climax in the short space of two months when Congress passed two measures that could be a turning point of historic importance.

The Revenue Act of 1971 provides tax credits, or tax deductions, for political contributions at all levels, though one of its provisions—tax-checkoffs to subsidize Presidential campaigns during general elections—remains unsettled. In January, 1972, a month after passage of the Revenue Act of 1971, Congress also passed the Federal Election Campaign Act, requiring fuller disclosure of political funding than ever before and setting limits on advertising expenditures for candidates for federal office, during both nomination and general election campaigns.

Enactment of these laws, recommended ten years earlier by the President's Commission on Campaign Costs, owed much to growing concern about the high and increasing costs of political campaigns. The Democrats in particular had cause for alarm. They were unable to erase or decrease the debts of 1968-70. With the 1972 campaign just over the horizon, the many potential or announced Democratic candidates for President were not only competing with each other for dollars, but they were siphoning funds which might have found their way to the party itself or at least eventually to its nominee. Significantly, the Democratic nominees already in the field had voluntarily agreed to limit radio and TV time expenses in each primary state to 5 cents per registered voter.

While Democrats hungered for funds, the Republicans controlling the White House widened their financial advantage. The disparity, coupled with concern in both parties about the high costs of campaigning and the seemingly great incidence of wealthy candidates for high office, combined to produce the Federal Election Campaign Act. The Act:

• Limits the amounts candidates for federal offices can spend on radio, television, cable television, newspapers, magazines, billboards, and automated telephone systems in any primary, runoff, special or general election to 10 cents times the voting-age population of the geographical unit covered by the election, or $50,000, whichever is greater.

• Provides that no candidate can spend more than 60 percent of his media expenditure limit on broadcast advertising.

• Provides that the broadcast media cannot charge candidates more than the lowest unit rate charged any other advertiser for the same class and amount of time or space for a period extending 45 days preceding a primary election or 60 days preceding a general or special election. At other times, rates cannot exceed the charges made for comparable use for other purposes. Rates for newspaper or magazine advertising cannot exceed the charges made for comparable use for other purposes.

• Includes an escalator provision to reflect future increases in the Federal government's price index.

• Defines "election" to mean any general, special, primary or runoff election, nominating convention or caucus, delegate selection primary, Presidential preference primary or constitutional convention.

• Broadens the definition of "contribution" and "expenditure."

• Places a ceiling on contributions by any candidate or his immediate family to his own campaign of $50,000 for President or Vice-President; $35,000 for Senator, and $25,000 for Representative, Delegate, or Resident Commissioner.

• Stipulates that the appropriate federal supervisory officer to oversee election campaign practices, reporting and disclosure is the Clerk of the House for House candidates, the Secretary of the Senate for Senate candidates and the Comptroller General for Presidential candidates and miscellaneous other committees.

• Requires all political committees that anticipate receipts in excess of $1,000 during the calendar year to register with the appropriate federal supervisory officer, and to include such information as the names of all principal officers, the scope of the committee, the names of all candidates the committee supports and other information.

• Requires candidates and their committees for the Senate

and House to file duplicate copies of reports with the Secretary of State, or a comparable office, in each state for local inspection.

• Requires each political committee and candidate to report total cash on hand, total receipts, the total sum of individual contributions, as well as to itemize the full name and mailing address, occupation and principal place of business, date and amount for each person contributing in excess of $100; to itemize each transfer of funds to or from any committee; to itemize each loan to or from any person in excess of $100, including names, addresses and occupations of any lender or endorser.

• Requires each political committee and candidate to report total expenditures, as well as to itemize the full name and mailing address, occupation and principal place of business, date, amount, and purpose of each expenditure in excess of $100; to itemize the same for each expenditure for personal services, salaries, and reimbursed expenses in excess of $100.

• Requires each political committee and candidate to report the amount and nature of debts and obligations on a continuing basis until extinguished.

• Requires the supervisory officers to prepare an annual report for each committee registered with the supervisory officers and make such reports available for sale to the public.

• Requires candidates and committees to file reports of contributions and expenditures on the 10th day of March, June and September every year, on the 15th and 5th days preceding the date on which an election is held and on the 31st day of January. Any contribution of $5,000 or more is to be reported within 48 hours if received after the last pre-election report.

• Requires a full and complete financial statement of the costs of holding a Presidential nominating convention within 60 days after the end of the convention.

• Prohibits any contribution to a candidate or committee by one person in the name of another person.

• Defines more explicitly the role which unions and corporations can take in political campaigns, get-out-the-vote drives and voter registration activities.

• Authorizes the office of the Comptroller General to serve as a national clearinghouse for information on the administration of election practices.

• Requires the Civil Aeronautics Board, the Federal Communications Commission and the Interstate Commerce Commission to promulgate regulations with respect to the extension of credit without collateral by any person, business or industry regulated by the federal government to any person on behalf of any candidate for federal office.

• Prohibits funds appropriated for the Office of Economic Opportunity from being used for any political activity.

The events leading to the passage of the Federal Election Campaign Act have been detailed in Chapter 14. Of particular interest is the long history of efforts to improve legislation on disclosure—to better illuminate who gives how much to whom.

The Senate passed fuller disclosure bills in 1960, 1961, and 1967, but the House refused to go along. Then, in late 1971, the House Administration Committee reported out, favorably, the Hays-Abbitt bill which was clearly less desirable than the disclosure provisions of the bill which the Senate had already passed. Complex manuevering in the House finally resulted in a notable success: the House voted to accept the Senate's disclosure provisions, even though another Senate provision—for a Federal Elections Commission—was dropped. The ultimate result was a bill stronger than the House version and weaker than the Senate one, finally passed by both houses and signed by the President into law.

The bill which emerged was clearly influenced by public opinion because it is clear that some members of Congress went along with it only reluctantly. As it was, the final version represented considerable compromises between the Senate and the House and between the Republicans and the Democrats. One area of trading concerned the fate of the Federal Election Commission, which would have placed the responsibility for gathering the financial data under one roof. The House bill had put costs for mass mailings within the overall limit of 10 cents per eligible voter, but some Republicans wanted as few campaign expenditures limited as possible, on the grounds that, as the minority party, they needed to spend as much as possible in order to unseat the more numerous Democratic incumbents. A compromise was reached whereby mailings would be exempt from coverage, as many Republicans desired, in exchange for scuttling the Federal Elections Commission, which elements of the House leadership opposed.

Threats to delay or sidetrack the legislation were made frequently by Representative Wayne Hays, Chairman of the House Administration Committee and author of the Hays-Abbitt bill. In particular, Hays was insistent that the Clerk of the House and the Secretary of the Senate continue to receive the financial reports from their respective members, and Senate conferees and Republican leaders generally assented to this demand. The result was a kind of hybrid, a troika arrangement requiring that candidates for the House of Representatives file reports with the Clerk of the House, Senatorial candidates with the Secretary of the Senate, and candidates for President file with the Comptroller General. (The same stipulations apply to candidate committees.) With three different officers receiving the reports, responsibility will be dispersed, and it will be harder for the news media or interested persons to seek out information on spending, since they cannot get it in one place. Further, the Clerk and the Secretary are employees of legislative bodies and, as such, are probably not in the best position to be disinterested policemen of the new system. The uneven scrutiny and enforcement which might easily result could weaken key provisions of the bill.

Enforcement of the Federal Election Campaign Act depends upon whether the Comptroller General, the Secretary of the Senate, and the Clerk of the House all endeavor to carry out the spirit and intent of the law as well as its actual content.

Some failures are bound to occur at the outset, until procedures become better known and are refined by both campaigners and administrators. The press and interested groups will undoubtedly assume a watch-dog role, following closely the operation of the new law. Public interest law firms and citizen groups such as Common Cause may also be alert to the possibilities of litigation as a tool to ensure effective enforcement of limitation and disclosure provisions.

One target in litigation could well be the section limiting expenditures to those authorized by the candidate or his agent, which raises the constitutional question of free speech. If a citizen or group wishes to advertise in support of or against a candidate, it could be considered an unconstitutional curb to free expression if they are refused authorization and therefore cannot speak through the media. Effective speech in today's media-oriented society may rely on wide use of advertising, and this equation could be put to the test under the new law.

There are other implications of the new law which cannot, as yet, be fully anticipated. To ensure compliance with the limitations, candidates will probably have to centralize their campaign spending. This will simplify the disclosure process, but there may be side-effects. If the law does inhibit spending, as intended, it could lessen competition among the contenders and favor the incumbents, thus introducing new rigidities into politics. It may also lead to greater importance for the non-candidate committees, like labor's COPE, because the spending limitations do not cover educational activities, even when such activities clearly have an impact at the candidate level. Further, some ad hoc committees could exhort the citizen to vote for a peace, or a law and order, candidate, without mentioning any by name, and candidates could then hitch their campaigns to such issues. It also seems possible that the new law could lead to the proliferation of committees against specific candidates because the expenses of these committees could not be effectively limited.

Another area of significant trading concerned the broadcast provisions. The Senate version of the bill exempted all candidates for federal office from Section 315, the so-called equal time provision, but the House balked at giving broadcasters more freedom in deciding on access for political candidates. The White House made it known that President Nixon might veto a provision repealing Section 315 for Presidential candidates unless Senatorial and Congressional candidates were also included. Accordingly, the Senate conferees agreed to the House position, while the House conferees gave in to a Senate position which called for charging the lowest unit rate for political broadcasts.

The recent history of Section 315 is particularly interesting. In 1960 it was suspended for the Presidential campaigns, permitting the Kennedy-Nixon joint telecasts and other programs featuring Democrats and Republicans without requiring broadcasters to give equal time to minor candidates. In 1964 suspension was again proposed for the Presidential campaigns, but President Johnson did not want to debate or to give free exposure to Senator Goldwater and Congressional Democrats were able to kill suspension even though it had already passed both houses in different forms. In 1968, with Nixon leading the polls, the Republicans denied suspension for the same reason the Democrats had four years earlier. In 1971-72 Nixon and the House (including leading Democrats) joined to kill the possibility of suspension or repeal. But this time, unlike the earlier efforts, serious attention was paid to extending repeal to all campaigns for federal office, and this doomed it.

Truly bipartisan efforts went into the enactment of the legislation. The Democrats, generally, insisted on limiting advertising expenditures—they were fearful of the results of Republican financial superiority—while the Republicans, as the minority party, with notable exceptions fought to keep the advertising limits as high as possible, as well as to exempt as many kinds of campaign expenditures from coverage as they could. Ultimately, restrictions were placed on the amounts that candidates and their immediate families could spend on their own campaigns, but some members of Congress were unhappy with this provision and wondered how effective it would be. Neither party desired effective limitations on individual contributions.

Threats of a Presidential veto kept portions of the various bills out of the final version or got them toned down considerably. Although the White House role in the content of the final legislation was limited mainly to veto threats, and the White House position generally was negative, clearly the 1972 law is a vast improvement over the Political Broadcast bill that President Nixon vetoed in 1970. Whatever the motivations behind that veto, it may have served a useful purpose. It kept the issue alive and placed pressure on both the Congress and the President to avoid another one. The roles of the National Committee for an Effective Congress and Common Cause in lobbying for reform were also influential. The Common Cause law suit became moot because it was based on the old law, but it undoubtedly helped prod the Congress into action.

In terms of the political system, the implications of the Federal Election Campaign Act are profound. Improved public reporting of large contributions should put pressure on parties and candidates to raise more money in small sums. That purpose is abetted by the companion enactment in the Revenue Act of 1971 of tax incentives for political contributions. Presumably the tax credits and deductions, if accompanied by an educational campaign to acquaint the American people of their availability, and if the candidates and committees step up their solicitation campaigns accordingly, can bring in more small funds for several reasons: tax incentives signifying government encouragement of the act of giving are in effect a "sales tool" enabling solicitors to ask small contributors—say, those giving up to $25 in the past—to double the amount of their gifts since the government is now sharing in the cost. In short, the combination of disclosure of large contributions and of tax incentives could, if properly exploited, effectively broaden the financial base of politics.

As contained in the Revenue Act of 1971, the new law provides that political contributors, if they choose, can claim a tax credit against Federal income tax for 50 percent of their contributions, up to a maximum of $12.50 on a single return and $25 on a joint return; alternatively, the taxpayer can claim a deduction for the full amount of contributions up to a maximum of $50 on a single return and $100 on a joint return. Eligible as contributions are gifts to candidates for election to any federal, state or local elective office in any primary, general, or special election, and gifts to any committee, association, or organization operated exclusively for the purpose of influencing or attempting to influence the election of such candidates, for use to further such candidacy.

The Internal Revenue Service has estimated that revenue loss in a Presidential election year will be close to $100 million. It is ironic that tax incentives costing that amount in revenue loss passed Congress with little debate, whereas the checkoff which would have cost a maximum of perhaps $27 million (for the Democrats and George Wallace, assuming the Republicans did not use the funds and no fourth party qualified) raised a major controversy. Of course, principles as well as dollars were involved. The checkoff would have assured campaign funds for the Democrats; tax incentives give no assurance of adequate funds, but do give Democrats new incentive to broaden their financial base. Republicans will benefit more from tax incentives, because they have more contributors, so the reason for their preference, apart from the principle of voluntarism involved, is clear.

The tax credits and deductions had an easy passage, but the accompanying tax checkoff has had a long and stormy history. The tax provisions were offered during Senate debate on the tax bill which the Administration considered necessary to the improved functioning of the economy. The checkoff was a revised version of the Long Act of 1966-67 (discussed in Chapter 13), and it was combined in a separate title with a provision for the tax credit or tax deduction. But it was the checkoff which received the attention and made the controversy. Senator Long passed up the opportunity to sponsor his checkoff proposal this time, possibly feeling it would be improper for him as chairman of the Senate Finance Committee to lead in amending a major tax bill during floor debate. Senator John Pastore, who had been floor manager for the Federal Election Campaign Act, led the Democrats seeking the checkoff provision. The tax credit and deduction were not held in high favor by Senator Long or his House counterpart, Representative Wilbur Mills, but were considered a necessary sweetener to attract bipartisan support, since Republicans generally favored them.

In its original form the checkoff amendment would have provided that every individual whose tax liability for any taxable year was $1 or more could designate on his federal income tax form that $1 of his tax money be paid to the Presidential Election Campaign Fund. Married individuals filing joint returns could designate $2 of their tax money. Major candidates, defined as those nominated by political parties whose Presidential candidate received 25 percent or more of the popular vote in the preceding Presidential election, would have been entitled to receive from the fund 15 cents for each person over age 18; given the latest population data, that would have provided $20.4 million to a major party candidate in 1972. Minor candidates, defined as those nominated by a party or parties receiving 5 per cent or more but less than 25 percent of the total votes in the preceding Presidential election, would have been entitled to receive the same proportion of this $20.4 million which their vote was of the average major party vote; this would have yielded as much as $6.3 million for George Wallace in 1972. While a minor party candidate qualifying for the first time would have to campaign on loans or contributions, he would be reimbursed after the election and would be free to use the money to repay loans or to return contributions to donors.

Candidates accepting checkoff funds would be limited to that amount and could not raise or spend additional funds. Candidates not accepting checkoff funds could raise or spend money without limitation—although the Federal Election Campaign Act limitations would apply to media expenditures in any case. Total payments from the fund to a party, however, could not exceed the amounts actually incurred in running the campaign, and various reports and audits would be required.

The Comptroller General of the United States was delegated the responsibility of determining the amounts spent or incurred by each party. On the basis of these determinations, he would certify the amount payable to each party to the Secretary of the Treasury. The Comptroller General would be assisted in these functions by an advisory board consisting of 2 members representing each major party and 3 public members agreed upon by the other members.

If the amounts in the fund were insufficient to make the payments to which the political parties were entitled with respect to a Presidential campaign, payments would be allocated to the party accounts in the ratio of the balances in their accounts. Surpluses remaining in the fund after a campaign would be returned to the Treasury after all parties had been paid the amounts to which they were entitled.

This legislation, sprung by the Democrats, came as a surprise to the Republicans who rose in near-unanimous opposition. Helped by Administration draftsmen, Republican Senators offered a long series of amendments, each designed to delay passage of the checkoff provision in order to give Republicans time to counterattack. The Republicans charged that the checkoff amounted to a Democratic attempt to walk away with $20 million of the taxpayer's money, and, they said, it would ensure the candidacy of George Wallace in 1972.

In test votes on the various amendments, the Democrats defeated all but one they were persuaded to favor. That amendment, offered by Senator Charles Mathias, Republican of Maryland, permitted taxpayers to designate the party fund they desired their dollar(s) to go to, or, alternatively, to designate that the dollar(s) go to a neutral fund. In both cases, candidates would receive no more than the amounts determined by formula, but at least taxpayers would have the right to allocate their dollar(s) to the party of their choice. This was thought to be a compromise amendment that would attract some Republican support, which it did, but in the final vote on the checkoff with the new amendment only two Senate Republicans supported the tax subsidy—Mathias and Senator Clifford Case of New Jersey.

The Senate debate on the bill made clear that Republicans would not take their share of the checkoff funds if it became law, but would prefer to finance their Presidential campaign privately —and without the limitation to $20.4 million expenditures which the checkoff imposed. Spokesmen for the President also let it be known that he considered the checkoff as irresponsible legislation, and that if it remained in the tax bill, he would have to consider the possibility of a veto. The veto threat raised the stakes considerably, because the tax measure contained certain tax relief for elements of the business community, among others. The White House had a strategy to alert businessmen to the possibility of a veto which would delay tax relief such as the repeal of the automobile excise tax desired by the industry. At first, many Democrats thought the President was bluffing, that he would not dare to scuttle the tax package and his plans for economic recovery, particularly with the Christmas recess approaching. They believed it would be months before the tax provisions could be reenacted without the checkoff. However, Representative Mills, who apparently was under pressures from alarmed businessmen, became convinced that the tax bill would, indeed, be vetoed if it contained the checkoff. In addition, headcounts seemed to show that there would be serious Democratic defections in the House if the Senate-House conferees retained the provision. In order to save the tax bill, which he felt was essential to the economy, Mills persuaded the conference to accept the checkoff in principle while deferring its implementation until January 1, 1973. Mr. Nixon signed the bill with the post-poned checkoff, but pledged to work to kill the checkoff before it went into operation. The Senate-House conferees did agree to retain the tax incentives, which went into effect for contributions made after December 31, 1971.

The proposed checkoff brought an adverse reaction in 1966 when it was enacted as the Long amendment and an even greater controversy as formulated by Senator John Pastore in 1971. The public reaction in 1971 was generally more favorable than in 1966 in the media and elsewhere, because the Democratic debt and the Republican financial superiority were widely perceived in 1971 as possibly restricting any Democratic Presidential nominee to an inadequate campaign for want of dollars. In the course of Senate debates in 1966, 1967, and 1971, there were few Republicans voting in favor; none supported the checkoff in the final vote in 1967, and only two supported it in 1971. But the degree of Democratic solidarity was notable in 1971 with only four defections in the Senate; back in 1967, Democratic Senators Albert Gore and Robert Kennedy had led the fight for repeal. In the House in 1971, there was some doubt as to the number of Democratic defections that would have occurred had the conference committee retained the checkoff, so what might have happened will never be known. Interestingly, Lawrence O'Brien, Chairman of the Democratic National Committee, was intimately involved in devising strategy to achieve the checkoff and lobbied actively for it—one of the few times a national party has taken legislative initiatives with its Congressional delegations on party matters. O'Brien and the Senate Democrats thought they had a promise from Representative Mills to see the checkoff through, but the pressures of a threatened veto were stronger than Mills was willing to withstand.

The tax checkoff seems ill-fated, having come so close to operation both in 1966 and 1971, yet neither time quite making it for the next election. No doubt there will eventually be major partisan fights over it because, on the one hand, the proposal cannot function without Congressional appropriation and, on the other, the White House's opposition has been vehement. The Democrats could make it a major issue in the Presidential campaign of 1972 if they have trouble raising money. They might, however, decide to wait until 1973, thinking that then they might control the White House. In any case, the Democrats will probably make political finance as big an issue as possible in 1972. Their continuing debt, their difficulties in raising funds, the Republican financial advantage, and the fact that the Federal Communications Commission, the Civil Aeronautics Board, and the Interstate Commerce Commission will promulgate regulations with respect to the extension of credit—all are potential political issues. Also, the operation of the Federal Election Campaign Act will be closely watched as to how well it is working, thus increasing interest in the field of political finance in general.

But the fate of the checkoff merges into the broader issues of political finance. The question should be, how can we better finance our political system? Should there be a direct subsidy in some form? Ideally, a subsidy should not be established solely because one party needs the money, but rather because both parties realize the need to change the methods of financing the political system. Some Republicans might more readily accept other forms of subsidy; at least, the controversies encountered with the checkoff indicate that its operation would surely lead again to bitter and divisive argument which will not be conducive to increased public confidence in the political system. In these circumstances, more serious consideration should be given, perhaps, to other forms of subsidies, a voucher system, or voter's time over broadcast facilities, or some combination. In fact, the idea of a checkoff could be combined with a voucher or another system where the checked off tax revenue goes into funds for particular purposes and not necessarily for general use according to the formula proposed in the Revenue Act of 1971.

A related Congressional effort in the fall of 1971 serves as another illustration of the kinds of things the federal government could do. This was the idea for a national system of universal registration of voters for federal elections at government cost, designed to increase political participation by making it easier to register voters and keep them registered. Hearings were held and a bill reported out in the Senate, but no further action was taken in 1971. It is difficult to predict the future of the proposal, but it relates closely to the efforts to reduce cost burdens for parties and candidates by providing for government assumption of responsibility. It would reduce out-of-pocket costs for parties and candidates while also decreasing their dependence upon special groups, such as labor unions, to help get potential voters registered. It would be especially useful in getting minorities and 18-year olds registered and in overcoming the difficulties found in many state systems caused by a highly mobile population confronting antiquated registration procedures.

Improved registration, the possibility of a checkoff, and the workings of the laws regarding disclosure, setting limitations and providing tax incentives are all controversial enough to ensure that the regulation of political finance will continue to be a major issue in the 1970's.

INDEXES OF DIRECT CAMPAIGN EXPENDITURES BY NATIONAL-LEVEL COMMITTEES, CONSUMER PRICES, AND NUMBER OF VOTES CAST, 1912-1968

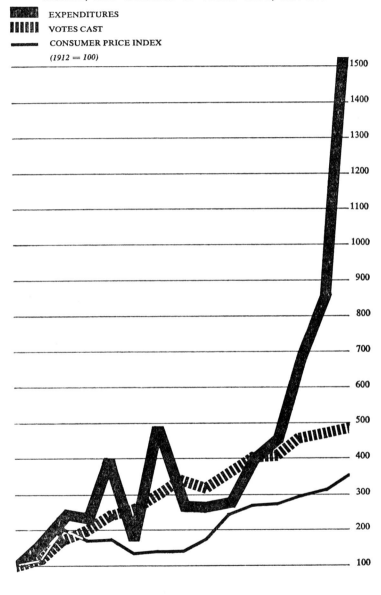

EXPENDITURES

VOTES CAST

CONSUMER PRICE INDEX

(1912 = 100)

1912 '16 '20 '24 '28 '32 '36 '40 '44 '48 '52 '56 '60 '64 1968

Reprinted from *Voters' Time*, a report of the Twentieth Century Fund Commission on Campaign Costs in the Electronic Era, 1969.

SUMMARY OF 1970 POLITICAL SUPPORT
FROM STEWART R. MOTT

SENATE CANDIDATES:

Quentin Burdick	N.D.	$ 500
Joe Duffey	Conn.	1,500*
Albert Gore	Tenn.	1,000*
Philip Hart	Mich.	1,769**
Philip Hoff	Vt.	1,000
Joe Josephson	Alas.	300
Ted Moss	Utah	500
Howard Metzenbaum	Ohio	1,000*
George Rawlings	Va.	1,000
Adlai Stevenson	Ill.	500
Stuart Symington	Mo.	500
Joe Tydings	Md.	1,000**
Harrison Williams	N.J.	500

PRE-PRIMARY:

Charles Goodell	N.Y.	1,000*
Ralph Yarborough	Texas	1,000
		$13,069

HOUSE CANDIDATES:

Herman Badillo	N.Y.	$ 1,500*
Ed Koch	N.Y.	1,500*&
Al Lowenstein	N.Y.	250
+ through NCEC	multiple	5,000
		$ 8,250

N.Y. STATE CANDIDATES:

Eugene Nickerson	$ 1,000*
Howard Samuels	2,000**
	$ 3,000

OTHER:

"Senators for Peace" — Mad. Sq. Gdn.	$ 1,000
New Democ Coalition — Fife	1,000
Referendum '70	1,000
Peace Inc. (loss)—approx.	12,000
	$15,000

Plus: staff expenses, postage printing, hospitality, travel, etc.	$10,000

TOTAL: $49,319

* — means I gave a get-acquainted or fund-raising party for the candidate.
** — means I gave two such.
& — does not include a $5,000 loan outstanding.

Source: *City East,* December, 1970

REFERENCES

CHAPTER 2

1. Robert J. McNeill, *Democratic Campaign Financing in Indiana, 1964* (Bloomington and Princeton: Institute of Public Administration, Indiana University and Citizens' Research Foundation, 1966), p. 28.

2. See Herbert E. Alexander, "Links and Contrasts Among American Parties and Party Subsystems," in Arnold J. Heidenheimer (ed.), *Comparative Political Finance*, (Boston: D. C. Heath and Co., 1970).

3. Gerald R. Elliott, *Financing Congressional Campaigns* (unpublished thesis, University of Minnesota, 1968), Appendix Two, pp. 337-349.

4. Alexander, *op. cit.* In 1970 incumbents were running for Governor and U. S. Senator in Massachusetts, and the primaries were not comparable.

5. *Survey of Political Broadcasting, Primary and General Election Campaigns of 1966* (Federal Communications Commission, 1967), Tables 1, 9, 16.

6. FCC, *Survey 1968*, Table 1.

CHAPTER 3

1. David Adamany, *Financing Politics: Recent Wisconsin Elections* (Madison, University of Wisconsin Press, 1969), Table 7, p. 57, based upon an index developed by Arnold J. Heidenheimer, "Comparative Party Finance: Notes on Practices and Toward a Theory," *Journal of Politics* (November, 1963), Table 1.

2. These and most of the subsequent figures, unless otherwise indicated, were collected by the Citizens' Research Foundation.

3. Bruce Winters, "Senate Races are Over; Debts Remain," *Baltimore Sun*, March 8, 1971.

4. Ottinger also reported a record high expenditure for his Congressional campaign in 1964. A candidate from the 25th Congressional District, located in Westchester County, New York, Ottinger publicly stated his expenditures were $193,582. A contested election case was brought against him, unsuccessfully, for alleged violations of federal and state laws. It was learned that $147,000 had been contributed to his campaign by his mother and sister, the sole contributors to 22 of 34 separate committees.

Since a federal gift tax provision effectively limits most individual contributions to a single committee to $3,000, numerous committees are established to receive gifts to that limit. The legal limitation in New York was $8,000 for a Congressional candidate and $8,000 on all committees taking part "solely in his election." A candidate can claim that the committees were set up for all Democratic candidates and to advance the cause of good government; by this interpretation of the law there was no violation.

Congressman Ottinger made public a breakdown of his expenditures: $37,633 for staff; $14,562 for office; $21,838 for billboards; $59,682 for mailings; $20,079 for newspaper advertising; $14,807 for radio; and $20,000 for miscellaneous (postage, travel, etc.). He made three mailings to each of the 168,000 families in his district; each mailing cost about $20,000 or 12 cents a family. While most candidates do without three mailings, they must have helped Ottinger win. Every campaign may have some urgency that will help improve its prospects, but at a financial cost. Much of the Ottinger case is summarized in *Congressional Record*, January 4, 1965, pp. 39-44, and January 25, 1965, pp. 1099-1103.

5. *Election Statistics, The Commonwealth of Massachusetts, 1966*, Public Document No. 43, published by the Secretary of the Commonwealth, 1966, p. 6.

6. *Summary Report of Campaign Contributions and Expenditures: 1968 Primary Election*, and also *1968 General Election*, both published by the Secretary of State of Oregon. Similar documents were published for 1966.

7. *Kentucky Primary Election, 1967* (Sept. 1967) and *Kentucky General Election, 1967* (Jan. 1968) Reports of Kentucky Registry of Election Finance. Similar documents were published for 1968.

8. "California Campaign Costs Pass $26 Million Mark," *California Journal*, December, 1970, p. 347, and "Late Campaign Spending Reports," *California Journal*, January, 1971, p. 22.

9. *Ibid.*

10. Warren Moscow, *What Have You Done For Me Lately?: The Ins and Outs of New York Politics* (Englewood Cliffs, N.J.: Prentice-Hall, Inc., 1967), p. 180.

11. William Buchanan, "Campaign Expenditures in Virginia," unpublished manuscript prepared for Tayloe Murphy Institute, University of Virginia, Charlottesville, 1970.

12. David K. Shipler, "Money Still Held Campaign Factor," *New York Times*, June 20. 1969.

13. FCC *Survey 1968*, Table 1.

14. In 1968, a special analysis of newspaper advertising was done for the Citizens' Research Foundation by Media Records, Inc., a firm that specializes in counting newspaper advertising linage. From rate charts, Media Records then determines the cost of the advertising. The analysis was made from July 1 through November 5, and covered daily newspapers in 139 cities.

15. "The Decade of Incentive: Marketing Review and Forecast, '65-'66," based on studies prepared by Marplan, a market research component of The Interpublic Group of Companies, Inc., New York, N. Y., January, 1966.

16. David Adamany, "We Should Spend More on Politics," a paper presented at the National Municipal League Conference on Government, Philadelphia, November 10, 1969.

17. Herbert E. Alexander, *Financing the 1964 Election* (Princeton: Citizens' Research Foundation, 1966), Table 6, p. 48.

18. See below, pp. 82, 254-62.

19. James K. Pollack, *Party Campaign Funds* (New York: Alfred A. Knopf, 1926), pp. 146-152.

20. See below, pp. 82, 254-62.

21. Figures for 1952 and 1956 are from Alexander Heard, *The Costs of Democracy* (Chapel Hill: University of North Carolina Press, 1960), pp. 7-8; and for 1960 and 1964 from Alexander, *Financing the 1964 Election, op. cit.*, p. 13.

22. Compiled from *Audit Report*, Democratic-Farmer-Labor Party of Minnesota, 1948-1966.

23. Adamany, *Financing Politics, op. cit.*, Table 4, p. 46.

24. Based on data in Riley Baker, "An Analysis of Some of the Generalizations in Alexander Heard's *The Costs of Democracy*," unpublished seminar paper, University of Texas, 1968-69.

25. *Voters' Time: Report of the Twentieth Century Fund Commission on Campaign Costs in the Electronic Era* (New York: The Twentieth Century Fund, 1969), Figure 1; p. 8a.

CHAPTER 4

1. Adamany, *Financing Politics, op. cit.*, Table 17, p. 87.

2. Heard, *op. cit.*, p. 21; for later data on Connecticut, see Adamany, "Political Finance: Notes for a Systematic Approach" (unpublished manuscript); and on Michigan, see John White and John R. Owens, *Parties, Group Interests and Campaign Finance: Michigan '56* (Princeton: Citizens' Research Foundation, 1960), p. 16. For Wisconsin, also see H. Gaylon Greenhill, *Labor Money in Wisconsin Politics, 1964* (Princeton: Citizens' Research Foundation, 1966), pp. 24-36.

3. "An Analysis of the 1966 Campaign for Governor of Pennsylvania," unpublished manuscript, 88 pp.

4. Tom Dearmore, "The Rocky of Little Rock," *The Reporter*, Oct. 5, 1967.

CHAPTER 5

1. *Memoirs of John Quincy Adams*, 1875, VII, entry of March 8, 1828; quoted in Jasper B. Shannon, *Money and Politics* (New York: Random House, 1959), p. 15.

2. Alexander Heard, *Money and Politics*, Public Affairs Pamphlet No. 242, Oct. 1956, p. 11.

3. Louise Overacker, *Money in Elections* (New York: The Macmillan Company, 1932), pp. 69-70.

4. Heard, *The Costs of Democracy, op. cit.*, pp. 334-35.

5. "Text of Taft's Analysis of G.O.P. Contest in 1952," *The New York Times*, November 25, 1959.

6. The totals do not include the substantial sums raised and spent statewide and locally (with the exception of Goldwater's California expenses, which are included); the Nixon expenditures are incomplete, and the campaign of Senator Margaret Chase Smith, though inexpensive, is not included at all.

The major discrepancy in the figures stems from significant understatements by the Rockefeller campaign. While Rockefeller associates admitted expenditures of nearly $3 million, the figure did not include the cost of personal staff, including much of the field staff throughout the country; travel for the candidate and his party; use of the family airplane; or use of the brownstone office in New York City which is maintained as a political headquarters for Rockefeller whether or not he is running for office. One Rockefeller operative said that the 1964 costs were about two times the admitted amount of $3 million, which was visible spending and could not be denied.

7. William Bradford Huie, "Wallace's Presidential Stakes," *New York Herald Tribune*, Oct. 3, 1965.

8. For a detailed analysis of the 1968 campaigns, see Herbert E. Alexander, *Financing the 1968 Election* (D. C. Heath & Co., 1971), pp. 7-72.

9. When travel costs for a campaign are given, there may be considerable inflation of amounts. When finance managers say, for example, that travel cost $1 million, the statement may be true but normally does not take into account the fact that as much as half of that is reimbursed by the media travellers—newspaper, radio, and television reporters—who are charged by the campaign for riding in the candidate's plane and even for ground transportation.

10. Alexander, *Financing the 1964 Election, op. cit.*, pp. 77-81.

11. An in-state fund of similar nature but larger amount, $250,000, also was maintained for costs of Reagan appearances at Republican functions in California and for the Governor's activities as a California party leader; this one was funded by a 22.5 percent assessment of gross income at in-state fund raising events he attended. A third fund was maintained for political travels of Lieutenant Governor Robert Finch.

12. Jerry Landauer, "Union's Political Gifts Follow Administration Aid to Fugitive Official," *Wall Street Journal*, July 19, 1968.

CHAPTER 6

1. State laws may require reporting for federal candidates, or committees supporting them, but collecting such data is costly.

2. In 1952 the Republicans claimed there were 16,000 Eisenhower-Nixon Clubs in operation.

3. This compilation is derived from a table for the years 1912 to 1952 (based on Pollock and Overacker studies) to be found in William Goodman, *The Two-Party System in the United States* (Princeton: D. Van Nostrand Company, 1956), Table 8, p. 517. Figures for 1952 and 1956 are derived from Heard, *op. cit.*, p. 20 with debts added; for 1960 from Alexander, *Financing the 1960 Election, op. cit.*, Table 1, p. 10; for 1964 from Alexander, *Financing the 1964 Election, op. cit.*, Table 1, p. 8; and for 1968 from Alexander, *Financing the 1968 Election, op. cit.*, pp. 117-21. 1960, 1964, and 1968 figures are adjusted for transfer of funds and leave out Congressional, labor, and miscellaneous committee spending. None of the figures includes spending at the state and local levels.

4. Heard, *The Costs of Democracy, op. cit.*, p. 376.

5. If the costs of the George Wallace campaign are deducted, the cost per vote for the two major parties came to 51 cents in 1968. This is a fairer comparison with earlier years in which minor party efforts were so minimal as not to distort the series.

6. For the specifics of polling in 1968, see "Political Polling, 1968," *The*

Analyst, March 1969, pp. 14-18, 44; Donald Oberdorfer, "Unsung Poll Helped GOP Chart Path to Victory," *Washington Post,* December 29, 1968; and *Congressional Quarterly,* April 29, 1968.

7. For a detailed analysis of the 1968 campaigns, see Herbert E. Alexander, *Financing the 1968 Election, op. cit.,* pp. 79-142.

8. Compared with more than $200,000 in 1952-3, and at least $360,000 in 1960-61 transitions, according to President's Commission on Campaign Costs, *Financing Presidential Campaigns* (Washington: Government Printing Office, April, 1962), pp. 23-24.

9. Mr. Stone also gave generously to the Nixon prenomination campaign.

10. News stories claimed the largest loans were for $250,000, but campaign fund statements filed with the Clerk of the House showed the highest to be $240,000.

11. Until 1972 federal law prohibited giving anything of value, including a loan, of more than $5,000 to any candidate or committee.

12. This practice was revealed in the March, 1969, official filings of eleven Republican committees, which showed six Illinois committees with similar names and contributing patterns, giving them a total of $268,610. None of the contributing committees had been listed in any of the Republican financial reports in 1968, and there was no information on who had contributed to the Illinois committees, or what if any function they had in the 1968 campaign. Illinois has no state reporting law, and press inquiries failed to turn up information.

13. To extrapolate from the figures given: $3,125,000 in loans was itemized by lenders; $2,800,000 was reported in "constructive receipts"; this totals $5,925,000, while Democratic reports admit contingent liabilities totalling $6,155,000. Accordingly, $230,000 is to be accounted for, but this may be explained in part by simple inadvertence or by double borrowing (to pay back old loans).

14. The United Citizens for Nixon-Agnew of Massachusetts was recorded on an official filing in Massachusetts as follows: "10/9/68 Proceeds of Loan First National Bank Secured by Signatures of Eugene Clapp, Richard R. Robie, John A. Volpe, Lloyd B. Waring $30,000." This loan from a national bank was illegal under federal law, but at least in this case the co-signers were listed. The co-signers later claimed they personally borrowed the money.

15. Alexander, *Financing the 1964 Election, op. cit.,* pp. 77-84, 112-115.

16. Heard, *The Costs of Democracy, op. cit.,* p. 54.

17. Overacker, *op. cit.,* pp. 79, 144-145. Overacker says LaFollette's Progressive Party in 1924 spent only $236,963.

18. Walter Pincus, "Suit Alleges Kickbacks for Wallace Campaign," *Washington Post,* April 15, 1968; J. M. McFadden, "Firm That Sued Alabama Gets State Asphalt Pact," *Washington Post,* May 30, 1968; "Agencies Weigh Price-Rigging, Kickback Charges in Alabama," *Washington Post,* April 29, 1968; Jerry Landauer and Kenneth Slocum, "Loss of Statehouse Control Cuts Donations To Alabamian's Drive: Pinch on Wallace," *Wall Street Journal,* June 10, 1968; Morton Mintz, "Liquor Sales to State Benefit Wallace Friends: Liquor and Favoritism Fund-Raiser, Payoff Linked," *Washington Post,* November 25, 1968; Jack Anderson, "Insiders Whisper Alabama Liquor Payoff," *Washing-*

ton Post, November 26, 1968; Drew Pearson, "Liquor Kickback Probe Backed," *Washington Post,* December 6, 1968.

19. *Congressional Quarterly,* October 25, 1968, p. 2954.

CHAPTER 7

1. For a fuller discussion of these matters, see Alexander, Herbert E., *Responsibility in Party Finance* (Princeton: Citizens' Research Foundation, 1963), 55 pages.

2. The Republicans compiled a listing of most President's Club members from 1964, 1965, and 1966 filings the Democrats had made under law with the Clerk of the House. See *Congressional Record,* Aug. 31, 1966, pp. 20516-33; also *Congressional Record,* Oct 20, 1966, pp. 27018-35. Democrats responded by publishing a listing of members of the Republican Congressional Boosters Club for 1965 through Aug. 31, 1966, in *Congressional Record,* Oct. 11, 1966, pp. 25054-60.

3. *Congressional Record,* July 14, 1966, pp. 15038-39; Aug. 1, 1966, pp. 17001-04; Aug. 30, 1966, pp. 20420-26; Aug. 31, 1966, pp. 20503-4.

4. *Congressional Record,* Aug. 18, 1966, pp. 19059-66.

5. "Transcript of President Johnson's News Conference," *The New York Times,* Aug. 25, 1966.

6. Mark R. Arnold, "The Ins and Outs of the President's Club," *The National Observer,* Aug. 29, 1966; also *Congressional Record,* Aug. 31, 1966, p. 20519.

7. James Deakin, "VA Work Done By President's Club Donor," *St. Louis Post-Dispatch,* Sept. 18, 1966; and Deakin, "Gift Made to President's Club After Firm Got VA Contract," *St. Louis Post-Dispatch,* Sept. 25, 1966.

8. Rowland Evans and Robert Novak, "The Mysterious $6,000," *Washington Post,* Oct. 9, 1966. Reportedly the money was returned when the criticism grew heavy.

9. Stat. 66 (1966).

10. *Washington Post,* Oct. 4, 1968.

11. This is an old custom that Republicans and others sometimes practice as well.

12. For detail, see Alexander, Herbert E., *Financing the 1968 Election* (Lexington, Mass.: D.C. Heath and Company, 1971).

13. See, for example, John Connally, "Why Kennedy Went to Texas," *Life,* Nov. 24, 1967.

14. *New York Herald Tribune,* Jan. 22, 1961.

15. When only one Congressional event is held, the profits are divided 60 percent to the House Committee and 40 percent to the Senate Committee.

16. See Ronald F. Stinnett, *Democrats, Dinners and Dollars: A History of the Democratic Party, Its Dinners, Its Ritual* (Ames, Iowa: The Iowa State University Press, 1967), 310 pages.

17. Jules Witcover, "White House Got Funds for Select Campaigns," *Washington Post,* Nov. 27, 1970.

18. James R. Polk, "7 Envoys Made Big Donations to GOP," *Washington Evening Star,* Dec. 27, 1970.

CHAPTER 8

1. Argumentation and documentation can be found in detail in Alexander, *Responsibility in Party Finance, op. cit.*

2. Categorized as follows: Printing ($1,051); Postage ($199); Publicity ($64); Kick-off picnic ($200); Awards and Certificates ($342); and Miscellaneous ($265).

3. For detail on these and other 1968 national-level committee data, see Herbert E. Alexander and Caroline D. Jones, editors, *Contributions of National-Level Political Committees to Incumbents and Candidates for Public Offices, 1968* (Princeton: Citizens' Research Foundation, 1971).

4. For some of the printed documents of the Nixon affair, see *U.S. News and World Report*, Oct.. 3, 1952. Also see Earl Mazo, "Richard Nixon: The Ordeal that Made Him," *Look,* June 9, 1959.

5. U. S. Senate Select Committee for Contribution Investigation, *Report* (Washington: Government Printing Office, 1956) (Senate Report No. 1724, 84th Congress, 2nd Session).

6. *Congressional Quarterly*, June 30, 1967, pp. 1106-08.

7. Robert Cahn, "Baker Conviction Spotlights System," *Christian Science Monitor,* Jan. 31, 1967.

8. Jerry Landauer, "Trial of Bobby Baker May Illustrate Dealings of Politics and Business," *Wall Street Journal,* Jan. 11, 1967.

9. For a useful summary, see U.S. Senate Select Committee on Standards and Conduct, Report No. 186, 80th Congress, 1st Session.

10. This was an income tax trial of former Governor William G. Stratton of Illinois. The federal government contended that Mr. Stratton should have paid income tax on $93,000 which he admitted receiving and spending during his last four years as Governor. Stratton's defense successfully argued that his use of the money for such things as his wife's clothing and for entertainment (on a houseboat and at a hunting lodge he bought or improved with the money) was a legitimate "political" expenditure in his role as party leader. His attorneys argued that the money represented gifts of political supporters and, as gifts, were not taxable because they were analogous to business expenses of a businessman. A jury acquitted Stratton. Auston C. Wehrwein, "Ex-Gov. Stratton Freed in Tax Case," *New York Times,* March 12, 1965.

11. In 1967 Senator Charles Percy of Illinois approved efforts of friends to raise $100,000 annually to help him defray his office expenses, which for his first year in office had run $75,000 above his Senate allowance. The special fund was announced publicly, but criticism was heavy and the group ended its activities. Donald Janson, "3-Month-Old Percy Fund Group is Ended at Request of Senator," *New York Times,* Jan. 18, 1968.

12. Minnesota permits candidates for specified offices, and certain party officials, to deduct from their gross state income tax liability limited parts of campaign expenditures or political costs they had personally paid. See Herbert E. Alexander, *Regulation of Political Finance* (Berkeley and Princeton: Institute of Governmental Studies, University of California and Citizens' Research Foundation, 1966), p. 25.

13. *New York Times*, Dec. 28, 1966. Also see Paul H. Douglas, *In Our Time*

(New York: Harcourt, Brace and World, 1967), pp. 85-93.

14. Don Irwin, "The High Cost of Being a U.S. Senator from N.Y.," *New York Herald Tribune,* July 16, 1961.

15. Gallup Report press release, May 3, 1967.

CHAPTER 9

1. Robert Bierstedt, "An Analysis of Social Power," *American Sociological Review,* (December, 1950), 737.

2. These and most of the following figures, unless otherwise indicated, were collected by the Citizens' Research Foundation. Some of the comparisons with citations can be found in Alexander, *Financing the 1964 Election, op. cit.,* pp. 68-95.

3. For lists and more detail, see Alexander, *Financing the 1968 Election, op. cit.*

4. *1956 General Election Campaigns,* Report to the Senate Committee on Rules and Administration, 85th Congress, 1st Session (1957). (Hereafter cited as Gore Committee.)

5. Heard, *The Costs of Democracy, op. cit.*

6. In comparison, in 1964 there were 130 individuals reported as giving sums aggregating $10,000 or more, for a total of $2,161,905. In 1960 there were only 95 persons identified as making reported gifts aggregating $10,000 or more, for a total of $1,552,009. Of these, 60 gave to the Republican cause and 35 to the Democratic. In 1952, 110 persons gave in aggregate sums of $10,000 or more, and in 1956, 111 persons gave similarly. In both cases the Republicans benefitted overwhelmingly. See Heard, *The Costs of Democracy, op. cit.,* and Gore Committee, *op. cit.*

7. The references are to Mr. and Mrs. C. Douglas Dillon (he is President of U. S. and International Securities Corporation) and to Arthur K. Watson and Thomas J. Watson, Jr., both of International Business Machines.

8. The references are to Patrick J. Frawley, Jr., Chairman, Eversharp, Inc. and to Henry Salvatori, founder of Western Geophysics Company.

9. Richard Austin Smith, "The Fifty-Million-Dollar Man," *Fortune,* November, 1957, pp. 176-177, 236.

10. Arthur M. Louis, "America's Centimillionaires," *Fortune,* May, 1968, pp. 152-157, 192-96.

11. Divided at $1,021,313+ for Republicans, $106,488 for Democrats, and $10,701 for miscellaneous committees.

12. Don Oberdorfer, "The New Political Non-Job," *Harper's Magazine,* October, 1965, p. 108.

13. Edward J. Flynn, *You're The Boss* (New York: Viking Press, 1947), p. 123.

14. James A. Farley, "Passing Out the Patronage," *American Magazine,* August, 1933, p. 77.

15. This analysis includes names in the non-career Chiefs of Foreign Missions analysis above.

16. Kevin L. McKeough and John F. Bibby, *The Costs of Political Partici-*

pation: A Study of National Convention Delegates (Princeton, N.J.: Citizens' Research Foundation, 1968), pp. 86-91.

17. Heard, "Money and Politics," *op. cit.*, p. 14.

18. *New York Times*, Dec. 15, 1956.

19. Ralph Nader, *Unsafe at Any Speed* (New York: Grossman, 1965).

20. Philip M. Stern, *The Great Treasury Raid* (New York: New American Library, 1965), pp. 56-71.

21. Heard, *The Costs of Democracy*, op cit., pp. 95-141.

22. These are the American Bar Association, American Medical Association, American Petroleum Institute, American Iron and Steel Institute, Association of American Railroads, Business Advisory Council, Chiefs of Foreign Missions and Special Missions, Manufacturing Chemists Association, National Association of Electric Companies, National Association of Manufacturers, National Association of Real Estate Boards, National Coal Association, and Chamber of Commerce of the United States.

23.

Year	Republicans	Democrats	Miscellaneous	Total
1968	$1,132,982+	$136,106	$11,967	$1,281,055+
1964	200,310	225,790	4,618	468,218
1960	425,710	63,255	2,500	493,465
1956	741,189	8,000	2,725	751,914

24. For example, it was revealed that in 1968, while the national-level AMPAC organization disclosed $451,000 in receipts and $682,000 in expenditures, between three and four times that amount was disbursed by state affiliates; since some states do not require public reports of campaign contributions, and some contributions are smaller than need be reported where required, the extent of the medical profession's political giving cannot be accurately measured. See *Congressional Quarterly*, July 4, 1969, pp. 1169-70; and *Newsweek*, July 28, 1969, p. 87. Including lobbying expenses in Washington, about $5 million is spent in an election year by doctors and their allies. Richard D. Lyons, "A.M.A. Discloses Political Outlay," *New York Times*, January 11, 1970.

25. In this and the following analyses, some of the Republicans and Democrats also gave to miscellaneous non-party committees, so the total amounts given are slightly higher than the sum of Republican and Democratic contributions.

26. The four lists of 25 corporations each were printed in Richard F. Kaufman, "As Eisenhower Was Saying . . . 'We Must Guard Against Unwarranted Influence by the Military-Industrial Complex,'" *New York Times Magazine*, June 22, 1969. These lists are derived from: for the Pentagon, 100 Companies and Their Subsidiary Corporations Listed According to Net Value of Military Prime Contract Awards (Fiscal Year 1968), Department of Defense; for AEC, Annual Report for 1968, Atomic Energy Commission; for National Aeronautics and Space Administration, Annual Procurement Report, (Fiscal Year 1968); for the industrial list, 500 Largest U. S. Industrial Corporations, *Fortune Directory* (1968).

27. Among these were 17 split contributors giving to both Republicans and

Democrats and six who gave to Republican and miscellaneous committees.

28. "1961-1962 Political Campaign Contributions and Expenditures," *Congressional Quarterly,* Special Report supplementing Weekly Report of July 26, 1963, p. 1193.

29. Quoted in Gustavus Myers, *History of the Great American Fortunes* (Chicago: C. H. Kerr and Co., 1911-17), Vol. II p. 316.

30. Nick Kotz in *Des Moines Register,* July 25, 1968.

31. Jerry Landauer, "Political Fund-Raising: A Murky World," *Wall Street Journal,* June 28, 1967.

32. Lester W. Milbrath, *The Washington Lobbyists* (Chicago: Rand McNally & Company, 1963), pp. 282-86.

33. Alexander Heard, "Giving to Both Sides: Some Observations on the Consequences of Democracy" (paper read at meeting of the American Political Science Association, September 7, 1957), pp. 13-14.

CHAPTER 10

1. For a brief introduction to labor political activity, see Greenhill, *op. cit.,* pp. 5-15. For an introduction to business political activity, see Edwin M. Epstein, *The Corporation in American Politics* (Englewood Cliffs, N.J.: Prentice-Hall, Inc., 1969).

2. In 1968 Maryland enacted a Fair Election Practices Act which permitted limited (up to $2,500) corporate contributions. No provision was made for making the contributions tax-deductible. Campaign fund reports thereafter began to show racetrack operations, state contractors, etc. contributing, which caused some press comment but no immediate change in the law.

3. Speech by Randolph W. Thrower (Commissioner of Internal Revenue), "Significant Developments in Tax Administration," before Tax Executives Institute, Atlantic City, Oct. 6, 1969, p. 6.

4. In a relevant case, the International Latex Corporation, pleading "no contest," was fined $5,000 for illegally contributing $8,000 to Senator Thomas J. Dodd's 1964 campaign, allegedly in return for Dodd's effort to get an ambassadorship for an officer of the company. Occasionally similar cases have been brought under state laws.

5. Thrower, *op. cit.,* pp. 5-6.

6. Gore Committee, *op. cit.,* pp. 16-17.

7. *Homefront* (newsletter of the Institute for American Democracy), "No. 1 Man on the Right," Sept., 1969, pp. 57, 59-64.

8. For an extended treatment, see John F. Bibby and Herbert E. Alexander, *The Politics of National Convention Finances and Arrangements* (Princeton: Citizens' Research Foundation, 1968), pp. 48-65.

9. In 1968 three union committees combined accounted for 46 percent of the $7.1 million reported; these were COPE, the International Ladies Garment Workers Union, and the Seafarers International Union.

10. Compared for Michigan and Wisconsin by Greenhill, *op. cit.,* p. 44.

11. For a case-by-case analysis of labor and early corporate litigation, see Edwin M. Epstein, *Corporations, Contributions, and Political Campaigns*:

Federal Regulation in Perspective (Berkeley: Institute of Governmental Studies, University of California, 1968), pp. 31-34.

12. Greenhill, *op. cit.*, pp. 26, 50-51.

13. Jerry Landauer, "The Shakedown Cruise," *Washington Monthly*, October, 1969, pp. 55-59.

14. Alexander E. Barkan, "Union Members Strong for LBJ," *Memo from COPE*, August 7, 1967.

15. Theodore H. White, *The Making of the President, 1968* (New York: Atheneum, 1969), p. 365.

16. *Financing Presidential Campaigns, op. cit.*, p. 12.

17. U. S. Office of Internal Revenue, *Internal Revenue Bulletin* (Washington: Government Printing Office, Sept. 24, 1962), pp. 7-10. State governments could also give tax incentives for these programs.

18. This notion was endorsed by the Commission on Political Activity of Government Personnel, in *Findings and Recommendations*, Vol. 1 (Washington: Government Printing Office, 1968), p. 32.

CHAPTER 11

1. Puerto Rico offers an example of a constructive effort to fill a gap left after a traditional source of political money was closed off. When Puerto Rico undertook to replace its system, in which the majority party was financed largely through assessments of government workers, the reduction in revenue was made up for in part by a system of partial government financing. This positive approach in replacing an outmoded practice is not often found in the American federal law or in the states. See Henry Wells, *Government Financing of Political Parties in Puerto Rico* (Princeton: Citizens' Research Foundation, 1962) and Henry Wells and Robert W. Anderson, a Supplement to the above, 1966.

2. This survey of federal law follows three publications: U. S. Congress, Senate Committee on Rules and Administration, Subcommittee on Privileges and Elections, *Federal Corrupt Practices and Political Activities;* U. S. Congress, Senate Library, *Factual Campaign Information;* and U. S. Congress, Senate Committee on Rules and Administration, Subcommittee on Privileges and Elections, *Law Guidebook*, 1968. Also see Herbert E. Alexander, *Money, Politics and Public Reporting* (Princeton: Citizens' Research Foundation, 1960).

3. "Campaign Laws Foster Cheating," *St. Louis Post-Dispatch*, March 16, 1969. Series continued on March 17-19.

4. "The Unknown Price of Office," *St. Louis Post-Dispatch*, March 20, 1969.

5. Gertrude S. Rubin, *Regulation of Campaign Finance: The Massachusetts Full Disclosure Law, 1962-1964.* Senior Honors Thesis, Smith College, 1965.

6. For a survey of state laws, see Alexander, *Regulation of Political Finance, op. cit.*

7. 163 Wis. 615, 158 N.W. 969.

8. *Smith v. Ervin*, 64 So. (2d) 166 (Fla. 1953).

9. McNeill, *Democratic Campaign Financing in Indiana, 1964, op. cit.*, pp. 15-19.

10. *Ibid.*, pp. 19-21.

11. "Oregon Official Cleared by Court," *New York Times,* April 17, 1969.

12. Overacker, *Money in Elections, op. cit.,* p. 353.

CHAPTER 12

1. This section draws on: Pollock, *Party Campaign Funds, op. cit.*; Overacker, *Money in Elections, op. cit.*; S. Sydney Minault, *Corrupt Practices Legislation in the Forty-eight States* (Chicago: The Council of State Governments, 1942); Pamela Ford, *Regulation of Campaign Finance* ("1955 Legislative Problems, No. 6"; Berkeley: Bureau of Public Administration, University of California, 1955); Heard, *The Costs of Democracy, op. cit.*

2. A lump sum exemption of $30,000 which may be taken only once in a lifetime is granted on gifts made after 1932.

3. House Special Committee to Investigate Campaign Expenditures, *Report* No. 3252, 81st Congress, 2nd Session, 1951, pp. 21 and 22.

4. For a fuller exposition of the events, see Heard, *The Costs of Democracy, op. cit.*, pp. 105-06.

5. "The Ticklish Problem of Political Fund Raising—and Spending," *Reader's Digest,* January, 1968.

6. White House Press Release, October 4, 1961, announcing the appointment of the Commission on Campaign Costs.

7. *Financing Presidential Campaigns, op. cit.* The seven other recommendations were:

• That the existing law forbidding partisan campaign contributions and expenditures by corporations and labor unions be maintained and strictly enforced.

• That all other statutes regulating the financing of political parties and candidates be vigorously enforced.

• That the parties take full advantage of opportunities to modernize and increase the effectiveness of their fund-raising practices.

• That research to increase campaign efficiency and help reduce campaign waste be encouraged among public and private organizations and individuals.

• That a nonpartisan White House Conference on Campaign Finance be called by the President to launch broad solicitation programs by all parties following the adoption of measures to stimulate such giving; such a conference to include representatives designated by the important political parties, as well as representatives from various segments of the population and the communications media, and to lay the groundwork for further continuing efforts to encourage voluntary private action in meeting campaign costs.

• That the states consider measures similar to those recommended in the report along with others that would help to reduce the costs of campaigning and make it easier for the parties and candidates to meet them; and that the Post Office Department make its change-of-address files available to the parties as well as to election boards as a way of assisting in local registration drives.

• That, after a trial period with the measures proposed, the President should provide for another nonpartisan evaluation of Presidential campaign finance, and that, if the objectives sought by the proposals have not been realized, study be given to additional measures to achieve them.

8. U. S. Office of Internal Revenue, Internal Revenue Bulletin (Washington: Government Printing Office, Sept. 24, 1962), pp. 7-10.

9. *White House Press Release*, May 29, 1962.

10. *White House Press Release*, April 30, 1963.

11. Alexander Heard, "A New Approach to Campaign Finances," *The New York Times Magazine*, October 6, 1963.

12. The total of $950,000 for the incoming party, $500,000 of it non-governmental, can be compared to total costs of $200,000 in 1952-53 and at least $360,-000 in the 1960-61 transition.

13. *White House Press Release*, May 26, 1966.

14. *Election Reform Act of 1966*, Committee Print of the Committee on House Administration, 89th Congress, 2nd Session, October 3, 1966.

15. Cannon stepped down as chairman in 1964, briefly, as is the custom, when up for re-election. The reason is that this Subcommittee also handles election recounts, and it is not proper for a contestant to chair a judging committee.

16. For a full account of the Long Amendment, see Herbert E. Alexander, "The Presidential Election Campaign Fund Act: The American Subsidy that Wasn't," paper presented at the Political Finance Panel of the 7th World Congress of the International Political Science Association, held in Brussels, Belgium, September 23, 1967.

17. *Broadcasting*, October 31, 1966, p. 102.

18. *The New York Times*, November 2, 1966.

19. *The Washington Post*, November 3, 1966.

20. Robert B. Semple, Jr., "President Signs Foreign Tax Bill, With Objections," *The New York Times*, November 14, 1966.

21. *White House Press Release*, May 25, 1967.

22. Submitted as H.R. 4890, 90th Congress, the Committee Report, No. 698, was not released until November 1, 1967.

23. *Election Reform Act of 1968*, Report No. 1593, Committee on House Administration, 90th Congress, 2nd Session, June 27, 1968.

24. Overacker, *Money in Elections, op. cit.*, pp. 241-48, 277-84.

25. "Censure of Dodd Opposed by Long," *The New York Times*, April 29, 1967.

26. *Report of the Special Committee to Investigate Campaign Expenditures*, 1970, House of Representatives, 91st Congress, 2nd Session (Washington: Government Printing Office, 1971).

CHAPTER 13

1. *Financing Presidential Campaigns, op. cit.*

2. *Financing a Better Election System*, A Statement by the Research and Policy Committee of the Committee for Economic Development (New York: Committee for Economic Development, 1968).

3. *Voter's Time, op. cit.*

4. *Electing Congress, The Financial Dilemma,* Report of the Twentieth Century Fund Task Force on Financing Congressional Campaigns (New York: The Twentieth Century Fund, 1970).

5. James C. Kirby, et al., *Congress and the Public Trust,* Report of the Association of the Bar of the City of New York Special Committee on Congressional Ethics (New York: Atheneum, 1970), pp. 118-154.

6. "Electoral Reform," *The Center Magazine,* January, 1969, pp. 2-11. Additional remarks by Ashmore, replying to criticisms of his proposal, can be found in the March, 1969, issue of the magazine.

7. Testimony of Philip M. Stern, Hearings, U. S. Senate, Committee on Commerce, March 4, 1971, pp. 448-451.

8. *Financing Presidential Campaigns, op. cit.,* p. 17.

9. See Gallup Poll releases for December, 1968, and January, November, and December, 1970.

10. *Electing Congress, The Financial Dilemma, op. cit.,* p. 3.

11. Kirby, *Congress and the Public Trust, op. cit.,* pp. 118-154.

12. White House press release, January 12, 1966, on the State of the Union address.

13. Rather than a single national primary, the CED recommended that a preferential Presidential primary be held in all states on the same date. This would have the same effect as a single national one and the arguments given in the text would apply as well.

14. At and after the 1968 convention, the Democrats moved to democraticize and open the delegate selection process through a commission headed by Senator George McGovern. The commission has recognized that the caucus-convention method of choosing national convention delegates can be just as fair as a primary, provided participation is open to all party registrants and certain basic rules of representation and timeliness are followed. The commission has also recognized that in those states with primaries the vote of the people should be binding on that state's delegates. If these kinds of reforms are adopted by the Democrats and the Republicans move in a similar direction, it will be a major advance in equal participation in the nomination process.

15. *Electing the President,* A Report of the Commission on Electoral College Reform of the American Bar Association, January 7, 1967. Also see Neal R. Peirce, *The People's President* (New York: Simon and Schuster, 1968).

16. This is disputed by some opponents of direct election. See Theodore H. White, "Direct Elections: An Invitation to National Chaos," *Life,* January 30, 1970, p. 4; and Alexander M. Bickel, *The New Age of Political Reform* (New York: Harper Colophon Books, 1968).

17. See especially White, *ibid.*

18. In a letter to the author, November 5, 1969.

19. Efforts in Kentucky resulted in the establishment of a Registry of Election Finance that publicizes the data.

20. Herbert E. Alexander and Kevin L. McKeough, *Financing Campaigns for Governor: New Jersey 1965* (Citizens' Research Foundation, 1969), p. 90.

21. Martin and Susan Tolchin, *To the Victor . . . Political Patronage from the Clubhouse to the White House* (New York: Random House, 1971), p. 146.

22. "Judges Elected by Popular Inattention," study by Citizens' Union Research Foundation cited in *National Civic Review*, May, 1967, p. 274.

CHAPTER 14

1. For various aspects of the Great Debates, see Sidney Kraus (ed.), *The Great Debates: Background, Perspective, Effects* (Bloomington: Indiana University Press, 1962).
2. Arthur Schlesinger, Jr., "How Drastically Has TV Changed Our Politics?" in *TV Guide*, Oct. 18-22, 1966, p. 9.
3. "Who on the Hill Own What in Broadcasting," *Broadcasting*, Dec. 15, 1969, pp. 64-5.
4. Hyman H. Goldin, "Time Free and for Sale: The Implications of the 1964 FCC Survey for the Future of Political Broadcasting," unpublished paper delivered at National Conference on Broadcasting and Election Campaigns, Washington, D. C., Oct. 13, 1965, p. 5.
5. "Statement by National Citizens Committee for Broadcasting Concerning Commercial Network Presidential Election Year Coverage," dated Oct. 22, 1968.
6. *Voters' Time, op. cit.*
7. E. William Henry, address before the Commonwealth Club, San Francisco, Jan. 15, 1965, p. 6.
8. From NCEC press release, dated October 21, 1969.
9. "The Equal Opportunities and Fairness Doctrines in Broadcasting: Pillars in the Forum of Democracy," *University of Cincinnati Law Review*, 37 (Summer, 1968), 447-549.
10. Red Lion Broadcasting Co. v. FCC, 395 U. S. 367, 390 (1969).

CHAPTER 15

1. *Giving USA*, A Compilation of Facts and Trends on American Philanthropy for the Year 1970, American Association of Fund Raising Counsel, New York, 1971, p. 28.
2. Figures are derived from the following:

PERCENTAGE OF NATIONAL ADULT POPULATION
SOLICITED AND MAKING CONTRIBUTIONS

Organ.	Year	Solicited by:			Contributed to:		
		Repub- licans	Demo- crats	Either	Repub- licans	Demo- crats	Either
SRC	1952				3	1	4
Gallup	1955	5	5	10	3	3	6
Gallup	1956	8	11	19	3	6	9
SRC	1956				5	5	10
Gallup	1958	8	8	16	3	3	6
Gallup	1958	5	5	11	2	3	5
Gallup	1960	9	8	15	4	4	9
SRC	1960				7	4	12

SRC	1962				4	5	9
SRC	1964	8	4	15[1]	6	4	11[2]
Gallup	1964				6	4	12
SRC	1966			18			8
SRC	1968	8	6	20[3]	3	2	6[4]

Sources: Survey Research Center, University of Michigan data, direct from Center or from Angus Campbell, Philip E. Converse, Warren E. Miller, Donald E. Stokes, *The American Voter* (New York: John Wiley and Sons, 1960), p. 91; Gallup data direct or from Roper Opinion Research Center.

[1]3 percent solicited by both parties.

[2]This 1964 percentage is combined for individuals who said they gave and for those who said they knew another member of their household had given.

[3]Includes 3 percent solicited by both parties, 1 percent solicited by Wallace's American Independent Party, and other solicited by non-party groups and combinations of parties and groups.

[4]Includes 0.5 percent contributed to Wallace and other contributions to other parties, groups, or combinations.

3. *Ibid.*

4. A Gallup series gives some rough indication of the potential. Gallup has made projections from the following question: "If you were asked, would you contribute $5 to the campaign fund of the political party you prefer?" The results are shown below:

NATIONAL PROJECTION OF $5 GIVERS IF SOLICITED

Year	Yes	No	Reject	Don't Know	No Opinion	Qualified Yes
1943	29%	69%	2%			
1947	29	71				
1949	31	62	1		4%	2%
1952	34	55		11%		
1955	34	53	1	12		
1955	32	56		12		
1956	35	50		15		
1956	31	59	1	9		
1957	39	47	2	12		
1958	23	66	1	10		
1958[1]	12	72				
1960[1]	17	53		12		
1966	41	46		13		

Source: Roper Public Opinion Research Center, Williams College.

[1]Does not total 100% because the question was asked only of the respondents answering in the negative a previous question regarding whether they had been solicited.

The question must be understood to elicit attitudinal responses, rather than giving grounds for confident prediction of behavior. However, the heavy and consistent "No" responses when a prestige "Yes" answer would not cost the respondent a cent, lead one to believe respondent's answers may be considered a reasonable gauge. Since the question was normally asked in conjunction with another question asking about contributions, the givers were already filtered out, and the "Yes" responses are an additional potential that can be added to those already giving. The range would be from 6 to 20 million who say they would give, which could add a maximum of $100 million in political income if fully tapped. Even assuming some overreporting, the potential looks promising.

Gallup projections are interesting. A typical breakdown shows that:

Proportionally more Republicans than Democrats say that they will give if asked;

Persons with incomes in the upper brackets are more inclined to say they will give;

Close to 4 out of 10 in professional and business categories say they will give;

Persons in cities of 50,000 and over appear more willing to give.

5. Derived from Campbell, *The American Voter, op. cit.*

6. *Giving USA, op. cit.*, p. 11.

7. The American Broadcasting Company, Columbia Broadcasting System, and National Educational Television networks have devoted prime-time television programs to political finance.

8. Neil O. Staebler, "A National Foundation for Political Finance," in Herbert E. Alexander (ed.), *Money For Politics: A Miscellany of Ideas* (Princeton: Citizens' Research Foundation, 1963), pp. 36-37.

9. Byron G. Allen, "Political Parties Should Be Chartered for Financial Stability," in *ibid.*, pp. 33-35.

10. "A Study of the Effectiveness of the 1960 Program of the American Heritage Foundation," The Gallup Organization, December, 1960, pp. 20-23.

11. Data from Survey Research Center, University of Michigan.

12. Overacker, *Money in Elections, op. cit.*, pp. 236-38.

CHAPTER 16

1. *Financing Presidential Campaigns, op. cit.*, p. 2.

2. Impediments to participation as candidates in the South and elsewhere may serve as screening devices. In recent years, the Democratic Party of South Carolina has assessed up to $2,000 as a qualifying fee for candidates for Governor and U. S. Senator in the primary elections. In Indiana in 1964, before a candidate's name could be placed before the Democratic State Conventon, he had to pay a filing fee to the party, ranging from $2,500 to $7,500 for statewide offices, $2,000 for certain judicial offices, and down to $250 for delegates and $100 for alternates to the Democratic National Convention.

INDEX

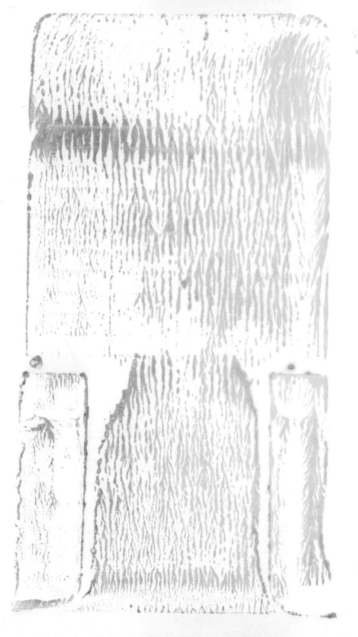

COM